CHANGING POLICING THEORIES

for 21st Century Societies

CHANGING POLICING THEORIES

for 21st Century Societies

Second edition

Charles Edwards

BA (Open University, UK), MA, MPhil (London University)
Quondam Lecturer in Justice Studies, Edith Cowan University

THE FEDERATION PRESS
2005

Published in Sydney by

The Federation Press
71 John St, Leichhardt, NSW, 2040
PO Box 45, Annandale, NSW, 2038
Ph: (02) 9552 2200 Fax: (02) 9552 1681
E-mail: info@fedpress.aust.com
Website: http://www.fedpress.aust.com

First edition   1999
Second edition   2005

National Library of Australia Cataloguing-in-Publication data:
    Edwards, Charles J
        Changing policing theories for 21st century societies

    2nd ed.
    Bibliography
    Includes index.
    ISBN 1 86287 537 5

    1. Police – Australia. 2. Police – Great Britain. 3. Police – United States. 4. Law
    enforcement – Australia. 5. Law enforcement – Great Britain. 6. Law enforce-
    ment – United States. I. Title

363.2

Typeset by The Federation Press, Leichhardt, NSW.
    Printed by Ligare Pty Ltd, Riverwood, NSW

FOREWORD

Christine Nixon, APM
Chief Commissioner of Police, Victoria Police

It's a good sign when a book goes into its second edition. It reflects well on the author, and indicates a healthy market of readers. It is also an indication that the subject field of the book is changing.

That policing is changing there is no doubt. While, as Charles Edwards declares, the core values of good policing have remained firm, the world the public police operate within is changing in a rapid, complex and challenging way. If the public police are to remain relevant and effective in this tumultuous environment, they must make greater and greater intellectual investment into their policies and practices. There may have been a time when policing was in a stationary state and hardly needed to change at all. Or, more recently, stepped changes arrived in the wake of some great scandal, or some technological invention such as the car, the radio, or the internet. Now, though, change must be continuous and thoughtful, proactive and evidence-based.

All the evidence indicates that Australian policing is rising to the challenge of post-modernity and the post-September 11 environment. The slow stirrings of professionalisation that began in the late 1980s are now gathering pace. Australia is one of the few places in the English-speaking common law world where foundational and post-foundational police education is being relocated to the university system. Two full-time policing practice degrees are on offer in New South Wales, and there to become a police officer you have to enrol in a university diploma collaboratively taught by police and university teachers. Here in Victoria we are proceeding down the same path. No wonder, then, that the readership for good introductory texts on policing such as this is on the increase.

Australian policing is also getting more and more serious about its research base. Modern communications such as the internet means that we can almost instantly tap into police research and development across the world. However, we need to improve our effectiveness in the context of our own Australian way of life. To that end, across most, if not all, Australian police jurisdictions, police organisations are forming strong partnerships with the research community within the university system.

Here in Victoria we are actively conducting practical research with university partnerships in areas as diverse as counter terrorism, the investigative interviewing of children, youth safety, train safety, serious sex offender recidivism, integrity systems for high performance policing, the policing of sexual assault and child abuse, and the policing of the night-time entertainment industry. We are also using research to evaluate the ways in which we are reforming and improving the organisational environment for a modern police force of highly responsible professional officers.

I have no doubt that this text will contribute to a healthy, rigorous and continuing debate about policing. Its comparative analysis of policing in the United States, the United Kingdom and Australia illustrates both differences and similarities. Above all, it reveals that, in terms of accountability and integrity, the modern police force has to meet the highest of standards. To meet those standards, our knowledge and skills have to be deepened and honed. This book will contribute towards that important endeavour. I suspect a third edition will not be too far away.

December 2004

CONTENTS

Part III
Accountability

For Totty,
who made my efforts worthwhile

ACKNOWLEDGEMENTS

The request for a second edition of this book is both challenging and gratifying. Thanks must therefore go to those whose enormous help contributed to the success of the first edition, which led to the new edition. As I revised my work, almost every page awakened echoes of discussion and comments by these people. I must thank, once again, Andrew Stewart, Paul Omaji, Garry Kosovich, Vicki Marr, Sue King, the late Alex Marnoch whose contribution to change in policing in a number of nations is inestimable, Mike Gilbert, Bob Owens and Vincent Henry.

The second edition was helped enormously by comments and discussions from students and police officers who had read the first edition, by Vincent Henry's gift of his book on Compstat and Margaret Farmer's timely offer of Newburn's *Handbook of Policing*, which filled many lacunae in what is new in British policing. I am also enormously grateful to Bill Boaks of the Western Australia Police Service for sharing his own work with me over a number of years, and assisting with a number of points in the second edition: thanks also to Karl O'Callaghan, now Commissioner of Police for Western Australia, for advice on various issues. As always, though, thanks must go to the one who has shared the vicissitudes of police life and academic endeavour and has read, scrutinised and corrected every paragraph in both editions, chased references, constantly discovered new material and challenged my thinking with her own inimitable original contributions – my wife, Margaret.

The essence of this book is 20 years' policing experience in London and 10 years of reflection, revision, research and teaching of policing issues in Western Australia. While John Donne observed that "no man is an island … and every man's death diminishes me", the converse is true: contact and communication with others expands oneself and one's horizons. In this sense, every colleague and student with whom I have discussed or practised policing has augmented my knowledge. I am grateful for the help, advice and information I have received: the flaws that remain are mine alone.

Charles Edwards
December 2004

INTRODUCTION

This book investigates the social context of policing, in particular the ways in which philosophies of policing have changed since 1829 to accommodate changing societies, and the changing requirements and expectations that these societies have of their police. The focus is on the problems of policing a modern, democratic, multi-cultural society which is both aware of and oriented towards individual rights, that is, very broadly, an examination of the art of policing by consent rather than policing by the imposition and enforcement of regulations using superior force alone. The book analyses policing philosophies and the relationship between societies and their police, and contrasts the way that these philosophies are put into practice in three different English-speaking countries, Australia, Great Britain and the United States.

This book is thus both a critical analysis of changes in policing philosophies as a response to a changing society and a comparison of policing methods, accountability and discussion of the future of policing. As a discussion of the philosophy and practice of policing, the book will be of interest to police officers whose intention it is to provide the optimum police service to whatever community they police, students of university courses in police and justice studies, and others working within the criminal justice system who have an interest in, or bear responsibility for, efficient and effective policing, such as magistrates, community workers or leaders, criminal lawyers and members of government, local or otherwise.

It is worth at this stage remarking on perhaps the most obvious change in policing, that from "Force" to "Service". This is not merely a semantic change, but a crucial change in outlook within police organisations, as Avery makes clear (Avery, 1981).[1] Within this work, I will refer to a police agency as a force or a service in such a way as to ensure historical and contextual accuracy, or by using the neutral term police organisation. For example, the Metropolitan Police was established in London in 1829 as a Force, despite the service orientation of Mayne's primary objects,[2] and will be referred to as such in discussions of at least the first 150 years or so of its history. However, when discussing modern, service-oriented policing organisations, these will be referred to as services whether or not they have formally changed their nomenclature. Many policing agencies in the United States have always called themselves police departments, and references to these will use force, service or department according to context.

---

1   This is a seminal work by the first great figure in the reform of Australian policing.
2   Mayne, with Rowan, was appointed joint commissioner of the new Metropolitan Police in 1829. He set out the "primary objects of an efficient police" on taking office: these are quoted and discussed in Chapter 2.

The three chapters of Part 1 examine the social and historical context of police in a modern democracy. Tension always exists between the law, society and the police. In a rights-driven society, governments are ideologically and/or constitutionally committed to the principle of maximising individual liberty for all members of society, yet the biggest single source of restriction on individual liberty is government itself. These restrictions are normally expressed as directives in the form of law enacted by a parliament democratically elected by the people themselves, and, therefore, ultimately created by society. The most obvious restriction of liberty is imprisonment imposed as a court punishment or, more worrying, detentions imposed by the executive level of government. Such detentions are usually associated with dictatorial regimes, but since September 2001 it can be persuasively argued that the American government has sacrificed constitutional rights, the law and justice to expedience in detaining suspected terrorists without trial.

Police in society are both bound by the law and required to enforce the law, and are the main agency of direct control over society while being under its control. Police are required to stop, question and search individuals, and their legal authority so to do in itself diminishes the right of the individual to personal inviolability: likewise, any lawful arrest of a suspect involves a necessary diminution of that individual's right to liberty. Society itself is changing, and part of this is reflected in the changing nature of crime. If crime is symptomatic of change in society, then it is, in essence, a social problem in the same way that unemployment is a social problem. It will be argued that while police have an important role to play in counteracting crime, if the roots of crime are social then these cannot be addressed by police alone, nor should society hold police responsible for an increase in crime.

Part 2 examines the changing styles of policing. For the first hundred years or so after Peel, police officers on patrol were in very close contact with the community, but largely out of contact with their base stations, supervisors or colleagues. Furthermore, they normally patrolled on foot in towns and cities. Policing changed with improved communications, both radio and telephone, and improved mobility through the use of motor vehicles, resulting in a change in emphasis from the patrolling officer being in close touch with the community and meeting its requests directly, to vehicle patrols being directed by radio dispatch to incidents as a result of telephone calls from the public. Personal contact between police officers and the public deteriorated until the mid 1980s, since which time modern policing has rebuilt links by making police an integrated, recognised, part of the community.

The changing nature of crime has its effect on the role of police in the prevention of crime. The essence of community policing is to involve police with the community in a joint effort to reduce crime.[3] However, if

---

3   This is not to assert that police must be involved in all crime prevention, or that crime prevention is the sole aim of community policing. The "Concerned Men" group of Islamic African-Americans in Washington DC work with disaffected youth to find them jobs and self-respect, and reduction of crime is almost as a by-product of this.

communities have become used to the instant communication and fast cars which characterise reactive policing there is an expectation that police officers will appear virtually on demand whenever they are called. Chief officers of police throughout the world have had to come to terms with the fact that there is not a bottomless pit of money for policing, and the public likewise have to face the fact that police resources are finite, and adjust their expectations accordingly. One of the aspects of policing that may need to be sacrificed in implementing a long term, proactive policing strategy on crime, is the automatic dispatch of police officers to all requests from the public. Policing is changing rapidly, and organisational, ethical and management issues arise in the transition from the reactive, thief-taking and order-restoring model of the past to an approach which seeks to work with the community to prevent crime and answer society's needs within financial constraints in a culturally sensitive and ethical manner.

Part 3 discusses questions of police accountability. There is a major paradox here concerning control and autonomy which arises from the nature of the police as a body. The police, even those police agencies which have changed focus and are now designated as police services, are an armed, trained force (while police in Britain and New Zealand are almost alone in the world in not carrying guns routinely, batons and capsicum sprays are part of their equipment). Police agencies are the only civil force with both de facto and de jure power to enforce compliance with their instructions.

Three aspects of accountability are analysed in depth: financial accountability, which concerns whether the money allocated for policing is being used effectively; operational accountability, whether the policing strategies, tactics and aims are those that are required by and acceptable to the community;[4] and individual accountability, the provision of a mechanism by which individual police officers can be held accountable for their actions and behaviour. The widely differing approaches of Australian, British and American policing to these issues are examined.

The final part of the book looks at the future of policing, both as an extrapolation of current trends, and a discussion of the limits to a police response to crime. In some ways, the modern police service is too sophisticated and expensive to allow officers to spend their time carrying out some of its traditional functions: a plethora of security patrols are now doing what the officer on the beat traditionally used to do, and are doing it much cheaper than any modern police service can. Technology has changed society, and has also brought changes in the nature of crime: police must change to keep pace. No longer is fraud carried out with stolen cheque books, but with cloned credit cards, and identities can now be stolen as well as tangible property. These are new crimes for police to deal with, while traditional police work remains. People will still fight, steal,

---

4   "Community" as used here is a flexible term. What might suit the majority may have a serious impact on one small section of society. The whole question of what is the "community" to which police are accountable will be explored in detail in Part 2.

crash cars and have emergencies where, however serious or trivial the matter might appear to an observer, the first resort for those involved is the police.

Two important matters have arisen already in the 21st century which have called for large-scale police activity, but in which police may well be virtually powerless. The first is the need for a police response to terrorism, which transcends both police jurisdictional boundaries and national borders. The second is the increasing use of the Internet for criminal purposes. While almost every technological advance can be turned to criminal use, the very advantages Internet communication brings to business are also brought to criminals. The same digital camera and Internet technology that allows families and friends to share weddings and births almost instantly across the world also allows pornographers access to a world-wide market. While some websites may allow stamp collectors and budgerigar breeders to get in touch with each other and share information, other websites allow paedophiles, cannibals[5] and bomb-makers the same ease of communication.

There are, of course, many other problems facing police in the 21st century. Some are old crimes in new guises, there being trends and fashions in crime as everything else, but there are some wholly new crimes, brought into being by new technology. This book does not try to examine them all, but seeks to show how, by harking back to the fundamental principles and philosophy of the essential nature of policing, some at least may be addressed.

---

5   In a case in Germany in 2004, the person convicted of killing and eating another claimed to have found his victim on the Internet, and a number of other cannibal websites have since been identified.

PART I

THE SOCIAL AND HISTORICAL CONTEXTS OF POLICING

CHAPTER 1

THE TRIANGLE OF TENSION

Introduction

This chapter explores the tensions which exist within a modern democratic state between society, its law and its police: each in some way determines the other two, yet is at the same time dependent on them. The law may be viewed as a set of rules within which society operates, and to change the rules is to change society: the law determines society. However, the rules of society also contain a set of procedures, the rules for both creating and amending legislation and electing a legislature for changing these societal rules: hence society determines the law. The law may also include arbitrary rules, where regulation is needed, but there is no incontrovertibly correct procedure. For example Australian traffic law directs traffic to drive on the left-hand side of the road, while American traffic law directs traffic to drive on the right: neither regulation has any advantage over the other, all that matters is that traffic be regulated so that traffic in each direction stays on a particular side of the road. One of the major themes of this chapter is to explore the co-determinacy of society and its law, since these combine to provide the formal context of policing.

Society not only needs law, but needs a means of enforcing the law – the police. Police in a modern society have not only lawful authority to enforce the law, but a virtual monopoly in enforcing the law. Three factors combine to render the police the most effective means of control in society: the lawful power of the police; the structured, organised nature of the police organisation; and the fact that no other entity in the state has anything like the same general powers. Other law enforcement agencies like Customs, Tax Office, and Public Health may have stronger powers than police in specific circumstances, but all lack the patrolling omnipresence and wide general powers of police. In some circumstances, specialist law enforcement agencies need the presence of police for their actions to be lawful: security agencies may find evidence of espionage, but lack a power of arrest, and public health investigators may lack power of forcible entry. A free society needs, ultimately, to have its police acting for the benefit of all its members: the power of the police is too great for control to be entrusted to any single arm of government, and likewise too great to allow the police themselves total autonomy.

The relationship between the law and police is complex. While police must enforce the law, they must enforce the law as it is, and may use only those powers granted under the law so to do. However, police work is largely discretionary: although the law gives police powers, it does not make the exercise of these powers mandatory – the law customarily says "any officer may arrest" rather than "any officer must arrest". The judiciary has a role in the supervision of the exercise of police powers in those cases which result in a prosecution, but must also decide solely on the case before it at the moment, rather than on a pattern of behaviour. For example, a court considering the legality of a search procedure can hear evidence only of the particular search involved in the case before it – suggestions that others should have been searched but were not, or that the officer involved habitually exhibits racist behaviour, are beyond the purview of the court.[1] The relationship between police and the law, where police must work within the law and under the law in order to uphold the law is sometimes uneasy.

Society and the law

Perhaps the most widely known statement made by Aristotle is that "Man is a political animal". By this he meant that human beings, even in the fourth century BC, normally live in mutually supporting groups in one place, and are not usually solitary wanderers. The pinnacle of civilised living was, to Aristotle, the polis, the Greek city or island state, a "political animal" being simply one who lives in a polis. An Aristotelian polis was organised, the very organisation presupposing the existence of a set of rules and a means of enforcing those rules and settling disputes. At the very minimum, members of a polis require government, law and courts.

Rules pervade the lives of every individual who has anything to do with others, whether or not this is recognised. Quite often these rules are no more than ossified convention, and most rules or conventions are hardly recognised as such because there is widespread agreement to obey them. The rule that traffic in Australia and Britain keeps to the left of the road and in the United States and continental Europe to the right is a matter of convention, as is using the right hand to shake hands.

Many of the rules of society go beyond this matter of convention or general agreement. The first problem for society is that whenever there are a number of individuals together disputes will arise, and even the least sophisticated society needs a means of resolving these. In very broad terms, disputes which cannot be settled by the disputing parties need to be settled by arbitration or adjudication. Already the complexities of dispute resolution are growing, and the complexity increases when the need for a process of enforcement of the settlement decision on one or both of the disputing parties is taken into account. In general, all societies have a need for rules which are consistent and broadly in keeping with the mores of that society.

---

1   While a court cannot directly criticise or punish police for habitually racist behaviour, if an officer is shown to be racist it may taint the prosecution such that the jury acquits, as was seen in the OJ Simpson case.

There are conflicting accounts[2] among criminologists of the roots of law. The first is that societies are expected to have an individual or a group in charge (aptly illustrated by the cartoon alien whose opening words are "Take me to your leader") and that the rules are set by this individual or group, whose vested interests include remaining in a position of authority. The second account, following from the account of social complexity above, is that law is a consensus, a natural product of the way in which people live and their desire to perpetuate this pattern. Both accounts claim historical justification.

The early tribal and mediaeval ruler made the rules, was the ultimate arbiter or judge, and employed armed men to enforce the decisions made. The dangers of such autocracy have long been recognised, typically by Plato, who advocated a republic controlled by an assembly of philosopher kings whose worth had been proved in service to society in a variety of roles, and by Hobbes, whose ideal Commonwealth was ruled by a truly Christian prince.[3] In keeping, perhaps, with the way Hobbes saw society growing ever better from the "nasty, brutish and short" life in a state of nature, the law has changed with the passage of time, becoming more sophisticated, complex and more open to change than in the past.

Rule by a sovereign or an elite has been the norm throughout history, and even when kings in European countries started sharing power with parliaments, such parliaments were usually comprised of the rich and powerful members of the aristocracy. These historical facts do certainly support the arguments that the law is an instrument for maintaining control by one stratum of society over others. The alternative argument that law is a consensus of the rules members of society require everyone to live by is supported by the fact that different societies have different laws on certain topics. The laws on divorce and abortion are stringent in countries with a largely Catholic populace like Ireland and Spain, for example, and the laws restricting possession of firearms are minimal in Texas, where guns are considered an adjunct to normal life.

The modern democratic state has a much more open law-making process than earlier democracies, which, arguably, makes it more responsive to the needs and desires of society as a whole. Various factors may be considered contributory to this. Historically the earliest of these is the post-Enlightenment emphasis on individual rights which was first explicitly stated in the American Declaration of Independence of 1776 and the French Revolutionary Declaration of 1789. Individual rights have assumed such importance, and have become so much a part of life in the modern western state, that it is something of a shock to remember that they have a history of little more than 200 years, and are not universally accepted in all cultures, particularly those wherein this life is held to be transitory or worthless in itself, or those that insist the laws of man are subservient to those of God.

---

2   The two views outlined here are discussed substantially in Hagan (1985, Ch 2).

3   These dangers are at the heart of Plato's Republic and Hobbes' Leviathan. Plato's vision was rather more oligarchic than democratic, as he claimed that democracy was one step away from the descent into tyranny.

The second important factor is that the right to participate in selecting members of the legislative body or becoming a member of such a body has been granted to more and more members of society. 1997 marked the centenary of the right to vote first being granted to women (in New Zealand), and throughout the 20th century gender and property restrictions on the right to vote have been relaxed until virtually universal adult suffrage has been achieved in most democracies.

The third factor which is of interest is that modern societies are more culturally egalitarian than ever before. Ethnic minority groups have frequently been marginalised both by discriminatory treatment by society and by reduced legal rights. Until 1744, for example, recourse to the English law was not available to Jews, Moslems, Catholics and others by the simple expedient of only allowing evidence from a witness who was willing to take an oath on the gospels.[4] The latter half of this century has seen an almost complete legal recognition of the equal status of different cultures in Western-style democracies: while this may not have been followed by the disappearance of discriminatory practices, such practices are no longer supported or encouraged by the law.

There is a co-determinacy between society and its law. The justification that governments claim for their actions is that their election gives them a mandate to take particular legislative action, whether or not it is popular with various sections of the population. Democratic theory holds that the people are infallible in electing governments to enact the law that society needs – if a government acts against the wishes of the people, it will lose the next election. However, the law itself is one of the determinants of the nature of society: individuals will refrain from certain acts because they are punishable under the law, but these acts are punishable under the law because society in general finds such acts unacceptable. The law reflects social mores to a large extent, even though these mores are liable to change over time. Patrick Devlin, an English judge, argued strongly against the decriminalisation of homosexual behaviour suggested by the Wolfenden Report in 1959, claiming that it is contrary to the Christian moral principles which underpin the law (Devlin, 1965). Although this argument may seem to many to be untenable now, his general argument that changes in the law irrevocably change the nature of society are undeniable.[5]

---

4   The relevant case is *Omychund v Barker* (1744) 1 Atk 21; 26 ER 15. The gospels required by common law were the Bible of the Established Church, ie the King James Bible, which was not the version acceptable to Catholics or certain other groups, for example strict Calvinists. No Christian Bible was considered sacred by other religions.

5   Devlin feels strongly that morals are at the heart of the law, and that English law reflects the fact that England is essentially a Christian country. Non-Christians have, therefore, no right to disapprove of English law because it fails to take into account their beliefs, or prohibits some of the practices acceptable to their religion. For Devlin, the multicultural nation would have been anathema, but he does show presciently how apparently slight changes in the law to accommodate minorities have a major effect, changing society radically.

Rules and rights

Modern democracies are both rights-driven and rule-governed, even though the two are often in conflict. The essence of statements of human rights[6] is the principle of individual liberty, the freedom to choose for oneself and not be oppressed, coerced, constrained or restricted in one's actions. However, the main restrictions and constraints on any individual are those imposed by the law, and many are enforced by the police. One cannot drive a car, build a house, marry, or even own a dog without conforming to the conditions set by legislation. Despite the stated commitment to liberty of the modern state, the uncomfortable fact is that government itself is the biggest single restriction on liberty.[7] The sheer volume of legislation enacted by modern parliaments shows how rule-bound societies have become, and although a parliament attuned to public opinion is unlikely to pass law which impinges too noticeably on the liberty of the majority of individuals, it is incontrovertible that we are more and more constrained by law in more and more aspects of our daily lives.

If the consensus theory of law is correct, that the law reflects and codifies the general behaviour patterns of society, then the law does not run counter to the choices the majority would make. If I respect other people's property, then the law of theft does not prevent me from doing anything I would choose to do, nor demand of me actions I would rather not take. If I habitually drive carefully at a reasonable speed, then I shall not contravene the traffic law unless I am uncharacteristically careless or in a hurry. For most individuals most of the time the law which enforces normal behaviour is like a good suit, which fits closely without being tight in places or restricting movement. Nevertheless, even for the person who views the law as fair and reasonable, and believes it enforces behaviour which should be required of everyone, the law can sometimes constrict.

The problem of the law's imposition of constraints on individual liberty is compounded in a multicultural society. The law's enforcement of general patterns of behaviour is acceptable only if general patterns of behaviour across society are actually identifiable. If society is homogeneous, that is if all its members are broadly similar in way of life, background and outlook, then such standards of behaviour are likely to be agreed. If, however, there is no such homogeneity, then there can be no general agreement over behavioural standards. Unless there is consensus in society over what is approved, acceptable, or tolerated and what is unacceptable or offensive to the point of needing society's disapproval to be shown, there can be no law equally acceptable to all.

To the conflict theorist of law the lack of general behaviour patterns is unproblematic. The law is determined by the ruling group within society, and that group is likely to reach consensus over what behaviour is to be

---

6   As expressed in declarations from the late 18th century French Revolutionary Declaration, the American Constitutional "Bill of Rights", many later State Constitutions and the United Nations Declarations of Human Rights from 1948 on.

7   This is most persuasively argued by Nozick (1974) amongst others.

declared unlawful, while the rest of society is expected to abide by this. This is summed up by Devlin, in the work mentioned earlier, where he takes as an example the English law on marriage:

> In England we believe in the Christian idea of marriage and therefore adopt monogamy as a moral principle. Consequently the Christian institution of marriage has become the basis of family life and so part of the structure of our society. It is there not because it is Christian. It has got there because it is Christian, but it remains there because it is built into the house in which we live and could not be removed without bringing it down ... [A] non-Christian is bound by it, not because it is part of Christianity but because, rightly or wrongly, it has been adopted by the society in which he lives. (Devlin, 1965 p 9)

For Devlin, England is a Christian nation, its rulers are Christian, and no allowance can be made for those who do not share the outlook of the Christian tradition.

Law which appears sound to the majority may well have a severe and deleterious impact on minority groups. Among the rights which are typically taken most seriously are those which allow freedom of religious belief and expression, and the maintenance of cultural identity within the larger society. Even this can clash with the law at times. The Amish people, for example, generally coexist peacefully yet separately with mainstream America, but were troubled by education requirements under the law, a matter eventually decided by the Supreme Court.[8] The law against murder effectively bans human sacrifice, and one might not take too seriously the claim by devil worshippers that this affects their rights of religious expression, on the grounds that Satanism is not acceptable as a religion. Mutilation, however, is a religious or cultural requirement of a variety of groups ranging from the circumcision of male infants in Judaism and Islam, through ritual scarification among some African tribes, initiation rituals in Australian Aboriginal culture, to the female genital mutilation practised by some African Islamic groups.

In strict Western legal terms, any of the requirements mentioned can constitute an assault, unless medical necessity can be proved, and, if it involves someone who has not reached adulthood, can be argued to constitute child abuse. Not many people would be prepared to argue that the law of a secular or Christian state should make criminals of those who circumcise male infants, while few would find female genital mutilation legally acceptable. These examples represent two extremes of the extent to which the majority in society is prepared to tolerate or curtail the religious practices of minorities, and illustrate the deep waters that surround law and rights issues. There remains the danger that the group that dominates the legislature will create law which permits only those religious expressions

---

8   *Wisconsin v Yoder*, 406 US 305 (1972) US Supreme Court. It may well be that some of the Amish felt compromised through having to leave their community for mainstream America by participating in the court case itself.

and rituals that that group agrees are acceptable, and enforces these laws upon the minority.[9]

There is, of course, much more which can be said about the relation between a society and its law. Society itself is in a state of constant change, as is the law, and each impels or impairs change in the other. Equal opportunities legislation, for example, has forced society and its institutions into adopting egalitarian employment practices, but can do little to change the opinions of individuals within society. However, the experience of working with people of other races and gender can affect the opinions of individuals, or reinforce their prejudices. Rarely is society and its law entirely of one voice, although there is usually general agreement. On the occasions when the law is broken, police are called upon to enforce it, which means that the views of the majority, once translated into law, are imposed upon minorities by the police.

Society and the police

Societies in which rights are of major importance are keen to guard against the imposition of power from any quarter, particularly government. Montesquieu noted with approval the system in 18th century England which he termed the separation of powers, where the Crown had power as executive, but parliament had power to create laws and control money, while the administration of justice was accomplished by the judiciary. Each of these had significant power and while each was independent of the others, each was constrained by the others. The emerging democratic republics of the late 18th century all followed the pattern of separating government powers, and Constitutions were written so as to restrict rather than empower governments, like Jefferson's claim that:

> Free government is founded in jealousy, not in confidence, it is jealousy not confidence which prescribes our limited constitutions, to bind those we are obliged to trust with power ... In questions of power, let no more be heard of confidence in man, but bind him down from mischief by the chains of the Constitution. (Jefferson, 1789)[10]

The most serious and obvious practice of power within modern society is that exercised by police. Before the rights-based political theories of the late 18th century, those who ruled societies employed their own forces to keep order, often without reference to the wants and needs of society as a whole. A modern society which values individual liberty will look very closely at any infringement of that liberty by government, and at the particular arm of government whose actions are seen to be restrictive. The power wielded by police is all the more worrying to members of society if they feel they have no means of controlling the police and their powers.

---

9   The argument here is discussed in more depth in Edwards (1997). In effect, though, a state which permits male circumcision but not female circumcision is making paternalistic regulations on how far groups are permitted to maintain their cultural practices.

10   This, the Kentucky Declaration, was, in effect, that State's first constitutional document.

Police powers

It is worth considering briefly the extent of police powers, and the almost complete monopoly police have of direct power over the individual in civil society. In the course of a day individuals have choice on how their time is spent, where they go, whom they speak to, and so on. Even when there is constraint, for example at work, individuals may still choose to report sick, strike, or even tell the boss where to put the job and take the consequences. A police officer has lawful power under certain circumstances to deny all these choices to an individual, and take away individual liberty. Police powers allow the search of a person in the street or at a police station, deprivation of liberty by arrest, questioning as to movements, name, address and proof of identity may be demanded and so on. More importantly, police powers frequently authorise officers to use force if necessary to exercise them.

To put police powers in context, no other individual or body has anything like the general powers police have. Customs officers have powers to search, but only with regard to a particular small category of offence, and these are most commonly exercised at ports. Immigration officers likewise have powers of detention, but only of persons who are unlawfully in the country. With very few exceptions, lawful powers to search, arrest and detain are given to police and only to police. Police are not only authorised to use force, but are both equipped and trained so to do. In Britain this is absolute: no person is allowed a loaded firearm in a public place except police, and no offensive weapons may be carried, even for personal protection. Police on general patrol rarely carry firearms (although they are more commonly issued now for particular operations), but are equipped with batons and capsicum spray and trained in their use. In Australia the rules are less rigid and exceptions may be made, for example for security guards, but in general police are the only persons lawfully armed on the streets. In the United States, firearms laws are extremely relaxed, and many people are licensed to carry firearms, and are equipped, if not authorised, to use force against their fellow citizens.

The lawful use of force by police is discretionary, the decision being made by individual officers without reference to supervisors. This is also true of the power to arrest, which means that the momentous question of the suspension of individual rights is often decided by the most junior and inexperienced members of the police service. The use of police powers which is of most concern to the community is that which is fruitless, and it is this which is the least likely to come to official notice. Any exercise of police power which results in a prosecution automatically permits review by the courts: any exercise of power which does not result in arrest does not normally even come to the notice of a supervising officer. The conviction of a suspect for an offence can easily be seen by police and some members of the public as post hoc justification for minor infractions of police powers, whereas the exercise of police powers which have no positive result, such as a search which reveals no prohibited item, can be a source of worry to the public while rarely being subject to supervision at the time or later, unless a formal complaint is made.

While police powers of search in the street may, when exercised, result in embarrassment and inconvenience for the individual concerned, police powers of detention are a direct and fundamental revocation of the right to liberty. This is not to claim that police should have no authority to arrest and detain, but shows how strong police powers are. To be detained in a police cell is not just to be deprived of liberty, but to be completely within the power of police, since few but police officers are present (except for other persons arrested) and contact with others may be severely limited if not denied completely, even when statutory prisoner's rights are met.

The power of police to operate as a body is limited only by the size of the police force itself. The Metropolitan Police in London each August puts thousands of police officers onto the few square miles of Notting Hill to police sometimes more than a million people at the West Indian carnival,[11] with all the tactics, planning, logistics and communications of a military operation. Combined operations of the various police forces through England and Wales during the miners' strike of 1983 showed, in the picket lines of Orgreave and elsewhere, a far more controlled and effective display of power involving far more manpower than many battles of the Boer War. News reports from around the world frequently show police dispersing rioters by force in times of civil unrest: rarely do the rioters overrun the police, despite their usually vastly superior numbers.

There are two conclusions which may be drawn from this. The first is that society has given to police officers as individuals enormous personal authority to act on its behalf to enforce the law. The second is that society has also created an organisation with the power and resources to take over and run that society against the wishes of society. In the Nazi era in Germany, the militaristic and oppressive police organisations of the SS and Gestapo held the power, as did the KGB in the Soviet Union. During the Franco era in Spain, the Guarda Civil were the main instrument of stifling insurrection and dissent, and the South African police were instrumental in maintaining apartheid. All of these, of course, were national policing bodies, and one way of reducing the power of the police as a body is to limit the size of that body. The American policing structure of each county having its sheriff and any municipality being entitled to appoint police produces a plethora of small policing bodies (and, of course, some large ones) which lack cohesive power as a body. In normal policing this works well, but in times of unrest or in major disasters, policing must be supplemented by the National Guard.[12]

---

11   The 1998 carnival was attended by 2 million people, and policed by 3800 officers. Numbers have been falling, 1.4 million in 2002 and 600,000 in 2003, although 9715 police were on duty.

12   This may in itself cause problems, as was seen in the public disorder during the 1960s at, for example, Kent State University. This is discussed more fully in Chapter 3.

Control and autonomy

The power that police can exercise, both as a body and by individual officers is such that it can impinge upon human rights and liberties. A police organisation which is controlled is a source of great power to its controllers, while a police service which controls itself is equally dangerous to the community. Society needs to monitor the power of police carefully, and harness it for the good of all. It follows, then, that there is a need for society as a whole to have some involvement in policing. The bald fact is that some level of control over police is claimed and exercised by government at the national, state or local level, and not infrequently there will be a multiplicity of police organisations with national, state, local, municipal, traffic and even tourist police agencies all answering to different levels of government. The reasons for, and consequences of, this government control of police bears close examination.

To place police, and the power they wield in the state, under the sole direction of executive government is to give that arm of government power to enforce its will on society and overrule opposition. It is also to give the individual police officer carte blanche to abuse, bully, or act outside the law to a degree acceptable to government, even if society, or certain sections of it, finds such activities unacceptable. This is not to say that to place a police force under the control of the government is to create a police state, but it can make any society's descent into totalitarianism much easier. A national police force, particularly if it is the sole police force, will have a large number of officers, and therefore a greater ability to coerce society. Control of police is embedded in the functioning political system of whichever society one chooses, and Montesquieu's separation of powers doctrine in its modern form must allow police some autonomy from government.

Consider some examples of police controlled by government. The Spanish Guarda Civil were a major instrument of repression in Spain throughout the Franco era. Although there were many other municipal, traffic and other police bodies, including incredibly benign tourist police in the Balearics and Costas who were prepared to tolerate all sorts of drunken and rowdy behaviour from numerous visitors from Northern Europe, the Guarda operated entirely to the satisfaction of their political masters and themselves. Complaints of corruption, violence or oppression against them were disregarded, and complainants risked being labelled dissidents, and open to investigation by the Guarda itself. The Italian Carabinieri are likewise a national police force – indeed, young Italians may opt to do their compulsory national service in the Carabinieri rather than the Army, Navy or Air Force. Italy too has local, municipal and tourist police agencies, the Carabinieri being one policing body amongst many, yet they are by no means an instrument of oppression. Nations with a federal system, wherein the component States have different laws and their own policing, still need a national police. This is the case with America's FBI and Australia's Federal Police (AFP), both of which are investigative agencies (although the AFP has a street policing role in the nation's capital and at international airports) to deal with federal crimes or interstate matters. Finally, very small nations may well be prevented by their very size from separating police from government. The peaceful and idyllic Republic of Maldives, for example, has but a few hundred of its citizens in the National Security Service, which is comprised of the Army, the Navy (which doubles as a coastguard), Air Force (which is the inter-island air link) and the Police, all of it military, and all under the control of the government.

Governments are, however, entitled to have some control over police activities. Financially, police will always be under the control of government, be it national, state or local, and to that extent be an arm of the executive branch of that tier of government.[13] If the government that exercises financial control also has the power of appointment or dismissal over the chief officer of police, then that person may well feel even more tightly controlled.[14] In places where the government is not democratically elected, then the politicians' vested interest is to keep the police as closely under their control as possible in order to maintain their grip on power, on the principle that the stronger police are, and the more closely controlled by the government they are, the better are the chances of the government continuing. While not imputing such motives to, for example, the Police Ministers of the States of Australia, the British Home Secretary, or Mayors of American cities, nevertheless elected politicians incline to the paternalistic view that, once elected, they have a mandate to do whatever they consider necessary, short of using the power of police directly to remain in office.

If policing is the responsibility of local government, then slightly different problems concerning the misuse of police power may occur. If those responsible for police are selected (or elected) from a small section of the actual population, then this group could exemplify the conflict theorists' description of how the whole corpus of law is used. Local oligarchic control of police was seen in Britain before the *Police Act* 1964, when every county and city and many towns had their own police force controlled by a Watch Committee, which appointed a Chief Constable to run the police force with a significant level of autonomy concerning operational control.

However, the members of the watch committee were, like the elected councillors, magistrates, and the local Chamber of Commerce, drawn from one small pool of local worthies of the affluent middle-class. Police officers soon learned whose cars it was wiser not to notice when they were illegally parked, and sergeants learned which individuals' calls for police should be dealt with promptly and unquestioningly. A similar misuse of police power in small societies was also to be seen in small communities in America, particularly in the south before the civil rights era. Sheriffs would be elected on the strength of their promise of the sort of policing the electorate required, and their re-election relied on their delivery of such policing.

---

13 This will be discussed in full in Chapter 9.
14 Police commissioners in Australia no longer have tenure, further limiting their independence from government, but are now appointed on a contract. New South Wales in 2002 dismissed an Assistant Commissioner, and Western Australia appoints inspectors and above on contract.

It is undoubtedly right that a police body should have autonomy from its political masters. There may well be occasions when police investigations involve members of the government, local or national, and the chief officers of police have a duty to continue their investigations and refuse to divulge details even to those who appoint them.[15] It is also right that individual officers have discretion whether or not to instigate a prosecution by infringement, summons or arrest if the facts warrant, without taking into account the status of the alleged offender or complainant. However, it has already been shown that the police are far too powerful a body to have complete autonomy, where individual officers are answerable to no-one but the chief officer, and the chief officer is answerable to no-one at all.

Answerability

If it is equally dangerous for police to be controlled by government or to be autonomous, then society itself must have some means of controlling its police. Direct control by the whole populace is not feasible, but it is possible for the police to be answerable to the public. Police organisational answerability exists when the society or community policed feels that it has some recourse if it is dissatisfied with the performance of its police. It is particularly important that police be answerable to society in some way for operational decisions and for the manner in which individual officers carry out their duties. All sections of society may be seriously affected by operational decisions taken by chief officers, or by senior officers responsible for geographical or strategic areas. The way police are armed and dressed, for example, may have a significant effect on the way they are perceived by the public. The police officer dressed for motor cycle duty with long boots, jodhpurs, leather jacket, helmet concealing the face and a large and visible sidearm is a far more menacing sight than the same officer dressed for foot or car patrol.

Every police service probably has its horror stories of operational decisions which were ill-conceived from the outset, or went disastrously wrong in operation. One such is Operation Swamp in Brixton, South London in 1981, which was an attempt to deal with a drug problem using large numbers of police in an extended stop-and-search operation. This was seen by the parts of the community, particularly those of Caribbean origin, as unfairly targeting young West Indian males. The build-up of resentment went unnoticed or was ignored by local police until it culminated in rioting, and a siege of the police station. The population of Brixton held its police answerable then by violent action, and, eventually, police acknowledged community concerns and ceased the operation. However, the power of the Metropolitan Police may well have been such that violence could have been met with violence, and the civil disturbances quelled by main force. In Queensland, ill-conceived and heavy-handed policing of anti-Vietnam war

---

15 This was illustrated in 1959 by the attempt by the Watch Committee of Nottingham, UK to suspend their Chief Constable, who was carrying out a criminal investigation into councillors. The matter is discussed in Marshall (1965).

protests in the late 1960s caused uproar, as did police public order tactics at the Chicago Democratic Party convention in 1968.

Clearly a less damaging form of communication between police and the community is necessary for police to take community feelings into account in operational decision-making. For police as an organisation to be answerable to society, they need to forge closer links with the community, and with community leaders. In a multicultural society, this involves contact with leaders of all community and ethnic groups by police at the level at which operational decisions are made. It is worth noting here that not all groups are easily identified, in that there may be more than just ethnic and racial distinctions involved and a lack of agreement among groups as to who actually represents them.

Aside from the question of the answerability of police as an organisation is the question of the answerability of individual police officers. These two may sometimes fuse. If a member of the public is dealt with badly, is abused or manhandled by a police officer but does nothing because that is the way in which police always behave, then the matter is less a question of the standards of an individual officer than of the standards of the organisation itself for its acceptance of such behaviour. Of crucial importance here is the question of the public perception of the complaints system as much as the efficacy of the system itself. The components of an effective system for police complaints must be such that they provide for full investigation of allegations, and for the result of the investigation to be open and publicly justified. Since society's most highly skilled and experienced investigators are to be found within its police, it follows that it is unavoidable that most of the investigation of complaints against police be carried out by police themselves. It also follows that if public confidence in the process is to be maintained, some high degree of involvement by persons or a body independent of police is required, and that this non-police presence must have the authority to criticise, overturn, or re-investigate the conclusions of the police investigators if that independent body is dissatisfied.

Police and the law

There are three particular areas wherein an uneasy tension may arise between police and the law or, more specifically, the criminal law. First, police can only enforce the law as it stands, not as they or the public might prefer it to be, and, conversely, they have a duty to enforce the law as it stands, and not ignore inconvenient or unpalatable issues. Secondly, the police must enforce the law using the powers granted them under the law, and, as prosecutors or investigators for the prosecution, must assemble sufficient evidence in a form which is acceptable to the courts. Finally, the arbiters of whether police powers are used correctly and lawfully and whether the evidence is legally acceptable are the judges and magistrates of the courts themselves. Each of these areas needs some analysis and explanation.

In the majority of cases in which police are requested by the public to attend incidents it is clear whether or not there has been a breach of the law, and whether there is some credible evidence to substantiate this. In many incidents either the action complained of does not amount to a breach of the law, or, if it does, there is no hard evidence to prove wrongdoing by the suspect. Consider, for example, a continuing dispute between neighbours over a barking dog, which culminates in the dog's being found dead, apparently poisoned. There is a great deal of difference between the dog-owner's belief that the neighbour was responsible, a belief shared by all who know the characters of the parties concerned and the history of the dispute, and there being evidence available to the police officer to prove the matter in court beyond reasonable doubt. Repetitive minor nuisances, phone calls, etc may cause extreme distress but not be contrary to any criminal statute.[16] In these sorts of case, police cannot act, however much they might wish to. In some instances, the opposite is the case. If, having been told police can take no action in the dog-poisoning case above, the distressed dog owner punches the presumed culprit, there might be ample evidence to support a charge of assault. Even if police feel that the dog owner is essentially the wronged party, they cannot refuse to take action provided that evidence is available to justify proceedings and the person punched demands it. Although police have some degree of discretion in prosecutorial decision-making, this discretion is limited, and will be considered shortly.

Police powers are clearly set out in the law, and include, under various forms in various jurisdictions, powers to stop, question, search, detain for the purpose of search, arrest for an offence, admit a person to bail or refuse bail pending court appearance, seize property, order a mechanical inspection of a motor vehicle, etc. Improper use of police powers may arise from police exceeding their powers or abusing their powers, two very different actions, and viewed very differently by the courts. Let us consider first cases of police exceeding their powers.

Although police powers are very clear, they all include some such phrase as "reasonable cause", "probable cause", "well founded suspicion" as a basis for the exercise of the power. There are various tests for this,[17] and within common law systems there is a considerable volume of precedent setting out examples of what does and does not constitute cause or suspicion enough to exercise the power. Clearly, if no justification exists for the exercise of the power, then the police officer has exceeded those powers and acted unlawfully. Suppose the power exercised was a stop and search in the street. If some prohibited item is found in such a search, then the

---

16   Many jurisdictions have recently passed legislation against stalkers and other forms of harassment, but the possibilities for petty vindictiveness are legion, and may not amount to offences under any legislation.

17   The most common is the "reasonable man" test, expressed in some detail under the *Police and Criminal Evidence Act* 1984 (UK). In general, exercise of police powers is justified if a hypothetical impartial observer would find it justified, or the action taken complies with stated legal criteria.

search will be followed by an arrest, prosecution, and a court case. Only if the defendant challenges the validity of the search as part of the defence will the court be able to consider whether or not the search was lawful. If the search is found to be unjustified, then the court may rule it inadmissible as evidence, and the prosecution will be lost.[18]

The problem that arises is that there is no adjudication at the time of the search as to its permissibility. In cases where a prohibited item is found, the question is ultimately decided by the court at a much later date, which leaves time for police to prepare a justification for court, the officer working backwards to find reasons for the search which will persuade the judge or magistrate that the search was valid. In cases where nothing is found, then there is unlikely to be an arrest, and the matter generally does not come to the notice of the court. Most members of society are aware, in general terms, that police have power to search individuals without being aware of the precise extent of these powers, so few persons against whom these powers are exercised are likely to be aware when the powers are exceeded. There may well be a feeling on the part of the aggrieved person that the search ought never to have taken place, but this does not amount to a clear realisation that the officer exceeded the powers available.

The situation then, with regard to police officers exceeding their powers, is that officers can usually only be held to account in law if the search is successful, or if the person against whom the powers are used is sufficiently aware of the law, or has sufficient legal advice, to mount some form of civil suit. Even if the individual makes a formal complaint against police, there is time and opportunity for the police officer concerned to prepare a justification. It is a frequent police complaint that the delay between the laying of a charge and the hearing of a case before a jury gives the defendant time to concoct a spurious defence once access is given to the prosecution case: the same applies when complaints are made against police, since any delay gives police officers time to produce a superficially acceptable, if totally fallacious, account of their actions.

Abuse of police power is rather different. Typically, police powers may be used in a way which may fall completely within the requirements of the law, and pass all the tests of reasonableness as a single incident, but be part of a pattern of discriminatory use against a particular individual or section of the community. An exercise of police powers must be justified, as we have seen, but, even when the exercise is justified, individual police officers have discretion whether or not to exercise their powers. If some police officers develop the habit of only exercising their powers with regard to certain sections of the population, or certain individuals, then there is an

---

18   There is some variation on the stance courts take in such matters. Clearly, if the search does turn up a prohibited item, then there is some feeling that there is post hoc justification for it. Australian courts are likely to give more weight to this post hoc justification, and only rule the evidence inadmissible if there is some glaring police malpractice. British courts are more likely to consider the good faith of the officer in carrying out the search, while American courts hold that an unlawful search is a violation of constitutional rights, therefore it, and all that follows from it, is inadmissible.

abuse of power. Frequent searches of members of a particular racial group may all be individually justifiable, and, if a prohibited item is found, the court may well find that the search was well within the requirements of the law. However, the fact that that particular group was singled out for searching may suggest abuse of power, despite the police claims that those searched were persons whom experience in similar circumstances had shown to be more likely than most to be carrying prohibited items.

The courts are powerless to deal with many abuses of power. Each case must be dealt with separately, and, in the same way that previous behaviour of a defendant is largely irrelevant to the incident before the courts, so the officer's exercise of power with regard to others is irrelevant when considering whether or not, on this particular occasion, the power was lawfully exercised. Only when an abuse of power is coupled with powers being exceeded can the courts exercise any control over the matter, for example when the search is both discriminatory and unjustified.

While in some cases, such as the use of lawful powers, there are opportunities for police officers to "rewrite the script" in self-justification, there are also cases where the law itself can be seen as preventing a richly deserved conviction. There is, of course, a need for procedural justice in the courts, whereby cases are decided on the evidence, and that evidence must comply with the rules necessary for its acceptance. Witnesses must be called, the truth must be told, methods of obtaining evidence must be fair, and the benefit of any doubt given to the defendant. Nevertheless, society is concerned that justice be seen to be done according to the facts of the case. Decisions which rest primarily on the arcana of legal argument concerning procedural fairness rather than evidence are seen as less than satisfactory. Police officers not infrequently prepare cases where all the information points to the guilt of the suspect and there is no reason to doubt that the right person is accused, yet that information is not all acceptable as evidence in court. It is, of course, part of police duty to collect sufficient information in a form that is acceptable as evidence, which is by no means an easy task. We have all seen fictional detectives who unmask the villain by a train of brilliant logical deduction from facts dismissed by others as irrelevant and an elaborate trap; the villain then obligingly fills in the missing details of the crime. In most courts, almost none of this would even be admissible, and certainly insufficient as evidence to convince a jury beyond reasonable doubt. Parties to the case who do not have a background in law are inclined to see the rules of procedural justice as unduly pedantic, and blame police for failing to prosecute effectively.

Police are seen by society as representative of the law itself. As such, they are in the front line for criticism when the public fear an increase in crime.[19] While police have an appreciation of the rules of evidence and

---

19   Crime statistics over the past 10 years generally show a falling crime rate, although public perception, perhaps led by bad news stories in the media, is the opposite. In 1998, for example, the British Home Office Crime Survey showed that crime has dropped by 8 per cent over previous years, although 75 per cent of the public surveyed on crime thought it had risen. The fear of crime, unfortunately, is as problematic for society as crime itself.

procedure, and recognise a need for fair procedures, in some cases the public may see rulings with regard to crucial evidence as legal hairsplitting and contrary to the need to put the facts as fully as possible before the court.[20] Even before the case reaches court, a prosecution may be stopped by a public prosecutor, not always with the agreement of the police. The effect may be to bring the justice system into some disrepute with the public, and since the police are an integral part of the system, they share some of the opprobrium.

The law provides considerable discretion to police officers. There is no legal obligation on police to carry out a search or arrest a suspect just because the conditions authorising such a search or arrest are met. This means that officers on patrol have some choice of whom they question, if indeed they question anyone, or how they deal with offences they discover themselves. However, in dealing with incidents where there is a complainant or independent witness, the needs and wishes of these individuals must be taken into account. Discretion needs to be properly exercised, otherwise police officers run the risk of either dealing lawfully but unfairly with individuals or sections of the community, or pre-empting the decisions of the judge and jury rather than acting as prosecutor.

Consider police powers of arrest. Each power of arrest carries its own parameters and conditions, not least of which is that there must be some prima facie evidence that a stipulated offence has been committed by the person arrested. However, arrest powers typically start with the rubric "any officer *may* arrest" (my italics), which indicates clearly that the law has no expectation that an arrest is an automatic consequence of the presence of conditions which would render the arrest lawful. Clearly, if the incident is fully investigated by a police officer but found to be trivial, and the victim has no great desire for a prosecution, the matter can be dealt with by way of caution. In many minor incidents, there is nothing to be gained from taking the matter before the courts.

However, cases do arise where a police officer, having investigated the facts fully, not only finds prima facie evidence of the offence, but also some evidence which is likely to give rise to a reasonable doubt in the minds of the jury. Suppose that there is clear evidence that an individual accused of theft took the property, but the suspect's claim that it was taken by mistake has some plausibility. Discretion in the power of arrest means that there is no obligation on the officer to arrest, but failure to do so decides the issue in favour of the suspect. The question arises whether or not this is a proper

---

20 An example worth considering here is the case put together in the mid-1990s by the Australian National Crime Authority against John Elliott and others. The investigation took many years to come to trial, at an extremely high financial cost, but at an early stage of the proceedings the trial judge ruled that a large and crucial part of the prosecution case was inadmissible. The case was sufficiently weakened by this that the prosecution was withdrawn. The Victorian Court of Appeal later expressed some disquiet at the validity of the ruling. The main point at issue is that contentious decisions on procedural issues benefit no-one: the prosecution case, particularly its evidence, has not been fully tested, the public decide the matter on prejudice rather than fact, and the conclusion is highly unsatisfactory.

exercise of police discretion, and there are unpalatable consequences of both arrest and failure to arrest. To arrest and charge leaves the matter for the court to decide, and the argument in favour of arrest is that these matters should be decided in the correct legal forum, the courts. However, if the officer is personally persuaded by the suspect's claim that the taking was a mistake not dishonesty, and this is the subsequent finding of the court, then to arrest causes a loss of liberty and some trauma for an innocent person. However, for the police officer to decline to arrest because the defence is plausible is to deny the complainant effective access to the courts – in effect, the police officer has heard the evidence and taken on the role of jury to acquit. There are very fine distinctions between making a judgement on whether there is enough evidence for a conviction to be possible, whether there is enough evidence for a conviction to be likely, and what a jury is likely to decide on the facts revealed.

There is an imbalance in the supervision of a police officer's exercise of discretion. As has been shown, if a police officer chooses to carry out a search and make an arrest, then the matter appears before the court where the officer's actions can be ratified or criticised. If the officer exercises the discretion to refrain from acting then the matter is ended. No-one is aware of the matter, nothing has happened so there is nothing to report to senior officers, and there is no possibility of criticising the officer later. The decision of an officer not to exercise police powers may not be a good one for society or for justice, but it is one which is extremely hard to prove to be malpractice. This use of discretion by the patrolling officer on the street is a matter which is frequently the subject of dispute by individuals who are stopped, searched or arrested, and will be discussed again under the topic of ethics.

Once a police officer has made a decision to arrest, the law provides a number of levels where that decision can be ratified or overturned before a full hearing in court. The United States and Britain have a public prosecutions department for all cases, which means that every prosecution, for whatever offence, however trivial, is undertaken by lawyers for the state. The American district attorney is involved in prosecutions at a very early stage, even before a charge is laid, and the discretion of police to prosecute beyond the decision to arrest is very limited. In Britain, the arresting officer's actions are immediately subject to scrutiny when the prisoner is brought to the police station, as the designated custody officer (of the rank of sergeant or above) must authorise detention.[21] Although the charge is decided by police, the matter is prosecuted at court by the Crown Prosecution Service who have the right, even at the first court appearance, to withdraw or change the charges laid. Australian police have significantly more discretion and power in prosecutions, since matters before magistrates are usually prosecuted by police themselves, and the Director of Public Prosecutions or Crown Law Department are only involved in cases which are sent for trial by judge and jury.

---

21   *Police and Criminal Evidence Act* 1984 (UK) s 37.

Conclusion

This chapter has only scratched the surface of some of the issues that arise between a society, its law and its police. The relation between a society and its law has been discussed at length by legal philosophers, sociologists and anthropologists amongst others, all with a different perspective, but all illustrating the problems of the relationship. The law defines society, but perhaps only in the way in which society would wish to define itself. Islamic societies can prohibit alcohol, pigs and dogs because those societies believe there is something inherently wrong or unclean about them, whereas the prohibition of alcohol failed in the United States because too large a proportion of the population enjoyed drinking. Stringent gun control works in Britain because the majority of the population have no wish to shoot anything, and can see no good reason for possessing something which, with the exception of shotguns and hunting rifles, is designed for the express purpose of killing people, while many Americans view gun ownership as a fundamental right.

Although modern policing in democratic countries is moving towards the concept of community service and many chief officers are proud to call their organisation a "Police Service", as an agency of social control the police are still a force. When called upon to effect an arrest, and by their nature as armed, uniformed citizens authorised to coerce, the police are a force, even though that force is unequivocally directed towards the service of the community. The unease in the relationship between police and society is perhaps encapsulated in this force / service dichotomy, where the community desires the services of police and is uncomfortable with force being used against it, yet the powers of police are a necessary evil in dealing with the criminal part of the community. A similar relationship exists between police and the law itself, whereby all a police officer's powers and all the constraints on police action come from the law: the law gives authority to police with one hand, while restraining them with the other.

A society, its police and its law are all inextricably interdependent, yet with a dynamic tension between the three which restricts each with regard to the other two. The power of the people and the rights of the individual rely heavily on the maintenance of this dynamic tension. It is within this context that the role and accountability of police will be examined in this book.

CHAPTER 2

THE HISTORY OF POLICING

Introduction

The most important year in the history of modern policing is 1829, the year in which the Metropolitan Police was founded in London by the then Home Secretary, Sir Robert Peel. Although there had been bodies responsible for good order in society before, the Metropolitan Police are usually said to be the first modern police force, and set the pattern for civil policing elsewhere. Using that date as a starting point, this chapter looks at the history of police and the subsequent development of Peel's concept of a civil force to maintain law and order in Australia, Britain and the United States.

Changes in society in the early 19th century prompted the establishment of the modern police force. The industrial revolution, which affected all of Europe and the northern States of America, caused many major social changes which were in large part responsible for the need for policing in cities and towns. Another contributory factor to the need for police, especially in Britain, was the civil disorder caused by returning soldiers and sailors from the Napoleonic wars who were largely homeless, unemployed, and often disabled by wounds. The need for police was not, therefore, peculiar to London, but the model of police established in the Metropolis became a model for the police in town and country areas throughout Britain, and in numerous other countries.

The British Parliament engaged in heated debate before Peel's proposal was accepted, and there was significant resistance among those who feared the power of an organised, uniformed police force. The only existing alternative to the outdated British system of the watch and parish constables was the European system of armed men paid by rulers to keep order, and the even more fearsome system of spies and informers that went with the larger kingdoms. As a result, the first British police force was established with clear rules of conduct and control, and all possible steps were taken to prevent it becoming the tool of autocratic oppression that policing bodies commonly were in European states. As the police force became accepted, a particular view of the non-threatening "Bobby" prevailed, and was perpetuated in fact and fiction.

Australia at the time of the establishment of the British police was a British colony ultimately subject to the direct rule of the Westminster Parliament, which significantly influenced the establishment of policing in

Australia. The United States had been a British colony from the 16th century through to the late 18th century and many of the institutions of American life were subsequent adaptations of established mediaeval and Tudor models. Their British heritage underlay the political and cultural history of the United States and Australia and had a significant effect on the development of police in these nations.

Peel's police force

The English common law developed quirks and complexities from simple and sound basic principles: so too did the administration of this law, including the early powers of constables, sheriffs and Justices of the Peace, or magistrates. The Constable was an individual appointed by the parish to keep order and take offenders into custody, while the office of sheriff was even older, pre-dating the Norman Conquest. The Sheriff, or Shire Reeve, was responsible originally for keeping the peace, imprisoning felons, collecting fines and acting as an officer of the sovereign with particular regard to fiscal matters. With the institution of Justices of the Peace and parish constables, much of the maintenance of law and order had devolved to local officials answerable directly to at least the land-holding members of local communities.

The British system of sheriffs, parish constables, local magistrates and circuit judges attending Courts of Assize and Quarter Sessions worked reasonably well while Britain remained a largely agricultural society, where even the large towns like York and Canterbury had populations numbered in the thousands. The late 18th century saw the establishment of mechanised, steam-driven industry, and the wholesale movement of population to the cities. Indeed, whole new centres of population sprang up, overtaking long-established cities in importance.[1] With the growth of cities came high density, poor quality housing for the poor, which, then as now, were areas where street crime proliferated. The poor have, perhaps, always outnumbered the rich, but the proximity of the hordes in the rookeries of London's St Giles were sufficient to strike fear into the hearts of the gentry of St James 30 minutes walk away. Perhaps for the first time, urban growth meant that parts of cities like London, Paris and Rome were effectively no-go areas for "respectable" people.

The Industrial Revolution had an immediate effect on all European countries except the most agrarian, like Russia. An additional problem faced by Britain, France and Prussia was that the aftermath of the Napoleonic Wars brought the return to peacetime conditions for thousands of ex-soldiers and sailors, many of whom were disabled, and without means of

---

1   Manchester, the second largest city in Britain, owes its existence to the establishment of cotton mills (Manchester, as a generic term for towels, sheets and household cotton goods, is still common in Australia), and Liverpool grew in importance as a dock city because of its proximity to Manchester. Older cities, such as King Alfred's capital Winchester, grew very little, and their importance waned.

support.[2] The vast majority of these ex-servicemen gravitated to the cities,[3] bringing additional problems to large centres of population, while imposing no urgent need for reform in rural areas. British cities, in particular, grew enormously in population size, as did the class of the urban rich and affluent who owned property but not land, while the old peacekeeping systems which had evolved for smaller centres of population were unable to deal with crime in these new and changing conditions. The cities, starting with London, were in desperate need of a new means of maintaining law and order. Rural Britain was still little changed, which accounts in part for the opposition to police from aristocratic Tories, who, from their landed estates in the shires, saw no need to reform a system which had worked well for centuries: still less did they wish such reforms to be at their expense.

Another important factor in the opposition to the establishment of police in Britain stemmed from observation of the administration of justice in mainland Europe. Policing functions on the continental model were carried out by a government controlled system of militaristic enforcement agents and paid spies and informers. The fear of the institution of such police in Britain was a fear of the oppressive form of government that a powerful king could impose, or that a weak king could be manipulated into. The Atlantic Democratic Revolution, as the late 18th century establishment of the new republics of the United States and France has been termed, may well have leap-frogged the democracy of Britain in setting out constitutional rights and principles, but did use many principles long established in Britain, for example the separation of powers.[4] Nevertheless, the only way that Peel could persuade parliament to accept his innovation was to overcome the misgivings of the Parliamentary Committee on Policing in 1822, which had commented: "It is difficult to reconcile an effective system of police, with that perfect freedom of action and exemption from interference, which are the great privileges and blessings of society in this country". This Committee, like its forerunners of 1812, 1816, 1817 and 1818, declined to recommend Peel's police to parliament.

The acceptable face of police

Although the conventional belief is that the "British Bobby" established by Robert Peel and named after him has always been beloved of the British

---

2 Sailors were, perhaps, a little better off than soldiers, particularly if they had served under a successful Captain. They were awarded prize money, a proportion of the value of any enemy ships captured. The careful ones saved that and invested it, hence the number of pubs called "The Lord Nelson", but many squandered, gambled or drank it away. Soldiers had no such bounty system.

3 The *Vagrancy Act* of 1824 is a good indication of this. It gives power to arrest those sleeping outdoors and failing to give a good account of themselves, and includes in the offence of begging "exposing wounds or deformities to gather alms".

4 It is interesting to note that Montesquieu, who coined the term "doctrine of the separation of powers" in approval of what he saw happening in 18th century Britain, himself bought a French magistracy under the king. A century later, Tocqueville wrote approvingly of democracy in operation in America, yet he, too, had bought a judicial post in France. Both saw it as part of their civic duty to participate in judicial matters, and were prepared to pay so to do.

people, this is far from the truth. There was considerable difficulty in getting the measure through parliament, and resistance to it from various levels of society. The need for the force, and the grounds for opposition to it, both had their effect in determining the nature of the police force which eventuated (Reiner, 1992).[5] If the opponents were vociferous in what attributes they did not want of their police, the question arises as to what precisely were the attributes of the police force that Peel persuaded them to accept. The principal requirement was that the force be an organised, disciplined body, concerned primarily with crime and its prevention. The mould was set by the first two Commissioners, Colonel Charles Rowan, formerly of the cavalry, and Sir Richard Mayne, a barrister. Mayne stated the primary objects of their police force:

> It should be understood at the outset that the principal object to be attained is the prevention of crime. To this great end every effort of the police is to be directed. The security of person and property, the preservation of the public tranquillity and all other objects of a police establishment will thus be better effected than by detection and punishment of an offender after he has succeeded in committing the crime.

These words of Mayne, written in 1829, were considered so explicit a summation of the duties of police that over a century and a half later new recruits to the Metropolitan Police were expected to learn them, almost on their first day at Training School. The ideals, if not the terminology, were incorporated in the Statement of Common Purpose established in 1989 by the Plus Programme, perhaps the most radical change in policing London since 1829.

Also crucial is the independence of the police as an institution. This has been discussed as a necessary part of democratic policing, and, as Ascoli puts it, the Commissioner of Police is "the servant of the Crown and people, answerable to Parliament, in its capacity as *vox populi* ... He is, by definition, as impartial in his field as the judiciary" (Ascoli, 1979, p 11). As Ascoli approvingly states, Rowan and Mayne saw themselves as public servants, and, at a very early stage established the relationship with the Home Secretary (then the Police Authority for the Metropolis[6]) which kept the holder of that political office of state out of the internal workings of the force, and prevented interference in operational concerns.

Much of British public life is a matter of tradition and precedent, the latter, of course, being at the heart of its common law. At worst, this leads to an unwillingness to change practices which "have always been done this way" but at best it establishes parameters and guides which provide sound practice, but can be changed or modified if a sufficient reason can be shown so to do. Certainly, Rowan and Mayne established de facto independence for themselves as Commissioners of Police which was not misused by their

---

5   Chapter 1, The Birth of the Blues, covers the political debate concerning the establishment of a police force, and modern analyses of it.

6   London was given its own police authority like other police agencies under the *Police Reform Act* 2002. This is discussed in some detail in Chapter 14.

immediate successors and thus became established practice. It must also be remembered that Peel's police force in London, led by Rowan and Mayne, was the only such institution in Britain for a number of years. Once parliament accepted the worth of the new police, it was extended throughout the nation to other urban areas by the *Municipal Corporations Act* 1835. Three years later a commission enquired into the desirability of rural constabularies, and a resulting Act authorised their establishment. However, only half the counties and not all cities chose to establish police forces, so police conforming loosely to the same system and standards were not established throughout the nation until after legislation in 1856.

Despite the military background of Rowan himself and many of his successors,[7] and that of many of the Chief Constables of Constabulary, the police managed to avoid being a paramilitary organisation in manner or appearance. The police uniform was distinctively different from that of contemporary military personnel. The "Bobby's helmet", perhaps the most potent symbol of British policing, was a heavily modified version of one of two military patterns. Even today, the helmets of some forces bear a raised ridge from centre to back, the echo of the cavalry plume, while the Metropolitan Police and others bear a silvered metal rose on the top, said to be the compromise reached to satisfy Albert, Prince Consort, who favoured the Prussian spiked *pickelhaube* for police. Rank nomenclature was similarly unmilitary: sergeant has military connotations, but is also used in the Law Courts and Westminster, while the choice of inspector and superintendent avoided the more militaristic sounding lieutenant and captain, although both these ranks are found in American policing.

Although Rowan and Mayne established the independence of the police as a body, this is by no means the same as establishing the autonomy of the police officer on patrol. The Metropolitan Police was to be established as a professional body, and, although largely eschewing gentlemen, it sought to avoid translating the rag-tag, inefficient individuals from the watch and other precursors of policing into the new body. The rigid class structure of Victorian England ensured that the Constable "knew his place". Reiner (1992) suggests that the urban middle class, who had most to lose from crime in the cities and no country estate to escape to, had been most in favour of the police originally (and whose pressure eventually persuaded parliament to pass the acts establishing police) became the group were most likely to expect deferential behaviour from the Constable. There was considerable resistance to police from the working class, which is to this day not entirely absent. Brogden (1982) claims the riots in Toxteth in 1981 were

---

7   Many chief officers had a military background, including Lord Trenchard, an ardent reformer of the Metropolitan Police in the 1930s, who was a soldier then a founding figure of the Royal Air Force, being its first Air Vice Marshal. In policing, Trenchard is best remembered for his scheme to appoint an officer class, gentlemen entering policing as sub-inspectors. It was very late indeed in British police history before it became practice to appoint professional police officers to chief officer status. Sir Joseph Simpson, a 1960s Commissioner, is remembered as the first Metropolitan Police Commissioner to have risen to the office from a Constable's beat, although now every chief officer must do so, frequently through an accelerated promotion scheme.

a modern version of the anti-police riots in the 19th century, and the pitched battles between police and striking miners at Orgreave and elsewhere during the 1983 pits dispute showed the antipathy between the working people and the police when perceived as establishment oppressors.

The police were originally established as a virtually unarmed body and the British public has expected police to defend themselves and others without having immediate resort to deadly weapons. Although truncheons have always been carried, these were concealed from a fairly early stage, and it is only since the mid-1990s that British police have adopted the longer batons which must be hung visibly from the belt. Guns have been available when needed, though never carried on normal street patrol, and in the latter half of the 19th century sabres could be used. Police were also expected to be visible, and for much of their history, British police were expected to wear uniform both on and off duty, a band on the cuff signifying that the wearer was on duty, and its absence showing the officer was off duty. This is a clear reaction to the fear of a network of police spies and informers springing up to interfere with civil liberties. It was not until the 1870s that a detective, plain-clothes, branch of the police was established, and that in the face of very strong parliamentary opposition.

By the end of the 19th century, the British public and its police had settled into a comfortable relationship. The large figure in a blue uniform, tall helmet and heavy boots had become a familiar figure in the streets, and, with a few minor changes (electric torches replacing bullseye lanterns, and the acquisition of bicycles), would remain so for at least another half century. Familiarity in this case did not breed contempt, but a certain fondness, especially among the middle classes. The individual officer was well aware that he answered first to his sergeant and inspector but ultimately to his commissioner or chief constable: persons of respectability and substance might very well be known to these very senior officers, and in a small force such relationships were almost certain. It was sensible, therefore, to treat the middle classes with some deference, and they responded by treating the officer as a public servant whose role it was to serve them individually, not just as members of the public.

Policing at the end of the 19th century

To the working class, the police officer as an individual had certainly proved himself useful in dealing with crime and local disorder. The police were authorised to take action to deal with the minor irritants of everyday life, although it was not so pleasant when one's own actions were regarded as minor irritants by others. The *Metropolitan Police Act* 1839 created various offences out of actions which at the time must have caused disharmony between neighbours, such as scalding casks and barrels in the street, beating carpets before 8am, furious driving of a cart and doing a moonlight flit (packing one's belongings and moving home at dead of night, leaving rent and bills unpaid) which have long fallen into desuetude. Even in cases of disputes between neighbours, in shops or the workplace, the police officer was and is an independent arbiter who could do anything from negotiate a truce to arrest an offender.[8]

As important as the nature of police and policing is its perception by the community being policed. One way of assessing this in hindsight, it not being possible to survey the 19th century public, is to see how police are portrayed in contemporary writing. Victorian detective stories usually portray the police investigator as honest, trustworthy but none too bright, and the uniform constable is useful only to convey messages to his superiors or handcuff a villain. Representations of police in 19th century cartoons in the humorous magazine *Punch* almost invariably depict a corpulent, bewhiskered figure whose main interests seem to be food, beer and servant girls. Although this cannot be relied on as a true picture, such humour will only work if it is an exaggeration or comic distortion of a generally accepted truth. It follows then that the readers of Punch, who for the whole history of the journal were overwhelmingly middle-class, viewed their police force as their servants, benign social inferiors whose sins were largely venial. We shall return to the portrayal of police in media and fiction shortly.

Neither the reality of policing nor its perception suggests that Peel's new police were the dangerous gang that their early detractors feared. In no real sense did the police officer on the beat impinge on the liberty of the public in general. As an organised body, they could, did and still do act for the establishment, but this has never been central to police duty. In London Rowan and Mayne established the autonomy of the commissioner from the police authority, and this has largely remained.[9] The principle of autonomy was carried over to the new constabularies and usually observed, at least formally, insofar as the police authority or watch committee was a separate body to elected local government. In practice, however, particularly in small boroughs, the police authority and elected councillors were all members of the same local oligarchy, and there could be considerable overlap of posts. The mayor may not have any ex officio power over police, but as friend, business partner or relative of members of the watch committee, mayoral influence was considerable.

The establishment of police in Australia

The first British colony in Australia was that of New South Wales, established at Sydney Cove in 1788 with both convicts and free settlers. Coincidentally, the year of the founding of the Metropolitan Police in

---

8   Bittner examines this role of police in 1970s Chicago, where he argues that "calling the cops" is done in the belief that the police officer as an authority figure will act to enforce the caller's desires. If one has sufficient faith in the civil police system that involving the police will not usually result in one's own arrest for time-wasting, the arbitration of a police officer can be an cheap, quick and easy means for the public to resolve disputes. See Bittner (1990) pp 38-59.

9   This may be changing, however, as is discussed in Chapter 14.

London, 1829, was also the year of the establishment of the Swan River colony at Perth, later to become capital of the State of Western Australia. While the Westminster Parliament was debating the establishment of police on its doorstep, it was responsible for the administration of one convict colony half a world away, and the establishment of a new free colony on the opposite side of what was not yet proven to be a single continent. Policing Australia probably never entered Peel's mind.

New South Wales, although it had free settlers, was under the military rule of a governor appointed by the King at the behest of the government of Britain. The loss of the American colonies (which had been useful depositories for malefactors) in 1776 made the establishment of a convict settlement in Australia a necessity to empty the prison hulks and cut prison populations, but also, perhaps, prompted Westminster to keep much closer control over this replacement. Maintaining order and upholding the law was a task for the military, and it could reasonably be expected that keeping sufficient control over the convicts would be an adequate way of dealing with crime. Nevertheless, convicts do complete their sentences, and as early as 1810 settlers and released convicts persuaded Governor Macquarie to establish and appoint Constables to maintain order in Sydney.

The first Act giving any sort of self-government by an elected body in New South Wales came in 1823, but even then much of the real power to rule remained with the Governor. The legal structure of Australia until the *Australia Acts* of 1986 allowed the Westminster Parliament to pass legislation binding on Australia, although since Federation in 1901 this has only happened at the request of the Australian government.[10] Until the establishment of self-governing status for New South Wales in 1855, all Acts passed at Westminster were applicable in Australia. The *Municipal Corporations Act* 1835 permitted the establishment of a new police force in Australia, and some of the larger centres took this up. However, there were few of these, although by the 1840s New South Wales had six separate and independently run policing bodies, the Sydney Police, the Sydney Water Police, the Mounted Police, the Rural Police, the Border Police and the Native Police (King, 1956).

These small police forces under British legislation did not last long. South Australia in 1844 passed a *Police Act* establishing a single police force for the colony: this was followed in 1853 by Victoria, 1861 by Western Australia, 1862 by New South Wales and 1863 by Queensland.[11] Only Tasmania continued the experiment of decentralised policing until finally

---

10   Australia has, in fact, moved steadily towards self-government since 1823. The establishment of parliaments in the colonies during the 19th century gave power to legislate for those colonies, provided that such legislation was not inconsistent with British legislation. Of course, such acts as were necessary to establish a Federation required consent by Act of Parliament in Westminster, and the final tie was cut by the *Australia Acts* 1986 – one Act passed in Canberra to exercise power, and one simultaneously in Westminster to formally cede it.

11   Despite their being a single force, some police even today maintain the city / country distinction: in Western Australia, for example, a khaki rather than blue uniform is worn outside the Perth Metropolitan area.

establishing a single State police force in 1898 (Finnane, 1994, p 9). This pattern remains today, that each State has a single police service, and, since 1979, a Federal Police responsible for policing Canberra and the Australian Capital Territory and the investigation of offences under Federal law from offices in each State capital and regional centres. From the outset, as can be seen from the names of the early New South Wales police forces and from the extraordinary nature of the Australian colonies, the tasks of police in Australia had significant differences from those of British police.

The nature of early Australian policing

There are four particular factors which, from the outset, have rendered the practice of policing significantly different in Australia from Britain. The first is a simple matter of geography: Australia has a vast area, roughly that of the mainland United States, containing a population about that of Holland, 60 per cent of whom live in one of five capital cities on river estuaries: even today, bush communities are small, isolated and are often hours from each other or the nearest city. The second is a matter of history: Australia has a convict past, and the penal colonies established first at Sydney Cove, then up the coast at Brisbane, across the Bass Straight in Tasmania, and at a later stage in Western Australia, had their effect on policing. Australia in the 19th century was a frontier land, and the settlers pushing further and further out from the cities displaced, and frequently came into conflict with, the indigenous Aboriginal people. Unlike the American expansion into Indian Territory, there was no significant military force or system of cavalry forts, thus the need for the New South Wales Native Police, later subsumed into the State police force. Finally, Australia was discovered to be an auriferous land, and towns like Ballarat and Kalgoorlie owe their existence to gold. Australian gold rushes, like gold rushes elsewhere, brought rogues and charlatans, thieves and prostitutes hard on the heels of the miner, to separate him, one way or another, from his hard-earned cash. As Finnane states: "Police on the goldfields were responsible for managing some of the most difficult and volatile sections of the Australian colonial population in the nineteenth century" (Finnane, 1994, p 28).

The question of distance prompted the need for central control of police. If constables were to be appointed by magistrates, most of whom were settlers, and were responsible for policing a small and isolated community far from the State capital, then there was a danger that they would be no more than the lord of the manor's men-at-arms of feudal England. Indeed, examples were found in the Kimberley in Western Australia in the 1890s where police meted out "justice" summarily at the behest of magistrates who were large land-owners (Gill, 1977). There was also the very real problem that a small community might only need one or two police officers at normal times but if something major and untoward happened the police strength would need augmentation: even today, country police stations with one or two officers are common. However, if the extra officers needed were to be drafted in from a separate area, or from several different communities, then this meant that negotiations had to be undertaken with several sets of magistrates, with consequent delay before assistance could be had. Even after the centralisation of State policing, police assistance from the capital could take days to arrive.

Although policing has changed its nature over the past century and a half and is still changing, the history of institutionalised and often legally sanctioned mistreatment of Aboriginal people has left its mark on modern police-Aboriginal relations. Although Aboriginals might win skirmishes against settlers encroaching on land to which the Aboriginals felt spiritual attachment, against the guns of the settlers and the power of the police their struggle was doomed. The police came to be viewed by Aboriginals as violent oppressors, while the police viewed the Aboriginals as wild and uncivilised, who had to be moved off the land to be settled then dispersed, and if necessary shot. By the end of the 19th century, the basis for fear and distrust of the police was laid, and early in the 20th century, most States passed legislation protecting Aboriginals. This did anything but protect, but established a paid government post of "Protector of Aborigines" whose role, in a nutshell, was to administer the Aboriginal people who were seen as vastly inferior to the white Australians. These official policies have been fully documented and discussed elsewhere,[12] and the details are not relevant here.

What is of overwhelming importance to any study of policing in Australia is that the execution of protective policies towards Aboriginals, which included the removal of children, relocation of communities, suppression of traditional practices and establishment of native reserves, was the duty of the police. Since, as has already been made clear, the police are the sole holders of the de facto power to coerce within the State, then the lawful directions of the Protector of Aborigines can only be enforced by police. Wherever one points the finger of blame for the institution of legislation to protect Aboriginals, it is clear that the onus was placed upon police to carry out the legislation, and that what the Aboriginal people saw, and were affected by, was police carrying out their duties. It would be facile to disclaim police responsibility on the grounds that police cannot help the flaws in the law they enforce and that police discretion is limited. Police are not responsible for what the law is, but they are responsible for the manner and zeal with which they choose to enforce it. The protection policies worsened rather than ameliorated the fear and suspicion of police felt by Aboriginal people. Although it was the system that required Aboriginal children to be taken from their homes, and the Protector of Aborigines and his staff who decided which children should be taken and where they should be placed, these were abstractions for the Aboriginal families who saw only the police officers forcibly removing their children.

---

12   An excellent source is Beresford and Omaji (1998).

The establishment of police in the United States

The system of law enforcement in America also had its roots in the British system, but the divergence came at an earlier time and for different reasons. The early British colonies in America date back to the sixteenth century: Virginia was named in honour of Queen Elizabeth I and the Carolinas for King Charles I. Consequently, the system of constables and sheriffs established in the American colonies were largely on the model of those of Tudor and Stuart England. The expansion of the United States from the eastern seaboard across the continent brought with it many of the problems of distance faced by Australian policing, but this was addressed in a markedly different way. Here, too, there are critical issues which strongly affected the nature of policing in the United States – these are:

- the underlying sentiments of the Declaration of Independence, which stressed the people's desire to be free of any government control;
- westward expansion and settlers' local government;
- mass immigration.

Each of these will be discussed in turn.

The leaders of the colonies who signed the Declaration of Independence in 1776 wished to be free of the yoke of British rule, but they were equally virulently opposed to accepting the strong rule of a central government, even one they had elected themselves, as a substitute. The intention was that each of the States of the union (of which there were 13 in 1790) would be self-governing, and that the national government would be restricted, as far as possible, in its power to do anything other than represent the United States in its dealings with foreign governments, and provide security against invasion.[13] The War of Independence had driven out King George's redcoat soldiers, which the American people had no wish to replace with an alternative form of lawful government oppression. This principle applied on a State level also: the power of those leaders of colonies who called themselves American rather than British had been restricted while the governor was appointed from Westminster. After independence there was no wish to strengthen the role of State governments. This is the basis of Jefferson's call, quoted in the previous chapter, for a constitution to limit rather than empower government, and to "bind in chains" those who are permitted to rule over others.

The next influence on American policing was the great 19th century expansion westward. As people headed west and created their own settlements which grew into towns they were entering territory beyond the borders of the earlier States. Thus they were responsible for themselves and their communities, and appointed or elected individuals to keep the peace as needed. The policing models were an amalgam of what people knew, ie

---

13   This can be seen very clearly in early political tracts discussing the nature and powers of national government. See, for example, articles from the political pamphlet, "The Federalist", collected and reprinted as Hamilton, Madison and Jay (1992).

what they had left behind in the eastern States, and what they could devise suitable for their needs. Washington was too far away to affect them, and a community that was beyond the boundaries of all established States was the responsibility of no State government. The new States had very different backgrounds: Louisiana was a colony purchased from the French in 1803, while Texas was originally a province of Mexico, then an independent republic for 10 years before being admitted to the Union in 1846, and the Mormon religious enclave in the South-west grew and flourished to become the State of Utah.

The base of the Statue of Liberty in New York proclaims "Give me your tired, your poor, your huddled masses yearning to breathe free, the wretched refuse of your teeming shore", and through the 19th century many thousands of European poor crossed the Atlantic in search of a better life. While some headed west, many joined and swelled the existing immigrant communities from their homelands in the ghettos of American cities. While the drift from the countryside caused the growth of industrial cities in Europe, in America the cities expanded both through industrialisation and immigration. The growth of cities like New York, Boston and Philadelphia rendered the sort of policing that was a throwback to colonial days inadequate, and a new type of policing was needed.

New police in America

In the cities of the eastern States in the early 19th century, the old system of night watchmen and Constables became ineffective. A police force was established to patrol and supplement the night watch, which eventually became a unified police force. New York was the first city to make such an amalgamation in 1844, followed by Boston 10 years later. By the end of the century most cities, whether in the original States or newly founded, had their own police force. There were, however, no directives from national or State government about policing styles or standards: each city made its own decision whether or not to have a police force, and what form of policing to have. While at an early stage the Westminster parliament had at first permitted, then in 1856 insisted, that constabularies be instituted, and had set national parameters for them to be examined by Her Majesty's Inspector of Constabularies, American policing was established piecemeal to suit the needs and wishes of the local population only. Although some States have accreditation standards for police officers, no such accreditation, State or national, has ever been implemented for police organisations.

Since independence, there was considerable overlapping of policing functions in the United States, and this has grown more rather than less complicated ever since. Every county had its sheriff who was responsible for law enforcement, courts, juries and imprisoning felons. After the War of Independence, the office of sheriff became an elected position. When a town or city needed a police force, it was established following a vote by the town council, and the mayor was given responsibility for appointing a chief of police. In some cases, the post of police chief was itself an elected position.

As the century went on, more and more settlements were established, each of which soon required local government, a mayor, and a sheriff to keep the peace. Perhaps an example of such development will clarify the evolution of law enforcement from its colonial heritage to modern multiplicity.

Texas joined the Union in 1846, and with it the county of Bexar containing the small town of San Antonio, which had an elected sheriff responsible for law and order, who ran the jail and maintained public order. San Antonio grew in size, established a city council which then appointed its own police force. At a later stage, several other municipal centres within Bexar County established independent local government and their own police departments. The State government in Austin established the Texas Rangers to patrol and enforce the law in those parts of the State which were not otherwise policed, but of course their powers could also be applied in areas covered by local police and sheriffs. At a later stage, Bexar County became home to a number of military bases, each on Federal Government land and patrolled by military police. Today, San Antonio has grown into the eighth largest city in America, whose city limits stretch almost to the Bexar County line, and totally surrounds those municipal centres with their own local government and police force, and the various military bases. Other police agencies exist to complicate matters further, such as the campus police at the University of Texas at San Antonio, whose officers are fully armed and empowered to act on any of the university's campuses. As a State university, its police are also a State body, ultimately controlled from the capital, Austin. The San Antonio Police Department has jurisdiction only within the city boundaries, which excludes the University campuses, self-contained municipalities and federal land (the military bases), while the Sheriff's Department and Texas Rangers have jurisdiction over the whole county, excluding military bases.

This rather ad hoc arrangement characterises policing throughout the United States. In some places, towns have chosen to leave most of the policing with the sheriff, and let the Sheriff's Department grow rather than introduce a police department. However matters are arranged, policing answers directly to the populace for its efficiency: sheriffs are directly elected by the people, and, where a mayor appoints the chief of police, a change of mayor can result in the appointment of a new chief. Since the mid-19th century, whenever and wherever a police force was deemed necessary, one has been instituted, resulting in a plethora of policing agencies such that, on at least one somewhat exaggerated estimate, there are more police agencies in the United States than police officers in Australia:

> [In 1996] there are about 40,000 police forces in the country. ... 90% of all municipalities with more than 2,500 inhabitants have their own force, and 80% of all forces employ fewer than 10 policemen. About 3,000 forces are based on counties, 3,000 in cities and the remaining 33,000 are distributed throughout boroughs, towns and villages. (Brewer et al, 1996)[14]

---

14   The most generally accepted estimate of the number of police agencies is 14,000-15,000.

During the 19th century urban police in the United States found themselves responsible for many non-policing tasks. In New York the Chief of Police was responsible for street cleaning until 1881, and police also from time to time provided lodgings for the homeless and ran soup kitchens (Lane, 1992). Despite carrying out these humanitarian tasks, American police have, to this day, never been accorded the respect that British police have received. From the outset, they have been an armed body, in some places very heavily armed. The strongly local control of police by elected local politicians should have established the credentials of police absolutely, but did not. Lane (1992, pp 18 et seq) explains this with the suggestion that the partisan nature of local politics rendered police answerable to their political masters so that they could never be seen as neutral law enforcers. Where police are closely linked with the local government (and in Boston, for example, they were named after successive mayors, for example Fox's police), they could be tainted by political corruption. This effect spread, in that not only the police of a city where local government corruption came to light were suspect, but doubt by association was cast on other police forces. This is not just an American problem – incidents of corruption or violence in one force inevitably leads to suspicion of police elsewhere in the nation. Scandals in Worcester, Brighton, Thurso and elsewhere in Britain in the late 1950s and early 1960s led to a revision of policing by parliament in 1964, and the Australian public in all States have concerns about their police following the disclosures of the 1989 report of the Fitzgerald inquiry in Queensland and the 1996 Wood Royal Commission in New South Wales.

Twentieth century changes in policing

The 20th century was one of great changes, many of which have affected police. Some, like scientific and technological advances, have affected all police forces in one way or another: others, particularly legislative or constitutional change, have affected different nations' police in different ways. The 20th century is also the century of mass communication and, since crime, police and detective work are the subject of a great deal of news reporting, cinema and television, and detective fiction has almost as long a history as policing, the way police are portrayed in fact and fiction has an important effect on public perception, and police relations with the public.

The impact of science and technology

Modern science makes more and more hypotheses into conclusive facts. In the early years of the 20th century, many post-mortem examinations were carried out by general medical practitioners, who gave their findings about cause of death, etc from their own knowledge and experience. Spilsbury commenced the grisly speciality of forensic pathology before the First World War, and, a later pioneer in the field, Simpson, practised from the 1930s for some 40 years. They both examined bodies and crime scenes with a specialist eye, finding a great deal more evidence than ever before, providing police with the advantage of more detailed and accurate information. Even an narrow estimate of the time of death can help an investigation enormously, particularly if this estimate is sufficiently certain to be used as evidence in court. Modern forensic pathology can claim to be an exact science, and a dead body can yield a great deal more information today than was dreamt of by Simpson or Spilsbury. Fibres, tissue samples, hair and even dust can be subjected to analysis and positively identified.

At its best, forensic science can prove independently and conclusively facts about which the courts previously had to rely on verbal evidence, which was always subject to challenge or rebuttal. In a rape case in the 19th century, for example, the prosecution case relied almost completely upon the victim's evidence: by the early years of the 20th century, medical evidence could usually be relied on to prove whether or not the victim had had sexual intercourse recently, while today tissue typing can prove unequivocally that the defendant had had sex with the victim. If the rape victim is unable to pick the suspect from an identity parade this no longer matters.[15] What forensic science can show it can usually prove conclusively: what it cannot do is provide a suspect, or indicate mens rea. The victim or witnesses must still provide a description of the suspect, and the victim's evidence is still crucial if the trial hinges on the issue of consent.

The power of forensic science relies upon an uncontaminated crime scene. Sherlock Holmes' frequent complaint about the constabulary trampling about and destroying evidence has even more force today, when crime scenes must be preserved carefully. Although many things are possible in forensic science, there are organisational and financial limitations. For example, there may well be a great deal of potentially useful forensic evidence left at a minor domestic burglary, but the very prevalence of such crimes renders it impossible for all scenes to be examined fully, and the cost of forensic testing can be considerable. While theoretically many more crimes could be solved, restricted police resources mean that only the most serious matters receive full scientific investigation.

While science has had a tremendous impact on detective work, of which the above is a very sketchy account, technology has changed all aspects of policing. The two most important areas of technological impact are communications and transport. The first triumph of modern communication occurred in 1910, when the use of radio to a ship crossing the Atlantic resulted in the arrest of the murderer Crippen, but most communications are far more mundane. When a 19th century police officer set out on patrol, all he had for communication and transport was a whistle, a voice and a pair of feet. He was on his own, and was equally unable to obtain assistance without returning to the station or sending a message there, or to be directed by the station to a particular task. Supervision was problematic,

---

15   Since he was convicted and hanged in 1962 for murder and rape in the A6 layby case, largely on identification in court by the surviving victim, there were sporadic attempts to prove James Hanratty's innocence. Forty years later, DNA tests on the victim's underwear and Hanratty's exhumed body conclusively confirmed the jury's verdict.

as sergeants could only patrol on foot themselves, in the hope of coming across an officer.

The invention of the telephone and the provision of public phone boxes helped both the public contact the police and the police contact each other. Most city and town police forces in Britain established a network of police boxes, usually on street corners, with direct phone lines to the police station. Little larger than a telephone kiosk, there was a telephone handset accessible from outside for members of the public to call the station, room for the officer to sit inside and write reports or contact the station himself, and a flashing light on the top to summon the attention of patrolling police officers. As a means of supervision, officers were frequently directed to call the station at set times from particular boxes. This police box system operated in British cities until the early 1960s. The modern version of this system is, perhaps, Surrey Constabulary's unmanned, computerised, fully automated police station with its video link to the control centre.

Police have always seemed to have access to new equipment as it became available, and the motor car was no exception. A few privileged people had cars in the 1920s, and most police forces, depending on their size and financial capability, also bought at least one or two cars since motor vehicles could transport officers from the station to a particular place more rapidly than anything else. Cars had the advantage of being able to move officers quickly, but once a car full of officers had left the station it could not be redirected without permanent contact with the station. By the 1930s this became possible: vehicle patrols commenced using motor cars with large metal apparatus on the roof to transmit and receive messages, and the passenger had a morse tapper and earphones to maintain permanent communication with the control room. Having the use of motor vehicles was highly prestigious for police officers, and the London Flying Squad got its name in the 1930s as a group of detectives travelling in fast cars. Vehicle patrols augmented the officer on foot or bicycle, who was still the key figure in policing, familiar and accessible to all, and the most likely person to attend calls from the public until the 1960s.

Police and the public

One of the problems that arises from close contact between police and the public is the possibility of corruption. There is, in fact, an almost insuperable difficulty in determining whether the benefits of an officer's close knowledge of the community policed outweigh the disadvantages of too close a relationship between an officer and the community. There is a similar problem in detective work which arises when the intimate knowledge of the criminal world, which is crucial to identifying and arresting the perpetrators of crime, becomes an intimate involvement in the criminal world which can lead to corrupt practice. The dangers of too close an association between police and public became more and more evident during the early 20th century.

By the beginning of the 20th century, the patrolling system of large American cities like New York typically allowed an officer to have a beat and keep it throughout his police career. Quite clearly, with a small beat the officer rapidly came to know most of the people living or working on it by sight or by name, and certainly knew important figures such as shop-keepers, bar owners, criminals and local politicians or property owners. While this has advantages in that the patrolling officer knows what is hap-pening and who is likely to be causing trouble or crime, it has the disad-vantage of leaving the way open for corruption. This could be as venial as an officer turning a blind eye to minor offences such as obstruction by a shop-keeper loading or unloading a vehicle, or the more serious matter of receiving a regular payoff for turning a blind eye to unlawful gambling or drinking.

The same sort of problem occurs in smaller communities. The village police officer in rural England should have a finger on the community's pulse, and be well able to clear up policing problems and minor crime through use of this local knowledge. It was often the case that the village pub stayed open well outside licensing hours with or without the police officer inside, the constable being well aware that no sergeant or inspector was likely to call. The community always outnumbers the police, so the only way police can be effective is with the co-operation of the community. For the first part of the 20th century, the officer, working alone and without a radio or other means of calling assistance, had to be part of the com-munity. This is true even today of police in isolated communities in outback Australia, or members of police departments with only a handful of officers in parts of the United States.

During the first half of the 20th century, policing became more specialised, certainly with regard to crime investigation. Specialist detec-tives became a feature of almost all police organisations, and their work required frequent contact with criminals and informants in the criminal world. A detective who did not make such contacts was likely to be comparatively ineffective in solving crime, yet such contacts could easily lead to condoning some crimes in order to clear up others. Once again, police organisations had to establish procedures to make their detectives efficient while preventing them descending into venial or corrupt practices. These problems slowly became apparent over the first half of the century and would not go away, but were often ignored, or, when corruption came to light, treated as isolated phenomena. As we shall see in the next chapter, in the 1960s the abandonment of almost all foot patrols and the use of communications technology promised to improve police efficiency while removing officers from dangerously close contact with the community.

Media portrayals of police

Crime fascinates people. This applies to both real and fictional crime, details of which are always in demand by the public. Public executions and floggings have always attracted spectators, the public galleries of courts always attract crowds, and certain criminals have always been famous. One can think here of British characters like Robin Hood and Dick Turpin the highwayman, 19th century American outlaws like Jesse James and Billy the Kid, and, in Australia, Ned Kelly, Moondyne Joe and others. The establishment usually viewed such people as thugs and murderers, and they were almost certainly not the folk heroes that they have become, but nevertheless, their stories fascinated the public. No less fascinating, of course, were those whose job it was to keep the peace. Wyatt Earp, the 19th century American sheriff, Treasury Agent Eliot Ness and Fabian of the Yard were all real people, yet became the stuff of legend. All too frequently the facts were overtaken by fiction built around these individuals, and it became difficult to know where the true stories ended and the fiction began. From the middle of the 19th century, the popular press was full of the grisliest details of crime.

The fictional detective genre started with Edgar Alan Poe's hero C August Dupin in the story "The Murders in the Rue Morgue" published in 1841. During the 20th century, the detective of literature was supplemented by cinema, radio and television detectives. The uniformed officer on patrol was not highly regarded in fictional portrayals during the early 20th century. In truth, such officers were probably working class in origin, educated to little more than statutory minimum school-leaving age, often with previous service in the armed forces, but rarely reaching beyond the rank of sergeant. In contrast, very senior police officers, at least in Britain and Australia, may well have held senior rank in the armed services, and be treated accordingly. Agatha Christie's fictional detective Miss Marple treats police in a way which shows very clearly how they were perceived in Britain: the uniformed constable or sergeant was useful insofar as he could be persuaded to obey instructions, while the detective chief inspector could be kept in his place (which was to arrest the criminal unmasked by Miss Marple) by her implied threat of recourse to the chief constable, who was, of course, a gentleman. From the 19th century cartoonists' depiction of police as having a taste for beer through to detective writers' portrayals, the public perception of the uniform officer as of little worth or intelligence has been coloured by fiction, such that even today a policing debacle invites the comment "Keystone Cops", a reminder of the comedies of the silent film era of the 1920s which only a few cinema aficionados have actually seen.

One classic police figure of early British television is Dixon of Dock Green. This avuncular figure lived and worked in the same dock area, knew everyone, was a friend to all honest people but any villain he came across was also treated fairly, and his compendious local knowledge and insight into character solved any policing puzzle. George Dixon became so much a part of policing folklore that 20 years and more after the program ended small boys would whistle the theme tune behind the backs of police officers walking British streets. Since the 1980s drama setting out to provide a realistic portrayal of police has become popular. In Britain "The Bill" (although this has gradually become more of a soap opera), in Australia "Blue Heelers", and in the United States "Hill Street Blues" and "NYPD Blue" all set out to show the mundane in policing, and portray police officers as credible people rather than stereotyped characters. Whether this serves to improve public perception of police is unclear, but such programs do provide powerful images of police which are not in absolute contrast to the reality.

Media interest and the newsworthy nature of police have made senior police officers intro reasonably well known public figures. Chief officers of large police services are recognised nationally and perhaps even internationally, and are frequently quoted and interviewed in the press and on television.[16] The level of awareness of policing has risen tremendously, but crime is, perhaps, one area where facts, fiction, perception and reality are so intertwined as to be very difficult for the public to sort out. Even more disturbingly, problems that arise in one area of policing do not necessarily arise in others. Each police service has its problems, although these problems are not always common to all police services. The public, however, are often all too ready to ascribe to their local police the wrongdoings which come to light in other police agencies, and hold them to account for the misdeeds of others or treat them with unwarranted suspicion.

Conclusion

This chapter has tried to set out the different starting points for the institution of policing in Britain, Australia and the United States, and the different early histories of police in those countries, relating these to the differing social and political histories of each during the 19th century. Since the police deal directly with some of the murkier depths of society, the relationship between police and community is a very difficult one. This relationship is coloured by the public perception of police, which is in turn strongly affected by media portrayals of police, both fictional and factual. The roots of policing have been explored here, in an attempt to explain how policing reached the position in which it stands today.

Despite the differing histories, by the 1960s social change had raised many similar problems for policing the developed, Western world. Although the phrase "global village" may be an exaggeration, police everywhere have sought to harness technology and dispense with the traditional foot patrol. This policy, what it sought to achieve and why it failed, will be addressed in Chapter 4. In addition to technological change, the 1960s marked an increasing public awareness of rights, and mass protest about public and international affairs. The reaction of police to peaceful protests of civil rights marchers in the United States and ban-the-bomb marchers in Britain at the start of the decade culminated in the violent clashes at its end, particularly those in all three countries concerning the war in Vietnam. These continuing changes in society brought with them changes in policing, which will be examined in the next few chapters.

---

16   Since the early 1970s, Sir Robert Mark's corruption-busting era, the Commissioner of Police for London has been in the spotlight. Commissioners of large American cities like New York and Los Angeles are similarly well known nationally, and most Australians can probably name and identify their own State police commissioner.

CHAPTER 3

CRIME – A POLICE PROBLEM OR A SOCIAL PROBLEM?

Introduction

This chapter examines various aspects of crime, and whether it is primarily a police problem or a social problem. This is particularly important when considering crime prevention: although in 1829 Mayne stated clearly that crime prevention was the primary object of the new police force, police powers are limited with regard to preventative action. It is incontrovertible that crime, once it has occurred, is police business. The police service is the agency responsible for recording and investigating that crime, collecting evidence for a prosecution and instigating that prosecution by summons or arrest. The extent to which police are responsible for crime prevention is by no means as clear. It was certainly felt by Mayne, and by many others up to about 1960, that the mere presence of uniformed police officers on the streets was a major deterrent to individuals who were about to commit crime, and that this in itself was the most useful crime prevention strategy. The call for "more police on the streets" echoes this feeling, even though, short of swamping an area with police, extra officers have little effect on the crime rate so new methods of policing are needed.

This chapter looks at crime, and its relation both to police and to society. As society has changed since 1829, so has crime changed with it, and also the public perception of what constitutes crime. Since much of the focus of community policing styles involves police working with the community to prevent crime, then an analysis of what lies within the ambit of police and what is society's responsibility is required. This chapter looks first at crime and society, then at police and crime, and finally looks at crime prevention to complete this analysis. A useful analogy to the division of responsibility for crime and crime prevention between police and community is the shift of responsibility between medical services and community in recent advances in community health and health education.

The health simile

The medical profession is making enormous progress in its ability to cure or ameliorate many diseases previously considered fatal. Heart disease is a useful example: by-pass operations are commonplace, as are less invasive treatments like angioplasty for victims of heart attacks, which enable many people to continue a normal life who would, as late as the 1980s, have spent a few years as an invalid before an early death. However, medical research has identified many causes of heart attacks, and there are a number of simple, relatively inexpensive, tests like blood pressure and cholesterol checks which can identify individuals at risk of heart disease. Few diseases are totally eradicable, but many, like heart disease, are largely preventable.

The public is now well aware of preventative measures to avoid heart disease, such as reducing consumption of particular foods, regular exercise, reducing weight and not smoking, and many individuals are prepared to take responsibility for preventing coronary problems and avoiding heart disease,[1] although they still expect the health services to intervene should a heart attack occur. The medical profession has two responsibilities for health: first, offering expert advice on the likely causes of disease and their prevention, although no guarantees are offered or expected since even health-conscious athletes may succumb to heart attacks, and almost every-one gets colds and flu however hard they try to avoid them; secondly, attempting to cure diseases when they do occur, insofar as the knowledge and technology exists so to do. However, there is rarely any criticism of the medical profession for the number of heart attacks suffered, or for the number of persons who cannot be saved after a heart attack, nor is the medical profession called upon to defend itself when skin cancer rates rise, nor to explain why there is no cure for HIV / AIDS or even for the common cold.

Part of the argument in this chapter will be that there is much that police can do to prevent crime by giving expert advice, much as the medical profession gives health care advice, but that there is little at the moment that police can do to force society to act on that advice.[2] Likewise, the police and criminal justice system can be brought into action to identify, prosecute and sentence the person responsible when a crime has been committed, but the efficacy of the action is no more guaranteed than is medical treatment guaranteed to save the life of a heart attack victim. However, unlike the medical profession which is never considered to be responsible for health problems in the community, or for certain diseases still being incurable, the police service is frequently held blameworthy by the press, public and politicians for the perceived increase in crime, and its failure single-handedly to prevent crime, while the courts and justice system are frequently criticised and blamed for failing to deal effectively with criminals to prevent them re-offending.

---

1   This, of course, applies to all sorts of other diseases too, although heart disease is a clear example. Awareness of and screening for susceptibility to diseases range through various types of cancer, osteoporosis and diabetes. These are all accompanied by strategies suggested by health professionals to reduce the chance of such disease.

2   This is changing, at least in Britain. The *Crime and Disorder Act* 1998 enforces statutory partnerships between police and local bodies to develop crime prevention strategies.

Homer Simpson has many counterparts in real life many of whom may well be shortening their lives, especially if they smoke heavily, but this is a matter of personal choice: in a free society no-one can be forced to give up beer, fries or cigarettes, or be handcuffed to an exercise bicycle; when the inevitable heart attack occurs, however, they do not blame the medical services.[3] A child who spends long hours in Internet chat rooms risks the attention of a paedophile, and a young woman dressed-up for a Saturday evening may attract a rapist on her way home alone at the end of the night: parental supervision could prevent a child abduction, and the foresight to pre-arrange transport could prevent a rape (as could a curfew on males unaccompanied by females), but blame for such offences is often put on the lack of police patrols or insufficient legislative control over the Internet.

Crime and society

Crime has always been present, and probably always will be present in society, although the patterns of crime change significantly over time. There are two separate but linked phenomena of equal importance in considering crime and society: the first is the reality of crime, what crime is actually happening, and the second is the public perception of crime, the fear of crime. One of the factors that affects the public perception of crime is the fact that crime has become a political issue, particularly since the mid-1970s, and crime itself, rather than particular crimes, is subject to a great deal of media coverage.

The politicisation of crime has a significant effect on information regarding crime. The utterances of politicians are always newsworthy, whether or not they are of any real value. Therefore, any statement made by a politician about crime becomes news, and any plan put forward or promise made becomes a matter of public record and raises the expectations of the public that something will be done. There is another parallel here with health. In the early years of the welfare state, the very provision of health care was the most important issue, but in the 50 years or so that state-funded medical treatment has been a right, the cost to the taxpayer of treatment, waiting lists, and the possibility of individuals funding their own treatment through insurance, have become major political issues. The crime prevention equivalent to private health insurance is the employment of security guards by businesses or by householders in private residential estates.

The public gets its information on most topics through the media. However, the press, radio and television are part of a highly competitive industry and, like any other industry, the media exists to make a profit. This profit, of course, comes from persuading sufficient numbers of people to buy the newspaper, or tune in to a particular radio or television channel, so the media's objective with regard to information is to transform it into a story that will generate public interest. General crime information, unlike

---

3   They may, however, try to sue tobacco companies and fast food suppliers.

horrific murder, lurid sex crime and crime involving famous persons, does not increase circulation or audience figures unless it can be reworked to seem more exciting or important. The media is not, primarily, a public information service, and the goals and ethics of journalism do not require that reporting of crime should provide a factual basis for crime prevention.

The public can easily see the newsworthy, which is frequently unusual or serious crime, as the norm, leading to significant and dangerous misperceptions of crime. These misperceptions can be alarming: in a year recorded crime had fallen by 8 per cent, 75 per cent of respondents felt it was increasing and, although respondents believed violent and sexual crime accounted for one-third of all crimes, the actual figure was 6 per cent (British Crime Survey, 1997).

Since crime has become a political issue, policing has been swept into the politicisation of crime, in that chief officers of police are, more than ever before, public figures and are expected to account for crime and show strategies (within a restricted budget) for dealing with and preventing it. Although crime figures have always been published, and chief officers of police produced annual reports, these formerly had very little publicity compared with the attention-grabbing murders or high-value thefts or robberies, and general, run-of-the-mill crime went largely unreported. Now crime itself is the issue, a matter upon which politicians make statements, and a matter on which the media are constantly looking for information that will increase sales. Not only is media revenue generated by increased circulation, but also by increased advertising for security equipment shown to be necessary by crime reporting itself.

Changing patterns of crime

The type of crime which most worries members of the public is that of which individuals can readily imagine themselves the victims. These are personal crimes, whether they are crimes of physical or sexual assault against the individual or property crimes, home burglary, handbag-snatch or mugging. The fact that such crimes are commonplace now is usually taken to suggest that society is rather more lawless than ever before, and that crime as a whole is more prevalent, and a more serious problem. What is suggested in this analysis is that change in society has resulted in changing patterns of crime, rather than that crime is out of control, as the media is wont to claim.

Consider how social change has affected domestic burglary. Typically, the modern burglar will take high-value electrical equipment like the TV, stereo, computer, cash, and perhaps jewellery and CDs. This property will most often be taken during the day while the house is empty and the proceeds taken away by car, which itself is often stolen. The burglary is unlikely to be reported until the owners return, since in most dormitory suburbs few people are about during the working day. Compare this to the situation in the 1950s and 1960s: neither computers nor CDs had been invented, the average TV needed two people to lift it, many stereos were the size of a coffin, and neither would fit into the average family car. Far fewer houses were empty for the long periods common today, and there would almost always have been someone about within half a dozen houses in any direction to notice a strange car in the street. Domestic burglary is now an altogether a more viable option than it was 30 years ago, changing social patterns having made it more profitable and easier to commit.

Social change has meant also that certain types of crime have all but disappeared. Traditional cargo handling methods in any of the world's ports used to rely upon large numbers of dockers engaging in the hard physical labour of unloading ships and loading trucks or warehouses. A fair amount of property "fell over the dockyard fence". Even outside the docks, packages, crates and boxes were frequently taken from commercial vehicles in transit or while delivering. Modern goods handling tends to involve larger units, and both trucks and ships are constructed to handle the ubiquitous container. It is, of course, possible to steal a container, but this requires a level of planning and organisation of transport and storage radically different from the opportunistic pilferage of an earlier generation. Another and more violent crime which is now consigned to history is the payroll robbery: few people are now paid in cash, most wages being paid through banks, so there are now few security vans full of cash to be held up on their way to the workplace.

While salary payments through banks have almost eliminated payroll robberies, modern electronic banking and shopping has brought with it previously unknown crimes. Credit cards can be duplicated and used without the owner's knowledge, and such fraud is easier to commit and much less easy to prove against the offender in court than the traditional passing of forged, stolen cheques or credit cards. It involves limited personal contact which can assist in identifying the offender, and can even operate across national boundaries. Obtaining cash is no longer done in the privacy of the bank, but in public from a machine. Thefts or robbery from individuals using these machines is increasing (although the use of drive-in ATMs in the United States has helped reduce such crime there) as are cases of individuals being forced to draw money from their accounts. Each advance which is convenient for the consumer also brings with it an opportunity for crime, and any form of transaction which falls into disuse reduces the criminal possibilities connected with it. Crime is part of the fabric of society, and as society changes so too does the nature of crime: a change in the pattern of crime is not necessarily an increase in crime.

Causes of crime

When considering any phenomenon which it is hoped to prevent or mini-mise (or even to maximise), an analysis of its causes is always a good starting point. This generalisation is true of crime. Hobbes' argument that society needs organisation and direction, and his famous dictum that life in a state of nature is "nasty, brutish and short" perhaps indicates that an unrestrained consideration of self leads to quarrelling and violence. The Russian anarchist, Bakunin, claimed that "property is theft": setting aside the political rhetoric here, it is clear that without the concept of ownership by an individual or body corporate there can be no property crime.[4] Without delving into the metaphysics of crime, all crime involves an individual, the offender, who acts in a way that society (or its lawmakers) forbids: usually that action involves another person, the victim, and frequently also involves property. Although there are steps that can be taken by the victim to prevent a crime occurring, all crime requires an offender who commits a criminal act: in all cases, that individual could have chosen to act in a non-criminal way. An analysis of the causes of crime therefore becomes an examination of the reasons why offending individuals act in the particular way that is designated "criminal".

A detailed analysis of possible causes of crime, or discussion of particular factors as causes of crime, would lead far from issues relevant to theories of policing. It is, however, incontrovertible that such symptoms of social deprivation as drug or alcohol dependence, poor educational attainment, family breakdown, and physical or other abuse as a child are present at a much higher frequency in the antecedents of individuals who are convicted of crime than of those who are not: more importantly, individuals who commit crime frequently show a combination of many of those factors. Another health analogy is valid here: not every person who eats in a restaurant with a dirty kitchen will suffer gastric problems – however, individuals who frequently eat in a restaurant whose kitchen is inhabited by cockroaches, flies and mice, where food is not refrigerated, utensils are dirty and the cook coughs over the saucepans are far more likely to be ill than if they had eaten at home.

It is important to make a caveat here about the type of crime being discussed. I am concerned here with crime which impinges directly upon the public, most of which are small-scale crimes. These matters include all street crime, public disorder, petty thefts, autocrime and most burglaries. Small-scale crime has a very serious effect on the quality of life in the community, as although individuals may be at worst occasional victims of crime, all are affected directly by newspaper reports of car theft, burglary and drugs on the streets. Much street crime, in particular, is found to be drug or alcohol related, for example property crime to obtain money for drugs, and crimes committed while under the influence of various substances. The regular appearance of graffiti, drug addicts and street prostitutes, persons behaving in a disorderly fashion and the signs of drug abuse in particular places rapidly leads to these places becoming "no-go" areas, avoided by the law-abiding and more nervous members of the public, and gives rise to a significant community concern with crime. Although the cost of white-collar crime may be much higher than that of street crime (if the average burglary involves $3000[5] worth of property it

---

4   This is borne out by studies of traditional Australian Aboriginal societies, which hold property in common throughout the group. Although disputes arise and are settled, only about 3 per cent of these are property disputes, as opposed to about 90 per cent of crimes reported to Australian police.

5     $3000 is not an unreasonable estimate for an Australian burglary, since the figure for UK burglaries of £1378 was cited in British research. See Ekblom P (1998).

takes 2000 of these offences for the total loss to be equal to that of a single $6 million dollar fraud), it is the frequency and personal victimisation of muggings and burglary that causes members of society to perceive street crime as more serious.

Certain minority ethnic groups are statistically over-represented in prisons and in indicators of social deprivation. The Aboriginal people of Australia represent 2 per cent of the population, but comprise over 30 per cent of the prison population (there is an Aboriginal imprisonment rate 13 times that of the population as a whole), have a higher infant mortality rate, lower life expectancy, less likelihood of completing school or entering university than any other group in Australia, and similar facts are true of African and Hispanic Americans and Britain's West Indian population: certain racial groups are over-represented at the bottom end of almost all indices. It is probably as accurate to say that an increased likelihood of imprisonment is one among many indices of social deprivation as to claim social deprivation as a causal factor in criminality. It is pointless to argue that certain factors are causal and some consequential when the indicators of social deprivation appear inter-related, and the presence of some factors justifies the prediction that various others are likely to be present also. Neither social deprivation nor crime can be dealt with efficiently by addressing their individual symptoms separately.

If one looks at the prison population, it is possible to build a picture of the typical street offender. It is likely that at least some of the following characteristics will be found: the offender will have below average intelligence, be poorly educated or illiterate, rarely in employment, a smoker, a heavy drinker or an alcoholic, a substance abuser, from a one-parent or dysfunctional family, neglected or abused as a child, a member of a particular ethnic minority group, be heavily tattooed or garishly pierced, suffer physical or mental health problems, and someone whose family and friends also share many of these characteristics. It is to be emphasised that I do not argue that any or all of these characteristics causes an individual to commit crime, nor even that their presence is the mark of a criminal, merely that having been in trouble with the law can be as much an indicator of social deprivation as minimal education.

All of these characteristics are common in the wider population: plenty of people smoke, probably most drink and tattoos are common. The point here is that these characteristics are far more common in the prison population, the proportion of smokers in prison being well above the average,[6] and they are often found in combination: the chances of an abused child who grows up illiterate with psychological and drink problems being able to keep a job and avoid trouble with the law are very low. These factors of social deprivation will be the subject of further

---

6 Although only about 25 per cent of the Australian population as a whole smoke, an ad hoc survey in 1998 of the population of one unit in the Western Australian prison system revealed 37 out of 61 prisoners were smokers – 60.6 per cent, well over twice the national average. There is no reason to suppose this is anything but a random sample. I am grateful to Maeve Barry for this statistic.

discussion a little later when examining possible approaches for crime prevention.

Police and crime

Although crime is, in many respects, police business, it is by no means clear what effect police can have upon the occurrence of crime. Once again there is a health parallel: the survival rates of individuals who suffer heart attacks show the effectiveness of medical science in treating heart disease, but the incidence of heart disease is not the responsibility of the medical profession. If there is an epidemic of a disease which fills the hospitals, or if insufficient facilities are available to treat all patients immediately, then persons who could, in better times, have been saved may well die. Hospitals in particular react to health problems, and their preventative role is concerned with recurrence rather than occurrence of ill health.

The justice system as a whole is geared towards dealing in some way or other with offenders. The justice system can do nothing with an individual until that person can be classified as an offender, and here the police role is clear: after a crime has been committed, police investigate it, identify and collect evidence against a suspect, prepare the case and bring the suspect before the court. The criminal justice system cannot operate unless police supply both a suspect and credible evidence collected against that suspect, but what happens after police have fulfilled this function, even the finding of guilt by the court, is beyond their control. The only function that the justice system can perform which has any role in the prevention of further crime is the manner in which it deals with an offender, the sentence it imposes. This may be preventative through rehabilitating the offender, through salutary punishment which dissuades the offender from repeating the behaviour, or which deters others from behaving in a like fashion, or simply by removing the offender from society by a term of imprisonment to prevent re-offending during the period of incarceration. Proponents of harsh sentences claim their preventative effect lies in the ability of individuals to calculate that the benefits of committing the crime are out-weighed by the severity of the sentence,[7] while rehabilitationists claim that offending behaviour can be changed in more positive ways.

This is not the place to discuss the efficacy or otherwise of particular types of sentence in preventing crime, but to examine the specific and limited role of the police in the operation of the justice system. Police powers are not preventative of crime (except insofar as they relate to

---

7   There is a flaw in the logic here, as it relies upon a level of rationality in making behavioural choices which is at the very least questionable. The argument requires that if the consequences of an action (crime) are sufficiently unpleasant (a long prison sentence), individuals will be deterred from that action and will not commit crimes. However, future unpleasant consequences of a course of action are no guaranteed deterrent, as the example of smoking shows: the proven health consequences are well known, and significantly more unpleasant than any sentence a court can impose, yet still do not deter the 25 percent of the (Australian) population who smoke.

preparatory offences such as conspiracy, criminal attempts and possession of offensive weapons), allowing police to deal with an offender or suspected offender only after a crime has been committed: insofar as they can prevent crime, they can only prevent further offences. There are no police powers to deal with any social factors connected with crime, and putatively causal of it, and none concerning what happens to an offender after the evidence has been presented to the court. The effectiveness of police in detection and collection of evidence is, however, crucial to the justice system. Whether one believes the function of a sentence is to rehabilitate, to punish or to deter by example, if offenders can evade prosecution they automatically evade sentence. While carrying out their function as part of the justice system, police can have only a minimal role in preventing crime, as their function is to provide grist to the mill of justice in the form of identifying and charging a suspect against whom a sound case has been prepared.

Detection and prosecution

It is no part of police duty to relieve whatever social pressures exist to cause some individuals to commit crime. In that sense, crime is a social rather than a police problem. Most crime that is committed, certainly minor crime, is opportunistic in the sense that the offender does not have a specific plan to steal a particular car or burgle a particular house or assault a particular person, but there is a certain rudimentary calculus in the offender's mind concerning the viability of the offence. The offender will consider the likely profit from stealing a car or property and the ease with which this can be carried out, or will assault an individual if the reasons to cause injury, in the offender's mind, outweigh the risk of retaliation by the victim. The risk of punishment follows from detection, so if an individual perceives the chance of arrest is high, that particular crime may well be averted. This, of course, is not to say that crime will be prevented – the chance of detection may well be high if a police car is in the street, but as soon as it turns the corner, the chance of detection drops considerably. Opportunistic crime is more likely to be relocated or delayed than prevented by police presence.

One major part of police action on crime, then, should be directed towards improving the chances of detection of offenders. Increased detection rates have several effects on crime. First, and most importantly, without detection, as has been shown, the other parts of the justice system have no raw material to deal with. Secondly, an increased detection rate may well affect the individual offender's calculus on whether to commit the crime, although this may well result in diversion to another geographical area or type of crime where the detection rate is lower. Finally, it is not unreasonable to suppose that the number of active criminals in any area is finite, and that if detection can lead to a significant, even if only temporary, reduction in that number then the incidence of crime will be reduced.

If much crime is opportunistic, the offender roaming until a chance to commit crime is seen, so too is random police patrolling opportunistic.

Police officers cruising the streets may well, in stopping, questioning and searching characters they perceive as suspicious (whatever a "suspicious character" might be) frequently discover property recently stolen, drugs or weapons, but this is no less opportunistic than the burglar looking for an easy target who eventually comes across a temporarily unoccupied house with an open window. Modern crime detection strategies are moving away from this sort of action into more productive, targeted use of manpower and resources, which is referred to as directed patrolling.

Petty crime is increasingly, but by no means exclusively, the province of the young. Studies of young offender patterns suggest that many child-ren commit one or two offences (or, more correctly perhaps, are detected once or twice for offences) but do not re-offend. However, those 10 per cent or so who persistently re-offend (or are consistently detected) may well be responsible for 90 per cent of juvenile crime. Extrapolating this to adult offenders (there is little to suggest that juvenile offenders cease to offend on reaching adulthood, although there are some indications that criminality reduces as offenders approach the age of 30) a relatively small group of persistent offenders between the ages of 15 and 25 is responsible for much of the crime committed (see, for example, Mukherjee and Dagger, 1990).

Information about offenders is of increasing importance to police crime detection strategies. The changing nature of crime has increased its visibility: when an individual's house is burgled, or a handbag stolen, the incident has touched the victim, a person with friends and relatives who soon are told, and the actuality of crime affects society. Formerly, pilfering from docks or workplaces had disembodied victims, anonymous com-panies who often did not know that their property had been stolen, and often some admiration from the public when an enterprising criminal managed to defraud a company of millions.[8] Few people disapproved enough of this type of crime to pass information to police, and many pro-fited by it. Now, though, police are aware of the identities of many active criminals, not least through their criminal records, and it can be easier to target them rather than locations to prevent criminal activity.

Computers are of enormous help in compiling accurate information about crime and criminals. Police stations, and indeed police services, have boundaries that may well be arbitrary and are completely irrelevant to the criminal. An individual might frequent a number of different places and commit burglaries within easy walking distance of each of them which might easily be recorded at three or four different police stations. A pattern of offending may therefore go unnoticed unless the crime reports are all

---

8   The feeling that "it is OK if no-one is hurt" may be changing. The British Great Train Robbers attracted considerable admiration, despite the fact that the train driver who was assaulted later died. Alan Bond, a West Australian business high flier of the 1980s, became bankrupt and was convicted and imprisoned over dishonest business dealings which had made him a multi-millionaire, but still retained some popular support. He did, however, attract some vociferous opprobrium mainly because he had persuaded many ordinary people to invest with him, who had lost most of their savings. Similar dislike is felt for those responsible for the Enron and Parmalat financial mismanagement, which has caused losses, particularly of pension entitlements, for ordinary workers.

analysed by a single computer. This problem was illustrated in Britain some years ago, where a number of rapes occurred miles apart, in different police areas. This resulted in a number of independent enquiries which were only later brought together when it was realised that each offence was committed reasonably close to one of Britain's major motorways. The eventual major inquiry resulted in the arrest and conviction of the offender when all the information on each individual case was pooled. The problem is increased in the United States, where, although almost every American has fingerprints on record somewhere, it can take so long for a suspect's prints to be checked on every database, especially if the case is dealt with by one of the smaller police agencies, that a wanted person can be granted bail and disappear once more.

Equally relevant is the targeting of criminals. Detectives have, of course, always used good information about crime that is about to be committed to maintain surveillance on criminals and premises in order to apprehend offenders just as they are committing the offence, but before anyone is hurt. In sufficiently serious cases, resources have been deployed to keep individuals under surveillance for some time in order to gain evidence of crime, but, of course, full 24-hour surveillance is expensive of manpower. If, however, a person who is believed to be a frequent offender is watched and monitored lightly over a period of time, then the chances of finding that person committing a crime is increased. This is a method that British police, in London for example, developed in the late 1990s with some success: every month a handful of known local criminals believed to be currently active by their local stations became designated targets. All officers at that and surrounding stations maintain an informal watch for those individuals, reporting any scrap of information but not exercising police powers in such a way as to amount to harassment. Plain clothes officers may from time to time keep that person under observation. The chances of arresting a target, if indeed that individual is an active criminal, are much enhanced by this.

Prosecution of a persistent offender requires care. When passing sentence, the court can sentence the defendant only for the offences proved or admitted, and on the basis of the defendant's antecedent history which includes previous convictions as well as family and social background information. However, just because a defendant has previous convictions for burglary and is to be sentenced for another burglary, the court is neither morally nor legally entitled to assume that that individual has committed any burglaries other than those brought to the court's attention. If police target a known burglar and arrest for a single burglary, the court can deal only with that offence, however many other offences that individual is believed to have committed. If the justice system is to deal with a persistent offender as a persistent offender then the court must be shown a pattern of offending by multiple offences being charged, or must wait until the individual amasses a large number of convictions.

The effect of policing on the incidence of crime

From previous comments concerning the causes of crime, doubts may be cast on the actual effect that policing has on the crime rate. If individuals commit crime as a result of social pressure, poor education, drug addiction or some other such cause beyond the ambit of police, then clearly police can have no effect on preventing these occurrences. Society will always have crime, and there will always be detection and prosecution work for police to carry out. However, when there is a complete breakdown of society (perhaps as a result of civil war or invasion, as has been seen in this century in Liberia, Haiti and Afghanistan) and there is no justice system and no police, murder, rape and looting are commonplace. This can be seen in stable societies on the rare occasions that policing and public order breaks down completely, if temporarily, when opportunists who would not normally commit crime may do so,[9] and crime increases as normally law-abiding citizens seize the opportunity to steal or loot property.

Lowering the incidence of crime is, of course, crime prevention. Since dealing with crime is the original *raison d'être* of policing,[10] then the effective role of police in crime prevention needs to be examined. There is one aspect of crime about which the police as a professional body have an absolute advantage over any other agency: police have almost a monopoly of knowledge about current crime and criminals in any given area. There are two formal sources for this knowledge: all reported crime is initially reported to police – no other agency maintains records of crime; and interviewing and recording information about individuals arrested for crime gives individual police officers significant knowledge of the area's criminal fraternity. The less formal source of information about crime is the community itself, where individuals frequently have information which may relate to crime and criminals. The alienation of police from the public by the emphasis on vehicle patrol and reactive policing methods has significantly reduced this less formal flow of information, and it is gaining access to this source of information which is one of the principles of community policing, what Bayley terms "grass-roots feedback from the community" (Bayley, 1989).

The knowledge that police have about crime can be used in two ways. The police may use the knowledge to be more effective in the arrest and prosecution of offenders, or the knowledge may be shared with the public in order that people may take informed action to prevent themselves becoming victims of crime. The great challenge to any crime prevention

---

9   During the police strike in Liverpool in 1919, for example, there was a serious outbreak of looting. This also follows natural disasters such as floods or cyclones where houses and shops are damaged, and police are engaged elsewhere. Looting may also follow in the wake of riots, for example after the Rodney King assault in Los Angeles.

10 Crime prevention is still cited by most police agencies among their primary objectives, although, in Britain at least, it is losing ground. It had primacy from 1829 until the 1980s, became second item in ACPO's Police Service Statement of Common Purpose and Values (1990), but is implicit rather than explicit in the Home Office National Policing Plan 2003-2006 (Mawby & Wright, 2003).

strategy or police operation against crime is to show that the incidence of crime has actually been reduced, not relocated or changed in its nature. One of the more frequent criticisms of some early community policing strategies, which were often introduced piecemeal and experimentally in various parts of cities, was that they relocated, rather than prevented, crime. Some community policing schemes claimed spectacular success by reclaiming derelict blocks or public spaces which had been avoided by most people as the haunts of thieves, drug dealers and prostitutes, and returning them to community use. There were, however, indications that the criminal operations had merely moved elsewhere to another part of the city, or even to a different police district. Community policing provides no real solution if the problem is moved rather than removed.

If the knowledge that police have about crime is used to improve detection and prosecution of offenders, then the effectiveness of this as a crime prevention device depends on the effectiveness of the other parts of the criminal justice system at dealing with offenders in a way that prevents their re-offending. This can range from effective rehabilitation to lifetime incarceration. Suppose, hypothetically, that the courts sentence wisely and the corrections system is effective in rehabilitating offenders and reintegrating them into the community, so that recidivism is low: improved policing will result in offenders being detected, prosecuted, fed through the system and released to offend no more, the number of offenders will drop, and crime will be reduced. If, more realistically, there is a high recidivism rate of offenders within the justice system, then improved policing can only result in increasing numbers of individuals entering and re-entering the system. If the only way to prevent recidivists committing crime is by increasing the length of their incarceration, then improved policing will only hasten the collapse of the justice system through overload. Another medical analogy suggests itself here: improved early detection of cancer is only of value if both the knowledge and the capacity are available to treat it. There is no point in being able to inform someone in apparently good health that they have a incurable disease, and still less in perfecting diagnostic procedures only to make patients wait months for treatment which must be given immediately to be effective.

If police are to disseminate their knowledge about crime to the community, then they must develop effective ways of doing this. A modern police service should maintain a clear picture of the crime situation within its area, and even in particular suburbs or streets. One of the advantages of computerised recording is that it enables links and trends to be shown clearly, and it is usually the trends that are important for crime prevention purposes. The police service has, with a few exceptions, no vested interest in suppressing information about crime, and therefore police crime figures are in the public domain. Those areas where police do not divulge information are matters where full details might prejudice a continuing inquiry, for example a task force investigating a murder, or where the victim of the crime requests that details be withheld. Accurate information on reported crime is collected, collated and made available by police with these few restrictions, so that the required information for informed crime prevention decisions does, therefore, exist.

The means of disseminating information about crime to the public can be problematic for police. The media disseminate information about crime and have access to accurate and recent police data, but have different interests: while police seek to give the public clear information about crime in general, the media seek a story which will increase circulation by attracting public attention. Since crime and policing feature high on the modern political agenda, politicians also use police information about crime to claim the success of their crime policies if in government, or to criticise lack of action if in opposition. Crime figures themselves, as supplied by police, may well form the basis for praise or censure (more often the latter) of police action by both politicians and media commentators. Police record incidents of crime, and while their information may well be of great value to the public as a crime prevention tool, they have no control over the context of its dissemination. Media information about crime is frequently sensationalised or used for political purposes.

Whatever use police make of their knowledge of crime, its effectiveness will be enhanced by increasing the accuracy of that knowledge. The raw facts of crimes reported or persons arrested need collation and analysis, and the more facts that can be added the more complete the collation and the more accurate the results of the analysis will be. Increasingly, police are making use of computer analysis in both major crime investigation, for example the HOLMES system in use in Britain and parts of Australia, and in day-to-day analysis of crime reports, for example the British NCIS and NIM systems and the COMPSTAT system originated by the New York Police Department, which will be discussed more fully below.

Compstat

In the mid-1990s the New York Police Department underwent great change under its new Commissioner, William Bratton, appointed in 1994 by the new mayor, Rudolph Giuliani, who had been elected largely on a law and order platform. The phrase which caught the world's attention was "zero-tolerance policing", the intellectual roots of which lay in the so-called "broken windows" theory (Wilson and Kelling, 1982), and the driving force was the statistics-driven management approach known as Compstat. This new era of policing in New York City claimed dramatic reductions in reported crime, the year 2000 recording a 57 per cent drop in the seven major crimes,[11] and a 65 per cent drop in murders (Henry, 2002). Ten years on, Giuliani's term in office has ended, Commissioner Bratton has moved on and the term "zero tolerance" is mentioned once only in Vincent Henry's highly detailed analysis of the changes in the NYPD, *The Compstat Paradigm*. What remains after the political and media hyperbole is a valid social theory and a highly influential management process.

---

11   Murder, robbery, rape, felony assault, burglary, larceny and grand larceny auto under New York penal law.

The broken windows theory claims that if the early signs of urban or social decay are ignored, then much more serious problems will follow very swiftly. The analogy is with a vacant house: if the windows break, rain enters, the wood starts to rot, the unkempt garden is a sign that no-one cares, the house soon becomes a target for graffiti and squatters and it is rapidly reduced to ruin. Even if empty, if the place is cared for and the odd broken window repaired, the house is less likely to be vandalised and destroyed piece by piece. Applying this theory to policing, if minor disorder is ignored, more serious disorder will follow, and eventually major crime will grow. If groups of rowdy drunks habitually linger unchallenged on the foreshore after a beach-side pub has closed, then, over a period of time, the groups will get bigger, noisier, more aggressive and more of a social problem: eventually, fights will break out, and someone may eventually be found dead in the surf. An active police presence at closing time in the early stages may avert trouble later.

Broken windows theory provides a rationale for early police intervention in comparatively petty incidents. However, the tradition in British and Australian policing has always required officers on patrol to take just this sort of action without reference to supervising officers, rendering "broken windows" less of a ground-breaking rationale than a post hoc justification for action. Any officer who finds, or whose attention is drawn by the public to, an individual selling drugs has always been actively encouraged to investigate and arrest if evidence is found. Henry suggests that this was not the case in New York before 1993, where, on encountering a drug dealer on the street, an officer's "only officially approved recourse [was] to file an intelligence report and hope that the specialized narcotics unit will get around to making arrests" (Henry, 2002, p 94). It would appear from Henry's exegesis that only since the Bratton era have uniformed police officers at street level in New York been permitted to exercise their own discretion with regard to the drugs, street prostitution and alcohol offences which most concern the public in the same way that police in other places have always been able to do: in Britain, it has never been acceptable for a senior officer to forbid a junior officer to make an arrest, far less for a police organisation to establish policy preventing officers carrying out specific aspects of their duty.

The most important point to be remembered about Compstat is that it is "a management process through which the NYPD identifies problems and measures the results of its problem-solving activities" (Henry, 2002, p 5). Two aspects of this management process are the accurate collection and analysis of data, particularly, but not exclusively, crime statistics, and the devolution of responsibility for police performance to precinct level. A Compstat report is produced weekly, breaking down crime and arrest reports on a precinct basis, and allowing comparisons of each precinct's performance against previous weeks, months and years, and against other precinct's performances. The report is also intended to show changes in crime and types of crime, and emerging crime trends, as well as the success of particular strategies. In this respect it is a form of information-driven policing.

Perhaps the most provocative aspect of Compstat is the weekly Compstat meeting, and its challenging ethos towards precinct commanders. These meetings amount to "intensive monthly performance evaluations for every commander" (Henry, 2002, p 18) – a performance evaluation, moreover, held in the presence of each individual's peers. While these meetings are intended to provide praise as well as criticism, and to enable commanders to compare strategies and negotiate additional personnel for specific operations, the general ethos appears to be both confrontational between the executive and precinct commanders, and competitive between precincts. Positive results are sought each month, which leaves little opportunity for developing long-term strategies.

The best strategy within policing to achieve an immediate, positive result is an arrest. The next best strategy is to remove the problem from a particular area, in this case the precinct, even if this means relocating the problem elsewhere. Cynically, perhaps, a precinct commander can achieve a better personal result at a Compstat meeting by moving a problem rather than by making arrests, since in so doing that commander's crime statistics show an improvement while someone else's are worse: in a competitive environment, it is better for A if A is praised while B receives criticism than if A is praised and B does not attract comment. More seriously, though, the Compstat process does, by its nature, seem to foster a one-dimensional, short-term approach to crime problems. There is a place in modern policing for the swoop-and-arrest approach, as there is for almost every other power, strategy and tactic that police may employ. These strategies have been used in short bursts by police agencies since at least the 1950s, but there are various criteria which must be met to make it a valid and useful option. These criteria are:

- there is a clear end result required by the strategy;
- the strategy can reasonably be expected to achieve this result;
- police powers are exercised in a particular area for a particular purpose;
- the problem to be addressed is confined to a particular area, so use of the strategy will not result in simple displacement of crime;
- there are no long-term implications for police / public relations, for example the operation will not create even the appearance of racism or discrimination against any particular group or groups.

The first three of these criteria are really intended to prevent police powers being used as a harassing tactic to make life unpleasant for supposedly problematic individuals. If there is a particular problem in a particular place, for example rowdy behaviour in or near a sports stadium on match days, then extra officers and firm policing on two or three match days could be expected to solve the problem. However, putting in a snatch squad in a particular place to arrest drug dealers or prostitutes is unlikely to do more than cause them minor inconvenience, and result in their moving elsewhere with their clients.

Finally, there are often racial and ethical implications of police swoops and indiscriminate, if legal, arrests. These will be discussed in more detail in Chapter 7, but relate to the profile of persistent petty offenders mentioned earlier. Many of these tend to be members of minority racial groups, and zero tolerance approaches may well result in a higher arrest rate for these groups than their percentage of the overall population warrants. Racism in policing is still a very sensitive issue in many countries, not least in Australia, Britain and the United States: saturation policing and increased arrests in particular locations may be seen as racist in both their approach and their results. It should not be forgotten that one of London's most serious race riots was precipitated by Operation Swamp, the stop-and-search drug operation in Brixton, South London, an area with a high West Indian population, in 1981. Although West Indian youth were not explicitly targeted, a disproportionate number were searched and arrested which the community saw as evidence of police racism.

Community policing strategies

Community policing is largely concerned with the acquisition and dissemination of knowledge about crime. With regard to acquisition of knowledge, community policing seeks to involve police with communities so that information about people, crime, problems and issues that affect individuals on the street can come to police notice in a way that has not been possible since the shift to reactive policing in the 1960s. With regard to dissemination of knowledge, one of the police objectives must be to pass on to the public new and relevant information about current crime trends at a local community level and thus assist that community to take precautions against crime. Unlike the reactive policing which, of necessity, runs parallel with it, community policing is a long-term strategy with long-term objectives. The first task is to build good relations with all sections of the public, and to help all groups within society to feel that police are approachable. Unless the community both knows and trusts its police, individuals are unlikely to talk and give information, and, likewise, are unlikely to want to listen to information given by police. Good police-community relations are, therefore, crucial for the interchange of information. This is relatively easy to achieve in small towns and rural communities, but is much more difficult in large towns and cities, where each station may police a population of 100,000 people, and have several hundred officers. The sheer numbers of people involved can make police and community totally anonymous to each other, and personal contacts, where possible at all, may take considerable time to build.

One difficulty in building links between police and community has been that these links have traditionally involved liaison between office-holders rather than between individuals. If a senior officer is posted to a particular police station or district as a liaison officer to the local community, it is likely that most of this liaison will take the form of meetings with local politicians, business persons, church and ethnic leaders for the few years that the officer is in post. While, arguably, useful in its own way, this does little to develop links between police and community at street level, that is between officers on patrol and residents, shopkeepers and youth on the streets. Even if an individual has frequent dealings with police, this may easily involve a number of different officers over a period of time, which does not often lead to good relations. Still less can links be built between officers and the community if operational duties lead to missed appointments, for example. Officers at street rather than senior rank dedicated to working with local people can be of great long-term value for police-community relations.

Community policing should not, however, be divorced from the rest of policing in dealing with crime. Information must be shared: community police are not only a conduit to pass information to the community, but also to glean information from the community which may be of assistance to other officers investigating crime. If knowledge is power, then knowledge shared within the police organisation will give every officer more power to deal with crime. Similarly, if the knowledge is shared with the community, then the community is likewise empowered to prevent crime.

Community policing should be viewed as one strategy among others for dealing with crime, although it is perhaps the only viable long-term police crime prevention strategy. It certainly does not take the place of detection, arrest and charge of a suspect, and is by no means a soft option for police. Community policing can and should assist communities to police themselves, in that there are sufficient eyes and ears about to supplement the police and render undetected crime less likely. Democratic communities are policed by consent, in that the public will always outnumber the police, and even passive resistance will cripple police efforts: community policing seeks to enlist the active cooperation of the public by calling attention to crime-related social issues, rather than accepting society's passive consent to be policed.

Crime prevention

There are four major ways of attempting crime prevention, which can be defined as:

1. removal of the causes of crime;
2. removal of the opportunity for crime;
3. preventing the offender from committing further crime;
4. target hardening, or making the commission of the crime more difficult or less attractive.

For convenience, I will categorise crime into three types: large-scale crime; personal crime; and minor or street crime. It is this last which is both the most prevalent and which causes most distress to the community. Crime is a social problem, and, insofar as there are steps that society can take to prevent crime, thus far is crime prevention a social responsibility.

Earlier parts of this chapter have looked at the effect that police can have upon crime, and this section looks at the impact that society can have in crime prevention. Crime can never be eliminated, as there will always be the violent, the unscrupulous, the greedy and the dishonest in society who will commit offences against others, but crime can be reduced.

Removing the causes of crime

Large-scale crime which is carefully planned, with the risk of detection and conviction evaluated, is committed from a combination of greed and hubris, neither of which cause is amenable to elimination. Removal of the opportunity for large-scale crime is difficult, as two examples will show. Computer crime cannot exist without computers, so to dispense with them would remove the opportunity to commit a whole range of highly lucrative, almost undetectable frauds. However, such is the reliance of the modern world on computers that this is not a valid option. Likewise, the import and manufacture of illegal drugs would cease overnight if such substances were available legally and cheaply or if society rid itself of its drug culture. Unfortunately, society has enough addicts to make large-scale drug offences profitable, although arguments for decriminalising drug abuse include the reduction of associated crime (Marks, 1990). Large-scale criminal enterprises have multiple offenders and removing them is not easy, but action during the 1990s in America and Italy against organised crime (particularly the Mafia) demonstrates that prevention requires more than just the removal of one, or even several, of the main offenders (Trahair, 1987).[12]

The causes of personal crime lie mainly within individuals. There is nothing society can do to prevent a conflict between two or more people, other than making it more difficult for those individuals to come into contact with each other. Most violence is committed within the home, as are most murders in countries like Australia and Britain, since inter-personal conflict is most likely to arise amongst those people to whom an individual is closest, the family. Crime prevention for personal crime is probably a by-product of individuals undertaking counselling or other strategies concerned with relationships. However, the sort of problems of social deprivation, powerlessness, and an inability to express oneself may well be as much a cause of violence as of other petty crime, and many assaults, both domestically and against comparative strangers, are committed by persons under the influence of drink or drugs.

The link between various forms of social deprivation and crime has already been shown, but the question was left as to how this could be dealt with to prevent crime. Factors such as ethnicity, illiteracy, unemployment, child abuse and family breakdown are deeply rooted in society itself, and are beyond the ambit of any one agency to deal with: while they present problems for members of society individually, they can only be dealt with effectively by

---

12   The issue of organised crime is discussed in more detail in Chapter 15.

society as a whole. While police may become aware before many other agencies of the existence of social deprivation, dealing with such social issues directly is usually well outside the role of police. Social deprivation is also a problem to be dealt with holistically: to deal with a single individual's drug problems, health problems and history of abuse is unlikely to be successful if that individual remains in a milieu where many of that person's relatives and friends have similar problems. Likewise, if an agency is established to deal with the drug problems of individuals in a particular group, and has no resources or authority to address their literacy and employment problems also, then it may be ineffective in achieving its goals and as a crime prevention strategy.

Addressing social deprivation on all fronts for groups of people is no easy task, but strategies which attempt to deal with all the issues simultaneously are the most likely to be successful. The largest problem in rehabilitating offenders, especially those with drug problems, is that upon release from prison or substance abuse programs they return home where they are likely to find themselves in the same drug and crime milieu which caused their problems in the first place. The most successful claims for such holistic rehabilitation schemes rely on anecdotal evidence, and tend to be on a small scale within particular communities. In Washington, DC during the 1990s, for example, a team of Islamic former offenders and drug addicts of African American origin calling themselves the Group of Concerned Men commenced working with street kids and claimed success in drug rehabilitation, instilling pride and finding work.

Removal of the opportunity for crime

Removing the opportunity for crime is in theory possible, but, with regard to theft, the affluence of modern society increases the amount of property available to be stolen. Reducing the amount of property would reduce the opportunity to steal it, although rationing ownership of cars, for example, would be socially unacceptable. Some serious suggestions for removing the opportunity for crime are equally unacceptable to important sections of the community. For example, late evening attacks on women could be prevented if no woman was out after dark without a male escort – however effective this might be, it is, in effect, a curfew on women. Imagine the corollary: rather than remove the potential victim, remove the potential offender by placing any male about after dark without a female chaperone immediately under suspicion, thereby shifting the curfew to the male population. Uncontroversial steps can, however, be taken to remove the opportunity for crime: not leaving valuables in one's car in an open, public car park removes any chance of their being stolen.

One way suggested of removing the opportunity for crime is to decriminalise certain offences. One example which has had some success is the decriminalisation of certain offences connected with prostitution in order to prevent more serious crime. While in many jurisdictions prostitutes are legally permitted to work alone, this carries far more personal danger (particularly if they are working on the streets) than working with others: however, several prostitutes working together within premises may lead those premises to be considered a brothel, and therefore illegal. Legalising brothels in cities such as Melbourne, Sydney and Canberra has rendered prostitutes less open to exploitation by pimps, coercion or violent assault, and legislation which controls the premises prevents drug addicts, under-age girls or illegal immigrants detained against their will working as prostitutes and enforces regular health checks.

In many ways, removing the opportunity for crime is not possible without a significant change in the way of life of individuals within society or society as a whole. Some individuals, particularly the elderly, may be so frightened of crime that they reduce the likelihood of their becoming a victim by radically changing their lifestyle. One can never be mugged in the streets if one never goes out, for example. Such actions, which are usually prompted by unreasonable fear of crime, can have a deleterious effect on the lives of those affected. If police have an obligation to protect the community, then this must include protecting the more timid of its members from the level of fear which destroys their lives, and ensuring that effective, reasonable, but not excessive, precautions against crime are taken.

Preventing the offender from committing further crime

This aspect of crime prevention has already been mentioned. To prevent an individual from doing something is to coerce, which, in a free society, requires legal authority. Although some offenders may put themselves voluntarily into some sort of program to prevent their re-offending (for example, drug rehabilitation, counselling or psychological treatment), for most it is the sentence of the criminal court which carries out this preventative function with greater or less success.

It must, however, be borne in mind that a sentence might be sufficient to prevent a particular individual committing further offences, that is to meet its requirements as a crime prevention strategy, without necessarily meeting any of the other requirements of a sentence, for example punishment. An individual may commit horrendous crimes as a direct result of being under the influence of drugs: a drug rehabilitation program may well last six months and, if successful, may render that individual unlikely to re-offend. Even if this is the case, to release the offender after such a short sentence may not reflect the serious way in which society and the victim view the offences, and a much longer term of imprisonment is required as punishment, or as a mark of society's revulsion at the offence.

Target hardening

Target hardening as a crime prevention strategy includes the usual obvious precautions like locking house and car, installing alarms, and buying a dog to prevent burglary. The question with all such strategies to make crime more difficult is whether or not the cost of prevention is worthwhile.

Security technology may be improved, making commission of the crime more difficult, although it can never be rendered impossible, but it is futile to fit a security system worth more than the property it protects. Target hardening may relocate rather than prevent crime, as a determined burglar will eventually find an easy target unless everyone has locks, bolts, bars and alarms.

Large-scale crime by its nature is planned, and has two risk factors considered by the criminal: the risk of detection, and the risk of successful prosecution followed by a severe sentence. Considerable criminal effort is expended on remaining undetected or removing incriminating evidence, so if more resources are allocated to investigation and prosecution, the increased likelihood of arrest and conviction may have a deterrent effect. This, however, is expensive: the American government has expended huge resources in its war on drugs, with only limited success.

Effective target hardening strategies may result in a change in the nature of crime, an example of which arises from legislation passed by the West Australian Parliament concerning pawnbrokers. This legislation made it more difficult for individuals to sell property to pawnbrokers without some form of identification, and was intended to prevent burglars from easily disposing of stolen TVs, VCRs, CDs and other property in such stores. The tactic was successful up to a point, in that burglary of unattended homes and the taking of such items decreased, but the rate of handbag snatches and burglary of houses with the resident at home increased, with victims being forced to hand over cash or bankcards and PIN numbers. Likewise, carjacking was almost unknown until car security improved to the level at which it was virtually impossible to enter and start a motor vehicle without the correct key.

Conclusion

This chapter has looked at crime, its causes, and the respective roles of society and its police in dealing with it. The causes of crime, it is postulated, are largely social, insofar as the vast majority of criminal behaviour which impinges upon the population as a whole is largely determined by social deprivation and other factors. If these underlying causes of crime are to be addressed, this can only be done by society as a whole, or by a concerted approach by a number of agencies within society, not least health, education and social services. Police have very little part to play in addressing the causes of crime, but much to do with crime which has been committed, and the extent to which society permits itself to be policed, and will cooperate with police in reporting and solving crime. Crime, like death and taxes, will always be part of society, so the most that police can hope to do is maintain a level of control over, and reduce rather than eradicate, it.

Crime prevention strategies which rely on working with offenders to prevent their continuing criminal behaviour rely on police for the detection of offenders and the early stages of their prosecution, but for almost nothing further. The success or failure of these strategies does not depend on police. The matter in which police are paramount is that of knowledge about crime. Police are the sole agency dealing with crime as it happens, recording details, dealing with victims and, initially, with offenders, and of all agencies police have an unsurpassed knowledge about all aspects of criminal activity. This knowledge about crime can be used to increase police effectiveness in apprehending and prosecuting offenders directly, and also provided to the public or other agencies in order to prevent crime. Ethical issues also apply here, for example there is a real dilemma whether police are justified or not in giving information about an individual's criminal history or whereabouts to members of the public who may be at risk from that person. The most hotly debated problem in this context concerns information about the location of released paedophiles, which will be discussed fully in Chapter 7.

PART II

THE CHANGING STYLES OF POLICING

CHAPTER 4

THE 1960s ON – POLICING RESPONSES TO SOCIAL CHANGE

Introduction

The decade of the 1960s has come to be associated with change in many different aspects of society and culture in countries throughout the world. This chapter will examine the impact this change has had on policing, both directly and indirectly. The changes in policing which started in the 1960s continued into the 1970s and early 1980s when the shift towards community policing began. However, the change to community policing should not be seen as a reversion to the pre-war tradition of an officer on foot patrol, but a new approach altogether attempting to blend the best from traditional patrol with the most effective use of change, particularly in information technology which had partly fuelled and partly driven the changes of the previous 25 years.

The changes of the 1960s, like many changes in policing styles, was largely driven by technology. As Reiss observes "technology made possible the demise of foot patrol and the substitution of motor patrol" (Reiss, 1992, p 58). Better and smaller radios enabled every officer to carry one, rather than rely on communications built into police vehicles. Since officers could be located, called individually and given tasks by their stations with no delay, the next logical step was to ensure they got to their tasks quickly. The obvious way to do this was to put almost all police officers in cars, in the expectation that a quicker response time would provide a better service to the public. This trend towards the increasing reliance on better communications and transport and, later, on computerised dispatch systems, will be examined and its advantages and disadvantages assessed. Despite all the hopes, technology did not seem to provide a better solution to crime than the outmoded foot patrol, and the community felt a certain amount of alienation from its police. Police organisations have since addressed this by changing their focus to one of service, and instigated community policing schemes.

Not only did what British Prime Minister Harold Wilson refer to as the "white-hot technological revolution" evoke a change in policing, but police were also forced to respond to the great cultural changes of the 1960s. The civil rights marches in the United States resulted in constitutional change through the Equal Rights Amendments, and the same cultural shift led to the outlawing of discrimination in many nations, first on grounds of race and gender and subsequently on other grounds like sexual orientation. It will be argued here that this emphasis on equality and rights led to society taking a much closer interest in those in authority who had an effect on the rights of individuals, particularly the police, and police-watching and questioning of authority became commonplace, and, in some cases, almost a way of life. This public scrutiny helped bring to public awareness the enduring problem of police corruption. The British faith in its police was rocked by the Challenor affair, corruption was shown by Serpico to be endemic in the New York City Police,[1] and allegations and corruption enquiries have dogged policing in democratic nations ever since.

Closely allied to the expression of rights was the rise of popular protest. The phenomena of civil rights marches in the United States and anti-nuclear protests in Britain caused a problem for police. These protests were largely peaceful, and could not be treated as riots, yet they attracted crowds which were too large to be ignored. By the end of the 1960s the phenomenon of the peaceful protest which by its very size threatened public order was established, and led to major questioning of policing methods on the occasions when violence arose.

Immediate-response policing

The most noticeable effect of changes in policing styles in the 1960s was the virtual disappearance of the police officer walking the beat in cities and towns. In Britain, this was followed by the rather more gradual disappearance of the resident police officer in rural areas. This was made possible by radio technology and relatively cheap motor vehicles,[2] but was also a result of the increasing tendency towards specialisation. Although police management have always stated that the most important individual of any police organisation is the officer patrolling the streets, from the 1960s this officer has become the poor relation of policing.

The police officer patrolling a beat was expected to know, and be known by, members of the community, remain in an area for a considerable time if not until retirement, and be a repository of local knowledge and deal with almost everything that occurred. However, from the 1960s came increasing trends in specialisation – motor vehicle offences were largely dealt with by traffic officers on motor cycles or in fast cars, crime was dealt with by specialist detectives, and even responsibility for stationary motor

---

1   Serpico was a police officer who was so horrified by the graft and violence among his colleagues that he commenced a one-man crusade against corruption, suffering death threats and physical violence. His story later became a major feature film.

2   The first cheap motor vehicle, the Model T Ford, was sold in Britain in the 1920s for less than £100. In the 1960s, the Mini, a much more sophisticated small car, cost less than £500, in real terms a cheaper vehicle. The companies that supplied the 1930s police vehicles had either folded (Railton) or catered for the luxury market (Lagonda), while newer companies were supplying reliable, mass-produced, sturdy police vehicles. The invention of the transistor likewise made radio communications cheaper, smaller, more reliable and less easily damaged.

vehicle offences was devolved to local authorities.[3] These specialist officers had to come from somewhere, of course, and the largest source was the bulk of each force, variously termed the beat, general duties or patrol officers. As specialisation increased, the number and quality of officers on beats or patrols diminished. Apart from those few dedicated to patrol, beat officers tended to be those who were in one way or another not acceptable to any specialist group, or those who were too young and inexperienced to be considered for membership of them. Over a period of 20 or so years, the officer on patrol, "the backbone of the force", ceased to be the solid, upright worthy figure in the blue uniform but young, straight out of the police academy, and awaiting the chance to get off the beat and on to "better things".

The disappearance of the foot patrol officer was largely an urban problem in Australia and the United States, and, although it started as such in Britain, it soon became a rural problem there also. In the United States, where each community organised its own policing, very small police organisations[4] made specialisation impossible, and in rural Australia the distances between communities meant that each township either had a permanent police presence or none at all. While British constabularies could close a village police station and provide patrolling cover from a town 10 or 15 miles (16–24 kms) distant, closure of a rural Australian police station could easily mean the nearest police post was two or three hours' drive away. In towns and cities in almost every nation the police officers in uniform appeared to the public to lose the use of their feet, and were only ever to be seen in cars.

Although high-powered police vehicles remained on the streets, there were increasing numbers of smaller cars or commercial vehicles in police use. Relatively cheap models came to constitute the majority of vehicles used by police. Australian policing favours standard panel vans for ordinary patrol and plain family saloons for most other work, while Britain has since the 1960s used first purpose-built, low powered motor cycles (known as Noddy-bikes) then small cars in distinctive pale blue and white as "Pandas" and small to medium saloons as general purpose cars, and American police use fairly run-of-the-mill cars, usually in distinctive black and white or blue and white livery. Depending on the affluence of the police organisation and its community, American police vehicles in particular can, if necessary, be kept in service until they almost fall apart. The public grew used to the sight of these patrolling vehicles, and soon realised that they could be despatched to incidents by a control room, often as a result of requests for assistance made to that control room by the public. The relationship between the police and the public had changed.

---

3   It is, perhaps, interesting to note that, once traffic wardens were introduced in London and other British cities, public approval of police rose sharply. It would appear that no-one likes having parking tickets, and having someone other than police to blame them on is good for police / public relations.

4   Ten per cent of police organisations in the United States have less than 10 members, and over 1000 have just one officer (Geller and Morris, 1992).

A police officer with a car and a personal radio could get from place to place quickly, and could be directed easily from a control room. A member of the public could call the police control room which would assign a car to arrive within a few minutes. The public grew accustomed to calling police, and police officers received so many calls that they were doing little else but travelling from one call to the next, which became known, in Britain at least, as "fire-brigade policing". There was a certain inevitability about this less personal relationship (which suited no-one), in that the public learned to expect police attendance on demand, and the police patrol just filled in the time between calls. Lacking a known, approachable local officer on patrol, the public increasingly called the control room: the more calls that were received for assistance, the more police felt the need to put officers in cars to deal with them.

This alienation between police and the public was felt and regretted by both. The alienation did not occur in small American communities with few police officers, nor in rural Australia, and it took some time before the village bobby in Britain became an endangered species. Anecdotal evidence suggests that Australian police officers who have served in small stations in rural areas view such service as among the most satisfying of their careers, and similarly officers who had their own village station in Britain regret any transfer to the more anonymous large towns. Little research has been done on police in small communities, but major studies (for example, Graef, 1989) which have shown police anomie and dissatisfaction with the way they have to carry out their duties have all been conducted in large cities.

It is worth recalling that this shift in policing style to vehicle patrol was both intended and expected to improve policing. If the public needed a police officer to deal with a particular incident, then it follows that the quicker the officer can attend and deal with the matter, the better served the public would be. Cars and radios together enabled police to implement this rapid response to requests from the public. However, the public also had a need, which was not fully understood or articulated at the time, for a police presence, the feeling that police were about, and if not actually visible at least not far away. Unwittingly, but for the best of motives, the comforting police presence was exchanged for rapid police response.

In Britain, at least, this was not intended to happen. The Unit Beat System was envisaged as a means of providing a coherent police service to the public. Some officers would patrol dedicated beats, and maintain traditional links with residents on those beats. The long-established emergency call system would operate, and powerful patrol cars would answer these calls. Small "Panda" cars would be used by other patrolling officers, who were to drive to an area, park, patrol on foot then drive on and repeat the process. Detectives were to deal with crime, in close liaison with home beat and panda patrol officers. This plan was perhaps overambitious in its conception, and as the number of calls for police increased, there was little opportunity for foot patrol from a panda. Indeed, with the ethos that every call from the public would be attended by police as soon as possible, it became necessary for the cars to be manned above all other priorities. This reduced even further the number of officers walking, and even those who had been assigned dedicated beats would with increasing frequency be removed from them to drive a panda. By 1970, few areas remained which were patrolled on foot, and all of these were in the heart of the largest cities.

Increasing specialisation has led to a change in the demographics of police officers. Policing is a career where there is no lateral entry, except possibly from other police organisations, and every police officer starts at the bottom. The bottom of policing is uniform patrol, on foot in those few services where foot patrol remains. Specialist duties and promotion all have requirements stipulating minimum length of service, meaning that all officers newly out of the police academy are required to spend their first few years on patrol. Typically, in police organisations which have a number of police stations, new officers are rarely sent to those stations which, because they are suburban or rural and have fewer social or policing problems, are in the areas where most police officers choose to live.

Those police officers who are youngest in age and service frequently find themselves patrolling the areas which are the busiest and most difficult of all to police effectively, a point noted by Lord Scarman in his report on the Brixton and other inner city disturbances of 1981. Police officers with skill and experience are desirable assets to any police organisation, and therefore prime candidates for specialist branches, promotion and congenial police stations as well as being vital to assisting, supporting and setting an example to recruits at busy stations in less desirable parts of town. It is little wonder that such officers choose the option most desirable to them personally, which is unlikely to be the stress of the inner city. The face of policing that answers calls from the public is most likely to be less than 25 years old, and have less than four years' police experience.

The structure of rapid-response policing leads logically to the conclusion that the quicker police officers can respond, the better is the service given to the public. The response time is also easily and accurately measured. In a time when the cost of policing has become a political issue, and in a political climate driven by economic rationalism, the cost effectiveness of policing is being questioned. A major problem for police management is the matter of measuring performance and justifying costs, and developing indices for so doing. One such index is the measurement of response time. It is easy to record the time a call for police assistance is received: many computer-linked phone systems do this automatically. It is likewise easy to record the time an officer arrives at the scene. From the 1960s, the public have come to expect a quick police response to a call as a right, and both the technology and police management have encouraged this expectation.

One of the results of the response-time fetish has been that the immeasurable criterion of quality of service has been sacrificed, and a rapid response is expected even when it serves no useful purpose. For example, if a victim reports a burglary after returning home and finding the premises ransacked, then there is nothing to be gained from an immediate police response unless the burglars have been disturbed by the victim while the crime is in progress. Once the burglars have left the scene, it makes no difference whether police arrive within two or 20 minutes, or even two hours. In purely practical terms, there is often little point in a patrol car attending a burglary in the dark, and precious police time could be saved by leaving a message for a burglary investigator and scenes-of-crime officer to call the following day. This, of course, may not be feasible in a customer-focused police service where meeting public expectations is at least as important as meeting public needs.

By the 1980s, the switch to the reactive style of policing discussed above was seen to have failed to produce the improvements that it promised. Since that time, police organisations have developed a community-oriented focus, which will be discussed shortly. It should not be thought, however, that community policing is, or should be, a simple reversion to the patrol style of the 1950s and earlier. Neither should it be thought that policing outside urban areas remained unchanged, and has come back into fashion. In part, the change in policing to a rapid-response style was driven by a failure of policing at that time to meet the needs of society. Society itself has changed and evolved, and many of those changes impinge directly on policing. Some of these matters must be discussed before discussing community-oriented policing, as they are determining factors in policing in this, the 21st century.

Changes in society

Many of the social changes since the 1960s have become so quickly embedded in modern life that it sometimes comes as a shock to realise that so many radical changes are relatively recent. Discrimination on grounds of gender, race or sexual orientation is now so generally unacceptable and unlawful that it is hard to realise that in 1960 racial segregation was a part of life in the southern States of America, Aboriginal people were not entitled to vote in Australia (although British migrants could vote without having obtained citizenship), feminism had progressed little since women got the vote and homosexuality was considered unnatural and unlawful almost everywhere. With change in social attitudes came legislative and constitutional change enabling individual rights to be enforced. In addition, members of society started seriously questioning the values of their society, and both questioning and watching those in authority in a way never before done – one of the organisations whose authority and actions were questioned was the police, perhaps because the police themselves were the most visible and accessible symbols of authority within society.

Individual rights

The major thrust of the changes brought about by the Equal Rights Amendments to the American Constitution or the Equal Opportunity legislation in Australia and Britain has been to establish that each person is to be treated as an individual, according to his or her own personal merits, not in accordance with putative membership of any social group. The

American Constitution certainly stated in its preamble that "all men are free and equal" (a phrase which today would itself be deemed sexist), yet Thomas Jefferson, the prime drafter of the document, saw no inconsistency between this statement and his possession of several hundred slaves. Jefferson, in common with most people in the 18th and 19th centuries, believed that there were inherent differences between races and genders which rendered the principle of equality inapplicable in practice. This belief persisted until the second half of the 20th century, but is now generally, if not universally, considered untenable.

With the change in society's attitude came a change in legislation to express the belief in equality many people now held. Clearly, legislation by itself cannot force people to change the way they perceive the world, and no equal opportunity legislation can change any individual's beliefs. What the legislation achieved was a change in behaviour, ensuring that each person is treated as an individual, not as a representative of a type, and accorded the same rights and consideration as any other individual. Those who still believed that inherent differences made certain groups inferior per se were no longer allowed to act upon such beliefs.

With this emphasis on the individual and individual liberty and rights came what Berlin (1969) has called negative liberty, or freedom from interference. As has been pointed out earlier, the likeliest source of interference with the individual is the government, and the most visible and powerful of government agencies which affect individual liberty is the police. As the cult of the individual grew, with it grew the habit of watching suspiciously anything which posed a threat to the individual or harked back to the stereotyping of sections of society which had been the cultural norm at least until the 1950s and adversely affected some groups. Political consciousness also arose among those groups which challenged these cultural norms. Most noticeable among these groups were the feminist and the black power movements of the 1960s which exhibited a great deal of militancy in some of their activities. This militancy often transgressed the criminal law, and necessarily became the subject of police action.

Public order

Closely connected with the growth of political consciousness came the public expression of this in marches and demonstrations. This was, if not entirely new, a rather different type of public expression of mass disapproval of authority. The Reverend Martin Luther King claimed that "a riot is at bottom the language of the unheard": large-scale public disorder is a danger sign for governments that all is not well and that sections of the populace are disaffected. In part at least, American policing in the cities was established to prevent riots or disperse rioters, and riots have always been an occasional part of the British political scene. Poll tax protests in London in 1990 culminated in full-blown riots. The new 20th century phenomenon was the carefully organised peaceful protest, which, although it might end in disorder was usually intended by its organisers and most of its participants as a peaceful expression of their views. Perhaps the first such demonstration was the trade-union organised Jarrow hunger march of 1931, when thousands of unemployed and starving men from the north-east of England walked, over about two weeks, to Westminster to protest to parliament about conditions brought about by unemployment.

The spectre that hung over Europe in particular in the second half of the 20th century was that of a third, nuclear, world war. In Britain during the late 1950s the Committee of 100[5] (later to become the Campaign for Nuclear Disarmament or CND) adopted Ghandi's strategy of non-violent non-cooperation in a series of protest marches which always ended, usually in Trafalgar Square, with marchers sitting down and refusing to move. A few years later, in Australia, Britain and the United States, a second campaign started against the Vietnam War, which also was to last into the 1970s. As anti-war campaigns, these were inherently pacifist in intention, although they were by no means always non-violent.

A third wave of political activity was avowedly communist. This was largely European, culminating as it did in the establishment behind barricades of a Paris Commune in 1968, but it had its effect elsewhere, particularly among young British intellectuals who caused disorder within universities, most notably at Sussex and the London School of Economics. The darker side of this activity was outright terrorism, the Baader-Meinhof Gang in Germany, the Red Army Faction in Italy and the Symbionese Liberation Army in the United States, this last most famous for its kidnap of the heiress Patty Hearst and her subsequent involvement in its activities.

The vast majority of all the protests described above posed a new problem for policing. They were emphatically not riots, in that most were organised, the protesters peaceable in intention, voices to be heard but not a mob resorting to violence. Furthermore, the aims and intentions of one group excited the sympathies of some of the other groups, generating inter-change of participants of marches for the various causes. An Australian male, for example, who protested against his country's involvement in the Vietnam war would be more likely than not to be broadly sympathetic to nuclear disarmament also, to see women and indigenous people as unfairly treated, and disinclined to vote for the extremely conservative Menzies government. Similarly an American woman actively promoting the feminist cause would draw the obvious parallels between her case and that of a native American.

Police responses

The sort of public order matters described above are highly challenging to the status quo. Whether or not the established order of things needs to be

---

5   The committee was named because it consisted of 100 well respected and concerned citizens, of whom the two most prominent were Canon Collins, a prominent churchman, and the octogenarian atheist philosopher Bertrand Russell who had been imprisoned during the First World War as a pacifist campaigner and was imprisoned again nearly half a century later.

challenged or is no longer acceptable, in general the task of police is to prevent crime, which in its broadest sense includes the prevention of public disorder, and upholding the status quo. Society saw public political protests in a variety of ways. For the average member of the public, those taking part in such protests appeared reasonably ordinary, well-behaved people, perhaps young and foolish or ethnically different, but not obviously criminal. For some, these protests were a direct confrontation to governments in the western world, and provided help and comfort to the enemy in Russia and China, if not being actually communist-inspired and led.

The police, as conservative organisations largely composed of conservative-thinking individuals, were generally antipathetic to protests, whether or not they, as individuals, agreed with the protesters. The main aim of policing these events was to prevent crime and disorder, and this often led to very tight police control of marches. The whole point of such marches was to gain publicity for the cause, and many were dutifully accompanied by press and TV cameras. However, the most likely picture to be seen on the news was the disturbance in the crowd, and police officers dragging away protesters by main force. Whatever had gone before, and whatever the offence committed, the repeated picture the public had of protests was of police manhandling demonstrators, most of whom looked (and were) harmless.

Inevitably, in Australia, Britain and the United States some peaceful protests reached violent conclusions, and, in Britain and the United States at least, resulted in deaths. In Australia police brutality against Vietnam war protesters in Melbourne and Brisbane became a dominant image of public order policing, even though the force shown was largely a result of government policies. In Britain, the Metropolitan Police had hardly lived down the Grosvenor Square riot of 1968 (a protest against the Vietnam war outside the American Embassy) when two deaths of unarmed protesters occurred in the 1970s, first, at Red Lion Square and a few years later in Southall. In the United States, there were deaths at Kent State University and at the Chicago Democratic Convention of 1968 to choose a presidential candidate. However the public saw the political views of Canon Collins, Bertrand Russell, university student protesters or feminists, they did not see the individuals involved as criminals. When the police force is expected to maintain the peace, the image of policing is adversely affected when police themselves are perceived as acting with undue force against a peaceful public. The immediate image of police being violent or exceeding their authority shown on the television evening news is the one that lasts, whatever a subsequent inquiry shows. The public concern about police violence, and about police corruption and racism, became an issue no police body could ignore, and had a major impact on how police operated.

Violence, corruption and complaints

From the 1960s on, a sense of unease grew against policing methods. There had always been an awareness of a certain level of malpractice and violent behaviour by police officers, but this was, perhaps, seen as both justifiable and, in some cases, acceptable. Even today some sections of the public, particularly the older blue-collar generation, talk of youthful misdemeanours being dealt with by a "clip round the ear" from a police officer, and recommend this as a panacea for youth crime today. Officially sanctioned violence has only been outlawed comparatively recently: the cat was swung in British gaols into the 1940s[6] and children were regularly (and sometimes viciously) beaten in schools in many countries into the 1960s. In this social context, if a police officer caused injury to a miscreant there were few complaints unless the violence was excessive, or the victim demonstrably innocent.

The comfortable feeling that police violence was minimal, or meted out only to criminals who thoroughly deserved it, was thoroughly shaken by a number of incidents from the 1960s onwards. At Kent State University the National Guard fired on and killed several unarmed demonstrators who were not only innocent of any real crime, but were perceived as the privileged cream of young America, the nation's university students. A peaceful anti-Vietnam War protest outside the American Embassy in Grosvenor Square in 1968 degenerated into a riot, and the British public saw police officers hit out with truncheons randomly at the crowd. Once again, the protesters were not perceived as criminals or thugs, but young and middle-class. Even when the protesters did not evoke public sympathy, police methods could still be questioned. In 1979 the National Front organised a march through Southall, West London, a suburb populated predominantly by people from the Indian sub-continent. The fairly small number of marchers included crop-haired, tattooed, heavily booted neo-Nazis spoiling for a fight, who faced a counter-demonstration by the Anti-Nazi League. The two factions could not be kept apart, and a running battle started, as it had at several other National Front marches in previous months, and afterwards Blair Peach, a schoolteacher from New Zealand, was found dead from a blow to the head believed to have been inflicted by police.

These incidents demonstrated clearly that police could behave violently and have a direct effect on ordinary, law-abiding people. It had also become apparent during the 1960s that police officers could be corrupt. In 1964 British policing was rocked when would-be detectives at a central London police station were convicted of perverting the course of justice by planting evidence on totally innocent individuals at the behest of their squad commander, Detective Sergeant Challenor. An investigation into what became known as the Challenor affair showed such actions to be alarmingly pervasive throughout London's police force. Policing in the United States was shaken by Serpico, the New York City police officer who was so concerned about endemic corruption in his force that he acted as a one man anti-corruption undercover agent. In Australia, most of the matters involving police corruption concerned gambling and prostitution. A Victorian royal commission into off-course betting was told that illegal bookmaking

---

6   The *Criminal Justice Act* 1948 outlawed its use.

survived because of corruption within the police deputed to enforce gaming law, and enquiries in other States including most spectacularly the Fitzgerald inquiry in Queensland showed the corrupt involvement of some police officers in gaming and vice.[7]

By the 1970s, society in Australia, Britain and the United States was no longer prepared to turn a blind eye to violent or corrupt behaviour by its police and the general acceptance of the principle of equal rights meant that the public were unwilling to tolerate racist or sexist behaviour from its police either. All three countries had become effectively multicultural. Britain had accepted large numbers of migrants from nations that formerly were part of the British Empire, Australia's population, which since the 18th century had grown mainly on Anglo-Celtic then other European migration, now had a significant and growing Asian minority, and the cultural diversity of the United States also continued to grow.

Police-watching

The awareness of police wrong-doing was accompanied by a public belief that something could and should be done. Although for many years most police organisations had had a procedure for investigating complaints from the public about police behaviour, this now had to be seen to be effective. Questions were being raised not just about the behaviour of individual officers, but about training and policies of whole police forces. Suppose, for example, a complaint is made about the racist behaviour of a particular officer in a particular police organisation. On one level, this concerns that officer specifically. However, if there are a number of similar complaints about a number of officers in that organisation, then the organisation itself is open to question about its policy on racism, its training and even its recruiting policy if the demographics of the force do not bear comparison with the demographics of the society being policed.[8]

Legislative and constitutional change enforcing equal opportunities did much to empower minority groups to organise and challenge any diminution of their rights. Such groups kept a close watch on police, monitoring their activities closely and being always ready to make articulate complaints at a high level. In Britain during the 1970s, many cities had left-wing controlled local governments, and these councils often both encouraged and financially assisted police monitoring groups. Although there was a serious and valid intent in such monitoring, the monitoring escalated so that some of these groups seemed to be almost harassing the police, and the mainly right-wing tabloid press applied the label "loony left" to many councils and their leaders. This excoriation reached a crescendo just before

---

7   Finnane (1994, Ch 9) discusses this in more detail.
8   Much the same sort of issue gained prominence in Victoria, where over a 10-year period from the late 1980s, there were 24 shootings of individuals by police, significantly more than in the whole of the rest of Australia. In no individual case did the Coroner find police culpable, but public suspicion arose that officers were too quick to resort to lethal rather than non-lethal options for resolving incidents, suggesting an issue for police training in that State.

parliamentary reform of local government, and continued into the 1980s.[9] Larger city police departments in the United States also found that minority groups were both watching and complaining about police behaviour.

Both police and police authorities took action to deal with corruption and complaints of bad practice by police. In Britain, the *Police Act* 1964 established inter-force investigation procedures, and specialist branches to investigate complaints were established in Australia, Britain and the United States. Whatever these units were called they consisted of officers who had sufficient rank to be effective and whose sole job it was to police the police. Despite this, the public still feared the possibility of a cover-up if police investigated police, so various means have been tried of making complaints investigation open, by involving persons outside policing: the Ombudsman in Australia; the Police Complaints Authority in Britain and Police Boards in the United States.

Police authorities, those bodies to whom the chief officer of police is answerable, responded by setting up commissions of inquiry into police, and by appointing chief officers whose brief was to address corruption. The Knapp Commission in New York was a direct response to the revelations of Serpico, and American police authorities became adept at head-hunting chief officers who had shown a degree of success in achieving desired outcomes when problems arose, and in sacking chiefs whose performance failed to meet requirements. Appointing chief officers for particular problems happened in both Britain and Australia. An example of this was the appointment of Sir Robert Mark as Commissioner of the Metropolitan Police in 1972, who both established the Complaints Investigation Branch and restructured the CID in order to break up the cabals that had tainted detectives in London even before the Challenor scandal. In Queensland, Police Commissioner Ray Whitrod faced battles from both within the force and from the State government in his attempts to build an autonomous, corruption-free police force in the 1970s, but the futility of his endeavours was, perhaps, not fully realised until the Fitzgerald inquiry of 1989 showed the depth and pervasiveness of police and government corruption in that State.[10]

Community policing

By the early 1980s policing needed further re-assessment. The immediate-response, hi-tech strategies were having no effect on the crime rate, and calls for police assistance were reaching a level which stretched police resources to the utmost. Furthermore, the public were expressing a need for

---

9   For an insider's view of this, see Livingstone (1988), the political autobiography of the quintessential "loonie leftie" and *bête noire* of the tabloid press. Ken Livingstone was leader of the Greater London Council until its abolition, later an MP, before his election (and re-election in 2004) to the new post of London's Mayor.

10 The problems Whitrod faced had been entrenched over a long period of time, and even today are still recurrent. The clearest exposition of the police and political corruption in Queensland can be found in Dickie (1988).

more visible policing, that is officers patrolling the streets once more rather than rushing from one call to another. Although clear procedures existed for complaints to be made against police officers, there were underlying problems concerning their objectivity, since most investigations were carried out by police officers. Finally, there was a perception that police officers behaved generally in a racist, sexist manner, and were likely to subject the less powerful and inarticulate members of society to unnecessarily abusive treatment. This latter point was made very forcefully by Chan in her analysis of police culture in New South Wales, where such behaviour was still to be found in 1992,[11] despite its having been addressed consistently since at least 1984, when John Avery was appointed Commissioner.

In addition to the perceived failure of policing strategies over the previous 20 years, police were facing other problems. Many cities had expanded significantly into urban sprawl, with the rise of dormitory suburbs wherein few people were to be found during the day, as most adults worked and most children were in school. The high cost of policing became a political issue, as did rising crime, and police were, for the first time, expected to justify their performance. In Britain, the rather nebulous common law police powers were codified in the *Police and Criminal Evidence Act* 1984, which also covered matters like complaints investigation and strategic consultation with communities. Out of this came reform in all areas of policing, most noticeable of which was the institution of community policing and thorough-going organisational reform usually signalled by the change of terminology from police force to police service.[12]

The public's expressed desire seemed to be that policing should return to what it had been in the first half of the 20th century, with officers walking the streets, being highly visible on patrol, and thereby catching offenders in the act or preventing crime. Social conditions and the demography of cities and large towns had changed significantly since then, making that type of policing no longer possible. In city centres where land was at a premium, population growth was catered for by the demolition of small terraced back-to-back houses and the erection of blocks of flats of 20 and more storeys. Where space was not an issue, particularly in Australian cities like Perth and Adelaide, more and more bushland on the outskirts was bulldozed to build suburbs of houses with up to half an acre of land. Small towns on the outskirts of major cities also became swallowed up to become suburbs as cities grew. The distance between home and work became less of a problem as more people owned cars. While in the first half of the century a police officer could be seen walking through shopping and residential streets, it became impossible for an officer to be seen walking past a flat 15 floors up, or to be seen during the day in a suburb where most adult residents were out at work. Communities where everyone lives,

---

11   Although Chan's research was only in New South Wales, there is every reason to believe her conclusions hold for policing elsewhere in Australia, and much may well be applicable to other countries' police. See Chan (1997).
12   This was flagged, in Australia at least, by John Avery in his seminal work (Avery, 1981).

works and socialises within a very small geographical area have virtually ceased to exist within the modern city.[13]

A modern city cannot be policed the way it was 50 years ago. Any strategy for police to interact with the community must involve police working with people in their ordinary lives which is not easy given the diverse lifestyles of modern city residents. Even rural communities are changing, and villages several hours journey from the city may well be felt by some people to be within commuting distance. Furthermore, the public had grown to expect police to respond to calls for assistance and saw any diminution of this response for whatever reason as a further reduction in police services. The problem that community policing has been trying to address over the past 15 to 20 years is how to put police back into the community while still meeting increasing public demands: this is not so much a matter of getting a quart into a pint pot, but supplying a quart from a pint pot.

Strategies

Community policing has become so much a catch-phrase in modern policing throughout the world that hardly any police organisation wants to be seen as not participating. Consequently, almost anything that is not a reactive strategy to deal with a particular issue has been claimed as a community policing initiative, which has blurred the meaning of community policing. There is no clear definition of the term, but Bayley (1989) in his research in a number of countries has found:

> [F]our recurrent elements in 'community policing' when it is meaning-fully undertaken. They are:
> 1. community-based crime prevention;
> 2. patrol deployment for non-emergency interaction with the public;
> 3. active solicitation of requests for service not involving criminal matters;
> 4. creation of mechanisms for grass-roots feedback from the community.

This, certainly, is as good a working description of community policing as I have come across, and will be used consistently in this book.

The first criticism of community policing that is made by many police officers is that it is no more than just a re-invention of the wheel, returning to what had been done from the 19th century to the 1960s. Crime prevention, after all, had been stated by Mayne in 1829 to be the first of the primary objects of an efficient police force. Modern community policing certainly needs to be distinguished from early policing styles, the essential feature being that of its purpose. While an officer on the traditional beat did patrol, did talk to people, and did get to know and be known by them so

---

13   Close-knit community living is so far from modern living that it is now the subject of historical novels. It is rather sobering to realise that the world of, for example, Catherine Cookson's Newcastle with its mean streets and dire poverty, is based upon the personal experience of a novelist writing as late as 1997.

that the likely presence of the officer was a deterrent to crime, nevertheless the patrol was carried out according to the whim of the officer. Supervisors, for example sergeants, were only concerned that the officer did not stray from the geographical area assigned without good reason, and, where police boxes were used, responded to calls promptly and rang in according to the stipulated timetable.

Community policing strategies involve targeted involvement with the community, and officers do not patrol aimlessly, but visit particular people or patrol specific places for a particular reason. This is encapsulated in Bayley's elements 3 and 4 of active solicitation of requests and creation of mechanisms for feedback. In current terminology this is pro-active policing. The police force of a large city in 1935 required no more of its officers than that they stay on their beats to be visible and available. While they could expect to come across incidents or individuals, or be called directly by the public to deal with some matter, for the rest of the time officers patrolled with no specific purpose. The modern community police officer's patrol is more ordered and purposeful, with the intention of actively becoming involved in the community and both gaining knowledge of what is hap-pening and of passing on information about crime.

In some respects, community policing is the antithesis of what preceded it. A significant part of social interaction in all cultures involves sharing food and drink, so community policing can leave its practitioners awash with tea, coffee and biscuits. Throughout the history of policing, this has been officially discouraged, disciplinary proceedings often being taken against officers found "idling and gossipping". Too close a relationship between officers and certain individuals on their beat may, it was feared, lead to corruption. Community policing strategies require officers to become part of the community and have involvement with individuals, but to do so overtly and as a way of joining the police service and community rather than as two individuals forming bonds. Other aspects of community policing may not even involve patrol, but are community initiatives such as blue-light discos for young people. While this is not expressly about crime or its prevention, in Bayley's terms such strategies create mechanisms for feedback from the community about matters which may be of use in reducing crime.

It is not appropriate here to list or discuss specific community policing strategies, since there are so many variations, and so many schemes are not easily transferable from one jurisdiction to another. Neighbourhood Watch is, perhaps, almost worldwide in its principles, which rely on the fact that individuals within their own home areas are more likely to see and recog-nise unusual occurrences than anyone else, and can note or report them to police for action. Similarly, community policing always involves police in community councils or committees, with elected local politicians, ethnic groups or organisations, whether these committees are police organised or community bodies – normally both types of committee are involved. Although involvement with the community needs to be at the grass-roots level with individuals talking to patrolling officers, agencies and groups are best approached through formal engagement in committees or structured meetings.

The fear always raised about Neighbourhood Watch is that it can degenerate into vigilantism. It is a small step from citizens watching what is happening in their suburb passively, so to speak, as they go about their everyday business, to watching actively by patrolling. In Britain, police services are quick to stress that patrols are not appropriate to Neighbourhood Watch activities, since individual members of the public run the risk of assault or inadvertently breaking the law themselves by getting actively involved. However, San Antonio Police Department in Texas is quite happy for civilians in its Volunteers in Policing scheme, whatever their age and gender, to patrol their own neighbourhoods having had some training at the Police Academy, wearing identifiable shirts and carrying cellular phones supplied free by the local telephone company. In the prevailing gun culture of Texas there is a high risk that any suspect may have a gun or other weapon, an added incentive for these volunteers not to involve themselves directly in any incident but to use their cellular phones to call police, as they are themselves an unarmed patrol.

Community policing, then, is not about more police on the streets, or more police officers walking, but about police working in partnership with the community, and adopting a problem-solving approach to crime. Its importance is that it puts more police officers in direct contact with the public other than when responding to an emergency, and allows, and more importantly encourages, communication and cooperation between police and public. Although this can involve police on bicycles, these are no longer the heavy, pre-1960s pedal cycles being ridden slowly or pushed by officers in full foot-patrol uniform. Cycle patrols in places as far apart as San Antonio and Perth call for officers on all-terrain bikes, wearing cycling clothing but readily identifiable as police, using this means of patrol as a way of both patrolling areas otherwise inaccessible to vehicles and responding to a general public need for visible police patrolling.

The claim is still made, particularly by rural officers, that policing a small isolated community has always involved this interaction with the public. In the best of rural policing this is the case – the officer in outback Australia or a British village has no alternative but to be involved with the community: it is, after all, the officer's home. However, in small communities it is always possible for the officer to develop both friendships and enmities which affect the impartiality of policing, and possibly too close an involvement with one section of the community and too little involvement with others. Historically, this has always been an issue for rural policing in Australia, especially in areas where the white and Aboriginal populations live separately.

In most police services, community policing is seen as a separate branch of policing, to be done in addition to the reactive policing that the public has come to expect. This has led to various pejorative claims about it, that it is seen as somehow a soft option type of policing, suitable only for women officers, older lower-ranking officers, or sought after by those who wish to avoid the problems and dangers of "real policing". These issues are largely unresolved, not least because officers committed to community policing are no longer available to answer calls from the public or do emergency policing, yet community policing in itself has had no measurable effect on the number of calls for police assistance. The fact that some aspects of reactive policing may no longer be possible when sufficient manpower to make community policing effective is committed to it will be addressed in Chapter 6.

Organisational changes to policing

Police organisations have had to change significantly in order to accommodate the change in emphasis to service rather than force. Some of this change has been called for by legislation, constitutional change or government policy and direction which affects police whether or not directed specifically at policing. Examples may make this clearer. In Australia, the *Anunga* case[14] had a major impact on the interviewing of Aboriginal suspects. Cultural differences and the history of police–Aboriginal relations have created major difficulties for police in questioning Aboriginal suspects, particularly in ensuring that any statement they might make is truly voluntary.[15] In *Anunga*, Forster J of the Northern Territory Supreme Court set out nine points as guidelines which "are designed simply to remove or obviate some of the disadvantages which Aboriginal people suffer in their dealings with police". What have now become known as the "Anunga Rules", although not binding in law outside the Northern Territory, are persuasive precedent throughout Australia and have been used as a benchmark throughout Australian policing and courts as a test for admissibility of interview testimony, and incorporated, often with additional safeguards, in police commissioners' directions or regulations.

In Britain, the *Police and Criminal Evidence Act* 1984 (*PACE*) codified police powers and the rights of suspects and additional rights of persons at risk (juveniles, the intellectually impaired, non-English speakers etc) and enforced compliance. Perhaps not surprisingly, the rights of suspects under *PACE* bear strong similarities to the guidelines in the Anunga rules. In the United States, the Supreme Court's rulings in *Escobedo* and *Miranda*[16] have long ensured that suspects are told of their rights by police, and the strength of the constitutional rights of every citizen has influenced police practice.

---

14   *R v Anunga* (1976) 11 ALR 412.
15   Hazlehurst (1987) cites the transcript of an interview by police of two Aboriginal suspects in a murder inquiry. In an effort to explain to the caution, the officer says "Now I want to ask you some questions about that trouble out there but I want you to understand that you don't have to answer any questions at all. Do you understand that?" Suspect "Yes". Officer "Now. Do you have to tell me that story?" Suspect "Yes". Both suspects answer "yes" to every question, even though, as shown here, these answers are mutually contradictory.
16   *Escobedo v Illinois* 378 US 478 (1964) and *Miranda v Arizona* 384 US 436 (1966).

Policies and legislation which affect police no more and no less than other agencies are those connected with equal opportunities. A complaint frequently levelled at police is that they are not truly representative of the community, as officers are overwhelmingly male and members of the dominant ethnic group. In Australia and Britain this is still largely the case, and, although the number of women officers and officers from ethnic minorities is growing, it by no means matches the proportions of the general population. This is especially worrying when applied to minority groups who have frequent contact with police like Australia's Aboriginal people and Britain's young people of West Indian descent: generations of suspicion have made them reluctant recruits to policing, and often not particularly welcomed within the organisations. Although these issues are being addressed by police in both countries, and minority recruiting strategies are having some success, the time lag for recruits to gain promotion to senior rank has meant that Australia in particular has its commissioned ranks filled almost exclusively by white Anglo-Celtic males.

Aggressive American affirmative action programs have resulted in many police departments having ethnic demographics matching those of the people they police. Although the gender balance is not equal, there is a sufficient proportion of women in American policing to ensure that it is no longer male dominated, even if there is male preponderance.[17] One other difference between the three nations which might also have affected this is, curiously enough, the war in Vietnam. A significant number of police recruits in Australia, Britain and the United States come from the defence forces. In Australia and Britain these are largely, but not totally, a white male preserve. The draft during the Vietnam conflict drew Americans of all backgrounds into the armed forces, and thence, perhaps, into policing. However it came about, many African and Hispanic Americans have long seen policing as a valuable career, and many have progressed through the promotion structure to the most prestigious positions.

Internal change

With regard to policing, the last 20 years of the 20th century will be noted for its major change, even upheaval, of working practices. On the academic level, writers such as Goldstein and Bittner examined both how policing was done, and asked how it should be done. Police organisations in places as diverse as New South Wales under Avery and London under Newman and Imbert examined themselves with the premise that nothing should be taken for granted, and that anything was open for change. The change suggested was not just to accommodate community policing but was structural, and involved every aspect of policing and every police officer. In

---

17   In UK too, there is male preponderance, but not domination as there are significant but not equal number of female officers in all ranks and departments of British policing. However, there are few women in Australian policing, and a review of the Queensland police service in 1997 identified a bias in favour of male applicants in the physical competence tests for police recruits.

accordance with modern management practice, this change involved a statement of common purpose, and a code of ethics.

Two of the most radical change programs instituted into police at the end of the 20th century were the Plus Programme in the Metropolitan Police in London from the late 1980s, and the Delta Program in Western Australia from the mid-1990s. The dates are not exact for such programs as they each relied on the introduction of a climate for change, and changes and consultation in a number of areas over a period of time, rather than the direct and cataclysmic introduction of a completely different system from a certain date. Both Plus and Delta were open-ended programs in that they did not set out to establish a new system then ossify its precepts, but set out to institute change as a continuing process, in order that policing should always meet the needs of society. For this reason, a close examination of the detailed changes wrought by each program is otiose, as they continued to change as policing and society change, and the changes were made to fit the needs of specific places, and cannot necessarily be expected to be suitable for other communities.

There are some essential broad characteristics of successful programs for change. One is the devolution of authority to local senior officers in order that policing at the local level fits the requirements of the community being policed. In a large city, the population can change over a very short distance, sometimes even from one side of the road to the other, and these different types of people may well have different needs from police. In the hierarchic nature of earlier policing, the model imposed by the chief officer would be followed at each police station, whether or not it met the needs of the community. Under most modern police structural reforms, officers in charge of divisions or regions are expected to develop policing to meet the needs of those areas.

This devolution of authority is meaningless unless resources are also available to implement change. Within the confines of the money available, police budgets are increasingly being decentralised to local operational commanders who are asked to make their own hard choices on what initiatives must be shelved to pay for the schemes which will be implemented, and whether more staff are needed more urgently than a new vehicle.[18] While managers in private industry have been used to making budgetary decisions at different levels, and have recognised that promotion brings with it responsibility for an increased proportion of the company's finance, this is a new concept in policing, and officers with no background in accounting are suddenly asked to take responsibility for million-dollar budgets.

One problem with the devolution of authority is that the officers to whom authority is devolved must be capable of handling it. Many senior officers in the past have been eminently capable of running a police station within the parameters laid down by the chief officer, and have dealt with decision-making by referring difficult matters to headquarters. This

---

18   This issue will be discussed further in Chapter 15.

approach is not suitable when authority is devolved and original thought is required. Almost a *sine qua non* of structural change in policing is that the promotion system be overhauled, and, with an eye to the future, the recruiting system also. Avery puts it succinctly: "[I]f a major commitment of executive time is put into placing the right people in the right places for the right reasons, then the organisation will function effectively"(Avery, 1989, p 99). This point was echoed by the Christopher Commission in Los Angeles, which inquired into the Rodney King incident.

If, as had been general practice in Australia, the promotion system is based on seniority, then the right people find themselves in the right places only by chance. Unless the recruiting standards are sound, then the very availability of the right people in the organisation is equally a matter of chance. Policing is traditionally a blue-collar occupation, and promotion within it has traditionally recognised the values that the military recognises for non-commissioned officers: the modern requirements of a local operational commander are akin to asking a sergeant-major to become a colonel overnight. While an officer class in policing (whether or not following Trenchard's 1930s scheme) neither was nor is viable or necessary, there is an undoubted need for senior officers to have the capacity to think for themselves, and an increasing tendency for this to manifest itself by the requirement for an educational qualification at the tertiary level.

Reiner's 1991 study of chief constables in Britain produced some interesting facts on the educational qualifications of chief officers. While 25 per cent of those who were interviewed by Reiner had university degrees, none was a graduate before joining the police although threequarters had had a grammar-school education. Reiner also found that the number of graduates in senior positions was increasing, virtually all the chief constables appointed in the late 1980s being graduates. Tertiary education is a sought-after qualification for police recruits in many police services, and Reiner concludes: "The chief constables of tomorrow are not only likely to be graduates, but to an increasing extent are likely to have entered the force as graduates" (Reiner, 1991, p 60).

When a police service undergoes radical change, serious problems arise with officers who discover that the system has changed around them, and that the career path they have followed, possibly for decades, has, at the stroke of a pen, become a dead end. Such officers cause two major problems. Their feelings of alienation and disaffection, particularly if they are shared by a sizeable number of officers, or held by officers in the middle ranks, may well be serious enough to affect the change process adversely, or even destroy it completely. This is particularly true if those officers are to remain for a significant time in the organisation. The second problem is that there is no easy way to remove them from positions of influence: on a personal level, it is not humane management to dismiss those who through no fault of their own no longer fit the organisation, yet there may be no suitable posts left for such individuals. It can be argued that the best, though rather expensive, option is to create an attractive early retirement package for such persons.

Performance indicators

Part of new management thinking within police services, together with many other organisations, requires that achievement should be measured, and to that end a variety of performance indicators are required. There are two matters of concern when police achievement is considered: effectiveness and efficiency. Effectiveness is the extent to which police succeed in addressing their goals, while efficiency concerns the processes with which they address their tasks. In many respects it is easier to devise a performance indicator to measure efficiency than to devise one for effectiveness. For example, it is much easier to measure response times to calls, or the number of officers on duty, than it is to determine how much crime police action has prevented, or to develop a numerical scale of public order or disorder. However, the need to measure achievement requires that all aspects of policing be quantified by the development of performance indicators. New public management theory requires that the public should receive value for money, which requires that policing activities must not only be quantifiable, but also given a cash value. This is a constraint on policing that has been given extraordinary importance over the past 20 years, and requires chief officers of police to justify their funding constantly.

There are two aspects to developing performance indicators, as there are to any other form of evaluation. The first is to identify clearly what goal is to be achieved, ie to determine what specific activity police are expected to perform, and the second is to determine an objective means of measuring this activity. Problematically, the primary objectives of policing set out by Mayne such as "the prevention of crime" and "the preservation of public tranquillity" do not permit of quantitative assessment. The same problem of measuring effectiveness applies even more forcefully to modern policing methods: Bayley's elements of community policing, for example, are not easily quantified and the success or failure of community policing is neither easily measurable nor easily compared over time or between police agencies.

The biggest danger in developing an evaluation strategy is that of finding some pre-existing parameter that is easily measured, then in some way defining this as a satisfactory measure for indicating performance. This is a particular problem within policing as so many of its aspects are immeasurable, yet policing abounds with numerical records of one form or another: of crimes reported and crimes cleared up; of traffic accidents, summonses and tickets issued; of breath tests carried out; of arrests; of incidents attended by police; of time taken to attend calls; of sick days, police assaults and so on. It is extraordinarily tempting to try to find a way of using some, at least, of these to measure police performance, but, although they have some bearing on police efficiency and effectiveness, they are hardly adequate to quantify them.

Crime statistics are almost legendary in their fallibility, yet have an overwhelming appeal for politicians and the media as an indication of the state of society and the effectiveness of the police. If one relied solely on reported crime figures, then in 2004 countries like Haiti, Liberia and Iraq would seem to be virtually crime free by virtue of there being no effective police organisation to whom crime can be reported. The extent to which victims report crime varies enormously according to social or legal circumstances. Some examples: in many Islamic countries rape is the rarest of crimes reported, since because of prevailing religious attitudes the victim has almost more to lose than the perpetrator by reporting that she has been raped – the crime may, in fact, be extremely common, as rapists can rely on their victims' silence to offend with impunity. Vehicle owners in Britain report motor vehicle theft almost as soon as the loss is noticed, since strict owner liability for traffic violations would otherwise hold them responsible for a thief's bad driving, and there is a legal requirement for every vehicle to have theft insurance.

That crime is committed frequently is indisputable: how much crime, and how police affect the rate of commission of crime, are not so clear. It is this last question, how police affect the crime rate, that is the crucial one for determining the effectiveness of police. The most important performance issue in policing is to discover how police in a particular place or with a particular strategy are affecting the incidence of crime. If any index of measurement has a bearing on that question, then it is valid as an indicator of police performance – conversely, if it has no bearing on that question, then it is useless as an indicator of police performance. In Britain in the 1970s there was a well-founded perception among women that to report a rape would result in unpleasant questioning by sceptical police and, if the matter went to court, a public cross-examination under oath of the victim's sexual history. As a consequence, rape was a significantly under-reported offence. Changes in the law to protect rape victims and preserve their anonymity and special training for police in dealing with rape victims were followed by an increase in reports of rape during the 1980s. It may well be that in this instance an increase in the number of rapes reported showed that police were doing a better rather than a worse job in dealing with this particular crime.

Given the unreliability of crime reports as an accurate measurement of the incidence of crime, they can hardly be expected to be a reliable indicator of police performance. Consider the burglary rates for two hypothetical police station areas: area A has poor housing, high unemployment, few people earn good incomes, there is a general mistrust of police and a high incidence of crime, much of which is unreported. If the residents of A are burgled, they may well feel they will never see their property again, the perpetrators are likely to live nearby and, if by some chance they are caught, they or their families will cause trouble if the victims give evidence. Burglary reports are low because residents feel that there is nothing to be gained by reporting the crime. Area B is affluent, its population has a high regard for police, and there is little crime. The residents of area B report every burglary, not least because insurance companies require it (residents of A cannot afford insurance premiums). If reported burglary rates are used as police performance indicators, area B appears to be worse policed.

Let us carry this further and hypothesise that area A has a new police commander, who realises the dreadful crime problem that exists. Community policing is introduced and a neighbourhood watch established, the residents over a period of time have a new faith in their police and start reporting crime and other incidents to them. The burglary rate in A rises fivefold as a far higher proportion of the burglaries that are committed are reported, although the actual number of burglaries has fallen by half. Once more, the crime figures indicate that policing in area A has deteriorated, which is counter to the non-statistical facts. The point being made here is not that policing should be exempt from performance indicators, but that the criteria to be measured must be carefully chosen so as to be true indicators of police performance. Many of the measurable indices connected with policing are at best not particularly useful and at worst seriously flawed, and frequently are dangerously invalid as indicators of police effectiveness. Kelvin's dictum that "what cannot be counted is not worth knowing" may be true for the black-and-white world of physical science, but in the sphere of human activity it is better to avoid becoming Wilde's cynic, who knows "the price of everything and the value of nothing".

CHAPTER 5

CURRENT POLICE RESPONSES TO CRIME AND DISORDER

Introduction

The essential feature of a police service, which sets it apart from any other body, is the coercive power of police officers. Any discussion of the role of police must be set within the context of this coercive role. Discussion of coercion as an essential element of policing is not just a matter of the reality of the lawful powers that police are given, but of public perception, the expectation of members of the public that a police officer can behave authoritatively. There is an ambivalence here, in that police are expected to be authoritative, but not authoritarian. This has a great effect on measurement of police performance: of major concern to the public are the "quality-of-life" violations, particularly rowdy behaviour, petty vandalism, overt substance abuse and graffiti, where police are frequently roundly criticised for taking no action. However, the petty nature of such offences, and the youth and ethnicity of offenders, can equally lead to criticism of authoritarian behaviour when police action is taken.

The implementation of new strategies of policing has led to changes in the structure of police management. Each town and suburb is different and, although they may superficially appear to have identical problems, this may well not be the case, so different solutions for each may be needed. Problem-solving approaches rely on an individual officer or officers working with the local community in small groups to devise and implement solutions, which by no means lends itself to the development of a single strategy for a city, county or state. Police organisations have traditionally had a hierarchic structure and a chain of command which usually imposes the methods favoured by the executive at all operational levels. However, if problem-solving policing is implemented, some decision-making must be relinquished to lower levels in the organisation which might even mean the creation of a flatter rank structure.

The pressures on policing

The most serious pressures being brought to bear on police result from the impression among the general public that crime is out of control, and that police are unsuccessful both in preventing crime and arresting offenders. This is not restricted to one particular police organisation or even nation, but is a common perception throughout the world. There are probably few places in the world where it is true that crime is out of control, and these are places where the entire social structure has either broken down, or has changed radically over the past few years.[1] The pressure on police to perform is exacerbated by the existence of severe financial constraints: modern governments are increasingly concerned with the financial cost of public services, so police organisations now have to show value for money rather than being funded on the basis of their undeniable, but unquantifiable, social value.

Police are also required now more than ever to behave in a manner which is both authoritative and acceptable to a public that is more diverse and socially aware than ever before. Not only are police powers carefully monitored, but interpersonal skills training is now, in many police agencies, as important for police officers as driving or firearms skills. These pressures on police only have cogency because of the increasingly sophisticated mechanisms for public accountability within policing. Issues of accountability have, more than anything else, kept policing under the public gaze, and will be addressed in great detail in the next part of this book.

Dealing with the public

There is a great deal of confusion between the police and the public about the reality, perceptions and expectations of police and public interaction and communication. Police are given powers to coerce, and are expected to behave coercively, but are also expected to coerce using only minimal force. Similarly, police are called by the public to arbitrate disputes, and are expected to do so with authority, yet without being authoritarian. Police are trained and expected to act as a team wearing protective clothing, helmets and shields in dealing with riots, yet when their interpersonal skills fail and violence erupts on the streets they face the criticism that they are the product of "cop culture". Realistic police drama[2] has blurred the line between fact and fiction. When the human failings of a TV character strike a chord in us, the potential for seeing police officers as human can be attributed to all officers. However, damaging generalisations can also be made from news items like the arrest and trial of OJ Simpson or the highly publicised

---

1   One such example is Russia during the 1990s, where the collapse of communist repression and the destruction of criminal records allowed major criminal gangs and conspiracies to flourish. After the 2003 overthrow of Saddam, one of the first tasks of the American administration was to establish a police force in Iraq. The very existence of police and a judicial system presupposes a single government of some sort, which for a nation re-establishing itself may well not be the case.

2   The sort of drama considered here are those series which portray police officers as human, fallible, and with their own problems such as marriage breakdown, alcoholism, etc and/or pride themselves on the accuracy of police procedures, tasks and argot. Current examples include the Australian "Blue Heelers", the British "The Bill" and the American "NYPD Blue".

brutality of the Rodney King incident in Los Angeles,[3] which could be consciously or subconsciously attributed to police elsewhere in America, and even overseas. A malaise of some sort in one police organisation can easily enter the public's collective consciousness as a general disease throughout policing.

Police officers, like dentists, are members of the community that most people are glad to know are available, but hope never to need or have professional dealings with. For most people, police do not impinge upon their lives until something goes wrong in a manner that might be, from the individual's point of view, cataclysmic, trivial, or somewhere between the two. The most likely incidents for bringing people into contact with police are mundane traffic matters, either traffic offences or traffic accidents, followed by being a victim of or witness to a crime, then being arrested for an offence. Since no-one reacts well to being involved in an accident, being given a ticket, being robbed, assaulted or arrested few of these incidents are likely to result in the best aspect of an individual's character being presented to police. In the circumstances in which people meet police, the officers' interpersonal skills are frequently tested to the utmost, and give rise to judgments of the behaviour of police in general.

Interpersonal skills training is, however, high on the agenda in police training throughout the world. Closely connected with this is the need for training in intercultural awareness which, likewise, is being addressed with varying success in police organisations.[4] Interpersonal skills training emphasises negotiation and the avoidance of confrontation which is fundamentally at odds with the coercive aspects of policing and the antithesis of self-defence, weapons and riot control training. All these skills are essential to a police officer, yet they are generally taught separately and too little emphasis is put on thoroughly analysing the respective places for coercive and non-coercive approaches to the public. The public itself is of little help here, as the primacy of the coercive role of police is assumed, and wittingly or unwittingly taught from an early age. The police officer in children's entertainment is usually an authority figure, and all police officers who have walked the beat have encountered the harassed parent with a fractious toddler and overheard the discouraging words "There's a policeman. If you don't behave, he will take you away". There is a problem also for police in free and democratic societies when dealing with immigrants or refugees from repressive regimes. Their view of police is forever tainted by state corruption and violence in their home nation, and such immigrants find it difficult to overcome their deep-rooted suspicion and fear of police.

---

3   The Rodney King and OJ Simpson cases both took place in the early 1990s, yet despite the passage of time they are still vividly remembered and influential in the public's perception of police racism.

4   For one analysis of this, see Chan (1997). Chan's research was carried out in New South Wales, but the pervasiveness of the underlying issues suggests her findings can be extrapolated almost universally. However, although Chan argues that the police culture she investigated has not changed as much as had been hoped, she nevertheless had praise for the change that had been apparent during her lengthy observation of New South Wales police.

The fundamental principle of interpersonal skills and intercultural awareness is the recognition of equality between individuals and cultures. More will be said shortly about the coercive nature of policing, but at this point it needs to be noted that the legitimate power to coerce and the perception of the police officer as an authority figure combine to detract from the concept of equality between police officers and members of the public. While there might not be any actual coercion in any interaction between a police officer and a member of the public, there is more often than not both a potential for coercion and an awareness of that potential by both the police officer and the individual concerned. Members of the public will often act in a manner which unconsciously seeks approval from police, so that coercive powers will be directed against someone else, or seek to exert their own authority over police, particularly if they view their own status as high. Even in circumstances where police powers are irrelevant, such as a victim reporting a crime, individuals are uncomfortable in the presence of police making them less likely to behave in terms of equality. It can be difficult for police officers to maintain equality with a member of the public whose response is deferential, timorous or challenging, which are among the norms for behaviour towards police.

In most cases, of course, the importance of interpersonal skills training to police is to defuse anger or aggression and reduce the potential for violence – to keep or restore the peace. In police training, interpersonal skills are often taught as a way for police to maintain authority without formal coercion, rather than as being grounded in the context of equality between individuals. There is a significant difference between resolving an incident by negotiation, and resolving it by using the implied or explicit threat of arrest to modify an individual's behaviour. While the latter is preferable to an avoidable arrest for some minor offence, it still represents a misunderstanding of the fundamental principles of interpersonal skills. Senior police officers have traditionally used the phrase "lacks assertion" as shorthand to suggest that the officer so described is not a forceful personality or lacks drive and ambition, while interpersonal skills experts running assertion workshops teach assertion as no more than the empowerment of individuals to state their feelings or views.[5] Care should be taken that interpersonal skills are taught as a means of negotiating a compromise with intransigent individuals, rather than as techniques for coercion without resort to formal police powers.

Certainly the introduction of interpersonal skills and multicultural awareness into the police curriculum is an important move away from confrontation and police-imposed resolutions, and encourages the use of police authority without an authoritarian approach. Much more difficult, in an apparently more violent society, is the use of coercion without force. It is right that police officers should be sufficiently well equipped to defend themselves should the need arise, but at a time when the thrust of everyday

---

5   I am indebted to Dr James Kiltie and others in a number of workshops at the University
     of Surrey from 1985-1989 for clarification of the basis of interpersonal skills.

policing is towards building rapport with the community, the sight of police officers with the accoutrements of violence[6] may well be counter-productive to acceptance and trust of police by the community.

Full riot equipment of overalls, helmet, shields and batons are intended for use in case of violent mass public disorder, but may also be the most suitable protective equipment available for officers dealing with stones and bottles being thrown when a drunken party or sporting fixture gets out of control. These tend to evoke the image of policing in oppressive third-world regimes rather than policing by consent in a free society, particularly when police are seen to use force against people who appear to be ordinary members of the public behaving in a disorderly manner, rather than a rampaging criminal mob. Training in the use of riot equipment by the very meaning of the term riot involves the use of significant or extreme force by officers acting together to restore the peace, so to equip officers with riot gear then criticise them for using it in accordance with their training is both unfair and illogical. If there are major discrepancies between the way police are equipped to act and the way the public expect them to act, these mixed messages create confusion for both the public and police officers. Similar questions arise concerning the psychological effect on officers sent on patrol wearing protective vests and carrying CS gas or pepper sprays.

The problems of equipment and training are matters for police executives rather than for officers on the street. The principle governing police use of force has always been that only sufficient force to serve the purpose is to be used, and any force which is more than just enough to overcome the force being used against an officer is considered excessive. Police officers who are being assaulted will and must defend themselves, using whatever equipment the police organisation has issued to them. Violence directed at police officers should not be met by the automatic issue of more or better weapons and defensive equipment to police, since this starts an arms race, escalating the level of violence and further alienating the public from its police. The more heavily armed police are, the greater the likelihood of persons fighting or resisting arrest being seriously injured. However, an officer cannot be expected to carry a variety of weaponry to fit all eventualities and must be equipped for the most likely contingencies. If officers are over-equipped, in that an officer's use of the weapons issued will or may result in the use of far more force than that which is deemed just sufficient, then police may be seen by the public as being violent.[7] The problem, like too many problems in the relationship between police and public, is one of perception. If there is evidence of a police officer using any sort of weapon

---

6   British police long carried their truncheons in a concealed pocket inside the trousers, but, with the advent of the long baton, the replacement of the tunic with NATO pattern woollen jumpers and, often, body armour, they now present a more martial, armed appearance. It is not yet clear what effect this has had on police / public relations.

7   The most common and difficult case here, certainly for Australian policing, is whether it is acceptable to use a gun against a person carrying a knife. It may be possible to disarm an individual with a knife without shooting that person, but from the perspective of an officer who feels in deadly danger, if a firearm is issued, this offers the best guarantee of personal safety.

against a member of the public this gives rise to an immediate suspicion of police brutality or overreaction unless it is countered by evidence of injuries to police (who may well be wearing protective clothing) or that the suspect was armed.

Involving the public in policing

Community policing means that the community actively participates in policing, and not that the community is merely passively policed. For the community to be involved actively means, first and foremost, a better police liaison with the public, and a more effective police response to the public's needs. On an organisational level, this means creating a police service, rather than a force, which is an organisation that can be recognised as part of the community, responsive and answerable to society. As Avery puts it:

> We therefore need to take positive steps to reconstruct our processes of social control to allow for a very comprehensive involvement of the people in the task, now regarded by many as being almost the sole responsibility of the police. ... [P]owerful social forces have produced a state of affairs where social control no longer resides in the body of citizens and that some effort should be made to attempt to reverse the process. (Avery, 1981, p 77)

At least part of community involvement means generating within the public a high degree of trust in its police, a genuine feeling of ownership of policing (which must be distinguished from ownership of police, which implies corruption), and within police officers of all ranks a feeling that they are part of the community, not controllers of it. As Avery has suggested, if society has permitted itself to be controlled by its police, then its police cannot help but view themselves as controllers. An important means of establishing this relationship between police and community is through setting up mechanisms for police accountability to society: these mechanisms must work on several levels, and are discussed fully in Part 3.

At an operational level, community policing requires that local police work with local communities to address specific continuing local problems. This is an expression of Goldstein's paradigm of problem-oriented policing, but, since local needs and problems vary, there can be no clear set of criteria of what must be done. Both police and community have information and opinions (which may well differ) as to what constitute local problems, and these, together with ideas for possible solutions, can and should be shared. Some of these solutions might properly fall within the ambit of police to deal with, others might be shared solutions, and still others might be solely community issues. Since these problems and solutions are so local, many of the examples are anecdotal.

Crime prevention initiatives, like any other initiative, need coordination and organisation to keep them effective: for example, a British study (Morgan and Smith, 1989) found that Neighbourhood Watch worked most successfully where police co-ordinated it. It would seem to follow, then, that whether the bulk of the responsibility for a particular community policing project falls on police or on the community, a significant police input is necessary for it to be fully effective. Whether this is due to a need for leadership, which police are able to supply in the lack of any other obvious body, or for crime prevention projects to be given some legitimisation by the police organisation is unclear. Modern policing is certainly moving in the direction of organising crime prevention initiatives: the British *Crime and Disorder Act* 1998 creates a statutory responsibility for local authorities to create multi-agency partnerships with police and others, and the *Police and Criminal Evidence Act* 1984 requires superintendents in charge of Basic Command Units (formerly divisions) to establish local Consultative Committees. The Australian Crime Prevention Council has significant impact at both national and State level, and each State has a Community Police and Crime Prevention Council or similar body to provide high level formal joint enterprise between police and community.[8]

Police implementation devolves to lower ranks for specific schemes. In police organisations where patrolling officers have responsibility for specific areas, either their designated patch as a community policing officer, or as being sole officer at an isolated rural station, then local initiatives are the province of that officer. This devolution of strategic responsibility to officers of lower rank has its effect on traditional police management systems, as will be shown later in this chapter.

The critical nature of coercion

The coercive nature of policing is what sets the police apart from any other agency within society and what creates the ambivalent relationship between society and its police. Traditionally, society has made legitimate coercion a state monopoly which has been exercised by police, and this monopoly is threatened by attempts to devolve order maintenance or patrolling functions to private security companies, or even to members of the public engaged in anti-crime patrols in their own suburbs. There is a clear recognition within society that some form of coercion is necessary, yet any society which is thoroughly imbued with the concepts of individual liberty and personal rights will insist on the minimum necessary level of coercion, and rigorous safeguards against any abuse of coercive powers.

In many nations, police are the sole organised, armed body permitted to use force against the civil population,[9] and, as such, have a potential for great power within society. The safeguards and restraints put on the use of this power, and the higher level of accountability of police than any other

---

8 The particularly local nature of American policing both renders community policing much more a responsibility of chief officers, and renders State and national bodies much less relevant. This will be made clearer in Chapter 12.

9 The defence forces of most democratic nations are under the control of the executive, and have severe restrictions on their powers within the nation. Their use of weapons is restricted to military manoeuvres, and cannot be used against the public except in restricted circumstances, for example the use of the British Army in Northern Ireland during "the troubles".

organisation is indicative of both the uniqueness of police power and the restrictions incumbent upon it in a free society.

Public use of police coercion

Members of the public who are participants in disputes or problems which seem intractable need, as Punch and Naylor (1973) found, "a quick remedy from a reliable, authoritative, but fatherly figure". The requirement is not just for a resolution to the dispute to be found, but a binding resolution with some implicit or explicit means of enforcement behind it. To analyse this more thoroughly it is worth looking at the style of police action which is taught at Police Academies and expected by the public in responding to a dispute where police are called by a member of the public who might be either a participant or a witness.

Disputes between individuals, however trivial they might appear to the objective observer, rapidly assume great importance to the participants, can lead to the use of offensive language and escalating violence and are frequently exacerbated by the consumption of alcohol or drugs. The incident typically worsens until it reaches such an impasse that police are called, there is a further delay before police reach the incident, so that on arrival officers may well have evidence of minor public order offences confronting them. The participants can be presumed to have some awareness that they are liable to be arrested if the police officers so choose, and have some vested interest in settling the dispute in order to avoid this. For many disputants, of course, tempers are running sufficiently high for this consideration not to be foremost in their minds, but for the complainant who called police there is the chance of vindication if police arrest the other party.

The first thing police are taught in dealing with disputes is to quieten the parties and investigate. In practice, police officers insist that all parties are quiet initially, in order that each person in turn can tell their version of the facts: the person who called police traditionally speaks first, although if two officers are present the two main disputants can each speak to an officer simultaneously. The coercive power of police is a recognised factor, in that everyone knows that an individual who continues to shout, swear or behave violently in public risks immediate arrest. Once police have a clear picture in their own minds about the occurrence, then steps can be taken to resolve it. Although this may take time (unless the facts justify an immediate arrest) the matter is resolved, if only temporarily, and peace restored. Police will remain until hostilities cease, will enforce the truce if necessary, and will return if the resolution does not hold at least until the end of the officers' shift. Once again, the possibility of coercion by police is a factor in the resolution stage of the dispute.

There is no suggestion here that police training in resolving disputes is misconceived in principle or ineffective – quite the opposite, in fact, as police frequently find a quick, commonsense solution to the great majority of incidents to which they are called which do not result in criminal proceedings. What is claimed here is that the coercive power of police enables them to find and implement a solution more expediently than any other organisation. In most disputes almost any impartial observer could identify a sound, workable solution, at least in the short term, but would have no authority for implementing it. Some matters, of course, will require expert intervention (long-term counselling in family problems, for example) or even civil court proceedings, and thus are beyond the ambit of any agency to resolve immediately. Even in matters which require long-term solutions, crisis points may be reached where some sort of resolution is required temporarily until long-term analysis can be undertaken and a solution found.

The resolution needed when disputes reach a critical point must be, in Punch and Naylor's words, quick, reliable and authoritative. As has been suggested, almost any observer, whether or not professionally skilled, can suggest a reliable resolution, but this is not authoritative. Resorting to violence can provide a quick resolution, but this is hardly reliable, and a professional seeking a long-term solution is unlikely to achieve it quickly. Whoever is chosen to arbitrate, be it police officer, social worker, doctor, priest, psychologist or magistrate, a reasonable solution can be found but unless this can be agreed by the disputing parties it is worthless. No other arbiter but police can ensure that the parties maintain at least a semblance of order and discussion and can impose the solution agreed because no other arbitrator has any coercive power.

The public themselves welcome the authoritative intervention of police in disputes, and this, indeed, is implicit in the phenomenon of calling the cops as Bittner (1990) makes clear. Implicit in the act of calling police is a request that coercion be applied to the dispute and, if the caller is a disputant, there is a further expectation that coercion, when applied, will be applied on behalf of the caller. Even without this, disputants are usually disposed to comply with a police officer's adjudication, and few will challenge it to the point where they render themselves liable to arrest. Society's view of the role of police in arbitrating disputes is encapsulated in a statement by one of Punch and Naylor's interviewees "I always deal with the police – the others are useless. Those youngsters come along with their airy-fairy theories but never get anything done".

Coercion and non-police agencies

Part of the response to the increasing cost of policing and the perceived need for security has been a growth in the private security industry, which has developed into almost a private police force in some areas. A number of organisations and businesses have always employed security guards for their premises and for valuable property in transit, with few problems. Increasingly, security patrols are impinging upon the general public in various ways where these security officers have assumed, or been granted, coercive powers. Examples are security staff in shopping malls, on public transport and, increasingly, at pubs and nightclubs.

All individuals have a general right to eject anyone from their property if they so desire: any persons who are told that their presence is no longer acceptable are deemed to be trespassers and must leave or face ejection. Usually, police would be called if such an incident occurs in a shop or house, and the trespasser persuaded to leave with the minimum of force, if any, used. In shopping malls with security guards, it is likely that they would be called to any dispute. As they are the agents of the owner or occupier employed to keep order in what are private premises, albeit ones which grant unlimited public access during shopping hours, security personnel have the authority to eject trespassers and remove any undesirable individual or those causing trouble.

Any action taken by security guards within a shopping mall to regulate the behaviour of the public has some coercive element, the implied sanction not being arrest but ejection from the premises. The guards are answerable to their employers, in effect the mall's management, and, unlike police, have no responsibility to the public in general. While their powers may be limited, security guards can use ejection or the threat of ejection in ways which would not be tolerated in police officers, and possibly even cause problems for police elsewhere. Consider, for example, the problem of police dealing with a group of young people creating some annoyance but not behaving unlawfully in a public open space. Police would, in dealing with the incident, have to consider not only the needs and fears of the general public but also the rights of the particular young people involved. If, however, those same individuals were inside a shopping mall, then security personnel, answerable only to management who are concerned primarily with maximising profit, would unquestioningly carry out the wishes of businesses and their customers, and eject the group or threaten them with ejection. If ejected, the young people then become a police problem, particularly if their anger at the security guards is vented in the form of criminal or disorderly behaviour in a public place.

Security guards on public transport have an overt, if limited, policing role in checking tickets and enforcing the regulations which apply, most commonly regarding unruly behaviour and drunkenness. Typically, the sanctions which can be applied are a financial penalty by way of infringement notice for offences like riding without a ticket or swearing, ordering the passenger off the train or bus (this includes refusing permission to board), or calling police to deal with breaches of the peace. Although drunks, or young persons without a ticket, have no right to travel on a train, once they are put off or left at a station, especially late at night, they may cause much more serious problems unless there is good liaison between police and transport security. A drunk left on the platform might awaken just sufficiently to stagger out into the road, or roll off the edge of the platform under the next train, and a stranded young person might be at risk of physical or sexual abuse, or steal a car to get home. These are severe consequences for failing to buy a ticket, or misbehaviour on a train.

Coercion and community self-policing

The issue of coercion also arises when members of the community are involved in active policing of their suburbs, rather than maintaining a passive role in Neighbourhood Watch. The main danger is the rise of vigilantism, where members of the public patrol and mete out rough justice to those they perceive as wrongdoers. The Nazi Penal Code of 1936 deemed any act punishable if it offended against the "healthy sentiment of the German people": the Nazi Party claimed to define this healthy sentiment and used this law as an instrument of repression. Vigilantism at its worst deals with those whom the vigilantes see as acting against popular sentiment in a way which they feel the law fails to punish: anything in the slightest reminiscent of *Krystalnacht* must never be allowed to happen again.

A similar problem arises from time to time with regard to self-defence, or defence of one's property. The law quite explicitly expects any individual who is attacked to fight back, and to use whatever force is necessary in self-defence, and also to use reasonable force to deter or apprehend a thief or a burglar. What is by no means clear, certainly in Australian and British law, is the extent to which weapons or deadly force may be used for this purpose. If a burglar is shot or the occupier of the premises uses a baseball bat against an unarmed juvenile's skull, courts are not easily convinced that only the minimum necessary force was used.

While police may be accountable for their actions towards suspects and other members of the public, the public itself is not accountable except under the criminal law. While involving the public in activities like Neighbourhood Watch or other crime prevention activities is both useful and does not involve any confrontation with offenders, proactive citizen patrols do increase significantly the chances of the public being brought into contact with offenders, and thus increase the possibility of concerned citizens breaking the law with the best of motives. In Britain, citizen patrols are actively discouraged by police, while the only citizen patrols tolerated in Australia are the patrols by Aboriginal community groups to find and take home or to a place of safety Aboriginal people considered to be at risk. These patrols are, in fact, having considerable success in many country towns throughout Australia.

The American experience is rather different, in that a number of towns encourage and assist community patrols. In San Antonio, Texas, for example, the "Volunteers in Policing" are identifiable by their shirts, have significant levels of training at the Police Academy, and patrol their own neighbourhoods equipped with mobile phones to call police at the first sign of trouble. There is little fear of vigilantism, and the nature of the volunteers in general suggests they are unlikely to take the law into their own hands. The reason that citizen patrols are not tempted to tackle putative offenders may, perversely, be related to the gun culture of the United States.

The situation is changing somewhat now, but in both Australia and Britain it is unlikely that any street criminal will be carrying any sort of firearm, although knives are more common than a few years ago. Gun control regulations are strict in both countries, and positively draconian in Britain such that judges will virtually double the sentence for any offence if it is demonstrated that a firearm is even present, much less used. As a consequence there is no real expectation in the minds of police officers dealing with individuals in the street that they are carrying a gun. The expectation and training of American police officers is quite the reverse, in that it is viewed as a sensible precaution to confirm that any person spoken to is unarmed. This expectation is also, presumably, in the minds of volunteer patrols, who are unarmed, and removes any temptation for them to deal with suspects personally, but rather inclines them to call police then stand back and allow sworn officers to deal with the matter.

Although there are significant steps that can be taken to involve the community or other patrolling or security agencies in police tasks, the problem of the extent to which those other than police may coerce must be addressed properly. It is clearly counter-productive for society to reduce the possibility of excessive force or discrimination by police through sophisticated accountability systems, only to allow others who have no sanction or public answerability to coerce using force. While it might not be in the public interest to allow any organisation to guard its traditional role jealously, it most certainly is in the public interest to ensure that society's coercive power remains wholly in the hands of agents who are fully accountable to society.

Strategic patrolling

The traditional police patrol system ensured that every part of the police area is patrolled at some time during each shift by posted officers on foot or in vehicles. This has led to police being spread too thinly, having officers patrol in places where their presence is unnecessary leaving insufficient officers to be available where their presence could make a difference. Modern methods of patrolling have led to the realisation that some areas do not need a 24-hour police presence, and the growth of private security and structural changes to places where the public work or shop have led to police patrols being redundant in many parts of modern cities. Some quiet areas which have little need of police may go almost unpatrolled, provided that officers can attend there quickly in reaction to a call from a member of the public, in order that a larger and more obvious police presence can be maintained in the areas of highest need.

Alternative patrols

Police organisations have been forced into various forms of compromise patrolling in order to meet the needs of communities and budget constraints. Nostalgia is just as strong in its perception of policing as in everything else, and there is a very real feeling that in the recent past there was more community feeling and less crime when police officers walked the beat and knew their residents and their criminals. Both modern lifestyles and the design of modern cities lower the probability of this being a viable option, despite the desire from the public (and from some police officers) for this type of policing to return. Other ways are being sought by police organisations to put the police officer back in regular, non-confrontational contact with the public, which is becoming known, in Britain at least, as directed or high visibility patrolling.

There is a frequently expressed sentiment among officers on rural patrols in Australia, Britain and the United States that community policing offers no more than country police officers have been doing since the establishment of rural policing. It is worth considering why officers on isolated or rural patrols are seen to be so effective, and one obvious answer seems to be that police are able to get to know people better when the community is easily identifiable, reasonably stable and comparatively small in size. This certainly is true of isolated villages or towns with only a few police officers, all of whom live and work in the community. It is more difficult for beat officers to get to know a reasonable proportion of their local population in cities, where people travel between suburbs to work, and move house reasonably frequently. City communities are rarely easily identifiable, stable or small unless they consist of ethnic or religious groups.

Changes in social patterns have meant that in towns and cities few people live, work and socialise in the same small area. Before the Second World War, extended families would live close together in one part of a city or town, and their work would lie within walking or cycling distance, or perhaps a short bus ride from their homes. With the increasing suburban sprawl of the 1950s onward and the trend towards personal car ownership, this local cohesion has weakened, and population densities have changed. Inner cities still have a high population density, but areas that were, within living memory, small villages or countryside outside cities have become commuter belt suburbs, with a population density higher than before, but not matching that of the inner cities. Many city suburbs have floating populations, in that people will rent homes for a year or two, or buy and sell and move on, and, even while living in one suburb, work in another part of town. The need for two incomes in a family renders some suburbs almost empty during the day, so that even if the traditional police officer returned to the beat, there would hardly be anyone about to talk to.

One of the foci of life in a community is its shops – sooner or later, and often several times a day, everyone needs a carton of milk or a newspaper, and visits the local shop for it. It follows that a police officer who spends a fair amount of time in the vicinity of the local shops is likely to encounter most of the local population. If, however, people choose to visit a mall which is not patrolled by police, then the chance of police meeting local residents is diminished, and the public sees less of its police. Police can no longer rely on frequent chance encounters with members of the community in order to build a cooperative relationship for interchange of information, but must be actively encouraged to go out into the community to establish such links. An alternative focus of life in a modern, secular community is the local school which provides a useful means for police to get in touch with the community. Most police services concentrate heavily on school programs, not only to provide a counter to juvenile crime, but also because concerned parents who attend parent / teacher groups are helpful contacts within the community.

Many areas of public open space are suitable for bicycle patrol, which is a valuable intermediate means of patrol being quicker than foot patrol and hardly restricted by footpaths too small for any other vehicle, yet still close enough to the public for the officer to stop or be stopped, and much less isolated from the community than car patrol. This should not be seen as a reversion to the ponderous combination from the past of the constable with a large, heavy cycle, slow-moving and authoritarian, since more often than not modern cycle patrols employ fit officers on modern all-terrain bikes in an easily identified police uniform which is designed for cycling. Police cycle patrols do, however, suffer from the twin perils of all cyclists, traffic and inclement weather. There is little sense in a cycle patrol in places where the traffic speed or density is too high for safety, and the health hazards of an eight-hour cycle patrol in the snow and ice of a Boston winter, or the heat of an Australian summer, mean cycle patrols may not always be possible.

Policing and community problems

If modern policing is to take a problem-solving approach as Goldstein (1990) suggests, then the first difficulty police face is reaching agreement with the community itself as to what its crime problems are. While police analyses of recorded crime may indicate crime problems in a particular area, the public itself might see other issues as more important, and may not be prepared to cooperate fully with police strategies unless or until their own concerns are dealt with. Reaching a shared awareness of the importance of particular problems requires a flow of information from police to community and from community to police to develop shared strategies to deal with crime. It is not sufficient for police alone to determine what the crime problems are.

The ways in which police establish sufficient links with the community to determine problems and develop a shared approach towards addressing them are as varied as the communities themselves. One of the most difficult issues to be addressed is that the communities with the most intractable crime problems tend to have the deepest suspicion of police, and are among the most difficult to establish sufficient rapport with to develop effective strategies. In Australia, the colonial history of policing, the mono-cultural recruiting (until recently, almost all Australian police officers were males of Anglo-Celtic background) and the use of police to enforce legislation supporting the White Australia policy,[10] have all served to create a gulf

---

10   Australia had a number of statutes concerning Aboriginal people which, although ostensibly for their protection, served to deny their culture, and led to the forcible removal of children from their families to receive a "white" education. Immigration was encouraged from the British Isles and other English-speaking countries but discouraged from other countries in the early part of the 20th century, then expanded to allow southern European immigrants and from the 1970s onward, Asian migration.

between police and important sections of the community. In Britain the perception of police as the keepers of order has meant that residents of the more affluent suburbs with less crime have been more keen to join police committees than the less articulate residents of suburbs with rather worse crime problems. In the United States, the effects of the constitutional amendments for equal rights and the higher degree of control of police by local government have been instrumental in the development of community policing.[11]

The essential elements in community consultation are to discover who the de facto community leaders the might be, and to establish communication with these individuals. In small communities this is reasonably easy, and in the rural United States the local sheriff, as an elected officer, might well be one of the community leaders anyway. In larger towns and cities with a mix of cultures not all the community leaders may be so obvious, and some, indeed, may be reticent about having dealings with police. Police services have long claimed that they are open to suggestions from the community and allow members of all groups to participate, without actively canvassing the opinions of many sections of their community. Since the affluent middle classes feel both comfortable with police and on committees, it is that group whose voices have usually determined the community viewpoint by default. Police may then argue that all groups had a chance to state their views and any right to complain is lost through failure to participate. Since the 1990s police have moved from this position to one of actively seeking out the views of minority ethnic and cultural groups in society to ensure that as many people as possible participate in planning the policing of their society. It is also vital to include the views of the community's young people, as, whatever their ethnicity, they tend to come into more frequent contact with police than older generations.

Examples of means of involving numerous ethnic groups in policing communities are quite diverse. Many, of necessity, involve breaking down language barriers before cultural and other issues can be addressed. This task, indeed, can be enormous in a polyglot community. A scheme[12] to establish a police community liaison officer in the northern suburbs of Perth, Western Australia, identified over 20 immigrant groups with a significant number of members, few of whom were native English speakers.[13]

---

11   American police departments seem much more successful in establishing an ethnic mix amongst their personnel that reflects the cultural diversity of the population, although Boston and New York in particular have had a long tradition of recruiting police officers of Irish descent. Police departments everywhere have always found a high proportion of their recruits from the armed forces, and it may well be that a number of Hispanic and African Americans who were drafted for the Vietnam war and joined the police service on their return established a precedent for a career in policing in their racial groups.

12   Policing in a Multicultural Community Program, initiated in Mirrabooka, Perth in 1995.

13   The Migrant Resource Centre in Mirrabooka records groups from dozens of countries from Afghanistan to Zambia. There are few common languages or cultures, and indeed possible conflicts rooted in their histories between different groups like Serbs and Bosnians. Even from Southeast Asia there is little in common between Thai, Malaysian, Vietnamese and Cambodian immigrants. There are also many other ethnic groups with only a handful of representatives.

All five Australian cities with populations over one million have similar problems with immigrants from all over the world, and each State police organisation has established a community policing branch, responsible for coordinating such schemes while encouraging small scale local initiatives. There is a real need for information to be shared, because if police and community liaison takes place at many levels simultaneously, then multiple and possibly conflicting strategies might be introduced, and contradictory statements made by different parties to the confusion of all.

Local problems need local solutions and, if they are to be addressed by police and community, then the implementation has to involve individuals at grass-roots level: members of local communities, and police officers of constable and sergeant rank. However, the local community involved may well be members of a much larger and internally diverse group within the wider community. The Muslim community is not homogeneous: its members may be Sunni or Shia, have ethnic roots in one of many countries in Asia, the Middle East or Africa and have levels of faith from strictly fundamentalist to wholly secular. Any police service with a significant Islamic population will have Islamic representation on some if not all of its community policing committees, but these will not necessarily account for the whole spectrum of Muslim belief. At street level, patrolling officers deal with individuals, or at most the congregation of a single mosque and may be best placed to deal with particular crime problems for specific victims.

There are two particular areas where police have superiority over the community in solving crime problems: their particular expert knowledge of crime and criminals (including access to confidential records), and their powers to deal with suspects. The community has no such powers, but can set up programs and exert social pressure on individuals to participate in problem-solving. The community can also work to alleviate the symptoms of crime, for example by a clean-up campaign for graffiti: a combination of rapid removal and community murals can replace an eyesore with enhancement of the neighbourhood.[14] The paradigm example of police and community cooperation is that of Officer Orazem in Brooklyn (Farrell, 1988, discussed fully in Chapter 7). Sometimes, indeed, a public works initiative may have the unexpected but very welcome effect of reducing crime. In the mid-1990s, the public housing authority of Western Australia, Homeswest, instituted a housing amelioration program in Kwinana, one of the less salubrious suburbs of Perth. Painting, improved lighting and accumulated rubbish removal were undertaken and residents were offered equipment and materials to make their own improvements at minimal cost to themselves. Not only did the area look better, but property values improved and the crime rate dropped significantly: this effect was a wholly unexpected result.

---

14   This strategy has been used very successfully in parts of San Antonio by its SAFFE officers.

Enhancing police performance

The crime rate has two repercussions for policing and the justice system in general: the figures themselves are taken as objective performance measures of the police and justice system, but, perhaps more importantly, the public perception of the crime rate affects how the public view their police, which in turn affects the relationship between police and public. It cannot be restated too frequently that the public perception of crime is as important as crime itself, and that the fear of crime can be as damaging to society as the actual rate of crime committed.

Police performance is judged by the general public as a combination of how safe from crime people feel, and how much of a police presence they perceive in their streets. Modern police strategies which attempt to improve the relationship between police and citizens in the long term may reduce the actual occurrence of crime, and in the short term improve public confidence and thereby reduce the fear of crime by making police more visible in the streets. Police services are both improving their performance in addressing crime and giving these efforts a great deal of publicity. Modern strategies are far more sophisticated than the older tradition of reactively forming a squad to deal with a crime problem, and often make good use of modern information technology for grounds on which to make decisions. This can be very effective, as can scientific investigative methods. Unfortunately, publicity raises the public's expectations of what can be achieved, and if the public's perception of crime is coloured by alarming reports of a rise in crime in the media the public may then feel cheated and betrayed.

Technology is also of enormous help in crime investigation and has the potential to solve many crimes but at some financial cost. It is axiomatic in forensic science that a person cannot be in a room or car or in contact with another person without leaving some physical trace, and that trace can be analysed, compared with the individual's own tissue and proved conclusively to belong to that person. Collection and analysis of samples are theoretically applicable to many crimes but are both labour intensive and expensive, so, in practice, financial constraints limit the use of most scientific forensic examinations to the investigation of the most serious crimes which involve death or critical injury, serious sexual assault or large amounts of property. In the sorts of major crime where forensic science is used to the full, police have improved their success rate in identifying offenders and amassing sufficient evidence to improve the chances of conviction by the courts. However, the very success of these modern scientific techniques can create further problems for police relations with victims of crime. It is very difficult to explain to victims of a burglary that the blood or hair sample found at the scene might well conclusively identify the offender, but the relatively low importance of the crime renders the tests unavailable because of their cost. Before the development of DNA and other tests, it was much easier to explain that the samples found at the crime scene could not be matched or identified.

The public perception of police performance is improved by the implementation of two strategies whose benefits in reducing crime are, at best, dubious. The public feel safer for seeing police on foot, even though uniform foot patrol has been shown not to be a particularly effective method of reducing crime. The public are also comforted by zero tolerance strategies which increase arrest rates, the phrase "zero tolerance" having a very satisfying ring to it. It is incontrovertible that much of the population of New York was tremendously pleased with the actions of its mayor and police during the 1990s: the effect of Compstat has been discussed, but for the public the mass arrests of squeegee-men at least gave the appearance that police were doing something. Chief officers may well be unable to resist calls to put officers more visibly on patrol in uniform, and to encourage arrests for petty offences even though these may not address the actual crime problem in any meaningful way.

Crime is a regrettable but accepted necessary concomitant of modern life, certainly in big cities, but the level at which crime becomes unacceptable varies between societies. Pollution used to be seen as aesthetically repugnant but a necessary evil, a by-product of modern life which just had to be endured, until some years ago when people in the western world realised the deleterious effects that pollution, particularly in cities, had on everyone's life and health. Different levels of pollution prompted this realisation in different societies, for example residents of Australian cities protest and take action about levels of river pollution which would be seen as utopian in some European cities. Similarly with crime: New York City celebrated a murder rate of 671 in the year 2000 (Henry, 2002, p 1) as proof of an enormous reduction in crime, while this number of deaths as a national murder rate would be unacceptable, or seen as appalling lawlessness, in many countries in Europe and elsewhere: it represents over three times Australia's national murder rate. Police are criticised for not being effective once crime passes a level which the public, wholly subjectively, considers to be unacceptable.

Implications of modern strategies for police management

The new policing strategies discussed here, and the questions of police accountability which will be discussed in Part 3, have serious implications for the structure of police management, especially in the larger police services with a complex hierarchical structure. Traditionally, police management has grown with a monolithic rank structure, with chains of command upwards so that most decisions were made, and all policy set, at the top. In many cases, decisions made at divisional command level had to be reported to the relevant headquarters branch for ratification. Since no step in the process could be by-passed, a report from a patrolling officer at a detached station might pass across many desks and be minuted by a number of people before authorisation was given by a decision-maker, only to return once more across the same desks before the initiating officer was made aware of the decision. The larger the force or the greater the area it covered, the more time-consuming was this process.

Devolution to middle ranks

Many police organisations in recent years[15] have devolved authority from the centre to local senior officers as a result of two differing types of pressure, that of financial constraint and that of providing the most suitable policing response to local communities. What was formerly considered to be a bottomless pit of public money for policing has been running dry for years: perhaps the last evidence of its existence in Britain was the restructuring of police pay in 1979 following the Edmund Davies report. One way of enforcing financial control from the top requires stringent rules and restrictions to be imposed and monitored, which has been attempted more than once. The alternative is to pass responsibility to local senior officers by allocating a set sum of money for policing their areas and leaving them the task of deciding how it is to be spent most usefully.

The more radically fiscal responsibility is passed down to middle management, the less control is left with the organisation itself. There is a qualitative difference between requiring a police superintendent to monitor a budget given for overtime for the district's police officers and giving that superintendent a one-line budget which requires decisions to be made whether the need for an extra patrol car is more urgent than the need for more officers or more computers. This extra responsibility adds a whole new dimension to the task of running a police district or a police station which was not faced by senior officers even, perhaps, 20 years ago.[16] Problems can arise if the police organisation, or the level of government which ultimately controls the funds, fears the autonomy given to middle ranks. One common hierarchic reflex to allay this fear is to institute an extra level of executive control so that budgetary responsibility rests at a higher rank level, but this serves only to increase the number of officers at that rank over those formerly deemed necessary, and defeats the initial object of the devolution of authority.

No less important a devolution of authority is the devolution of operational decision-making to middle management. This follows from the recognition that there are widely differing problems in different geographical areas policed by a single agency, and that there is probably no single approach which is adequate for all. In Britain there is also a statutory influence in this, as superintendents are obliged to establish Police Consultative

---

15 Two, in particular, were radical in such reforms during the 1990s: London's Metropolitan Police and the Western Australia Police Service.

16 This is not, however, a problem specific to police managers. Many areas of the public service have been forced by government to consider costs directly, or have been privatised. Examples are the establishment of National Health Trusts to run British public hospitals as businesses, and the cuts to university funding by governments in Britain and Australia particularly with the expectation that those institutions make up the shortfall by entrepreneurial arrangements with industry.

Committees with local representatives, and if superintendents were not empowered to act on these committees' policing requirements this method of addressing issues would fall into disrepute and the police service would be seen as lacking commitment to community problems. However, to allow a superintendent to make decisions in accordance with the requirements of a local committee reduces the power of a police organisation's head-quarters. Rather than making rigid policy decisions and insisting upon their implementation across the board, the police executive can only set general policy guidelines if operational implementation is to become a local management decision.[17]

True devolution of decision-making downwards marks a major change in the role of middle-rank police officers, giving more power and respon-sibility to inspectors and superintendents in Australia, superintendents in Britain and lieutenants and captains in the United States. They are no longer links in a chain of command with clearly circumscribed authority and enforcers of decisions made at a higher level, but with wider delegated responsibility they are now decision-makers in their own right. This new role requires officers to adopt a completely different approach to their rank, and to many it is an unwelcome culture shock with which it is difficult to come to terms.

The military has over the centuries nurtured the idea of an officer class and a chain of command which operates by senior officers communicating a plan wherein junior officers have their part to play, with initiative and cooperation encouraged as a means of achieving the objective, while non-commissioned ranks merely followed orders. This has always been anathema within policing, since junior police officers on patrol work alone with considerably autonomy and lawful authority, unlike their counter-parts in the armed forces. However, the traditional hierarchy of policing discouraged initiative among those on their way up the promotion ladder. The safe option for an inspector, superintendent or lieutenant was always to carry out as efficiently as possible the directions from headquarters, as innovation carries the risk of failure. Middle-ranking officers, who have obtained their position after 15 or 20 years of doing what they are told in this manner, can be expected to have difficulties in formulating strategic initiatives rather than merely implementing them.

In the short term, one of the most intractable problems faced within the change process in policing is that of changing the middle management, without whom little real progress in policing can be made.[18] On the one hand, no change is possible without a new selection system to identify

---

17 It may well be that, despite the appearance of control resting with divisional com-manders, a plethora of guidelines and directives can constrain middle management severely. This is discussed fully in Chapter 14.

18 Within British policing, the OSPRE promotion system has been introduced to achieve this, together with specialist training at the Police College Bramshill. In Australia, police management courses are run at Manly Police College, and each State is examining its promotion system carefully. The Delta reform of the Western Australia Police Service introduced a whole new set of promotion criteria in an attempt to appoint suitable officers to command positions in the restructured organisation.

individuals capable of interpreting broad policy to formulate effective local strategies, but on the other policing contains a considerable number of persons of rank and seniority who were promoted before the parameters changed: police services cannot afford the luxury of waiting until all these persons reach retirement to impose change.

Effect on rank structure

The logical consequence of devolving authority is that a flatter rank structure becomes possible. With the exception of those officers providing uniform policing for the nation's capital, the Australian Federal Police in 1995 discarded its rank structure completely, and now operates in investigative teams with team leaders and an area manager in each capital city, with some similarities to the American FBI. With regard to policing generally, there seems little need for a multiplicity of ranks between the operational decision-makers discussed above and chief officers who make policy decisions. If real authority is to be vested in, for example, superintendents then it is on the face of it difficult to find a decision-making role for chief superintendents or commanders, and these ranks become redundant.

The same argument operates downwards through the rank structure. Clearly, there is a need for supervision within the police service, but a hierarchy can no longer be justified on the grounds that each superintendent requires three chief inspectors, 12 inspectors, 36 sergeants, and so on. Patrol police officers are frequently the youngest and most inexperienced, yet, paradoxically, these are the most likely to be exercising their discretion as to whether or not to stop, search and arrest persons in the street. Decisions made with regard to local community policing initiatives may also be made at constable or sergeant level without an obvious need for ratification by senior officers. Once the hierarchic structure is challenged, as it has been in many policing organisations, then these organisations are forced into an analysis of the real rank requirements for any given post.

Quite clearly there are some posts which need an officer of intermediate substantive rank. Police stations need an officer in charge, as does each patrol shift, and officers in charge of larger shifts and stations need deputies. Legislation in some jurisdictions defines some duties as related to police rank,[19] so it is incumbent on police services to have such officers reasonably available at all times. Consideration of what posts are to be filled by what rank of officer can lead to a very different rank profile of a police organisation. Restructure of a police organisation leads inevitably to changes in the career prospects of officers within that organisation which disadvantages many, and can make the change painful and difficult to

---

19   The *Police and Criminal Evidence Act* 1984 in Britain is a prime example, giving specific powers to sergeants, inspectors and superintendents with regard to various duties. Child-protection and mental health statutes also give power to police to take the young or the mentally ill to a place of safety, but these powers are often restricted to officers of particular supervisory ranks.

implement. Although change itself is needed to meet the requirements of modern societies, a discussion of the process of change management takes us far from the question addressed in this work, which concerns only the policing needs of society.

Conclusion

This chapter has made no attempt to offer definitive solutions, or discuss successful strategies in detail, because the needs of different communities even within a single city may differ radically, and schemes that work in particular places may not easily be transplanted. Each suburb of each city is different, and an affluent, middle-class suburb of Melbourne may well have more in common with an affluent, middle-class suburb of Boston than it has with many other suburbs in Melbourne itself. Any police innovation that has been shown to work well in a particular place must be examined carefully to determine whether the factors that make it successful in one place also exist in the area where it is hoped to introduce it.

Many of the crime problems and quality of life issues addressed in this and other chapters of this book are particularly prevalent in cities and, while crime is not solely a city problem, it is certainly a much larger issue in the great conurbations. There may be no areas inhabited by the human race which are crime-free, but the lower incidence of crime is one of the first advantages claimed by people who live out of the cities or in fortress suburbs or gated estates. Although not explicit, some of the most intractable needs of society are those which pertain to city communities, and are to be addressed by police organisations responsible for cities, which, in turn, are among the larger policing agencies of the world.

CHAPTER 6

THE HIDDEN COST OF MODERN POLICING STRATEGIES

Introduction

Community policing is widely held to be the most promising fundamental change in policing, yet it is costly in resources to address the expressed wants of the public, if not in strictly monetary terms. The demands of the public for police attendance have already stretched the resources of most police services to such an extent that many are unable to cope adequately with the work: while community policing initiatives should reduce these emergency demands in the long term, in the short term finding officers for community policing strategies means that the already stretched resources of reactive policing are depleted even further. This chapter examines this problem in detail, showing that it is not possible for police organisations to offer effective community policing in addition to all the services currently expected and provided.

There are considerable demands on policing today. There are the demands of those responsible for allocating funds to police, who are highly desirous of seeing a measurable return for the money invested in policing. This has prompted a need to identify the essential functions of police, in order that police efficiency in these areas can be evaluated.[1] A modern police service currently attempts to fulfil all requirements made of it by the public and others: those of dealing effectively with those tasks which, by consensus, are essential police functions, those required by community policing strategies, and those demanded by members of the public in their requests for police attendance at all sorts of incidents. The art of police management in the 21st century is to meet the public's needs efficiently, in part by involving the public in policing and in part by targeting police resources to the most important issues.

None of the options for making sufficient police officers available to fulfil their various necessary tasks is without cost. Simply to employ more

---

[1] There are major issues about the possibility of evaluating policing which have been discussed in the previous chapter. Those responsible for providing police funding are concerned with the dollar value of police, although some of the aims of policing, like maintaining public order or prevention of crime, are not obviously amenable to quantitative measurement.

police increases the wages bill on a police budget – even to replace police officers in some jobs with unsworn personnel may increase the salary costs, and may reduce efficiency in some areas. Preventing police officers from carrying out certain tasks in the interests of essential tasks may well be resented by the community, and in any case there is a limit to the improvements that increased efficiency can provide. Aside from community policing, if crime analysis is used to provide information for offender targeting strategies or zero tolerance operations these, too, require police officers to be assigned who must be taken from some other duty. No police organisation has a significant pool of officers available who can be assigned to new duties, even temporarily, without a noticeable and deleterious reduction of efficiency in another area.

The essential tasks of policing

The clearest and least controvertible fact about policing is that police are expected to deal with crime. Since crime occurs at any hour of the day or night, and in any place, police are required to be available 24 hours a day everywhere. Mayne's primary objects gave the prevention of crime primacy over dealing with crime that had already been committed, but this objective may no longer be realistic. Indeed, many aspects of crime prevention have already been shown to be beyond the power of police to effect, and the reactive policing approaches for much of the past 40 years have effectively denied Mayne's dictum and shown that the de facto primary task of police is to deal with crime that is in progress or has just been found to have been committed.

Police powers are all directed towards dealing with offenders or suspects during or after the commission of a crime, and do not extend to permit the coercion of individuals before an offence has taken place, except for a very few statutes which do criminalise actions which are preparatory to an offence, for example criminal attempts and conspiracies and the possession of weapons and implements to commit substantive offences. Powers that may have formerly existed to arrest persons before a substantive offence is committed have been seen to be unsatisfactory and often discriminatory and repealed.[2] To some extent the essential tasks of policing might be implied by what police are given powers to do, and an analysis of police powers is at the heart of the argument of one review of the core business of British policing, the Home Office Review of Police Core and Ancillary Tasks (1995). This Review defined the essential functions of police as matters which police and police alone must do, which were those which required the special powers of police: any matter which required coercion in the broadest sense

---

2   The notorious British "sus" law, which was repealed by the *Criminal Attempts Act* 1981, is an example. The *Vagrancy Act* 1824 s 4 allowed any officer to arrest any "suspected person loitering with intent to commit an arrestable offence" when there was evidence of two or more overt acts, such as looking in cars, trying car door handles, etc. "Sus" charges were triable only summarily, the "overt acts" were often fairly nebulous and open to allegations of fabrication, and were a source of particular resentment among young West Indians who felt unduly victimised under this section.

114

was a matter which devolved to police, while any matter which did not involve coercion could safely be passed over to other agencies.

Although made in a far more general context, Hayek's dictum that the state should maintain a monopoly of coercion is relevant to the criminal law. Part of the distinction between civil and criminal proceedings is that in criminal proceedings society itself, personified either as "The Queen", "The People" or "The State" prosecutes one of its members, and, on conviction gives some form of punishment or formal order to enforce the offender's compliance with the requirements of society. At virtually every stage, force (coercion in Hayek's terminology) is applied by the state to express the will of society. Suspects can, with or without their consent, be searched, questioned, arrested and taken before the court, and power to do this is given to police. This sort of action, the exercise of coercive powers to arrest, detain etc which the Home Office Review defined as "Inner Core Functions", must not be devolved or delegated to any other agency.

There is a second level of action, normally the province of police, which involves what might be termed administrative coercion. Most jurisdictions allow for certain minor offences, particularly motoring offences, to be dealt with by payment of a financial penalty through the courts rather than a summons, court appearance and fine.[3] Within the terms stipulated above these are still coercive measures, although by no means as invasive of individual rights and liberty as the power of arrest. In an increasingly technological age, traffic offences are proved by devices which do not rely on human judgment, such as cameras, fixed or hand-held radar or instruments to measure blood or breath alcohol. Although these result in coercion by way of prosecution if the legal limit is breached, there is no convincing argument for these matters to be dealt with wholly and solely by police officers unless the question of arrest arises.

This level of exercise of coercive powers the Review terms "Outer Core Functions", which can be carried out by suitably trained staff who need not be sworn police officers, but which do need to be exercised under the aegis of the police organisation. Ultimate responsibility for use of such powers remains with the police service, and in some cases there should perhaps be direct police supervision, but the use and servicing of speed and traffic light cameras, for example, may safely be entrusted to unsworn personnel. In order to maintain the state's monopoly of coercive power, the police, as the coercive arm of society, are required to have some involvement in the exercise of these outer core functions, and, ultimately, the responsibility for use or misuse of such powers must remain with the police as an organisation.

Clearly, police carry out many other tasks, such as dealing with lost property and found dogs, which do not involve coercion, and which are

---

3   These may be termed infringement notices, fixed penalty notices, or, more colloquially "tickets". Formally, they are a device whereby a summons, court hearing, entry of a plea and disposition of the matter by the court can be averted by acknowledgment of wrongdoing and payment of a stated penalty, which is less than the maximum penalty that can be inflicted by the court. It is always open to the alleged offender to challenge the penalty by exercising the right to have the matter heard by a court.

termed by the Review "ancillary". These tasks could safely be delegated to other agencies. Few of the matters were defined as non-police tasks: one exception, mentioned in the Home Office Review, is the use of police to control traffic while escorting unusual loads. Most of the tasks that police are called upon to perform involve minor crises or emergencies which are part of the duties of some agency which does not operate an emergency system, or matters which the parties involved can deal with by themselves, but need authoritative advice on how the matter should be resolved. Examples are family disputes, which require expert counselling and mediation which is available by appointment during working hours, and those disputes which are best resolved by negotiation or, ultimately, as civil wrongs, which are the province of civil courts and require lawsuits rather than criminal charges.

Not all analyses of the essential business of police are premised upon police powers. The Western Australia Police Service committed itself to a continuing reassessment throughout the mid-1990s, and as part of its purpose and direction statement listed its five core functions as:

- prevention and control of crime;
- maintenance of the peace;
- traffic management and road safety;
- emergency management co-ordination;
- assisting members of the community in times of emergency and need.[4]

This is a much more inclusive list of the essential elements of policing, and far more in keeping with what police actually do rather than what police should do. The British model of core functions sets out to exclude matters which, in practice, it is impossible to keep out of policing, whereas the Western Australian model is based upon public expectations of police. The coercive powers of police are, nevertheless, central to the Western Australian Police core functions, as can be seen by examining each of the functions in turn.

Maintenance of the peace and control of crime clearly involves, at least potentially, most of the powers given to police. Police probably carry out most of their order maintenance role on the streets by the arrest or threat of arrest of individuals behaving in a disorderly fashion in public. Bittner's analysis (1990) of the police role is that it involves order maintenance as much, if not more, than it involves dealing with crime, and that this order maintenance, particularly on Skid Row, is carried out by police officers directing recalcitrant individuals with the implied assertion that arrests will result from continued disorder or non-compliance with police directions. Traffic management likewise often relies upon the use of punishment for infringements of the law detected by technological devices whose record-

---

4   These are taken from the undated Purpose and Direction statement, which, itself, was part of a continuing review, the Delta Program, commenced in the mid-1990s into all aspects of policing. Current policing priorities are little different.

ings are almost irrefutable. This technology can be operated by police, or other persons working under the aegis of police, and the level of coercion involved renders these matters part of overall police responsibility in Britain[5] as in Australia. Thus the first three core functions of policing in Western Australia meet the definition of core business suggested by the British Home Office Review.

The last two core functions of the Western Australia Police Service do not obviously meet the criteria of core functions set out by the British Home Office. Emergency management coordination is rather less problematic in this scheme than the blanket "assisting members of the community in times of emergency or need". What is implied by emergency management coordination is that when crises or disasters occur a number of agencies are involved, and some sort of liaison needs to be established. For example, in a serious fire, a chemical spill, or a train crash, fire services, paramedics, statutory authorities, the media, and other agencies all have a part to play, and, since police are likely to be among the first of the services to be notified of the incident by the public, police are the most obvious agency to assume control of the emergency response on the scene first.

It is not easy to imagine any sort of major incident where there is no other role for police but coordination. Most major incidents involve at least the possibility of criminal offences, such that a police investigation is required. Few incidents fail to attract a crowd, which in itself is a public order issue, and many, particularly in cities, cause traffic congestion. Different sorts of incident all have different agencies who will have primary responsibility for dealing with it, fire service for fires, rail board for train crashes, etc, but the common factor is that police are likely to be amongst the first persons to the scene, and likeliest to be able to supply sufficient personnel trained and experienced in dealing with major incidents. Initial emergency coordination in itself is not highly expensive in terms of police manpower, provided that the police organisation is large enough and has the ability to deal with it efficiently. The important point about emergency coordination is that it must be immediate, but is not usually a long-lasting commitment of resources. Suppose a train crashes in a city suburb: coordination of various agencies must start immediately, but within 24 hours all necessary steps to save life and prevent further harm will have been taken, and the action at the scene will usually be no more than clear-up operations undertaken largely by the railway authority. Although 50 or 60 police may have been involved in the incident, the financial cost to police of co-ordinating the incident is limited to 50 or 60 officer days pay and use of resources.[6]

Assisting members of the public in time of emergency and need is rather more difficult to equate with the Home Office core functions. Indeed, it is a wide enough definition to allow almost every call for police assistance

---

5   Increasing, the British government is putting responsibility for traffic management onto local authorities as far as possible. This will be discussed further in Chapter 14.

6   If there is any sort of police inquiry following the incident, this, of course, may be extremely expensive: an Incident Room for some investigations can remain open for years.

to be justified as a core function, which is, perhaps, something that any review of policing which seeks to cut the police workload would seek to avoid. In the United States, some police departments maintain the ethic of being total response services, in that police attend every request for their assistance, whatever it might be and whether or not it appears to the despatcher to be genuinely police business, whereas others allow despatchers to filter calls, and refuse to send a car to some requests on the grounds that it does not appear to be police business.[7]

In the areas of crime, public order and major incidents, there is little argument about whether these should be part of the police role. However, police spend much of their time answering calls to matters which do not fit into any of these categories. In any analysis of policing which seeks to measure the effectiveness or value for money of policing within the parameters of the police role as strictly defined, any tasks which are not core functions do not count, and therefore are considered as a waste of time and resources. Unfortunately, the public has grown to expect police to be available 24 hours a day, and will call for their assistance anyway, in which case it may take as much if not more time to explain why the request for assistance is refused as being no part of police duty than to comply with the request, whatever it might be. In some instances, police may be called to a matter which is not police business, but common humanity may well prompt the officer to take action if there is no agency nominated or available to assist with the matter.

The acknowledgment by the Western Australia Police Service and others that assistance to the community with unspecified emergencies is a core function of policing does no more than recognise that members of the community may often require assistance at times when only the police and fire services are available. While the fire services get their share of calls which do not fall within the official ambit of their duties, the public see their abilities as more specialised than those of police, and they consequently receive fewer calls. Attempts to define the core business of police are either restrictive, as analysis of the British model has shown, or allow a catch-all component which fails to define a core at all. Any strictly defined core of functions will actually eliminate many police activities important to both public and police.

The requirements of community policing

Community policing itself exacts a very high internal cost on the police service. Its fundamental principle is to develop improved communication and a relationship of trust between police and public, which means that individual police officers must build a professional rapport with individuals

---

7   In Texas, for example, the San Antonio Police Department prides itself on being a total response service, attending every call however trivial it might sound, while Dallas police despatchers are expected to assess the content of calls and point out to some callers that their requests appear not to be a police matter and that police will not assist.

and groups within the community. Whether a police service establishes community policing as a specialist branch or encourages every officer on patrol to be a community police officer, community policing necessitates non-emergency interaction with the public. Two issues arise immediately from this: first, establishing how non-emergency interaction can fall within the definition of core police business; and, secondly, given the level of demand from the public for what it, if not always the police, considers to be emergency interaction, finding police resources and time to allow non-emergency interaction to take place.

The first of these issues can be answered easily, if cynically. In the broader definitions of core business which allow for meeting the needs of the public, then community policing falls within the definition for any society which is keen to have its police highly visible and in touch with the community. Where core business is defined more narrowly as dealing with crime, community policing is not too closely scrutinised as a strategy if it can be shown to have an immediate effect on crime, even if only through particular schemes in particular areas. There is a certain amount of leeway allowed in what strategies police use to address core business, and the sole criterion for acceptance of any strategy is a measurable positive effect on that core business.

The second issue, the matter of finding time for community policing, is critical to the success of community policing in general. Community policing in all its aspects is both expensive in police time and a long-term strategic approach rather than offering a quick fix to an immediate problem. On occasions, of course, community policing does have its startling successes in reducing crime,[8] but often this is in a particular small area as a result of a specific project which may do no more than relocate the problem rather than solve it.

The change process in policing

Policing is in a process of major change to meet the needs of modern society. The appointment of John Avery[9] as Commissioner of Police in 1984 initiated the process of change in policing New South Wales, and other police agencies have been no less rigorous in their own programs for change. Some police agencies have even given the process a title of its own: the "Plus Programme" instituted in the mid-1980s by Commissioner Imbert in London's Metropolitan Police, and Commissioner Falconer's Delta Program of the 1990s in Western Australia are examples. Implicit in these change processes is the shift in focus of policing. The change from force to service discussed by Avery is no cosmetic change, but a real attitudinal

---

8   See, for example, the work of Officer Orazem in Brooklyn reported by Farrell (1988), and
     discussed in full in the next chapter.
9   Avery himself was the author of one of the most influential books on police change
     (Avery, 1981) and, indeed, made the New South Wales Police into a service. The process
     of change continued under the commissionership of Peter Ryan, and the effect of the
     change, particularly with regard to racism, is examined in Chan (1997).

change within policing towards addressing the needs and concerns of the public.

One of the unforeseen consequences of distancing police from the public during the era of reactive policing was that the public no longer felt any responsibility for public order and the prevention of crime – all that seemed necessary then was simply to call the police and leave it to them. A Royal Commission into policing in Britain refuted this view:

> It is destructive both of police and public social health to attempt to pass over to the police the obligations and duties associated with the pre-vention of crime and the preservation of public tranquillity. These are obligations and duties of the public, aided by the police and not the police, occasionally aided by some public spirited citizens. (The *Report of the Royal Commission on Police*, 1967, conclusion)

However, the public have been extremely reluctant to shoulder these obligations and duties. It is perhaps ironic that Avery's concept of a police service consists of the police officer on the street as a crime specialist assisting the public in maintaining the peace and reducing crime, which changes the status of police in modern parlance to that of "crime consultants". The police officer who was expected to arrive and deal expeditiously with the problems that members of the public could off-load with a single phone call was far more of a servant as a member of a police force than the provider of expert assistance which is the police officer's role in a police service.

The American perspective on policing change is far more robust, largely due to police accountability to local government. In areas where the chief of police is an elected sheriff, the public of the county can ensure their needs are met at the ballot box. In areas where the chief of police is appointed by the mayor, then the ballot box is a slightly less direct weapon for the public to get the policing it wants. There are two important aspects to the change process in the United States which differ markedly from the change process in Australia and Britain. Change in American policing is enforced from the top down, as chiefs of police are appointed or elected specifically to engineer change in a particular fashion, and within a specific time limit which is certainly before the next election. Examples here are the replacement of Darryl Gates in Los Angeles by Willie Williams as a reaction to the Rodney King incident, despite his 17 years of maintaining the traditional hard line on crime. In New York, the election of Mayor Giuliani on a manifesto which included a crusade against crime required the replacement of Mayor Dinkin's appointee Raymond Kelly[10] as chief of police by William Bratton.

A further difference between American policing and Australian or British policing is the geographical extent of single police agencies. If a particular policing strategy results in the displacement of crime in Australia

---

10   Dinkins' first Commissioner, Lee Brown, was actually responsible for the introduction of community policing in New York at Mayor Dinkins' behest, but after his mid-1992 resignation he was replaced for the remainder of Dinkins' mayoral term by Raymond Kelly.

or Britain nothing is achieved, as the displacement is usually from one part of a particular police agency's area to another. A policing initiative in New South Wales which merely displaces crime is likely to shift it from one part of Sydney to another, or at best to a centre like Wollongong or Newcastle: street criminals are unlikely to uproot en masse for the 10-hour drive across the State border to Brisbane or Melbourne. Similarly in Britain: a crime initiative in Birmingham which displaces criminal activity is most likely to displace it to neighbouring cities like Wolverhampton or Coventry, but all three are patrolled by the West Midlands Police.[11] In the United States, police boundaries are contiguous with local government boundaries, so crime displaced from New York City will be displaced into a different police area, even though it may only be across the river into New Jersey or into one of the commuter-belt counties of New York State. The same applies elsewhere, in that Oakland abuts San Francisco, and Dallas and Fort Worth are reasonably close together. If crime is displaced from one municipality to another, or into a neighbouring county, then the effect on the voting population is the same as if crime had been prevented, so displacement is as good as prevention in ensuring a chief of police keeps his job.

The effect of a community policing focus

Whether community policing is carried out by specialist officers or responsibility for it is shared across the service, community policing has a major impact on the way policing is actually performed. Community policing is a major cost in resources, as it requires officers to be available to the community consistently and over a sufficient period of time to become known to individuals within it, and for officers to be committed to building long-term relationships with the community, providing a source of information to the community about crime, and to other police officers about the community.

Few, if any, police services have officers to spare to put into community policing as a specialist unit, so such officers must be taken from some other area of policing unless an increase in manpower (with a consequent increase in budget) can be agreed. Since staffing levels are set in most police agencies for specialist groups such as detectives, dog section and mounted branch, officers for new or temporary specialist areas can only come from the ranks of general duties or patrol officers. For many years, the reaction of police management to new problems has been to form a squad to deal with

---

11 Although big cities like London, Los Angeles and New York may be a magnet for disaffected young people who then often get involved in crime, nevertheless there is little reason to expect those who commit crime to be more significantly mobile than the population in general. Census data in Britain shows that a high percentage of people live within 10 miles of the place where they are born – intuitively this seems surprising, yet the continued existence of British regional accents, even given the increase in population mobility since the Second World War, tends to bear this out. The high percentage of impenetrable Geordie accents noted by a visitor to Newcastle is evidence than many of the city's residents were born there, and Mancunians and Liverpudlians have vastly different accents despite Manchester and Liverpool being only 40 miles (64 km) apart.

it, and whether this squad has been of a permanent or temporary nature, its members have almost always been drawn from the only pool available, general patrol officers. Whatever success such squads have had, there has been no diminution in the workload of officers on patrol even though each new squad formed reduces the number of officers available for patrol duty. Specialist community policing units, however effective they are, make no appreciable impact on the number of calls for police which are dealt with by patrolling officers, yet serve to reduce the number of officers on patrol.

There is no less of a problem if all officers on patrol are expected to fulfil the role of community police. Emergency calls from the public will always take precedence over non-emergency interaction, and if patrolling officers spend most of their time dealing with calls for assistance, there is little or none left over for building links with the community. While there is the possibility, if not the likelihood, that an emergency will arise to take precedence, officers on patrol who are not dedicated community police will be unable to keep appointments or make follow-up visits with a sufficient level of reliability.[12] This is a vital point, in that unless police can keep appointments and spend time with members of the community no useful working relationships can be made, and police will further alienate themselves from the public by their perceived failure to make and comply with arrangements.

Even where community policing is the province of a dedicated team of officers, the workload may well increase for others. Some police services are experimenting with the use of computer communications to provide crime information to the public: the San Antonio Police Department home page on the Internet has updates on current crime trends, including the modus operandi and description of active criminals, and the PCCOPS system in Western Australia provides crime information suburb by suburb via interactive phone links to a police computer to anyone interested enough to call. For this information to be useful it needs to be both accurate and kept up to date regularly and frequently, which is time consuming. Furthermore, if members of the public call local police as a result of this information, for example when a suspect is seen, confidence in police will be lost if the officers on patrol are unaware of the computer information, or fail to act on the new information given. Community policing, then, requires the commitment of sufficient resources, which means that sufficient numbers of police officers be made available both for community policing itself, and for the issues that will arise as a result of increased participation in police matters by the public.

---

12 One means of addressing this problem has been sector policing in London. Each police station area is divided into sectors, each sector having its dedicated team of officers under a sergeant. The team is responsible for community-oriented policing on that sector, and, although some members of the team may be absent for a week or so to provide night duty cover for the station area, in general there will always be some member of the team available for non-urgent interaction with the public.

Public expectations of police

The public as a whole do not understand, nor, perhaps, do they have any wish to understand, the concept of core police business or the requirements of community policing, but they do have generally held expectations of police. If positive expectations of police are met, then relations between the police and the public are maintained and perhaps improved, but if police fail to live up to public expectation then suspicion and bad feeling are generated which do nothing to ameliorate social problems. Without public support the difficult task of policing by consent is rendered even more difficult: with overt public antipathy, policing by consent is impossible.

The first and major expectation that society has of its police is that police should be there and available. This expectation is certainly addressed – police do indeed provide 24 hour coverage, seven days a week, all year round. The constant availability of police is, perhaps, responsible for many of the other expectations that the public has of its police. All members of the public can expect that at some stage things will go wrong in their lives, and at least some of these will be major, unexpected crises for which help is needed. Modern society is geared towards providing help to its members, and there is almost no aspect of life's problems which is not addressed by social workers, counsellors, self-help and support groups of fellow suffe-rers. This is not to minimise the validity or usefulness of these approaches: one need only consider the services of Alcoholics Anonymous, one of the earliest of such self-help groups, to see they can be of immense value.

The state, however, provides only a few emergency services with full 24-hour cover. There are emergency medical services, namely hospital accident and emergency departments and public ambulance services, fire services, coastguard and police. The first three of these are relatively closely defined: any person who goes to a hospital at any hour of the day or night will be medically examined (although there may well be some delay) and if there is no medical problem, sent away. Similarly, fire services will attend calls, but unless there is a conflagration, or some individual is trapped and needs rescue, will leave the scene, and coastguard services are reserved for problems at sea. Although all these services receive a proportion of trivial calls, these can relatively easily be dismissed as not the type of emergency for which that particular service is trained or equipped. The police service is left to deal with all other matters – as Punch and Naylor (1973) comment, "the police could well be described as the only 24 hour, fully mobile, social service".

Punch and Naylor's study shows clearly the public expectation of police: they are there when no-one else is available to help, and provide a quick remedy from an authoritative source. Often calls are made to police for reasons which even the caller realises are not strictly police business, but police are called because no-one else is available. Of 30 people interviewed by Punch and Naylor about their reasons for calling police:

> Five people saw the police as the obvious choice when problems came up. Twelve said they were aware that some other organisation could or

should have dealt with their particular incident, but either that service could not be contacted or else they did not know where to locate it. Generally, it just seemed quicker and easier to call the police than anyone else. In every case, [police were] sent to the scene in response to the call.

Punch and Naylor's conclusions would, perhaps, be even more forceful had their study been conducted 30 years later. As the extended family unit has been superseded by the nuclear family, the support and help that extended families formerly gave is now expected of the state. However, almost every aspect of the state's social services has been cut back, or at the very least is under stringent financial constraints. Reduction of in-patient treatment for the mentally ill and its replacement by care in the community, for example, has brought many individuals who are in no real sense criminals to the notice of police, or even incarceration in prison. Emergency social problems which are no part of police duty fall to police for action when the specialist agency responsible is unavailable outside office hours or there is a waiting list for appointments.

The lack of emergency specialist social services increases the workload for police. Emergencies will still occur, even if no relevant professionals are available to deal with them, so such matters fall to police to provide a temporary solution. The hospital system itself suffers overload in a similar way, as accident and emergency departments fill with individuals who do not need immediate treatment, but are unable to get prompt treatment from any other source, and wards fill with the elderly for whom no temporary residential care during convalescence is available. The public who see "care in the community" as government shorthand for "look after your own mentally sick and physically handicapped" may well be wary of community policing if it appears to be yet another do-it-yourself solution enabling the state to cut its service to the public.

Bittner (1990, pp 120ff) provides a useful analysis of the phenomenon which he refers to as "calling the cops" as a means of dispute resolution. When disputes arise, members of the public need them to be resolved, and, if this cannot be done by negotiation between the parties present or involved, some impartial arbitrator is required. The formal system of such adjudication in society is to be found in the courts, and the binding nature of such adjudication is provided by the power given to judges and magistrates to enforce their decisions. The power to coerce ensures court judgments are followed. When police are called to a dispute, Bittner argues that this is because the parties to the dispute require a resolution which is binding on the protagonists. Police are authorised to coerce as a last resort, and this is at the heart of the phenomenon of "calling the cops". It is the potential for coercion that makes police more valuable than any other service, as they have, in Bittner's words, the "capacity and authority to overpower resistance to an attempted solution in the native habitat of the problem".

Even when there is no dispute, the authority of police in other contexts enables police to cut many gordian knots to effect a solution to difficulties.

Where social workers may fear for the safety of a child within a house but are refused access, police may have legal power to force entry to the premises. Police frequently have temporary emergency powers to remove children in need of care to a place of safety, or persons considered a danger to themselves or to others to hospital for compulsory psychiatric assessment. At the very least, police can pacify situations by the implied threat of arrest for disorderly conduct or similar public order offence if protagonists are too vociferous in their disagreement, and hope that such a truce holds until the relevant professional agency is available to deal with the matter.

The public have also been encouraged over many years to seek help from the police in case of need. This is a message put across by police themselves, and reinforced by police attendance at every request for assistance. Whether or not the matter is within the ambit of police duty, police officers will normally do something to assist, and leave the caller in a better frame of mind than when the call was made.[13] Calls from the public have increased police workloads tremendously, but to stop answering such calls would be counter-productive. The whole rationale of community policing requires better cooperation between police and public, and this can never be achieved by police declining to answer calls for assistance made in good faith by members of the public. However, it is precisely the time spent attending non-urgent calls or those which do not relate to core functions which make the police appear to be inefficient. There is a paradox here: the demand for more efficient police services with particular regard to crime and its prevention cannot be met while as much time as is currently the case is spent in answering specific demands from individual members of the public for police assistance in matters other than crime, yet the non-crime demands on police show more signs of increasing then decreasing.

How police time is actually spent

There have been numerous analyses of what police actually do, in an attempt to discover whether any police time could be diverted to other tasks: however, whatever measure is made of police activity, no researcher has ever found that police are, to any significant extent, idle. Police may spend much of their time carrying out tasks which are not directly related to crime or public order or any other core task, but their time is fully accounted for by carrying out tasks legitimately required by somebody. There are two separate issues to be examined if police management is seeking to divert extra officer hours to core functions of policing or some form of pro-active or targeted strategy: the management problem of identifying officers in administrative or other roles who can be re-assigned to

---

13   Punch and Naylor cite police officers humanely killing injured cats, providing accommodation for the destitute, obtaining voluntary help for the elderly, and there is a wealth of anecdotal evidence from police officers of everything from mending bicycles to performing exorcisms.

active policing, and the strategic problem of ensuring the officers on patrol who are in contact with the public are effective in their duty.

The vast majority of the police budget is spent on wages and overtime: 80 per cent is probably a fair average figure. Any chief officer of police who claims an increase of staff is necessary can expect to answer very hard questions from police paymasters concerning the efficient deployment of all officers currently employed. Even when the number of officers notionally on patrol duty is calculated, these numbers will be depleted further by holidays, sick leave, suspensions, court attendance, in-service training or temporary transfers to other duties. Much of this is true of other organisations also, but if modern policing requires that officers be both visible and available to the public, it is vital that police agencies ensure that officers are at their most effective.

Distribution of officers

Part of the trend during the reactive policing era was to establish specialists to deal with particular tasks or problems. This became a serious problem in police forces with several thousand officers, as to establish a modest squad of 10 or 20 officers would hardly seem to make a great deal of difference, but 10 or 20 such squads in different parts of the force area established by different senior officers could seriously weaken the police presence on the streets. For this reason, some police executives have questioned seriously the value of specialists, and most have reduced, or put time limits on, specialist squads.[14] It is difficult to see how any police service could cope effectively without proper training facilities with skilled instructors, or without a specialist drugs unit or dog section and it would be untenable to claim that there should be no, or fewer, specialist tasks in modern policing. The problem for police management is to maximise the use of the skills of these disparate specialists for the police service and wider community.

The scale of the problem can be illustrated. A police district containing a million people with a ratio of police : public of about 1 : 300, will have about 3000 police, of whom between 400 and 500 will be detectives. To establish a Murder Squad, Robbery Squad, Drugs Squad, Fraud Squad and Vice Squad of 20 to 25 detectives each would cut the number of detectives left to investigate all the other crimes committed and reported through the police district to around 300. A police organisation of this size will have an Academy, Mounted Branch, Dog Section, Traffic Section which together may account for 25 per cent of the total number of officers on the strength. Senior officers, that is those of inspector rank and above in Australia and Britain, lieutenant in the United States, account for perhaps 5 per cent of all

---

14   In 1976, Sir Robert Mark challenged the elitism of London's CID by insisting that every detective revert to uniform on promotion and wait at least a year before re-applying to CID. As part of the Delta Review, the Western Australia Police Service abolished some central squads like Liquor and Gaming and sought to distribute the expertise of their officers by transferring them to regions, where regional commanders may or may not find their permanent employment as specialists necessary.

officers.[15] Any large modern police service which has 60 per cent of its officers posted in uniform to police stations is doing well as many have a much lower proportion than that. Even then, many large police stations are microcosms of the organisation, and have officers carrying out specialist functions rather than being on patrol.

The actual tasks of police patrols

A number of studies have sought to break down the proportions of the working day spent by uniform patrol officers in the various tasks they perform. There have been problems of definition here, as it may well be unclear in many instances whether a particular matter may constitute a crime or not. Officers might be sent to an incident which can be variously described as "a person being assaulted", "a disturbance", "a fight" or "a domestic dispute". They may then discover the incident to be an alcohol-induced argument between two people known to each other, and deal with it either by mediation, or by one or two arrests for drunkenness or disorderly behaviour, or by a report and prosecution for assault. Neither the original call nor the eventual disposition of this matter indicates clearly the mixture of service role and crime investigation inherent in this example.

The sheer volume of calls made to police which are then allocated for patrolling officers to attend means that most of the work of police is generated in this fashion. The reactive role of police means that officers spend much of their time on tasks relating to or originating from calls from the public. Both Punch and Naylor (1973) and Cumming, Cumming and Edell (1964) found that no more than half the calls for police could be classified as law enforcement matters, the other half were for assistance with personal or inter-personal problems. Calls themselves generate what might be termed secondary tasks. Every incident that police attend must be reported in some way, so that every call has its share of paperwork to be completed. Writing the initial reports of incidents can easily take an hour or two of every shift. If any of the incidents result in an arrest or a prosecution by summons, then not only is the amount of paperwork to be done multiplied considerably, but more time is later to be spent in attending court. There is no such thing as a short court appearance: even attending magistrates court will take an officer off patrol for a morning or an afternoon at least, and attendance at higher courts can take several days.

There is what might be termed an iceberg effect in police duty. While the public expects police to be out catching criminals, and this is the very thing that police as portrayed by Hollywood and television do, the mere apprehension of a suspect is a very small, albeit the most highly visible, part of a police officer's duty with regard to that crime. Suppose police are called to a disturbance in or outside a bar, and, on arrival, find that two

---

15   In the Western Australia Police Service, inspectors and above comprise 3 per cent of the police strength, but many police stations in country towns such as Broome or Kalgoorlie which in Britain would be inspector or chief inspector posts are run by senior sergeants, a rank which does not exist in British policing.

young men have been fighting, and one has suffered slight facial injuries (cut lip, black eye, or broken nose). The most likely action for police at the scene is to call an ambulance and send the fight's loser to hospital, then arrest the winner. This incident will be familiar to all police officers, and attendance at the scene, the part of police duty which is visible to the public, will probably take no more than 10 minutes. The whole incident will, however, take several hours to deal with. Statements must be taken from friends of the participants, who usually offer alternative versions of blame, from the bar staff who probably saw only the fight and the final blow, and police may be no nearer understanding what the fight was really about. The victim's statement cannot be obtained until he has been examined by a doctor, often entailing several hours wait, then the suspect must be interviewed and fingerprinted, his identity confirmed and eventually charged or released. A brief of evidence has to be prepared for the person who will undertake the prosecution and at a later stage the officers may be required to attend court.

The problem is quite intractable. No analysis of core functions and designation of particular matters as no longer part of police duty can prevent members of the public calling police and requesting their attendance to deal with these non-core functions. Unless some other agency can be found to deal at the time, then public faith in police will be lost if a refusal to attend results, however politely that refusal is made. Clearly, also, full reports need to be made of police actions, and police cannot be absolved from the obligation of giving evidence in court. It may well be that no more than minor or cosmetic changes can be made to what patrolling police officers do that can allow them more time to engage in the non-emergency interaction with the public that is central to community policing. This problem may be exacerbated by zero-tolerance strategies. It has already been demonstrated that the time spent making an arrest is far less than the time spent completing the preparation for a prosecution at the station. If zero-tolerance is to be carried out by way of increased arrests and prosecutions, then this is a highly labour intensive strategy to implement, and yet the public will still keep calling police, and officers must be found to deal with these calls for assistance.

The real costs of possible options

Police agencies have been aware for some time of the problems of implementing new strategies where officers are already operating at full capacity. There are a number of possible options which have been suggested, and in some cases implemented, but these are not without their costs. These options, most of which will be considered in detail here, include:

- recruiting more police, or seeking better qualified recruits;
- recruiting unsworn staff to take over some tasks currently undertaken by police officers, in order to release those officers for core functions;

- obtaining volunteers to assist police in various tasks;
- improving police efficiency;[16]
- reducing the tasks that police actually undertake (which will need to take into account who will be nominated to deal with them).

Recruiting

The most obvious option to solving the difficulties of having too much for police to do, and the one championed most vociferously by chief officers during the 1980s, is to employ more police. However, financial constraints have made even the most law-and-order minded government reluctant to agree to this, in part because there is no clear indication of how many more police are needed, and in part because of doubts concerning the effectiveness of the police as a body in dealing with crime. The second part of the option, recruiting better qualified officers is rather easier to implement.

High levels of unemployment have allowed all employers to indulge in qualification inflation, by which they can demand higher qualifications than ever before of applicants to fill vacancies, whether or not those qualifications are relevant to the task. Modern policing is far more complex than it was 20 or 30 years ago, and officers on the streets need to be able to cope with this. An educated, articulate officer may have the interpersonal skills necessary to cope with disputes quickly and effectively, and therefore deal with more calls. If the pool of potential recruits is large, then it enables police agencies to select officers who have the potential to carry out their tasks more effectively. There is no suggestion that a university degree guarantees interpersonal skills or effective communication, but it does indicate that the holder has the capability of absorbing further education. Training in itself is expensive in police officers' time, but is justified if it enables officers to perform better. Following Lord Scarman's judicial inquiry into the Brixton riots (Scarman, 1981), the Metropolitan Police embarked on an ambitious program of two weeks' interpersonal skills training for the whole force of over 27,000 officers, but this was, perhaps, crucial to the later acceptance of the changes comprising the change from a police force to a police service.

Civilianisation

As has been shown earlier, a large number of the tasks which police actually do are peripheral to those duties connected directly to the use of coercion. If some of these tasks can be performed by personnel other than police officers, then police officers will be made available for other duties. This is in some respects an extension of many years of police practice, as police agencies have always employed unsworn staff in clerical roles, as cleaners and catering staff, or in specialist roles in forensic laboratories, etc. However, other police tasks which do not involve direct dealings with the

---

16   This matter is addressed in a variety of contexts throughout this book.

public, or where dealings with the public do not require coercion, may also be suitable for civilianisation. Most of the obvious office duties have long been passed from sworn to unsworn staff, and some of the non-coercive duties involving interaction with the public have also been passed over. Examples here are the use of clerks at the front desks of many busy police stations to answer queries from the public, check driving documents and other such matters, and the use of technical staff to service roadside camera and radar devices for speeding offences.

Various arguments have been raised in policing circles regarding the employment of civilian staff to deal with matters that were traditionally the preserve of police officers. One such reservation has been the matter of confidentiality. Clearly, some matters have a high level of confidentiality about them, others less so, but there is no compelling argument that a police officer is any less likely to discuss confidential information than a reasonably screened unsworn staff member. Many rooms in police stations have confidential information in them, including names and photographs of suspects, details of crimes like rape whose press reporting may be restricted, yet these rooms are visited every night by the station cleaners, who may never have been checked for security. Information obtained in major crime investigations is now routinely held on computers which are operated by unsworn staff, who are thereby privy to highly confidential, and sometimes speculative, personal information.

The argument for civilianisation is that there is no reason to suppose that any police task which does not at least potentially involve the need to apply coercive force to any member of society cannot be done equally well by an unsworn member of the police staff, or by sub-contracting the work to a non-police agency. The question is whether it can be done at a lower cost without loss of efficiency. The other important issue is whether the police officer thus released for other duties is adequate to perform those duties. Let us consider the economic issue first. Within the context of police training, for example, there is no good reason why a police recruit or a new detective should have to learn criminal law or other theoretical topics from a serving police officer: arguably, this could be taught by a lawyer: however, for a police organisation to employ lawyers full time on the staff of their Police Academy would be more expensive than to have police do it. Certain aspects of police training, especially practical matters and aspects of street duty, can probably only be taught effectively by police officers or ex police officers.[17]

Policing is a violent and sometimes dangerous occupation, requiring a reasonable standard of fitness from patrolling officers and operational detectives at least. Occasions arise when an officer recovering from sickness

---

17 Police education is increasingly carried out in conjunction with formal educational estab-lishments. The New South Wales Police Academy has a campus adjacent to Charles Sturt University, and the Western Australia Police Academy shares a campus with Edith Cowan University and TAFE integrating police training and tertiary education: similar arrangements exist in the United States. In Britain an agency known as Centrex, staffed in part at least by police officers on secondment is responsible for much police training.

or injury is insufficiently fit, physically or psychologically, for the rigours of patrol duties, but is capable of performing a useful role within the police service. As part of a duty of care towards employees, police services have frequently placed such officers in some administrative duties for varying lengths of time. If all such posts are filled by unsworn staff, then problems arise with the placement of officers who are temporarily unfit for full duty. Consider three hypothetical examples. Officer A has an accident on a police motor cycle and suffers serious leg injuries: the prognosis is that a full recovery is likely, but will take six to nine months, although A is mobile on crutches after 12 weeks. Officer B is within 18 months of a pension and suffers a heart attack, then is advised by a cardiologist to avoid active or stressful duties. Officer C suffers psychological trauma after a family tragedy, and is subject to depression, fits of rage and mood swings while under pressure, although this is unlikely to be permanent. All three are capable of carrying out administrative duties and, in the case of C, it is considered that working would be positively therapeutic. In all these cases, if the officers remain on sick leave then the police service would be responsible for sick pay, and for the wages of the unsworn staff member whose job A, B or C could otherwise do.

Since large police services can expect to have a small but not negligible number of officers at various times in the circumstances of these officers, then it follows that complete civilianisation may not be to the advantage of such officers as those described, or, indeed, the police service as a whole. There are two alternatives for A and B unless the possibility remains of administrative duties: they either collect sick pay for a lengthy period, which is wasteful if they could be doing something useful, or they are retired on medical grounds. In the case of A, medical retirement is inherently wasteful, as A is expected to recover, so an experienced, productive member of the service would be lost. In the case of B, compulsory retirement seems a poor way to treat an individual who has given long service, and may affect the long-term commitment of other members of the service if they feel that they, too, might be cast aside if their health fails.[18] For C, the possibility remains of an early return to active duty as C is physically if not psychologically fit, but if C is expected to carry a firearm whilst on duty, doubts must be raised about the safety of the public, colleagues and C personally if C is armed.

In the short term, many police services do have officers in some posts which may be suitable for unsworn officers, but whose age, health or temperament render them a potential liability on active police duty. They may well not be sick enough for a medical discharge, not recalcitrant enough for disciplinary dismissal, unwilling to accept early retirement themselves, yet are not prepared or are unable to meet the needs of a

---

18   There is a danger that this would be perceived as a return to a harsher era – there is a great deal of evidence that in 19th century London, sergeants and inspectors were expected to target long-service constables for disciplinary action in order to save money by having them dismissed before they were eligible for a pension.

modern police service. Such officers are, perhaps, best left where they are rather than placed back on the streets.

Obtaining volunteers

Many of the arguments which apply to civilianisation apply to the use of volunteers to assist in policing. A distinction needs to be made here between the use of volunteers to carry out some of the mundane tasks within police departments, and the community policing objectives of assisting members of the public to take responsibility for their own environment in Neighbourhood Watch or other such crime prevention schemes. Perhaps the most obvious use of volunteers in policing is the Special Constabulary instituted in Britain, originally during the First World War to enable police services to be maintained while many police officers were in the trenches, but retained ever since. "Specials" wear uniform with distinguishing shoulder patches, a flat cap rather than the traditional helmet, and patrol voluntarily once or twice a week. Although extremely useful during two world wars, the special constabulary is now of doubtful value. At its worst it suggests that policing is so simple that anyone could do it as a hobby, but at its best it is both a support to regular police, and a useful recruiting method.

The San Antonio Police Department in Texas has a volunteer scheme whereby citizens can assist police in clerical or computer or receptionist posts or in working on community projects. The volunteers make a yearly commitment, but only, perhaps, for a few days or half days per week, and are checked and cleared before being used. This is full involvement of volunteers in actual police support tasks, but volunteers are used in other police services rather more peripherally. Victim support groups are also often staffed by volunteers and have a close working relationship with police, although they are often not as closely associated with police as the San Antonio scheme permits. The economic costs of using volunteers are small: there are no wages, obviously, but some costs are incurred in recruiting and assessing volunteers, and also in making insurance provisions for volunteers who meet with an accident or illness while on police duties. Volunteers working with police will quickly encounter, even at second hand, the realities of policing, and can build links between police and the community. This applies to both civilian volunteers of the San Antonio variety, and the Special Constabulary in Britain.

Reducing the duties of police

This option is one which has been the subject of considerable scrutiny by both police management and national or local agencies responsible for police funding. There are some major tasks undertaken by police which are large-scale drains on resources that are not obviously police duty, but, nevertheless, involve police and need to be carried out correctly. There are other matters which police officers do for no other good reason than that society expects someone to do them, and that police are an agency which is always available.

One major task which in many jurisdictions falls to police is the transport of prisoners in custody, and court security. Police are responsible for the first part of this, in that they are the agency which arrests and charges suspects, and, often, makes the decision to keep them in custody until the court appearance the next morning. Prisoners need to be transferred early in the morning from police stations to court, and from remand prisons to courts, then later in the day, after the court has dealt with them, taken from court to prison once more. While at court, of course, security must be provided. In the United States, this is largely the task of the sheriff's department, which is responsible for courts and county jails, but in Australia and Britain this has traditionally been a task for the police.

The drain on police resources in prisoner transport in Britain was huge, and in 1992 the matter was contracted out to private security companies. This has been extremely successful, in that many police officers have been released for other duties, no significant drop in efficiency has been noticed overall, although in the early stages a handful of horrendous incidents received great publicity, and the vast majority of the public have not noticed that police are no longer carrying out prisoner transport and court security. These tasks have also been contracted out in parts of Australia, again with some spectacular initial failures. Another task for which police in Australia are responsible is the issue of driving licences, driving tests, register of motor vehicles and testing of used vehicles before relicensing. Although much of the actual work is carried out by unsworn staff, nevertheless some police officers are involved, and the costs of this service are part of the police budget. There is no reason why such responsibilities cannot be undertaken by government agencies, as they are in Britain.

When there is a major transfer of duties from police to another agency, no gains result for policing if savings are not passed on to police. Every police officer released from a duty like court security is in one sense an extra police officer for a police station, but the money spent on someone else to replace that officer is an extra, but lesser, cost elsewhere. If the police budget is reduced by the cost of court security paid elsewhere, the officers formerly employed in this task are still on the payroll but no longer assessed for the budget. Even if a civilian employee on a lower wage replaces a police officer in a particular task, then that task may be done more cheaply, but police costs go up, as there is an extra, but smaller, wage to be paid. When major tasks are taken from police, the money involved is extremely large, and care must be taken to ensure that cost-cutting does not reduce police services.

Smaller tasks which police just happen to be on hand to carry out may cause public disquiet if taken from police without an alternative agency being found. One such example is lost and found property, and, in Britain, stray dogs. Although stray dogs are now, rightly, a local authority responsibility, there are probably not enough stray dogs in any borough for there to be gainful employment for specialist dog wardens on duty 24 hours per day, seven days per week, and, given that most dogs' homes are registered charities (or run by animal charities), there is unlikely to be sufficient funding available either. If a dog is seen wandering, whether it looks lost or half-starved and vicious, it is likely that some member of the public will call police, and expect an officer to attend and coax and catch the dog.

Many of the ancillary tasks of police are those which fall to police because police are available and no other agency has clear responsibility or 24-hour facilities to undertake them. None may be particularly onerous in themselves but the amount of police resources directed to these activities in total may be quite considerable. If policing is to transform itself into a service, and in doing so refuses to provide these minor services to the public then the quality of life of the community will be diminished. The public probably understands very clearly that a well-trained, well-paid police officer is not a lost property officer, dog catcher, telegram boy or tour guide, yet welcomes and is reassured by the fact that police will deal with lost property and stray dogs, pass urgent messages and give directions. Police forces which refuse such tasks (who would ask a police officer the way in a third world dictatorship?) lack public trust and confidence, and cannot thus claim to either police by consent or to have established community policing.

Conclusion

This chapter has looked at what police should do, what police actually do, what is expected of police by the public, and what are the requirements of policing strategies like community policing. The problem which has been identified for policing is that currently calls from the public and the tasks actually carried out by police have police at full capacity, yet are not only impossible to reduce but are increasing. Police personnel are fully committed, yet new strategies will in themselves require a significant increase in police resources to be carried out effectively. Against this, there is a perception by the public that police are not as effective as they once were, and there is a continuing reluctance by various levels of government to increase police budgets.

CHAPTER 7

ETHICAL CONCERNS FOR MODERN POLICING STRATEGIES

Introduction

The modern policing strategies discussed here are all information driven, and proactive: they rely on information known to the police or obtained by police, and seek to take pre-emptive action before crime, or more serious crime, can occur. These strategies are a radical departure from policing as it was originally conceived, and with the reactive approaches which immediately preceded them.[1] If police are to take covert (criminal targeting) action against individuals who have as yet committed no crime, then libertarian and privacy issues arise, not only concerning the individual targeted, but other persons with whom the target might come into contact, criminally or otherwise. Ethical questions will also be raised about the methods by which targets are selected.

There are two problems which arise with zero tolerance strategies, or other crackdowns where police take overt action against those who have committed only minor crimes which would not otherwise have merited police action. The first question to be asked concerns the type of offence and offender targeted: in effect, which segment of society determines which crimes shall be the subject of special police activity. If there is a demonstrable and genuine public concern about a particular crime or disorder issue across the whole community, the use of zero tolerance might be a valid approach, but this widespread concern needs to be shown clearly, otherwise the intolerance of only some sections of the community is enforced. The second issue concerns the sort of people who are usually prosecuted in zero tolerance crackdowns: in many cases, they tend to be those persons whose characteristics have been discussed earlier in drawing profiles of street offenders. If too many of the persons arrested are from a particular ethnic group, then police may be open to complaints of racial harassment.[2]

---

1   Little is made of the uncomfortable fact that police, learning of a planned crime, could prevent it by alerting the criminals to the fact that their intentions are known. However, police operations usually entail surveillance until sufficient evidence has been collected to warrant a prosecution or until there is a likelihood of real imminent danger to members of the community.

2   It has been suggested that the policing operations which led to urban riots in Britain in the early 1980s might now be termed zero tolerance approaches.

With both overt and covert police strategies, police credibility and respect relies on the strategies themselves being seen by the public as fair, acceptable and successful. If surveillance results in unforeseen embarrassing or unwelcome intrusion into the privacy of persons not connected with the target individual, or if racial bias is perceived in zero tolerance strategies, then this will reflect badly on police. Public perception is what counts here, especially if police/public relations are an issue, so it matters not that the invasion of an innocent person's privacy was accidental, or that no racism was intended by a series of public disorder arrests: it is sufficient that there is public disquiet about such police action. Policing in a free society must always be by consent.

Ethical questions may arise for pro-active community policing, where police officers receive information that may be of interest to members of the community which may lead to action that in some way interferes with the liberties of an individual who has committed no crime. For example, should the parents of a young person of good behaviour who has struck up a friendship with, and is seen in the company of, a known offender be informed of the relationship? There are also privacy problems when police are aware of the criminal antecedents of individuals moving into an area. Public information about the location of convicted paedophiles is an emotive issue, and Australia, Britain and the United States have established registers of sex offenders. The ethical issues involving release of information for community policing is of a less inflammatory nature, but has many similar features.

Criminal targeting

For many criminal enterprises, there is a world of difference between police, and, indeed, the public, knowing who is responsible for a particular crime or crimes, and being able to prove this beyond reasonable doubt in the criminal courts. There are those persons in society who make a living from crime, and many of these are known to police, and to their family, friends and others in their own milieu as professional burglars or pickpockets or robbers. However, just because A is a habitual burglar the assumption that A has committed any given burglary is no more warranted than the knowledge that B is an electrician automatically leads to the assumption that B was responsible for rewiring a particular house.

In essence, criminal targeting rests on the assumption that if X is a known burglar (or drug dealer, or robber) then X is likely to continue to make a living from this chosen field of criminal enterprise. Rather than working backwards from recently reported burglaries to establish whether X has committed any of them, watching X carefully is likely to lead police to X's next burglary, where X can be arrested, and perhaps evidence found for previous offences also. There are always far fewer criminals than potential victims, and targeting likely offenders is potentially more fruitful and cost effective than targeting likely victims.

Surveillance

There are, in the main, three types of surveillance which can be used against an individual, two static and one mobile. Static surveillance involves seeing or hearing what an individual is doing at a particular place, and typically involves an observation point and camera to photograph or film activities at a particular spot, or listening devices placed at a particular location to relay conversations which may or may not be recorded for use as evidence, or even both at once. Each of these normally requires two officers on duty constantly while the surveillance is maintained, usually 24 hours per day. Mobile surveillance involves a team of officers who follow and watch the suspect for a period of time. For logistical reasons, all surveillance must be used sparingly, as it is labour intensive, requiring at least six officers per day on eight-hour shifts for static 24-hour surveillance and even more for mobile surveillance, especially if the person watched is likely to notice the watchers.

Any sort of surveillance amounts to an invasion of privacy. There are two categories of people whose rights need to be considered with regard to surveillance: those members of the public whose actions are likely to be seen and noted, even though they have no involvement with any offence, and the individuals who are the targets of surveillance and may later face prosecution. Although the rights of innocent members of the public may well be thought to be of more importance, nevertheless the target of the surveillance is entitled under law to the presumption of innocence, and, as a notionally innocent person, to individual liberty and privacy.

The ethical issues of some aspects of surveillance are addressed, at least in part, by the requirement to obtain a warrant for phone taps or listening devices, which are treated by the law as invasions of privacy akin to searches of premises, which have always required warrants. This is by no means the case for all methods of surveillance in all jurisdictions, for example the use of visual and photographic surveillance of an individual in public areas. Even when a warrant is required, the law's concerns are mainly that the rights of the suspect are not compromised, that there are good and sufficient reasons for suspecting the individual and that the surveillance is likely to turn up evidence against that person. In short the law provides the general power to invade an individual's privacy provided that certain specified conditions are met: those conditions usually have little to do with individuals who might be affected other than the suspect.

It is worthy of note that it may not be necessary for surveillance on an individual to be continuous. Criminals, like the rest of society, are creatures of habit, and tend to meet in particular places, visit particular pubs or clubs, and commit the same sort of offences time after time. If a particular criminal is a target, particularly if that individual is active in comparatively minor crime, then police resources will probably amount to light surveillance. This means that police will not sit outside the suspect's home waiting, but if the suspect is seen on the streets, then that person might be followed for a short time just to determine whether a crime is contemplated. Such surveillance requires no warrant, but relies on increased, and possibly covert, attention when the target happens to be seen while out and about.

Privacy issues in full surveillance

The television images of the destruction of the World Trade Center's twin towers repeated over weeks and months helped to sow the seeds of a world-wide fear of terrorism. Much as the visceral loathing of paedophiles swept aside ethical concerns of privacy to establish public registers of sex offenders, so the fear of terrorism has allowed governments to provide greater powers for intelligence gatherers, setting expedience, in some cases, above hard-won individuals' rights. This includes greater powers to detain suspects without a court appearance, and increased surveillance powers for use against terrorist suspects. Many countries have made or extended such provisions since September 2001.

The use of electronic listening devices in surveillance must generally be authorised at a very high level.[3] Although the subject of the surveillance must be named in the warrant, each use of the device involves surveillance of other persons: generally little harm is done as most calls are mundane. Nevertheless, telephone tapping is an invasion of privacy for both parties to the conversation, trivially so in many cases, in such cases as ordering a pizza, but many non-criminal conversations may nevertheless involve matters that innocent individuals would prefer to be kept confidential. The same, of course, applies to visual surveillance, especially if the place being watched allows access to the public where innocent people may be observed, and possibly even recorded, doing things they would rather keep private. If drug dealing is being carried out in a particular public lavatory, for example, then a surveillance camera may well be installed to catch the offenders, but collaterally record many individuals in what is essentially a private act. Whenever surveillance occurs, it risks including innocent, unwitting individuals.

The more surveillance increases, the more likely innocent individuals are to be subjected to it. Not all of the surveillance is carried out by police, and private security cameras pose a major threat to privacy. There have been cases of cameras installed for security being used to spy on (usually) female patrons in shop changing rooms, pub lavatories and casinos. While not under police control, security cameras can be used by police. Many city centres have surveillance cameras running more or less continuously, major roads have traffic cameras, and all of these are capable of providing evidence in serious cases,[4] but may also bring to notice individuals who are not breaking the law but who nevertheless would prefer their actions not to

---

3   In Australia, the power to insert listening devices is covered federally by the *Australian Federal Police Act* 1979 (Cth) and the *Customs Act* 1901 (Cth) and requires a warrant signed by a judge of the Federal Court. State law in Australia makes similar provisions, and in Britain the Home Secretary's consent is required for telephone tapping.

4   A goods vehicle used by the IRA in the City of London Bishopsgate bombing in 1993 was subsequently traced back along its route using traffic cameras.

come to light. The simplest example would be two people, married but not to each other, who are caught on camera near a serious crime, and who are believed to be witnesses to that crime. If that photograph is made public in an attempt to trace them, there are major implications for their right to privacy.

The first ethical issue is how to protect the privacy of those innocent individuals who just happen to be caught by surveillance, and who would rather not have their actions noted, recorded or publicised, especially as they have breached no law. To some extent this has always happened: a few people have always been unlucky enough to have a speeding or parking ticket, or be spotted on television as one of the crowd at a cricket match, in circumstances difficult to explain to a spouse or employer. Increased use of surveillance increases these risks, and real ethical problems arise about how such information is to be used. It demonstrates insufficient concern for individual rights and privacy for police to claim that a person who has committed no crime has nothing to fear, and that in order to deal with serious crime no thought should be given to what happens to persons collaterally involved who are not prosecuted. Care should be taken to ensure that no unpleasant consequence befalls any individual who is unfortunate enough to be involved in surveillance.

The question arises as to how the problem of the reluctant witnesses mentioned earlier should be handled. Just because they are photographed and identifiable does not give police the right to publish that photograph in order to trace them, although the interests of justice, if the crime is serious enough, might suggest otherwise. Police management must establish ethical guidelines for surveillance operations before this ceases to be a hypothetical problem and real instances occur where individuals are aggrieved by what, in military circles, is termed "collateral damage". It is noteworthy that a witness might only be shown to be reluctant if that individual fails to volunteer information to police after some publicity: it is probably wiser not to publish surveillance photographs of witnesses immediately, before the persons identifiable have an opportunity to offer information. If witnesses can be persuaded to come forward by publicising the fact that their photographs have been obtained their privacy can be retained and photographs only published in circumstances of absolute necessity.

The rights of the subject of the surveillance also need to be preserved. It may well be that the evidence which is brought before a judge as grounds for authorising a phone tap must be obtained by other forms of surveillance first. To become aware of being the object of police surveillance in itself is threatening, and from the perspective of the subject of surveillance, the feeling of being stalked may well occur before the realisation that the "stalker" is in fact a police surveillance officer. To assume from the outset that the suspect is guilty and to carry out surveillance in such a manner as to harass the suspect is, perhaps, a hi-tech equivalent of the use or threats of physical violence used to obtain admissions from suspects in the past. Surveillance is a breach of the privacy to which we are all entitled, and, whether or not it requires a warrant, police organisations must consider ethical guidelines and bounds for its use.[5] The ethical standards which are set should at the very least be sufficient to protect the privacy requirements of prevailing public sentiment and any directives or comments made by the courts.

Surveillance and offences revealed

Surveillance may sometimes provide evidence of other offences not connected with the operation being undertaken. Suppose a surveillance operation is under way which targets a major drug-dealing ring. The surveillance has involved 10-15 officers over several weeks, and is likely to lead to a number of arrests and very serious charges being laid. During the later stages of this surveillance, officers hidden in a vehicle in the street witness an offence being committed by two persons who are totally unconnected with the drugs observation. Ethical issues concern the extent to which the operation giving rise to the surveillance could or should be compromised by officers taking action on other offences, or the extent to which these officers are justified in turning a blind eye to matters on which they can give evidence sufficient to obtain a conviction for that offence in the courts in order to continue the surveillance.

The obvious answer is that the wider interests of the community are better served by ignoring minor offences, such as those which involve disorderly conduct, or are victimless crimes in which no member of the public suffers, in order to gain evidence against the drug dealers. Let us hypothesise that surveillance officers are unable to call other police officers to deal with the following incidents, so they and they alone are responsible for permitting or preventing the crime by exercising their discretion whether or not to effect an arrest:

- two persons are observed stealing from parked cars;
- two persons are observed stealing cars;
- two persons start fighting, and one is injured;
- two persons start fighting with knives, guns or other weapons;
- a woman is seen struggling with a man, who hits her;
- a woman is seen struggling with an man, who may be attempting to rape her.

In most police discipline codes, allowing an offence to take place is a clear dereliction of duty. Although in the first three and fifth of the examples above police observers might be justified in taking no action, of the fourth and sixth certainly it would seem hard to argue that the greater good of the community outweighed the likely harm about to be committed

---

5   Use of surveillance has been closely scrutinised by the courts also, resulting in some case law affecting police procedures and policy. In Australia, *Green v R* (1996) 85 A Crim R 229 in the WA Court of Criminal Appeal is particularly relevant. I am grateful to Andrew Stewart for bringing this case to my notice.

on its individual members. The same problem arises when the subject of the surveillance is seen to commit offences other than those connected with the operation. Clearly, the evidence gained by surveillance of minor drug offences or dealing with stolen property may be used later in court as these other offences may well become the subject of charges. However, the offences seen may involve serious harm or immediate potential harm to other individuals. Police may see the individual take quantities of alcohol and drugs, then drive a car putting innocent people's lives at risk. Indeed, an accident may happen, and the suspects drive off. Likewise, an assault on another gang member might result in serious injury, or even death. It is by no means clear at what point the surveillance team should stop being objective observers, and move in to arrest and prevent further harm. There is some anecdotal evidence that surveillance teams have become aware of quite serious offences taking place unconnected with their observation.

The more commonly that targeting of criminals and surveillance of any sort is adopted as a police strategy, the more likely it is that ethical questions arise about the involvement of surveillance officers who observe offences in progress. The matter is one which should exercise the minds of police executives, in order that guidelines or policy can be produced for officers undertaking surveillance duties, perhaps with the assistance of the judiciary who will increasingly have to decide on admissibility and other issues connected with evidence obtained by surveillance.

Selection of target criminals

If information-led policing strategies are to be carried out by targeting individual criminals, then police need to be able to justify their selection of targets. For many years, police officers have come to know their local criminals and vice versa. If officers stop, question or search a local criminal for no other reason than that that individual is known to have a criminal record, this exceeds the officer's powers, and, if done frequently, may constitute harassment. The police strategy of criminal targeting must have a more substantive basis for target selection than merely selecting targets from the known local criminal population in turn, as this may be perilously close to an officially authorised and institutionally approved policy of harassment of local criminals. At the very least, targets must be selected on the ground that they are currently actively involved in local crime.

Most legislation granting police powers stipulates that those powers cannot be exercised without a good reason antecedent to the exercise of the power, aptly expressed in the American phrase "probable cause". The grounds for the exercise of the power of search under *Police and Criminal Evidence Act* 1984 (UK) for example, must be present before the search, and, indeed, before the person is questioned before the search:

> The reasonable grounds for suspicion which are necessary for the exer-
> cise of the initial power to detain may be confirmed or eliminated as a
> result of the questioning of a person detained for the purposes of search

... but the reasonable grounds for suspicion without which any search is unlawful cannot be retrospectively provided by such questioning ... [or] refusal to answer any question.[6]

The principle behind this is clear: to maintain the civil liberties of all individuals, police may not exercise powers of search without a pre-existing reason to do so; police powers do not allow fishing expeditions using random searches in the hope that something will be found. By extension of this principle, if an individual is to become a target for any form of surveillance, there must be a pre-existing justification for selecting that individual as a target. It is casual police attention which is most likely to give rise to claims by the target of harassment or unjustified stops and searches. These are issues which police management would do well to consider before target selection, and perhaps even before targeting criminals is adopted as a strategy, rather than have to discover post hoc justifications when a target complains of police action.

Targeting active criminals is a sound, responsible policing strategy. However, targeting known criminals may well be harassment. The difference is the question of whether the criminal is truly active immediately before being targeted. If there are reasonable grounds for suspecting that an individual is active as a criminal, then there may be some justification for that person's nomination as a target. Even then, only half the selection issue has been addressed, that of showing that an individual is active: it is unlikely that the individual selected is the only active criminal in the area, and there should also be reasons for selecting that individual in preference to others. Of the criminals living within a police station area, any number of them might be known or suspected to be active. Unless all the active criminals can be targeted at once, police must be in a position to offer some objective justification for selecting those few who are targeted. Rightly or wrongly, allegations of selection on racial grounds may be made, or victimisation because an individual has complained against police, or because of a recent acquittal at court. It may, indeed should, be easy to justify the suspicion that an individual is an active criminal – it may be more difficult to justify the claim that that individual is more worthy of targeting than other active criminals.

The ethics of zero tolerance strategies

The term "zero tolerance" may be no longer popular in New York where it originated, but it has gained common currency to describe policing strategies which rely on making numbers of arrests for offences, usually fairly minor, in a particular area. Henry (1996) claims it is a problem-solving approach which differs from others "primarily in the emphasis it places on rapidly identifying and aggressively responding to crime problems and in the high-technology methods and information exchange

---

6   Codes of Practice Para 2.3 for the Exercise by Police Officers of Statutory Powers of Stop and Search, *Police and Criminal Evidence Act* 1984 (UK).

systems it uses".[7] Zero tolerance implies that police coercive powers are used against each and every perpetrator of a particular type of offence to stop the commission of those offences, which may be the best method, or at least an effective method, in dealing with some policing problems, but is not a panacea for every problem.

The theoretical justification for an aggressive response to crime problems lies in Wilson and Kelling's "broken windows" theory (Wilson and Kelling, 1982). This theory suggests that once a neighbourhood starts to suffer from unrepaired broken windows, unweeded gardens and graffiti, it will rapidly disintegrate to a level where it is perceived that nothing can be done, and residents sink into acceptance of petty theft, vandalism and a diminished quality of life. If the neighbourhood maintains the struggle against urban decay, and police do their part working with the community, then urban decay may be checked and reversed, and the quality of life improved. Significant disagreement arises about what, precisely, the role of police is. Community policing theorists approve of such strategies as police coordinating community and local government to deal with vacant or derelict premises used by drug dealers and prostitutes (see, for example, Farrell, 1988), while zero-tolerance theory suggests that the police role should be to give the community confidence by dealing firmly but lawfully with such offenders.

The issue revolves around police treatment of what are termed "quality-of-life" offences. While most people are concerned about being burgled, attacked or having their cars stolen, the actual likelihood of any given person being the victim of such a crime is quite low, although public perception may well be that it is high. However, an encounter with beggars, rowdy youths, drunks, or evidence of drugs is common, and graffiti is everywhere, so most city-dwellers are likely to be confronted with these sorts of crime almost daily. The unpleasantness of this pervasive criminality reduces the quality of life for members of society, and it is these petty offences rather than the more serious ones which cause most general disquiet.

Zero tolerance strategies address quality of life offences directly, by actively targeting perpetrators, and feeding them into the justice system by arrest or summons, however petty the offence may seem in itself. Previously, conventional wisdom had it that such minor offences were too numerous to be dealt with, and that police efforts were better conserved for more serious crimes. Zero tolerance theorists counter-claim that those people who are likely to commit serious crime are unlikely to baulk at minor crime, and if police stop the minor crime then in so doing they tend to apprehend serious offenders preparatory to a major offence. Superficially, there appears to be no ethical problem in dealing with offenders for minor offences, providing arrests are lawful, and the manner in which they are carried out is correct; however, there are underlying issues which may cause long-term problems for policing.

---

7   The "information exchange systems" Henry refers to is Compstat, discussed in detail in Henry, 2002.

Scales of tolerance

It is implicit in the exercise of zero tolerance that the anti-social behaviour against which action is to be taken is execrated by the majority, if not all, of the community. This assumption is questionable, but the rather weaker assumption that it encompasses, that the community in general welcomes police action against petty offenders, is also dubious. With regard to the first assumption, there are wildly differing views on acceptable behaviours throughout most communities often, but not always, on age, gender and ethnic divisions, and what one group sees as anti-social may well not be viewed in that fashion by others. Even more dubious is the assumption that the general community would accept that prosecution was the best answer to behaviour which was only mildly offensive.

One example of this is the unauthorised street musicians or buskers to be found in many shopping malls or thoroughfares. In London, for example, buskers are frequently found in Underground Stations, or in popular tourist areas like Covent Garden Market.[8] The buskers on the Underground show varying levels of musical ability and attempt an extraordinary range of musical styles, and passers-by may be either entertained or appalled by the noise: judging by the amount of money collected, the entertainment level varies markedly. All these buskers are operating illegally, but few travellers are incensed enough to demand their removal: in fact, the reverse seems to apply, in that whether or not they like the music, many passers-by are disturbed by efforts by London Transport staff to remove even the worst musicians.

The general feeling perhaps is that if persons are in breach of the law but doing no great harm, they should be left alone. Traditional police discretion allows officers to turn a blind eye (or ear) to buskers, however bad their rendition of Presley, Dylan or Mozart, but police will arrest those who wield a guitar as an excuse to beg, and to move on those who have outstayed their welcome. The same applies to other acts which vary from useful to nuisance: some young people with bucket and sponge who wash windscreens at traffic lights may be welcome and perform a service worth a dollar, others may be ineffective in clearing the dust and flies, while still others wield a filthy rag to extort money. Police discretion allows the public choice, and can sort the sheep from the goats in antisocial behaviour, while zero tolerance strategies would have all treated in the same manner.

Zero tolerance approaches to minor public disorder requires a policing decision to be made at, presumably, a fairly senior level, to address a particular problem by arrest or summons of offenders. The ethical issue concerns how that decision is made – in particular, who is to decide that a particular type of minor breach of the law is offensive enough to warrant police time and effort to eradicate it. If the concern is truly felt by all sections of the community, then it may justify a police initiative: if not all sections of the community view the matter with concern, especially if the

---

8   In Covent Garden, buskers are recognised as a tourist attraction and are auditioned first!

issue is confined to a particular neighbourhood where it is not seen as a problem, then police action might be both unnecessary and unwelcome. Certain "quality-of-life" offences such as graffiti and street drug abuse are seen as so generally unacceptable that the public welcomes action: even then, by no means all police action is approved of. Increased prosecutions may not be the best long-term solution, nor may the community approve of high arrest levels.

The concept of zero tolerance policing is associated most readily with New York, its Mayor Giuliani and its former Police Commissioner William Bratton. It remains unclear whether all of the particular targets for police operations were particularly execrated by the community of New York or whether some, at least, were the personal *bêtes noires* of the mayor, which he nominated as crime problems. There is a real danger that inappropriately selected target crimes for zero tolerance strategies may not reflect the needs or desires of the populace, or, worse, have a disproportionate effect on particular sections of the community. Community feeling may be measured in part by the level of complaints against police, which increased by 50 per cent in New York in the years after 1994.

Implications for the community of zero tolerance strategies

It is undeniable that the effect of Bratton's approach in New York has been a dramatic reduction in many categories of crime, but it is by no means clear how much of this can be attributed to the zero tolerance strategy and how much to the more efficient targeting of crime through use of Compstat and other initiatives, or to the increase in police strength by several thousand officers in recent years. An important issue that needs to be addressed is the effect of zero tolerance strategies on the community as a whole.

An apocryphal comment on zero tolerance made by a senior British police officer is "We had zero tolerance once – we called it Toxteth, Brixton and St Pauls". The reference here is to inner-city rioting in areas of Liverpool, London and Bristol with large populations of West Indian descent, triggered by major police drug stop-and-search operations. Although these operations were intended to inhibit street-level drug possession and trafficking offences which had become a problem of epidemic proportions in those areas, they were seen by the West Indian communities as a further example of the ingrained racism of policing because most of the persons stopped were young black males.

The moral to be drawn for zero tolerance strategies is clear: if an aggressive policing strategy is perceived to be racist in conception, or even to have an unfair deleterious impact on one section of the community rather than others, then the harm done to police/public relations may well outweigh the good done by removal of the nuisance, whether it be major or minor. What matters is not whether the strategy actually targets one particular section of the community, but whether it is perceived so to do: the public is frequently wary that police powers may be misused, and perceptions of lack of fairness may increase public unease.

It is worth looking back on some of the issues raised in Chapter 3 about the causes of crime, and some of the characteristics common amongst repeat petty offenders. Those features particularly relevant here are unemployment, illiteracy, drug or alcohol abuse, and membership of particular ethnic groups. With all these, almost of necessity, comes living in a neighbourhood of community deprivation amongst other people with social problems. Such neighbourhoods are likely to be those which suffer the highest incidence of crime, so are most likely to receive extra police attention. It is those neighbourhoods, too, which probably harbour most fear and suspicion of police, and where the most work needs to be done to create and maintain good relations between police and public. Such neighbourhoods are indeed typified by Toxteth, Brixton and St Pauls in Britain, Redfern in Sydney and Watts, South Central Los Angeles[9] or Harlem in the United States.

There is no doubt that the crime problems of poor city areas need to be addressed urgently, or that zero tolerance policing strategies may have an immediate significant impact on them. However, zero tolerance policing is in its very nature confrontational, and involves "aggressive enforcement",[10] sometimes accompanied by a temporary increase in police numbers in a particular area, which is hardly conducive to good relations with the community. Consider how a poor community with a high proportion of Aboriginals, Hispanics, or West Indians would perceive a sudden influx of police intent on prosecuting a disproportionate number of their teenage males in order to prevent a particular form of crime or disorder. If drunkenness is perceived as a nuisance on public transport, then the majority of travellers might well regard a zero tolerance strategy which prevents drunks travelling very highly. However, if the overwhelming preponderance of drunks belong to a particular ethnic group, then this strategy may well have the effect of barring persons of that ethnicity from public transport.

The effect of aggressive prosecution strategies to deal with public order problems may be very difficult to distinguish from the perceived police harassment that the young or members of racial minorities have received for little reason other than their youth or race for years. Police have worked hard to shake off their image as perpetrators of injustice, and much police training has revolved around sensitive treatment of minority groups and multicultural policing.[11] The whole ethos of recent reforms in policing is that of service to the whole community, and much is being done to improve police dealings with groups who have always been fearful of police. This

---

9   This area has been renamed South Los Angeles to erase the stigma that has dogged the area: whether this cosmetic change will affect the social problems is dubious.

10   The phrase "Zero tolerance aggressive policing" was used several times by Albrecht (1998). Less emphasis is placed on zero tolerance and much more on the Compstat process by another NYPD insider (Henry, 2002) to account for crime reduction in New York since 1994.

11   Chan (1997) documents some of these strategies in New South Wales. She observes that much has been done but there is still much to do to eliminate racism from policing in that service.

process could easily be put at risk by zero tolerance strategies, which are open to abuse by those officers who would see it as officially authorised licence to target members of particular groups. The need for police to be seen to be doing something by making arrests can also lead to police malpractice by concocting evidence in order to make the figures look good.

If police can expect that an aggressive policing strategy will result in a preponderance of the persons charged with offences belonging to a particular ethnic group, then it is wilful if not malicious blindness to ignore the possibility that such prosecutions will be seen by most members of that ethnic group as both intimidating and discriminatory. It is insufficient justification to claim that they were all committing offences and therefore merited prosecution. While these strategies may work, and have an appeal both for police and for those whose political platform is for a tough response to crime, it may well be counter-productive for the long-term goal of a safe, peaceful society. The Scarman Report into the Brixton riots in Britain acknowledged the existence of serious crime problems, but stated that public order must be maintained as a priority above upholding the law.[12] This echoes Mayne's insistence in 1829 on the "preservation of public tranquillity" as a primary object of policing.

If a particular problem is identified, then some sort of zero tolerance strategy may be appropriate. It is, however, one of many possibilities that can be used. Farrell's analysis of community policing cites several examples of non-aggressive strategies in community policing to deal with problems. Indeed, since Goldstein (1990), many police efforts have been directed towards identifying and addressing specific issues with the community rather than increasing police patrols, arrests and prosecutions. If a particular city park starts to attract drug dealers or prostitutes, then a few well-organised arrest teams and increased patrolling may, perhaps, nip the problem in the bud, but if an area has been notorious for sex and drugs for years, arrest swoops will have no long-term effect. Such an operation needs thought and planning to ensure that the problem is not merely relocated, and to avoid allegations of harassment or racial bias. There is, therefore, a place for zero tolerance methods, but they must be considered one weapon in the armoury of strategic policing, and not necessarily the weapon of first choice for any problem. The immediate positive results that an aggressive policing strategy has may make it very tempting, but the long-term effects remain when the immediate results are forgotten.

Pro-active intervention which avoids prosecution

The concern addressed in this section is that preventative measures, however effective they might be, may encroach unacceptably on civil liberties or

---

12   The primacy of public order is by no means universally accepted. In a 1998 wharf dispute affecting most Australian ports, some Commissioners of Police expressed a preparedness to risk violence from dockers to uphold the legal right of opposing groups to cross the picket line and collect containers.

individual privacy, and that the ethical implications must be considered very carefully before implementation. This is far from denying the efficacy or value of community policing strategies, but a plea to have two separate questions addressed independently when deciding whether a course of action is justified: first, whether that course of action works and, secondly, whether that course of action is ethically justifiable. A positive answer is required to both, rather than simply the former, before that course of action should be implemented.

There are four particular types of police pro-active intervention strategy which are considered here: social intervention, where police work with the community to deal with causes of crime; diversionary strategies intended to prevent first-time or petty offenders being prosecuted; intervention directed at particular individuals to prevent their engaging in crime; and coercive action taken on behalf of the community against particular recognisable groups within it who are identified by the majority as troublesome.

The ethical problems that arise concern the perception of police action by each section of the community, and the maintenance of individual rights. Police powers are coercive, and any non-coercive police action may well be seen as coercive whenever the member of the public addressed feels that there is no real option to complying with a police request, lest coercive action be taken in this or another matter then or later. If, for example, the manager of a business feels that refusal of a request made by police will result in parking tickets being issued outside the shop, or delayed attendance if the burglar alarm sounds, then a non-coercive request may be seen as coercive. There is a parallel here with the formulaic police statement that some person is "at the police station assisting with inquiries" when that individual has no real choice but to remain as long as police have questions to ask.

Social intervention

In many discussions of crime, public perception and police perception of a problem tally, and pro-active strategies are both worthy and effective. Consider the case of Police Officer Orazem, in New York, which is reported by Farrell in Greene and Mastrofski (1988). On Orazem's beat, burglaries, assaults and drug offences caused the respectable occupants of a small part of Brooklyn considerable problems, and police action by way of sporadic raids and arrests did little to help. After some analysis of the problem, Officer Orazem discovered that the focus of the offences was a derelict vacant corner block used by drug dealers. Deciding that conventional arrest sweeps were ineffective, Orazem sought help both from the local community and from City Hall to deal with the derelict block. Volunteers from the residents and community groups worked to clear the site of rubbish, and donations of materials enabled it to be fenced and a children's playground constructed, transforming the centre of criminal activity into a place benefiting the community. Although this anecdote is probably an extreme example of what community policing initiatives can do, it bears repeating as an example of a joint crime prevention initiative instigated by police to deal with a problem without arrests. Well-targeted police action can also work: community complaints in Railton Road in Brixton, South London in the early 1980s resulted in raids on unlicensed drinking and gambling clubs, and their closure contributed to a significant reduction in street crime in the area.

The claim made in rebuttal of the efficacy of such strategies is that there is nothing to show whether those committing offences at the site gave up or moved their operations elsewhere. Clearly, an individual who is addicted to drugs is not going to give them up because of community action in a particular area, but will find a new drug dealer in a new area. Unless this type of strategy is implemented simultaneously in every derelict block across the city and its environs then the problem will be relocated rather than removed. However, the existence of a known haven for drug dealers and prostitution can instigate additional crime in that area, for example the known availability of drugs at a particular location may encourage those wavering on the edge of the drug scene to experiment. Such strategies may reduce crime, in that it becomes less easy for the potential criminal to get involved, and every such action may result in a small number of offenders failing to relocate. At each successive removal of drug hot-spots, some addicts, at least, will seek treatment programs.

Such strategies as that used by Officer Orazem concern the crime environment rather than specific individuals who may or may not be concerned in crime. In such cases, there is, typically, little power given to police to act in the matter, but police officers become, in effect, co-ordinators of public activity with no power to coerce but authority and knowledge to persuade and advise. If police are genuinely non-coercive then the public can simply refuse to cooperate: Officer Orazem's initiative could have been blocked at almost any stage by a refusal to help on the part of one or more of the volunteer groups or City Hall. Many other community policing initiatives, such as "Blue Light Discos"[13] and sporting activities, rely as much if not more on community support and the willingness of their target groups in particular to participate as they rely on police activity. Directionless young people, for example, can be offered alternatives to the drift into drugs and crime, but cannot be forced to take them. The point is that such initiatives are only valid if the public are under no pressure to take part and only do so as genuinely willing volunteers.

Diversionary strategies

Many diversionary measures aimed at preventing crime in the long term work by avoiding formal prosecution of offenders: the danger here is that,

---

13   An Australian police initiative wherein police volunteers run alcohol and drug free discos for young teenagers when no similar recreation is available: these are also running now in Britain.

while the stigma of conviction is avoided, so too is the answerability of police to the courts. This is not to say that such diversionary measures are inherently dangerous, but that steps need to be taken to ensure such measures are properly supervised. Perhaps an example would be useful here.

In the early 1980s, to reduce pressure on courts, the Metropolitan Police in London were encouraged to give formal cautions to any person arrested for a petty offence with no previous record. The instructions clearly stipulated that the offence must be capable of proof in court before a caution could be considered. Individuals who agreed to accept a caution rather than be taken to court did so on the understanding that the matter would be kept on record for a number of years, and that to accept a caution was to admit the offence. The inherent danger is that an individual could be arrested when the evidence was insufficient, and where there might not, eventually, be enough to prove the case before a court. From the suspect's point of view, it may well be better and quicker to accept a caution, even for an offence that the suspect has not committed, rather than remain in custody while investigations continue, then insist on prosecution to demonstrate innocence which risks possible conviction and punishment for the matter. For police, a caution would seem an easy option to clear up a rather tricky matter expeditiously.

While such a system of cautioning is valid and useful, it requires considerable monitoring and supervision to prevent abuse. Cautions remain on file for a time, and if the suspect is re-arrested for a similar offence, previous cautions are taken into account in deciding whether subsequent matters should be taken to court. To caution without questioning the evidence seriously is to allow poor investigation: under the pressure of work most crime investigators are faced with, the bulk of their efforts must, of necessity, be directed to cases which are destined for the courts. While cautioning may save both time and public money over sending matters to court, the cautioning system must be seen to be effective in preventing further offending behaviour by the individual. Too often the cautions given are seen by all, offenders, police and community, as being no more than a formal indication of disapproval of the crime, rather than a serious attempt to change offending behaviour.[14] It is one thing to accept that a disadvantaged background was a critical factor in a particular offender's behaviour, but quite another to caution that offender without setting in train any procedure to help the offender overcome any underlying problems.[15]

Legislation may also be a means of preventing crime, or at least of diverting it into a less unpleasant form. The clearest example of this is gun

14 Crime prevention may not be the primary intention of cautioning offenders anyway. Western Australia's *Young Offenders Act* 1994, which sanctions the cautioning of juvenile offenders, is premised on diversion and restorative justice, and crime prevention is a secondary consideration.
15 British police, at least, have made some moves here. For many years juvenile bureaux have made inquiries about the home and educational circumstances of young offenders before recommending cautions, and in the late 1990s the Northumbria Constabulary claimed considerable success in assessing the risks offenders pose and their chances of success if helped by a project worker before cautioning.

control legislation in Australia and Britain after incidents in both countries of mass killings by mentally deranged individuals with lawfully obtained weapons. Clearly, any form of restrictive legislation reduces individual liberty to some extent, but in the case of gun control most people in both countries feel that a small restriction imposed upon a small minority is justified by the degree of public safety this encourages. Restrictions on keeping animals in both countries prohibit keeping snakes, tigers and crocodiles as pets, and this too restricts individual liberty: many Australians, and most Britons, consider an individual who desires to have a handgun or semi-automatic rifle as strange as one who desires to have a puff-adder as a pet.

Gun control legislation does reduce the possibility of gun crime and gun suicide. In nations where gun control is stringent people are probably no less violent or suicidal than where such controls are reduced or absent, but controlling guns takes away a remarkably easy way of causing death or serious injury. It is worth remembering that hand guns and assault rifles are made for the express purpose of killing human beings: since this is their design function, they should be expected to be effective for this purpose, albeit that this is usually illegal. In homes where there is a gun, this is likely to be a factor in any accidental death, suicide or homicide of one of the occupants. Individuals who fight with fists, bottles, sticks or even knives are far more likely to survive than those who have recourse to guns. Controlling guns diverts assaults and self-harm into more generally survivable forms.

Legislation intended to prevent crime may have an effect the antithesis of that desired. The *Pawnbrokers Act* 1994 passed in Western Australia to make it more difficult for offenders to sell the televisions, VCRs and other typical proceeds of domestic burglaries did reduce the number of domestic burglaries significantly, but it diverted property crime into significantly more unpleasant forms: the number of handbag snatches and street robberies for cash increased, as did incidents of victims being forced to draw money from ATMs, and hand over cash to the offenders. This is, fortunately, a rare example of legislation to ameliorate one problem actually creating a worse one.

Pre-emptive action against potential offenders

Western governments are, rightly, concerned with maintaining individual liberty and rights, and the principle that no individual should suffer punishment without a fair trial goes back to the Magna Carta. The Constitutions of liberal democratic political systems uphold the rights of the individual over government, but as Hayek (1960) and Nozick (1974) have shown, those governments in themselves constitute the largest single restrictive force on any individual in society. One of the most important organs of government power is the police force, which has always been subject to restrictions imposed through the judicial system.

The whole *raison d'être* of pro-active policing is that it involves police action being taken before a crime occurs, or to stop crime in general without necessarily taking action against specific criminals. This being so, pro-active police action is no longer controlled by the judicial supervision or legislative sanctions which exist whenever an offender is charged with an offence. This does not mean that pro-active policing against potential, rather than actual, offenders is necessarily wrong or undemocratic or unconstitutional, but that its ethical implications need to be very clearly analysed and understood. There are two particular examples of police action which will be considered here: one involves an analysis of the action that police are entitled to take when a young person who has committed no offence is frequently found in the company of known young offenders, and the second is the extent to which police are entitled to let the community know of the dangers posed by recently released prisoners.

Suppose a police officer in a community policing role sees a group of four young persons, three of whom the officer knows to have been involved in minor public order offences, possession of cannabis and petty theft. The fourth the officer does not know, but obtains the individual's name and address, and discovers that the person has never been involved in any criminal activity. The four are dealt with amicably, no offences being apparent on this occasion, although it is strongly suspected that the three who have previously come to notice are still actively engaged in crime. Several times over the next two weeks the same officer sees all four youths together, although never in circumstances to suggest that they have committed, or are about to commit, any offence together.

It is, perhaps, rather less likely that the young person of good character is an agent for change of the others and is leading them away from crime, than that the three known (and putatively active) young criminals are involving the other individual in the sort of misbehaviour that has previously brought them to notice. There is, however, no evidence of that individual committing crime. The ethical question concerns what the officer should do. Clearly, the officer cannot compel the young person to find new friends, but it is not clear whether it is justifiable for police to speak to the individual's parents. Police working with the community have a duty to give information relevant to preventing crime, and to obtain information for that purpose, but issues of privacy and individual rights and liberty apply when all that can be imputed is guilt by association.

The young person's parents are likely to see the matter in a quite different light if their child is later arrested with the others, and have not been informed by police that all four have been seen by police in company for some time. The ethics of giving or withholding information when no crime has been committed, but criminal action is anticipated, needs to be considered by community police officers. The more effective police are in the community, the more likely they are to have such information and the more frequently decisions will have to be made about whether or not it is to be divulged.

A similar problem arises with informing a community if a person with convictions for serious offences joins it. Australia, Britain and the United

States have all recently passed legislation concerned with informing communities about paedophiles released from prison, so for that particular type of offence informing the community may well be a statutory obligation. While it is wrong to assume that an individual released from prison is unlikely to re-offend, indeed the opposite is often more likely to be the case, individuals who have served their sentences will stand no chance in society unless there is some possibility of a fresh start with a clean slate for them to overcome the disadvantage of their criminal history. Once again, the privacy and individual liberty of a previous offender must be balanced against the needs of the community to be protected. Police in the community have the information, have a duty to the community, but are also bound by the law and the obligation to uphold individual rights. There is no clear answer to the problem – it is an ethical and civil libertarian issue which must be addressed by the police service as an organisation and by police officers as individuals.

This issue has indeed given rise to practical policing problems. In Britain, a group of paedophiles convicted in 1989 of offences concerning the disappearance of a young boy[16] served the sentences they were given, and were released. There was every indication that these individuals would commit further offences (the leader of the gang, Sidney Cooke, having never accepted treatment or admitted guilt), and were generally understood to be extremely dangerous to children. Local press publicity which warned parents that one of the men was in a particular area served only to cause him to disappear completely, while another spent some weeks in a police station under police protection. An individual who has served the sentence of the court is entitled under the law to liberty, privacy and freedom from harassment, however odious the crime and the perceived likelihood of that individual committing further offences. Once an offender is released, having served the full sentence, the slate is clean: if individuals present a real risk to the community, then legislation is required to prolong their detention.

Coercive requests made of groups

The police and the community may well agree on the need to take action against, for example, car theft and domestic burglary, but police attention may well also be drawn by the public to "quality-of-life" issues, where no specific offences have been committed, but some members of the public feel upset or threatened by others. The police, the public and the persons involved may well have radically different perceptions of what is actually going on, and whether the behaviour complained of is within the powers of

---

16 The Jason Swift case. Because of evidential issues a charge of murder was not possible, and the group responsible were convicted of manslaughter and given determinate sentences. While a person released from a life sentence would be on licence, and therefore liable to recall to prison, release at the expiry of a determinate sentence gives unconditional freedom. As a result of public disquiet over this case in 1998 legislation was introduced to provide indeterminate sentences for paedophiles.

police to deal with as anti-social. Consider, for example, groups of unemployed teenagers gathering and passing time in a particular public place. From the perspective of the respectable, middle-aged citizen, this is a group of teenagers who ought to be at school, university or work, who are creating noise and nuisance with, perhaps, bad language and horseplay, distressing people going about their lawful business in a shopping mall, park or thoroughfare for considerable periods of time. From the perspective of the teenagers, they have nothing particular to do, not a great deal of money to spend, and find that particular public place a convenient spot to meet their mates and pass the time in talk about football, surfing and music, with the occasional bout of minor misbehaviour. There is no inherent difference in behaviour between this group of teenagers and a group of an older generation meeting in a pub for a few beers, and talk about football, interest rates and motor-bikes.

Police who are endeavouring to establish a rapport with the local community are likely to have their attention drawn to groups of teenagers, and asked to deal with them. Owners of businesses, for example, may well feel that groups outside their shops drive away trade, and the elderly in particular may well be unwarrantedly frightened of groups of youths. It is quite possible that police will consider youthful bad behaviour unpleasant, and be inclined to assist by moving the youths on – some, at least, of the young people may be known to the officers from previous encounters. The public expectation that police should do something about the nuisance is high, especially if community policing in that area has strengthened the belief that police are there to help solve social problems. The police may have an equally strong desire to assist, in part because they disapprove of the young people's behaviour, and in part to increase public support.

The most attractive course of action for police may well be to exercise their coercive powers to the limit, or even somewhat past it, to deal with the problem by questioning, searching and moving on the youths involved. The short-term effect of this action is to restore peace, while the medium-term effect may be to relocate this particular group somewhere else. However, the long-term effect is deleterious to relations between police and young people, and can lead to even less co-operation with police from young people who are best placed to know more about juvenile crime than any other group. If this sort of action does not result in any formal court appearance by any of the teenagers, then the legality of the police action remains unchallenged as the accountability of police to the judiciary is sidestepped. Those who have requested the assistance of police in this matter are likely to approve, while the young people may well feel harassed.

The more difficult option for police is to decline to take any coercive action in this situation. To take no action leaves a public order problem of little importance to the criminal law, but of major concern to that section of the public with whom police often feel most sympathy, the respectable, hard-working majority. There is a significant difference between the sort of concerted action by police and community to change the environment to remove crime illustrated by the example of Officer Orazem, and police action in response to the wishes of one section of the community which coerces another section of the community into changing their behaviour, particularly when that behaviour, albeit anti-social, is not unlawful.

The ethical issue, then, comes down to this. Many community policing initiatives involve police officers as knowledgable authority figures who can co-ordinate action to remove or prevent criminal activity. Nevertheless, these same police officers, by virtue of their office, retain coercive powers to maintain public order in the widest sense, and in a healthy democracy these powers are properly used and carefully monitored. However, it is possible for occasions to arise when these powers can be misused, with the best of intentions, and the normal inhibitory factors waived. This problem is by no means insurmountable, and in no way detracts from the value of community policing. It is, however, a matter which needs to be addressed sooner rather than later, lest policing methods overtake policing ethics in the same way that technological advance has apparently overtaken ethical decision-making in medicine. Ethical questions must also consider whose ethical standards are to be adopted, whether they are those of the community at large, which is by no means easy to establish in a multicultural community, those of the chief officer of police, those of the mayor or town council, or some objective standards established by, for example, the International Court of Human Rights.

Management issues

Modern policing strategies are very much driven by the need to obtain measurable results, often in terms of an improvement in crime statistics. Both Albrecht (1998) and Henry (1996 and 2002), for example, insist that the New York Police Department's approach since 1994 has relied heavily on supervisory officers working with the crime patterns generated by the Compstat system and devising means of reducing the incidence of crime. Change in policing strategies elsewhere has involved middle police management in taking innovative measures and demonstrating the success of their innovation. Taken too far, this can result in panic management, rapid changes in style and direction, and unnecessary response to minor changes in crime patterns. At worst, this can also result in schemes directed at creating an impression of improvement by addressing the statistics alone, without any genuine effect on crime in the streets.

Modern management methods emphasise the setting of goals and objectives which are capable of measurement. While many of the objectives of policing are not obviously amenable to measurement, for example maintaining public tranquillity or allaying the fear of crime, reported crime and arrest rates are eminently suitable for quantitative evaluation. What management does need to ensure is that the goals and objectives chosen are those relevant to policing, and they are not chosen primarily because of their amenability to measurement. Consider the setting of goals concerning the answering of calls. It is relevant to a professional organisation that all telephone calls are answered promptly, not left to ring unanswered for several minutes, and also that a response is given to written communication, even if only an acknowledgment, within a short space of time. Both these are relevant and measurable criteria. What is also easily measurable, but much less relevant, is the time taken for police to attend a call from the public once it has been received.

Much stress is put by police management and the public on the time taken for police to attend calls for assistance. Certainly, if a serious criminal offence is taking place, a fight with knives or a burglary in progress, then police need to be at the scene as quickly as possible. However, most calls are to less serious incidents, or to crimes which have been committed some time before but have only just been discovered. If a person calls police from a car park to report a stolen car, there is little need for police to be at the scene in two or three minutes: arguably, there is little police can do there other than to give the victim a lift. If police management use time taken to respond to calls as a criterion of efficiency, this will do little to improve performance and may even impair it. A rush to attend non-urgent matters can leave too few police available to attend to more serious incidents, or encourage officers to spend too little time on one call to complete it effectively before leaving for the next one. There is, however, an important issue concerning public expectation of police, and, if police do not attend non-urgent matters immediately, there must be some public education explaining the rationale behind this decision.

Police management is being called upon to improve the performance of police organisations. It is required to do this through new or improved strategies, and to show it has been done by measurable criteria. The pace of change in policing is such that it is tempting for police management to change strategies too often, which can both prevent proper evaluation and also confuse the officers who have to implement new systems. A strategy needs to be given time to settle, minor running adjustments made, then left to develop and be assessed. Some strategies, particularly those associated with community policing, are designed for the long rather than the short term, and quick results cannot be expected. The issue for police management is, therefore, to determine what will count as a positive outcome for a policing strategy, and, equally importantly, when that outcome can reasonably be expected. The officers implementing it, if they are conscientious and committed, will be demoralised if expectations are too high and too immediate, or, worse, if the strategy is replaced before it has been given a chance to be productive. Timing is critical: a mistaken strategy should be revised or withdrawn as soon as it can be shown to be unproductive, but this may well take time to discover.

Police management has many opportunities to behave in a less than ethical fashion in a police service in a state of change where management is under pressure to succeed. The first and most obvious risk is that figures are manipulated in order to make schemes appear more successful than they are, or to produce apparent efficiencies where these do not really exist. The second possibility is to impose as a new strategy something which has been tried elsewhere, with a few minor variations, in order to play safe with a slight, but guaranteed, improvement where a more radical change might have been of greater benefit. The third, and most dangerous, policy is for a member of middle management to devise a strategy of startling immediate impact without thought being given to its long-term development, and using the claimed success of this before it is fully evaluated in order to gain kudos or a more prestigious post.[17]

The moral here is for police executives rather than police management. In order for strategies to be developed and assessed, the officers in charge should be given sufficient length of time in post to see the strategies through to the end, and accept responsibility, praise or blame for their success or failure. The tendency to reshuffle senior officers too frequently can be just as counterproductive to the development of a 21st century police service as leaving them in post to ossify over a number of years.

Conclusion

Developments in almost every field of human endeavour in the latter half of the 20th century brought with them ethical problems. The development of medical science which can save lives in previously hopeless disease and disability has led to questions of who should benefit and be saved, and who should be left untreated. Cloning of sheep has led to ethical questions on whether it could or should be used for humans, and the genetic mapping of inherited diseases has led to questions concerning the ethics of genetic engineering, and the ownership of patented genetic maps. It is insufficient for the developers of these technologies to concern themselves only with the techniques, and leave ethical concerns about their application to others.

The same problem arises with new developments in theories and strategies of policing. This chapter has demonstrated some of the issues which arise with some of the more popular new policing strategies, not to provide answers, but to demonstrate the dangers of implementing strategies without thought being given to the ethical and other problems which will, eventually, be raised concerning them. As every advance in technology can be used for good or ill, and many open the possibility of new forms of criminal activity (the pornography industry was revolutionised by the digital camera and the Internet) as well as being a source of information, so, too, every new police strategy can be open to abuse or misuse, and carry its own dangers. It is irresponsible for policing strategies to be put in place

---

17 There was rather a spate of this in the early 1990s in Britain, brought about perhaps by the recruitment of officers above the rank of chief inspector nationally, rather than within a single police organisation. The somewhat scathing title "butterflies" was coined for officers who developed a highly publicised strategy for one service, and claimed this "success" before it was fully evaluated as a stepping-stone for promotion into one of the other 43 services in England and Wales.

without thought being given to their potential hazards or foreseeable diffi-culties and policy or guidelines effectively communicated with regard to them.

CHAPTER 8

ETHICS, DISCIPLINE, AND THE BEHAVIOUR OF INDIVIDUAL POLICE OFFICERS

Introduction

Probably the issue of greatest public concern in policing after crime itself is the way in which individual officers behave. Media reports of police corruption and violent or racist behaviour used by individual officers and use of the term "cop culture" in an invariably negative way have led even people who have had no dealings with police at all to become armchair critics, and to have firm ideas about the need to eliminate such behaviour from policing. "Cop culture" implies that police officers can be expected to behave in a way that is to a greater or lesser extent racist or sexist, and liable to address members of the public in a manner that can be rude, over-bearing or even outright violent. Furthermore, even though not all police are given to strengthening or concocting evidence, nor are they all openly corrupt, "cop culture" (or so it is claimed) forces those officers who are honest, polite, non-violent, non-racist and non-sexist to appear to condone such behaviour by their peers by closing ranks and failing to speak out against their colleagues.

Underlying the public concern about police behaviour is the question of why, precisely, the behaviour of police causes so much more public concern than the behaviour of other groups within society. To a greater or lesser extent, every occupation or profession has its own culture and behavioural standards (computer culture seems even to have its own language), and although the spotlight falls from time to time on corruption in business or politics, or violence by night club bouncers or football stewards, or racism within service industries, there is no sustained public pressure to eradicate such behaviour. Surveys of how various groups and professions within society are seen by the public usually result in police being at or near the top in public confidence and approval, which is inconsistent with the belief that police are to be singled out for criticism as violent, racist and corrupt.

The police officer has, under the law, great power over individuals. Even in a modern democracy with an accessible and accountable police service, the first reaction of most people to an approach from the police is to wonder what they have done wrong. Police officers have authority and, irrespective of whether the individual or the uniform engenders respect, there is an awareness that challenging police authority has its dangers. It is this representation of authority and potential for exercise of lawful power that is clearly expressed by Goldstein:

> The police, by their very function, are an anomaly in a free society ... The specific form of their authority – to arrest, to search, to detain and to use force – is awesome in the degree to which it can be disruptive of freedom, invasive of privacy and sudden and direct in its impact on the individual. And this awesome authority, of necessity, is delegated to individuals at the lowest level of bureaucracy to be exercised, in most cases without prior review and control. (Goldstein, 1979)

Part, at least, of the basis for concern about police ethics is that the impact of instances of police malpractice is greater for both individuals and society as a whole than malpractice among, for example, car salesmen or accountants. Police officers are invested with a greater degree of directly applicable power over their fellow citizens than any other group in society: furthermore, the degree of autonomy given to individual officers in their exercise of that power allows even the most junior officer patrolling the streets a level of decision-making normally reserved for senior persons in any other government and non-government organisation. Every decision to stop, question or search an individual is an infringement of liberty, and every arrest is both an infringement of liberty and an exercise of force against the individual. Police officers are the only persons routinely armed to carry out their duties, and the use of handcuffs, for example, is unexceptional in carrying out an arrest in many jurisdictions, if not an actual procedural directive. A further cause for concern is that police powers are most likely to be exercised by those officers who have most to do with the public, that is officers on general patrol duties, who are, typically, junior in rank and young in both age and police experience.

If a restaurant owner refuses to serve an individual on grounds of race or sexist behaviour occurs in the workplace, it is unacceptable and may well be unlawful: the victim may, however, challenge this behaviour either immediately or by reporting the incident to the relevant authority. If a police officer exhibits racist behaviour, this usually takes the form of an abuse of authority or legal powers, for example routinely questioning or searching members of a particular ethnic group. A challenge to such police behaviour can escalate a poor interaction into a disastrous confrontation. A stop and search motivated by racist stereotyping, if challenged, can result in an enforced search, and if this is resisted and a scuffle ensues there may well be an arrest for assault on, or obstruction of, a police officer. Such police actions have implications for civil liberties which should, perhaps, be considered far more serious than the refusal of a racist restaurateur to serve a member of an ethnic minority, and a criminal conviction is a far worse outcome than a missed meal.[1]

---

1   This is not to suggest that any instance of racism within society is trivial, but to make the point that one incident involving a racist police officer can have a permanently damaging effect by leaving the victim with a criminal record.

It is the fact that much police malpractice has the form of an abuse of authority or a misuse of legal power with a direct effect upon individual members of the community which renders it significantly more serious than similar behaviour by other groups within society. Police organisations typically operate with both a Code of Ethics and a Discipline Code, and this chapter considers the roles of each of these. It also considers the standards of behaviour which should be expected of police or considered acceptable by the community, and ways of promoting these. Finally, the chapter reviews the individual and organisational issues involved in investigating complaints and the ethics of pro-active measures specifically intended to eliminate police corruption.

Ethics and discipline codes

There are three distinct influences which regulate the behaviour of individuals: their personal ethical system which is, in part, a product of their culture, the code of ethics which applies to them professionally and any discipline code within their terms of employment. The strongest of these is the personal code, which is founded in an individual's beliefs and values and manifested in the adoption of particular attitudes which in turn result in behaviour. To each individual the most important of these are the beliefs and values which in part determine identity, but to the rest of the world an individual's behaviour is most important, in that it alone impinges on other people. Some individuals may feel offended by encountering a woman in unduly skimpy clothing, or shrouded in an Islamic burqa, in their local shopping mall: their feelings are personal and real, but are only harmful if they are expressed in abuse of either woman, or an attempt to cover one or disrobe the other. Everyone, including police officers, is entitled to irrational likes or dislikes, of Fords, beetroot or persons from Texas. What matters is that an individual's behaviour towards others in the professional context does not betray feelings of bias. An individual's religious or ethical views may lead that person to see abortion as abhorrent and evil, and is entitled to hold and state those views in the strongest possible terms: nothing, however, can justify that individual in making a physical attack on an abortion clinic, its patients or its staff.

Professional codes of ethics and discipline codes mention various types of behaviour, some of which are proscribed as unacceptable, some prescribed as professional duties, and some described as recommended practices. There is a sharp distinction to be drawn between a code of ethics and an enforceable discipline code, although they may contain common elements, especially when proscribed behaviour is mentioned. The *raison d'être* of a code of ethics is to set a general standard of behaviour for those to whom it applies largely by voluntary self-regulation, in effect by requiring individuals to incorporate these standards for professional behaviour into their personal ethical systems. A discipline code, by contrast, enforces a standard of behaviour by punishment or threat of punishment for transgressions: an individual is not required to adopt any moral attitude towards a discipline code, merely recognise its existence and accept that transgression of it may attract punishment. Both codes can achieve consistency of conduct, a discipline code through enforceable rules where there is no individual autonomy, and a code of ethics when autonomous individuals are required to act consistently with each other.

That a code of ethics regulates the behaviour of autonomous individuals, while individuals whose working practices allow no autonomy have need only of a discipline code, can be illustrated by consideration of the armed forces. For the common soldier military discipline applies, and is such that, for the non-commissioned ranks at least, these rules suffice to control behaviour. Officers, by contrast, are expected to lead and to make decisions, and there is a need for them to be guided by a code of ethics. In making a military decision account must be taken of parallel decisions being made elsewhere – the army must be consistent in its decisions to be effective, in that on the battlefield one regiment cannot choose to retreat while another attacks. This can be contrasted to the medical profession, where, for a doctor, to behave professionally is to behave in a similar fashion and according to similar standards to doctors elsewhere. Such behavioural standards cannot be maintained through enforceable rules, since doctors are largely autonomous and rarely, except in large teaching hospitals, work under the direct control of another.

Few, if any, professions are directed solely by a code of ethics. Military officers can be court-martialled, and disciplinary proceedings can be taken against doctors: most professions which have a body for accreditation or licensing of practitioners have a procedure for revoking an individual's accreditation or licence if misconduct is proved. Whereas for many years the medical profession has had both a code of ethics and a formal disciplinary board, the police service had a discipline procedure from the outset, but has only recently attempted to introduce codes of ethics.[2] Intimately connected with this late move are the reasons seen for the necessity for an ethical code, and the success or failure of implementation of codes of ethics within policing involves a discussion of the term "cop culture" used earlier.

A code of ethics does not arrive, fully fledged, from the void, although long-standing codes of ethics within various professions arose more from an ad hoc recording and identification of good and bad practices, with the aim of encouraging the former and discouraging the latter, than from a governing body's drawing-up of a charter. Perhaps this is analogous to the common law, which evolved from the records of decisions made in specific cases to ensure consistency, to a highly sophisticated set of legal principles and rules, and guides for the application of those principles and rules in

---

2   London's Metropolitan Police, for example, had a discipline code from its inception in 1829, which was draconian in the extreme by mid-19th century, but its first attempt at a codified ethical system was not introduced until 1985, when each officer was issued with the "The Principles of Policing and Guidance for Professional Behaviour" produced by the Commissioner, Sir Kenneth Newman.

new contentious cases. While it is naive to expect a code of ethics to meet with universal acceptance and compliance, practitioners in general can be expected to comply with all of the injunctions most of the time and most of the injunctions all of the time. A well-established code of ethics becomes standard practice, therefore a safe and uncontroversial pattern of behaviour, from which conscientious individuals deviate only in exceptional circumstances, since to do so would be risky and likely to attract the disapproval of their peers.

Police officers have established practices and patterns of behaviour within the parameters of what is punishable under the discipline code, and a general consensus of what is acceptable. This is no more and no less than what individuals do in any workplace. Frequently, acceptable practice may break the rules or even the law: taking pens from an office, using the phone, fax or photocopier for personal matters, arriving late but booking in on time all cost one's employer money, are dishonest and can be technically punishable in court as theft or fraud, yet such practices are so pervasive as rarely to be seen as wrongdoing. Any working practice which the majority comply with, especially if it is not seriously challenged by management, is seen as a safe standard, and rapidly becomes the norm of behaviour. This consensus of behaviour can be termed according to the profession involved, cop culture, doc culture, computer culture, or second-hand-car-dealer culture. What is of concern here is, of course, cop culture.

Spectra of police behaviour

It must be said that many, if not most, of the working practices of police, in the western world at least, are uncontroversial and readily acceptable to the public: such practices need no discussion. What does need to be challenged is the use of gratuitous violence, the manufacturing of evidence and the acceptance of corrupt inducements as well as racism, sexism, and stereotyping of individuals. Certainly, cop culture is an important factor in the continued presence of such behaviour in policing – however, to expect such behaviour as a matter of course from police because every officer is a product of cop culture is to construct a cultural stereotype of a police officer in precisely the fashion that police are criticised for constructing cultural stereotypes of ethnic minority groups.

Many aspects of police culture, those that are stressed by police officers themselves and their unions, increase effectiveness and efficiency and have a beneficial effect on the public. Police officers take pride in quick attendance at the sort of dangerous incident which most other members of the public would rush away from: police culture expects all officers to do this, but in return all officers gain confidence in the knowledge that they will be supported by as many colleagues as are available in a potentially dangerous situation. Other agencies, for example the fire services and defence forces, develop a camaraderie which spreads the risk in dangerous situations, and while there may well be a strong element of machismo in risk-taking, real policing incidents like gang fights, fires and riots are more effectively dealt with by the deployment of sufficient numbers of well-equipped personnel rather than by a Hollywood hero acting alone.[3]

Some aspects of police culture, while not positively helpful, have little or no effect on the public at large. Police culture dictates that the proper place for a police officer is out on the streets fighting crime, leading to a form of guerrilla warfare with management over record-keeping, reports and paperwork in general.[4] This is no more and no less than occurs in other organisations – a large company's sales department is full of individuals who would rather be out meeting customers than completing worksheets or travel diaries. One might speculate that inflating expense claims may provide clandestine revenge on the bureaucracy as well as extra income.

The darker aspect of police culture is that it permits individuals to adopt rude, violent, racist or corrupt behaviour by creating an atmosphere where the duty to support one's follow officers takes precedence over wider responsibilities. In private, many police officers would condemn the behaviour of some of their peers while being unwilling to take a public stand, Serpico-style, against this. At worst, organisational culture insists on behaviour which an individual feels is wrong: more commonly, an individual is expected to tolerate if not to participate in such behaviour, certainly to the extent of not admitting wrong-doing to those outside the organisation, or even to its own management. The public itself is ambivalent about its police service, surveys indicating both a high level of trust in police and a feeling that police organisations are secretive, likely to target and harass the young and minority groups, and that complaints are routinely covered up rather than investigated. Police are not alone in having a secretive organisational culture, as anyone who has encountered the difficulties in proving negligence against the medical or legal profession will attest, but, as stated earlier, police malpractice has additional ramifications.

The controlling forces on police behaviour are the law itself, the discipline code, the code of ethics and police culture. As has been suggested, police culture is not always a malign influence, and is probably the most powerful force on police behaviour. To destroy police culture may well be impossible without destroying the police service, although the police service is indeed, as has already been shown, undergoing major changes. Police behaviour would be changed significantly by integrating the code of ethics into police culture, and perhaps this is a necessary part of achieving a police service to fit the needs of the 21st century. Ways of carrying out this integration will be examined shortly, but first three specific types of police

---

3   It is worth noting, in this context, that all of the police and fire officers killed in the destruction of the World Trade Center went to the scene after the first aeroplane struck, and could have saved their own lives just by staying away.

4   Various studies have been made of what police actually do. A significant result of all studies is that little police work is crime-directed, most consisting of various service calls to the public, but a high percentage of police time is spent in paperwork. Punch and Naylor (1973) is one of many explications of how little police time is actually spent catching criminals.

conduct will be examined, to show that police conduct cannot always be easily defined as good or bad.

From burgers to bribes

Clearly, a police officer who takes payment, however large or small, to act (or fail to act) in a way which is contrary to the duty of a police officer is corrupt: such an officer has no place in the police service, and deserves to be the subject of investigation if not criminal prosecution. A police officer who is given a sandwich and beer, having dealt with a road accident in which a child's dog is run over and killed, then spent half an hour burying the mangled remains before the child's return from school has done much for the image of police in the community. These two cases do represent the black and white aspects of gifts and bribes, but much of the area between may be various shades of grey. This is particularly true when issues of the greater good run counter to the absolute imperatives such as preservation of individual rights.[5]

It takes only a few minutes thought to postulate some intermediate cases:

- the offer of a very valuable gift to a police officer who finds a lost child;

- a gift for a caution rather than prosecution for a traffic offence where the officer involved never had any intention of writing an infringement notice;

- a take-away food chain routinely gives discount to police and always receives prompt attendance when disturbances occur;

- an officer feels there is not enough evidence to prosecute an individual for an offence and closes the investigation – a few months later while trading in the family car, the officer by chance encounters the earlier suspect, who offers a new car at a loss-making discount;

- although convinced that there is insufficient evidence, an officer lays a charge, having been induced to do so by the victim – the defendant is bailed and later acquitted.

There are various questions which arise concerning the above examples. The nature of the gift, the intentions of the parties and the circumstances of the offer all affect the legitimacy of the transaction.[6] If the gift is a friendly and commensurate expression of gratitude in all the circumstances, then there seems no element of corruption, but if the gift or offer is of great monetary value, or an inducement for a particular police action, then it does seem corrupt. The matter is further complicated if the offer is made corruptly by an individual who did not know the police officer's actions

---

5 In moral philosopher's terminology, this is a version of the gulf between utilitarian and deontological theories of ethics.

6 There are Kantian issues here which arise about doing good for its own sake, and whether or not doing what is right or one's duty is devalued if this is rewarded.

were not determined by the inducement, but that the officer intended that course of action anyway.

The most important aspect of corruption is, perhaps, the mental element of what the intentions of the parties were in giving or accepting the gift. The matter is even more difficult when the gift itself is not tangible or of monetary value – membership of an exclusive group, queue-jumping for medical treatment, or a favourable word for transfer or promotion may be, literally, gifts beyond price. However, corruption investigators find it much easier to prove the *actus reus* of giving and receiving gifts than the equally, if not more, important *mens rea* of the corrupt intention of the parties involved. I leave the individual reader to decide whether the examples above show acceptable behaviour, unacceptable behaviour, poor judgment or corruption, and to what extent the officers involved would deserve punishment, but will return to corruption and ethical considerations after two more sets of examples.[7]

From reasonable force to violence

The use of physical force, too, presents a whole spectrum of behaviour. An officer has lawful authority to handcuff a prisoner, and could hardly be criticised for doing so if the arrest is made a considerable distance from the nearest police station. Police officers whose opening gambit in dealing with any gang member is to take a swing with a baton to stamp their authority on the situation are clearly guilty of assault. Police officers represent the coercive power within society, and are given lawful authority to use force: indeed, insofar as an arrest is an application of force, police officers have a duty to use it against members of the public. The use of such force is subject to control, in that such formulae as "no more force than is reasonably necessary" are included in police powers, and all police services have directives on the use of firearms and other weapons, and the need to call warnings before firing etc. Nevertheless, the general test of "reasonable force" is whether it was justified in the circumstances at the time.

As with the corruption examples above, some grey areas can be hypothesised:

- a fairly small police officer fears a burly prisoner is becoming aggressive, and elbows the suspect in the ribs;
- a suspect is frightened by a police officer's unconscious body language, turns to run, is caught, flails about and is very vigorously subdued;
- a police officer goads a short-tempered individual into open aggression, then punches him in retaliation and to restrain him;
- a police officer carrying out an early morning search of a known violent offender's home bursts into the room, jumps on and

---

7   It must be noted that this discussion concerns ethical considerations only, not breaches of any discipline code. The *Police Act* 1964 (UK), for example, forbids acceptance of gratuities in any circumstances: other examples which follow may also be disciplinary offences.

handcuffs the suspect who is half asleep – a gun is later found readily to hand under the bed;

- a prisoner is subdued after a violent struggle in which two police officers are injured, and is kicked in the ribs while handcuffs are being applied.

Nothing, of course, justifies gratuitous violence against another person, but if actions are to be justified at a later stage as "reasonable" then the states of mind of all the individuals involved at the precise time of the incident are important. The police officer in the third example may have prompted the suspect to hit first to gain an excuse to strike the individual as a personal vendetta, or may just have been insensitive to the effect the words or actions would have on the member of the public. In due course the officers above may be called upon to demonstrate that their actions were reasonable, either to senior police officers investigating the incident or to a court. A conviction for assault requires that the prosecution proves beyond reasonable doubt that the officer's actions were unreasonable in the circumstances pertaining: given the subjective nature of the evidence of the various parties' states of mind, such a standard of proof is by no means easily attained in any but the most blatant cases.

From collating evidence to perverting justice

The adversarial nature of the common law system necessitates that the prosecution is required to put its case to the court, have its witnesses challenged individually and collectively by the defence, and, furthermore, prove its case beyond reasonable doubt. In all countries police have a major part to play in prosecutions as frequent prosecution witnesses if not as prosecutors. In Australia the vast majority of prosecutions (almost all summary matters) are conducted by police officers, while in Britain it is only since the mid-1980s that the Crown Prosecution Service has taken over all prosecutions. In many cases, especially minor matters, the bulk of the evidence is given by police officers, and the collection of evidence is the sole responsibility of the police officer in charge of the case.

Police, therefore, quickly develop an understanding of the points which must be proved in any particular type of case, and what their own local courts like to be told. The rules of evidence in common law systems can be Byzantine in their complexity, and adversarial proceedings of their very nature mean that the function of the court is not to discover the truth, but to judge by deciding between different versions of the event in question. While outright fabrication of evidence cannot be tolerated, some flimsy evidence may be burnished to appear better than it is. Consider these examples:

- a police officer chases a suspect who is believed to have a knife. While the suspect is momentarily out of sight, the officer hears metal against metal: the suspect is caught, the knife is found in a metal wastebin, and the officer says in court "I saw the suspect throw the knife in the bin";

- most of the evidence against a suspect is inadmissible, but the officer investigating leads the suspect to believe it is stronger than it is as a result of which the suspect volunteers an admission;

- a police officer undercover obtains evidence by means which would probably result in dismissal of the case – the officer's testimony subsequently suggests to the court that the evidence was obtained by legitimate means;

- two police officers write up their notes of an arrest together, and mutually reinforce each others' memories;

- an officer is told certain facts by an apparently trustworthy witness who declines to get involved, and, knowing that that evidence would otherwise be hearsay and inadmissible, includes those facts as personal observation.

The rationalisation commonly used by police officers for such strengthening of evidence is that it is the job of the defendant's lawyer to challenge the credibility of any and all aspects of the prosecution's evidence: if the value of police evidence is to be dropped by 10 per cent in cross-examination, then it is fair to have strengthened it by the same factor in written statements and evidence-in-chief. This argument suggests a parallel with the process of selling a car or a house, where the advertised price is inflated to allow for a bargaining process with potential buyers, allowing the seller to be beaten down to the price which is required or expected.

Slippery-slope theories of discipline

Of the 15 hypothetical examples of police behaviour listed under the various categories in the preceding few pages, it is probably true that most, if not all, police organisations would consider them specific breaches of the disciplinary code and some, if the facts could be proved, are criminal offences. It is probably equally true that actual examples of such behaviour are fairly common in policing, suggesting that they are part of normal working practices, and, in the widest sense, part of police culture. Codes of ethics typically discuss impropriety in general rather than mention specific matters and may, for example, exhort officers not to "participate in any activity which is improper or which may be construed as improper". Although codes of discipline and ethics are both ostensibly addressed to the elimination of misconduct within the police service, it will be argued that a discipline code is not particularly effective in so doing, and may even be counter-productive.

Police discipline codes typically proscribe specific defined actions without any discussion of the intention behind those actions. In some respects, this is strongly reminiscent of military discipline, and is an echo of the semi-military origin of policing. It is also part of the paradox of policing that while individual police officers in the lowest ranks are invested under the law with vast power over the public and almost total discretion in its application, they are more trivially constrained in their behaviour by the organisation itself than the most menial employee in many a commercial organisation. Police officers may be subject to disciplinary charges for such matters as accepting gifts, taking secondary employment (however temporary) without permission, losing or damaging an item of uniform, straying from an assigned beat or patrol, and may be required to have their new home approved as suitable before moving into it.

Such restrictions are intended to ensure not only that police behave properly, but are generally perceived as behaving properly, whether on or off duty. However, stringent regulations, especially those which are known to the public, may do little for the modern professional image the police service seeks to project. Consider this example, which recurs frequently in cinema and television portrayals of police officers. It is commonly known that police discipline codes forbid officers to consume alcohol whilst on duty: it is, however, a common social practice to offer visitors on professional business refreshment, which may or may not be alcoholic – this is frequently accepted. However, when a fictional detective visits to investigate the crime, individuals wishing to establish some social superiority frequently utter the line "Drink, officer, or not while you're on duty?" Such an offer could be accepted or rejected on face value by a visiting lawyer, doctor or plumber, but has implications for police. To refuse is to accept the role of a rule-bound petty functionary, and therefore of low status, while to accept is to take the role of one who openly and flagrantly flouts the rules and refuses to obey instructions, the maverick detective.

The hierarchic, multi-rank structure of traditional police agencies is justified in two ways. One, common to almost all organisations, is that setting policy and decision-making and authorising or carrying out certain specified tasks is a matter for senior persons. Within policing, a young constable can exercise far greater authority over the public in general, including making a decision to prosecute for many, if not all, offences, than a superintendent can exercise over lower ranks through policy-making decisions. The lawful authority to issue motoring infringement notices or summonses, or arrest for drink-drive offences, can be exercised by constables even over their senior officers, and constables who exercise their discretion not to do so make such a decision as a result of professional courtesy or prudence: a direct instruction not to proceed from the senior officer involved is not a lawful order. The law itself gives individual police officers autonomy in the important areas of arrest, summons, individual liberty and prosecution: it is frequently beyond the authority of even the most senior of police officers to interfere with this. Ironically, the further up the hierarchy an individual is in the police service, the less opportunity that person has to exercise police powers under the law.

The second explanation for the hierarchic structure of police agencies is that staff junior in rank or experience (or indeed both) need supervision and direction by those of a senior rank. This supervision does not extend to directing officers in their exercise of legal powers, the kernel of policing, but to every other part of an officer's working day. Such supervision traditionally shows itself by the requirement for officers to submit written reports to supervising patrol officers on almost every matter they deal with, and for a system of recording the activities of officers. This does not provide supervising officers with a way of affecting junior officers' decisions, but it does allow them to ensure that any subsequent report contains a justification for the action taken. A comprehensive discipline code gives teeth to such supervision.

Slippery-slope theories of discipline claim, in effect, that if trust is put in police officers to allow them to decide that acceptance of a gift is proper in particular circumstances, this may be the first step towards corruption. Obliging police officers to comply with a rigid disciplinary code restricts their scope for action, and reduces the opportunity for corrupt behaviour. Although the law itself places a great deal of faith in police to exercise discretion, the discipline code is a means for the police organisation to hold its members accountable for their actions. For example, if no gifts are to be accepted at all, then the fact that a gift was a corrupt inducement need not be proved: if all meetings are to be recorded in a diary, then while there may not be sufficient evidence to prove that a particular meeting with an individual was corrupt, if the meeting itself was not recorded, then the officer can be disciplined for failing to keep correct records. By making and enforcing strict rules police organisations can restrict police officers' actions – not in the major problem areas of how, when and whom to stop, search, arrest and question, but in the areas of record-keeping, radio contact and task allocation. It may be easier to deal with aberrant police behaviour by disciplining the officer for procedural rather than substantive malpractice. There may be a parallel here to the way Al Capone was dealt with: his involvement in organised crime was never charged or proved in court, but he was removed from society by convicting and sentencing him for tax evasion.

There are problems with the theory that a strict discipline code is necessary to prevent police corruption. Let us consider, first, the issue that to allow officers discretion over gratuities is to allow the first step towards corruption. There is a vast difference between accepting a free hamburger or other gift for routine duties or even supererogatory actions, and taking money for performing an action which it is clearly an officer's duty not to perform.[8] Any police organisation that believes that its officers are unable to draw such a distinction either has an unacceptably low expectation of their moral worth, or needs to examine the recruiting policies that allow officers who cannot make this distinction into the service. Police agencies frequently demonstrate ambivalent levels of trust towards their officers. FBI agents have great investigative authority and access to weaponry, yet their academy at Quantico bars alcohol: the organisation authorises them to use

---

8   There are other possible motivations, for example that half-price or free hamburgers are a legitimate perk for the rigours of police work, or that the expectation that such a gift will lead to preferential treatment does not imply a contractual (or even moral) obligation. Such claims may, in the accepting officer's mind, remove the taint from a potentially sordid offer.

lethal firearms and exercise police power over the public, but does not trust them to behave responsibly with a bottle of beer.

The effects of discipline codes

There are major counter-productive effects of a discipline code which creates offences out of activities which are neither corrupt nor inappropriate but are seen as common working practices. Any group will define its own norms of behaviour, and act in accordance with them rather than the norms of another group. In criminological terms, "crime is always relative to the norms of the group defining it as a crime – therefore it is a product of social definitions" (Gottfredson and Hirschi, 1990). Translated into the context of a police disciplinary code, such codes are devised and implemented by police management, but if parts are seen as antithetical to "getting the job done" then those parts might be rejected by street police officers, indicating that the norms of police officers are not those of police management. An example here is the acceptance of an alcoholic drink. Junior officers are likely to be charged under the disciplinary code if they accept alcohol on duty, while senior officers may be seen to imbibe after meetings with community leaders without comment. Many police officers see no real harm in drinking small quantities of alcohol, unless the officer may foreseeably be required to use a gun or drive a car.

If these sorts of provisions in the discipline code are strictly but selectively enforced, then a split may arise in the police organisation between street police and management (this has been remarked by Chan, 1997), which brings the discipline code into disrepute and leaves the way open for the worst aspects of police culture to arise. It cannot be stressed too highly that the law places great faith in individual police officers, giving wide powers and discretion, while a hierarchic, disciplinary police organisation displays little faith and trust in its officers. At best, a strict discipline code can produce officers who flout inconvenient regulations while behaving essentially correctly: at worst, it can produce officers who view police management as politically motivated and as much a hindrance to the good order of society as the criminals themselves. In some cases all aspects of the discipline code fall into disrepute, as do those who seek to enforce it.

Police officers themselves are as aware of fictional portrayals of police as the rest of the public, and fictional detectives do strike chords of recognition with real police. Fictional police heroes, of course, always need their trademark, but there are numerous examples of the detective who can and will solve the crime provided he (there are only a handful of cop heroines) is allowed to do so in his own inimitable way, wherein at least some of the battles which must be fought are against senior officers. The paradigm of this genre is almost every cop played by Clint Eastwood: few police officers have not felt some of the frustration of Harry Callaghan[9]

---

9   The reference here is to the 1970s series of films, the first being entitled "Dirty Harry". The "Dirty Harry Problem" has become widely discussed in the literature of police ethics.

who, having found the suspect, cannot persuade him to admit where the victim is hidden and dying. Luckily, even fewer police officers would consider Harry Callaghan's solution: blowing the suspect's kneecap off to obtain the information!

Any rule, however sound, will be inconvenient at times, or possibly even inappropriate in its application. Nevertheless, if such rules are generally approved as reasonable in most circumstances, then those to whom they apply will accept and keep them. If a set of rules is generally seen as unfair, unnecessary or inappropriate for whatever reason by those to whom they apply, then they are likely to be disregarded – if those whose task it is to apply the rules also find them unjustified, then the rules will fall into desuetude. In such cases, the rules, or parts of rules, which remain valid and valuable are at risk of being ignored with the rest.

A final indication of how a discipline code might be counter-productive is that it may well serve to increase rather than dispel the aspect of police culture which prevents officers reporting serious misconduct by others. If, as has been suggested, common working practices encompass breaches of the discipline code, then all police officers are likely to have committed disciplinary offences at some time in their careers. With regard to the strict letter of the discipline code, then, none has totally clean hands, although most are honest and maintain sound ethical standards. Suppose that officer A becomes aware that officer B has committed a corrupt act. If A reports this conduct, then B will be thoroughly investigated. This investigation will not just examine this incident, but B's actions over a long period of time, and other officers who have worked with B will also be drawn into the investigation. Suppose B had attended court with C, a friend of A's, and when the case finished early, B and C had treated themselves to a leisurely lunch rather than returned directly to the office.

This venial misbehaviour, harmless in itself, may well result in disciplinary action against B and C if subjected to the harsh light of a full inquiry: if everyone has something trivial to hide, no-one is willing to precipitate a major investigation which will result in all disciplinary infractions, however trivial, becoming the subject of disciplinary proceedings.

Promoting positive standards of behaviour

There are many factors which go towards determining any individual's behaviour, ethical standards and beliefs about what is right and wrong. Factors such as family, religion, psychological and intellectual development, peer group or groups all influence the way we behave. Apart from the pure psychopath, all individuals have some sense of right and wrong, however bizarre some aspects of this might be. It is, I hope, not unduly optimistic to claim that most members of society share the same broad moral principles, and act in accordance with them most of the time: it is not immediately clear how a society could exist in which there were no general agreements on, for example, property rights and the importance of human life. This is not to say that total agreement is required, and perhaps no two members of society would agree totally on all moral issues.

Formative influences on behaviour obviously have a much stronger effect than later behaviour influences, which serve to modify behaviour. The behaviour of a peer group affects the behaviour of individuals quite strongly, and this is perhaps the most important modifier of behaviour in adult life. As one's peer group changes, so one's behaviour may change with it: an individual who graduates from university, takes a commission in the army for some years, is cashiered and imprisoned then starts a new life and a new career spends time with a variety of disparate peer groups and undergoes changes of behaviour patterns accordingly. However, unless an individual undergoes some traumatic events, religious conversion or some extremely heavy and long-lasting peer pressure, the formative influences are still likely to have a very strong effect.

The person who enters the police milieu cannot fail to be affected by common working practices any more than a young doctor or army officer can reject out of hand all the working practices encountered in those environments. As has been shown, the new police officer also falls under the pressure of the disciplinary code, and the general reaction to this. Furthermore, the modern police officer will also be subject to a code of ethics. All of these pressures will tend to affect a police officer's behaviour – the main issue for police ethics is how these influences can modify behaviour positively. The operation of a police discipline code having been sufficiently explored, the elements of a code of ethics now need further examination.

The Code of Ethics of the Western Australia Police Service, for example, contains clear statements of the aims of the organisation, which amount to what is commonly termed a mission statement, and have the function of making clear the ends to which the organisation or profession is directed. It is easy for individuals within an organisation or profession to become overly concerned with the processes rather than the objects of their actions – every university lecturer could work more efficiently without the presence of students, and hospitals run more smoothly without patients.

Ethical codes typically adjure officers to "make every effort to respect and uphold the rights and freedom of all the people in the community". This is in the nature of a rule of best practice, or, as Oakeshott (1983) terms it, a prudential rule to guide behaviour. Such articles in the code neither describe behaviour which is insisted upon or forbidden by the profession or organisation, nor do they have the form of defining clear objectives to be attained. They do, however, describe clearly approved practices, and the manner in which members will conduct themselves. For some professions and all organisations it is important, as has been claimed, that there is consistency in approach when individuals have a level of autonomy in achieving their collective goals. The most important aspect of the function of any code of ethics is as a regulator of the behaviour of autonomous individuals rather than as a set of rules to enforce particular types of behaviour from subordinates.

Finally, codes of ethics frequently contain explicit rules forbidding certain broad types of behaviour, perhaps forbidding officers to "participate in any activity which is improper or which may be construed as improper". As a descriptive guide to right conduct such a rule is acceptable, setting aside Socratic problems of definition, but as a disciplinary measure definition becomes essential. In the context of a code of ethics, "improper behaviour" is left to the discretion of the individual, the peer group or the organisation to define: in practice the imprecision of the term "improper" renders it difficult to incorporate into an enforceable disciplinary rule. The dangers of such imprecision can be seen with the working of the 1936 Criminal Code of Germany, which stated that any act was punishable that was "contrary to the healthy sentiment of the people", and the definition of this term was supplied according to the whim of the Nazi party with disastrous consequences for justice.

Problems of implementation of codes of ethics

Stick-and-carrot approaches rely on the assumption that behaviour can be modified through a system of reward for compliance, and punishment for non-compliance. However, positive rewards for ethical conduct are far rarer than attempts at punishment for non-compliance with a code of ethics, which can only be possible insofar as the code of ethics is part of a discipline code or proscribes criminal acts. So, for example, a police officer who offers gratuitous violence to a prisoner breaches the professional code of ethics in that such behaviour is clearly improper, but also commits an assault, which is punishable in law. To ensure compliance with the ethical requirement to avoid improper activity by punishing any instance of improper behaviour is hardly possible. In general terms compliance is best ensured through general acceptance of the rationale of the code of ethics by the individuals to whom it applies, for which there are three prerequisites. These are that the code itself be known and understood, that individuals by and large comply with its demands, and that the persons to whom it applies accept its requirements. In effect this means that the professional code of ethics must become a part of both common working practices and each individual's personal ethical system.

A code of ethics, however, does not just appear from thin air – it has to be drafted and adopted, somehow, even if it is a pre-existing code of ethics from one organisation or profession which is taken by and adapted for another. Long established professions like doctors and lawyers have their codes of ethics which are the prerogative of members of those professions to set, implement or change. Any person joining these professions must learn and accept the ethical code, and acceptance is made easier by its being set by their peer group. While it is unreasonable to expect any individual, much less any group of people, to behave in complete accordance with any code of ethics all of the time, most people most of the time behave according to reasonable ethical standards. Professions and organisations which have a long tradition of demanding certain standards of behaviour have little difficulty maintaining those standards.

Police services which have been trying, over the past 10 or 20 years, to implement a code of ethics where previously none was explicit are in a different situation. At least in part, the drive to do so has come from a perception that something is amiss with the behaviour of at least some of the individuals involved, so that the code of ethics implies criticism of current practice, not a move towards best practice.[10] There is a sense of public unease at the behaviour of some officers towards some or all members of the community. Significantly, the police service of the new Republic of Slovenia is so keen to rid itself of its totalitarian image that within a few years of independence it published a Code of Ethics in a seven-page booklet in a number of languages, including English. In this sort of case, the implementation of a code of ethics is, in fact, an attempt to change the behaviour of individuals.

A code of ethics must be concise, clear, and a public document, and, especially if it is a new code of ethics, the organisation or profession involved must devote a reasonable amount of time to teaching the code and its implications. This drafting can be carried out either by discussion and agreement among the autonomous individuals whose behaviour it will regulate, or by imposition by the organisation, with or without consultation. It follows that the more involvement there is by individual members of the organisation in the drafting and adoption of the code of ethics, the more ownership members of the organisation will have of it, and therefore the more likely it is that it will be known and understood and the organisation will operate according to its precepts. A horror story here may make this point clear – in 1985 the London Metropolitan Police published (at great expense) a slim, hardcover book of some 60 pages, entitled "The Principles of Policing and Guidance for Professional Behaviour". During a single week all members of the police force, over 23,000 officers, received their own personal copy, with no training offered, no discussion and no feedback invited. Few officers, except those studying for promotion who were told there would be an examination question based on it, read this book, and it failed to modify the behaviour of any officer significantly.

If the implementation of a code of ethics is an attempt by the hierarchy of the organisation to modify the behaviour of its members to meet new standards that the hierarchy has imposed, a "top-down" code of ethics, then its degree of acceptance by members of the service may well be inversely proportional to the extent to which an individual's behaviour needs modification. The requirements for implementation, which have been stated, are knowledge, acceptance and compliance. Knowledge is the easiest issue to address, in that some formal or informal training can acquaint every member of the organisation with the new ethical code. Compliance can also be ensured up to a point through measures of sanction

10   There have been any number of inquiries into policing since mid-1960s in a number of countries which have criticised ethical standards and practices. These include Lusher (NSW), Fitzgerald (Queensland), Scarman (London, Bristol and Liverpool) and Knapp (New York). The changes that resulted, including training, codes of ethics, etc, have all been a reaction to bad practice rather than building on best practice.

and reward, although this is not possible with regard to some of the broader principles which are, arguably, the most important. There is a further danger with the imposition of sanctions for breaches of the code of ethics that the code itself becomes a further, "catch-all" addition to the discipline code.

The key to implementation is the full acceptance by individuals of the validity and necessity of the code of ethics. It may well be that certain individuals, those whose behaviour is less in need of modification than others, accept this with minimal training, and that these individuals are sufficiently large in number to ensure that peer group pressure ensures eventual acceptance by almost all. Should this, however, not be the case, then a considerable amount of training time and effort needs to be expended in gaining acceptance for the code. If the code of ethics is perceived as a new set of rules imposed from above, then one likely reaction will be that individuals reject it, pay lip service to acceptance, and evade rather than comply with its provisions. This, certainly, was the reaction to the "Principles of Policing" in London in 1985. This was soon seen as impossible to implement, and the project was recognised as stillborn, although there was no formal burial for almost five years. By contrast, the Plus Programme, which was successful in changing policing in London, had at its heart a Statement of Common Purpose and Values developed after a long period of consultation and the cooperation of many police officers.

It is implicit in remarks made about acceptance of a Code of Ethics that if such a code is accepted wholeheartedly by the individuals to whom it applies, then voluntary compliance generally follows. The difficulties of getting an imposed code accepted have been outlined – if a code of ethics is to be drafted by those to whom it will apply, then a different set of problems occur. First, if all members are to be involved in this process, then considerable time and money needs to be set aside for this. Alternatively, a code may be drafted by representatives of those involved, and then offered as a consultative document for further discussion. Although in the long run this has a better likelihood of success, in that the more individuals have been given ownership of the project at an early stage, the more likely they are to accept the result, the process is both long and expensive.

Dealing with unacceptable behaviour

No police service is, or ever can be, perfect – the effect of discipline and ethical codes on improving or maintaining standards has been shown, and this will be sufficient for most individuals within the police service. Inevitably, though, there are officers who are corrupt, dishonest, violent, aggressive or discriminatory to a degree unacceptable to their police service or to the public it serves. Such individuals have no place in policing, if only because they cannot be entrusted with the power the law gives to police, and there must be some means of removing them.

The spectre of corruption is one that haunts police officers of all ranks. It perhaps needs to be said that, although no police force is ever free of corruption, and that at times corruption exists at even the highest level of the force,[11] the majority of police officers are decent people attempting to give good service to the community. This is not to minimise in any way the matters brought to light by any royal commission or inquiry into policing practices, but to indicate that corruption in policing is as pervasive as cockroaches. Cockroaches can never be completely eradicated, but their numbers can and must be controlled. One of the intractable problems with the international drugs trade is that the sheer profitability of it encourages corruption since enormous sums are available to be laid out in bribes: enough, certainly, to tempt some members of the police, judiciary and legislature in any country in the world.

There are a number of aspects to dealing with unacceptable behaviour within the police service. The first is that allegations of such behaviour, whether they come from within the force or as complaints by members of the public, need careful investigation. The second issue concerns the disciplinary process. Before disciplinary action is taken, allegations of misconduct must be proven, but the question arises whether that proof should reach the criminal standard of beyond reasonable doubt, or the civil standard that the matter is shown on the balance of probabilities. Also of concern here is the need perceived by some senior police officers and sections of the public to dismiss officers who are strongly believed to be corrupt, but against whom insufficient evidence exists to put before a jury. Finally, some chief officers of police are in favour of sting operations which institute a set of controlled and recorded circumstances enticing officers who are believed to be open to bribery, etc to accept an inducement: the ethics and value of such operations are questionable, especially where such operations would be rejected as evidence in the criminal courts. British courts, in particular, are unwilling to accept evidence from an *agent provocateur*.

Police complaints procedures will be discussed fully in Part 3, but some outline of the parameters is worth noting here. The first and most obvious criterion for a system of investigating complaints about police behaviour is that it be stringent, effective, and capable of discovering the facts. This requires trained, experienced, skilled investigators and the largest number of such individuals is to be found within the police service itself. This is, of course, only one part of the picture. It is not sufficient that complaints against police be investigated rigorously, it is also necessary that the public have confidence in the rigour of the investigative process. This affects the credibility of the police service as a whole: the public needs to be given faith in the fact that allegations of unacceptable behaviour by police officers will be investigated and dealt with. However, credibility in the process is served

---

11   Examples are legion. After the Fitzgerald inquiry, the Queensland Police Commissioner Terry Lewis was imprisoned for corruption and in the 1950s, corruption scandals involved the Chief Constables of Cardiganshire, Brighton and Worcester in the UK.

not just by the public being shown that an officer the subject of a complaint is dismissed from the police service: credibility of the complaints investigation process within the police service also needs to be preserved, so that any officer dismissed or otherwise punished must be shown to be genuinely guilty, and that the punishment fits the conduct.

Disciplinary hearings, proof and dismissal

The whole purpose of a disciplinary hearing is to make some determination of the future of an individual police officer against whom some form of misconduct is proved. As with sentencing in criminal courts, a disciplinary decision needs to satisfy many disparate requirements. Complainants need to be shown that the matter has been treated seriously, and they are not made to feel diminished if the officer is treated leniently; the public as a whole (insofar as the matter is publicised) needs to be shown that the outcome is fair; officers punished need to be fairly treated, not singled out as scapegoats, and encouraged to modify their future behaviour, particularly if they are not dismissed from the police service; and, finally, members of the police service itself need to be shown that a discipline board is a just tribunal, not a kangaroo court.

Of vital importance in investigation and discipline is the issue of proof. The common law system of justice allows for two standards of proof. That used in criminal matters is that the prosecution is obliged to prove its case beyond a reasonable doubt, while civil courts accept a lower standard of proof, that the plaintiff's or defendant's case is the more likely to be true on the balance of probabilities. Police discipline boards traditionally operate to the more rigorous, criminal, standard of proof, while disciplinary bodies in most other professions operate to the civil standard of proof.[12] Each has advantages and disadvantages for the parties involved.

With regard to the sort of malpractice generally alleged at disciplinary tribunals of professional bodies, the matter is most likely to be one of negligence or poor judgment: for example, when a lawyer loses a case through an avoidable error, or when a vet gives advice about an animal over the phone and the animal then dies through misdiagnosis. The substance of such matters is tortious rather than criminal and cannot, except in the most blatant cases, be shown beyond reasonable doubt. Since a police discipline code has much of the form of a criminal code, the criminal standard of proof is intuitively more suitable for alleged breaches of it. An additional complication is that police officers, like prison officers and others working in the justice system, are more likely than most professionals to encounter dishonest individuals, so the credibility of a high proportion of those who complain against police may well be open to doubt. Malicious complaints can be made against any individual, but there is a very real fear among police officers of malicious or vexatious

---

12 This is no longer the case in British policing, where the *Police (Conduct) Regulations* 1999 allow a complaint against police to be substantiated "on the balance of probabilities" rather than "beyond reasonable doubt" (Sanders and Young, 2003).

complaints being made, which can be allayed to some extent by the need to prove complaints beyond reasonable doubt.

While many disciplinary matters are sufficiently clearly defined to admit of the criminal standard of proof, many of the complaints made by members of the public against police are difficult to prove to this standard. To compound the problem, these are the sorts of matters which cause most ill-will between police and public: matters like rudeness, rough handling of persons arrested which falls short of actual assault, harassment of young people, or derogatory remarks to members of ethnic or other minority groups. The investigator and the discipline board may well be reasonably satisfied that the behaviour complained of was broadly as the complainant and witnesses described it – but being reasonably satisfied is not being satisfied beyond reasonable doubt. Under the criminal standard of proof, reasonable doubt is raised by the production of some sort of plausible explanation, which should suffice to acquit the police officer.

There are various options here, some of which are not particularly appealing as they tip the balance too strongly for or against the police officer or complainant. The first option is to retain the status quo, wherein complaints of, for example, rough handling are investigated. Although the investigating officer may be convinced that the officer's actions towards the person arrested were unnecessarily forceful while falling short of actual violence, the claim that in the officer's judgement the action complained of was no more than was needful to deal with a difficult prisoner is sufficient to raise a reasonable doubt in the case. This results in the dismissal of disciplinary proceedings against an officer whose behaviour is unacceptable. The second alternative is to reduce the standard of proof to that required in civil cases, where the subjective views of a complainant are given greater weight, and an officer who did need to use force is open to punishment.

The problem of proof in discipline inquiries is compounded when the inquiry concerns an allegation of corruption. This arises when allegations of corruption against one or more police officers are investigated, and there are very clear indications that they are well founded. However, the clandestine nature of corruption is such that much of the evidence may well be circumstantial, direct witnesses are either unwilling to tell what they know, or of such character as to render their credibility open to challenge, and there is little hope of securing a conviction in the criminal courts. The same evidential problems are sufficient to render disciplinary proceedings for corrupt conduct unlikely to succeed to the criminal standard of proof. It is precisely this problem that leads the public to fear a cover-up in the wake of corruption allegations or inquiries. Examples are common – the Fitzgerald Royal Commission in Queensland and the Countryman inquiry in London may have achieved some successful prosecutions and persuaded some individuals to take early retirement, but left not a few other officers of doubtful character still ensconced in the police service.

One solution to this which has been adopted on many occasions is for the investigating officer to discover a technical offence under the discipline code which is capable of incontrovertible proof, and use that as an justification to dismiss an officer believed to have committed more serious misdemeanours. An example has been cited earlier: it may very well be a provable fact that an officer had a meeting with a particular individual, although the corrupt activities cannot be proved: failure to make an official record of that meeting may well constitute a disciplinary offence. While this is an effective way of ridding the police service of unsuitable officers (Al Capone's conviction for tax evasion springs to mind once more), it is hardly satisfactory as a means of openly dealing with corruption.

The last possibility, which has been raised on a number of occasions by chief officers of police is that of some form of administrative dismissal,[13] notably by Peter Ryan of New South Wales in the wake of the Wood Royal Commission, because of the problems envisaged in proving the highly publicised allegations made. This, while not without its problems, is a very attractive option. Suppose a number of complaints are made about the conduct of a particular individual, all citing the same sort of conduct, but none of which can be proven to the standard required. The existence of a number of allegations is corroborative of the unsuitability of the officer, although this, of course, is not admissible as evidence. Let us further suppose that the officer has been made aware of the allegations and has been sent on training programs, with no noticeable change in the officer's behaviour. Only the introduction of administrative dismissal can rid the police service of this individual.[14]

The police service is no place for individuals who are corrupt or dishonest, violent or aggressive (physically or verbally), racist, sexist, or otherwise discriminatory in their actions. The fear exists among police officers that a series of allegations might be made against a particular officer or group, none of which can be substantiated fully, but taken together creates sufficient smoke without which, proverbially, there is no fire, to lead to the dismissal of the officer who "no longer has the Commissioner's confidence". With the exception of corruption, dishonesty or violence, the police behaviour which causes most problems is as much a result of mental attitude and a lack of inter-personal skills as misconduct. While the public has a right to expect that police officers who are psychologically unsuitable should not remain in the police service (especially when those officers are authorised to carry firearms, long batons and other weaponry), it is demoralising for members of a police organisation to feel they may be dismissed on ill-defined terms, and particularly for the individuals who are dismissed after many years service when it is the police service, rather than they, which has changed.

---

13 Changes in the UK allow officers to be subject to dismissal for "inefficiency", once again under the *Police (Conduct) Regulations* 1999.

14 There is frequently provision for police officers to be dismissed purely on the grounds that they have been convicted of a criminal offence. Administrative dismissal without this proviso, for example the much resented s 26E of the *Australian Federal Police Act* 1979 (Cth) which allows the services of an officer in whom the Commissioner "has lost confidence" to be dispensed with, often preserves benefits, and can be seen as a reward for those who are escaping criminal charges.

It must also be noted that the introduction of administrative dismissal would be against the general flow of change in industrial relations. Industrial relations tribunals generally hold that a dismissal is unfair unless an employer can show that an employee was formally warned, usually in writing, about the conduct in question, and dismissal for that conduct was, eventually, justified. To introduce provision for administrative dismissal only to have it overturned in the industrial relations courts would be counter-productive. If administrative dismissal is to be introduced, it will require careful consideration, and the procedure itself must be shown to be scrupulously fair so that no officer is dismissed for political reasons. One can, perhaps, suggest some possible safeguards: for example, no hearing for administrative dismissal can be convened without the personal authority of the chief officer of police, the discipline board must contain a judge or magistrate, or a decision to dismiss an officer administratively must be reviewed by an independent panel, and proceedings and findings to be open to public scrutiny.

Pro-active anti-corruption measures

Clearly, the most suitable way of dealing with corruption is to have clear proof – such means as electronic surveillance, bugs, cameras and microphones carried by parties who admit their involvement can all provide this. If criminal proceedings are to be successful then the rules of evidence must be borne in mind, although these might be less stringent in purely disciplinary proceedings. Any legitimate means which serve to prove the involvement of police officers in continuing corruption are acceptable to most police services.

Pro-active strategies, which are growing in popularity among some chief officers of police, are often described as integrity tests but more colloquially known as sting operations. Officers on patrol, not necessarily suspected of any form of malpractice, are dispatched to deal with ostensibly routine police matters: to report a crime, perhaps, or deal with a motor accident. However, the incident is completely fake, the persons involved are actors, and the whole thing is recorded by concealed cameras. During the course of the incident an approach is made or temptation put in the way of the officer to commit a disciplinary offence to test the officer's reaction, and disciplinary action and dismissal may result from the wrong decision.

On the surface, this appears to be a sound strategy to identify and weed out unsuitable persons from the police service. However, questions need to be raised about the moral worth of such tactics, and also about the likely effect of them on police morale and relations between police and public in the longer term. The moral issue involves the extent to which such operations rely on entrapment of the officer, or the use of an *agent provocateur* to bring about an action the officer had not previously contemplated. Courts look very closely at such operations in criminal trials, and will dismiss cases where there is any suggestion that a prosecution witness has taken more than a minor or passive role in the commission of the offence.[15] Certainly the person who offers a bribe is equally as culpable as the person who accepts it. Sting operations always involve some deception being practised, and if they reach the point where evidence is gained for discipline proceedings in a manner which is essentially corrupt in itself then the moral worth of the organisation's management is called into question.

With regard to police morale, this can only suffer if police officers feel that the management does not trust them, and is out to set traps for them. There may well be an element of a police management culture as well as a cop culture,[16] and, unless they are very carefully handled and used sparingly, sting operations within the organisation against police officers could have a divisive effect on the police service. Within many police services, internal affairs or complaints investigations branches are viewed by other officers with some suspicion as to their methods. If senior police management were to authorise for use against police officers in disciplinary matters the sort of "dirty tricks" which police officers are forbidden to use against criminals, this is not likely to be seen as management support of police but as an attack on the majority of the service.

There may well be a deleterious effect on police public relations if police officers have reason to fear that not every incident they deal with is genuine. The argument in favour of sting operations, of course, is that officers should behave correctly at all times, and a good officer should exhibit no difference in standards whomsoever is involved. This, perhaps, is a simplistic view: individuals who feel they are under scrutiny will naturally be scrupulous about their behaviour. For example, someone who is normally smart, polite and respectful to superior officers is likely to put on a little more smartness and respect if the commissioner makes a visit. Officers who feel they are being watched may well behave differently to those who feel they are unobserved.

An officer who suspects that a matter is a sting rather than a genuine incident is likely to react by being extremely punctilious and aloof from persons involved in the incident. This may be interpreted as arrogance, and, especially if the interaction does not involve an individual being arrested or reported for a criminal offence, may create precisely the opposite image of police to that which community policing strategies would wish. Many incidents and individuals which respond to negotiation are often best dealt with by officers giving the tacit impression of agreement to some extraordinary statements. Police officers often encounter individuals suffering harmless delusions, who are best dealt with by good humour, and agreement with their often confused logic. A person who loudly blames everything from a rise in interest rates to global warming on a CIA conspiracy is most effectively dealt with by being humoured rather than contradicted. Suppose, however, the conspiracy alleged is Zionist, and the

---

15   This varies, of course, between jurisdictions, British courts being particularly reluctant to convict where a prosecution witness has been an *agent provocateur*.

16   There is a useful discussion on this point in Chan (1997).

officer has some suspicion that this might be an integrity test for racist attitudes, then feigning agreement with untenable views would not be good strategy. A trivial encounter may well lead to confrontation and possibly an unnecessary arrest.

Conclusion

This chapter has explored some of the methods available for maintaining and improving behavioural standards in the police service. Traditional policing required officers to keep order by their presence, with the implicit threat of arrest for the disorderly or dishonest. Police were themselves made to behave in accordance with the requirements of the organisation by the application of hierarchic supervision, and strict application of the discipline code. It needs to be said that only over the past 40 years or so have society's requirements included a widespread recognition of equal rights for all sections of the community, and even more recently has policing changed from a force which required of its officers little more than order maintenance and reactive strategies for dealing with offenders, to a service which requires officers to work with the community to keep the peace and prevent crime. It may well be that the traditional police discipline code is now of less use to a modern police service than a properly introduced code of ethics and sound training in its principles.

This change in policing ethos brings with it a new view of the police officer. Officers who are required to be culturally sensitive, are agents of assistance rather than control, and are accountable not just for what they do but how they do it, can no longer be unthinking, unquestioning functionaries responsible only to senior officers. The move towards police codes of ethics is a significant one, in keeping with modern expectations of police, but fits ill with older styles of discipline. However, it is dubious whether pro-active anti-corruption strategies are of value in the short or medium term. They are, perhaps, best seen in context as the last gambit of those who seek to change policing by imposing their will through force rather than managing change by leadership and consensus.

The most powerful influence on behaviour within a group or organisation is the pressure on an individual to conform, more or less, to the general behaviour patterns of that organisation. These behavioural norms should comply with the requirements of the organisation: to do this in policing, police culture must broadly conform to the code of ethics. The problem lies in how this is to be ensured. Training has a large part to play in modifying police culture to the mores required in modern policing, although this, clearly, has to be a long-term strategy. However impressive the training, reinforcement will always be needed, most obviously by the traditional "carrot and stick" reward and sanction process. The rewards are clear – promotion, pay increments or preferment within the police service for those whose actions merit it. Sanction is, perhaps, a matter of ridding the organisation of those whose behaviour is, ultimately, so seriously unacceptable as to merit their dismissal. Since the behavioural criteria at issue are matters like racial awareness, aggression and dis-honesty, consideration should be given to the chief officer of police having power of administrative dismissal, and discretion to dismiss an officer convicted of a criminal offence. Much as it requires a leap of faith to commit a police service to community policing in the face of public disquiet over crime rates, so it requires a leap of faith to move wholeheartedly from a strict discipline code in the face of public disquiet over police malpractice.

PART III

ACCOUNTABILITY

CHAPTER 9

CONTROL, INDEPENDENCE AND ACCOUNTABILITY IN POLICING

Introduction

The police of any state wield enormous power under the law: it follows that whosoever controls the police, controls the society it polices, and in a free democratic society the people themselves need to maintain this control. If control of the police is ceded to government, then the power of police may be used to enforce the government's wishes – in the true sense of the term, the civil state becomes a police state: it follows from this that police need to be independent of government. However, if removing police from the direct control of government results in the complete independence of the police, then this too has its dangers, as an armed, disciplined body of police answerable only to its chief officer is a formidable force within a civil society. J Edgar Hoover accumulated such a wealth of information on politicians that he rendered himself immune from criticism or removal from office.[1] Practical problems arise with regard to democratic control of police, since in most democracies control of public utilities and services is one of the functions of elected government. The three nations discussed in this book have developed different systems of monitoring police and holding them accountable which seek to maximise overall control of police by society as a whole while minimising the possibility of a single state or national body controlling policing and preserving police operational independence.

The police as a service and its individual officers need to maintain a high level of autonomous decision-making, while being controlled by society itself so as to act in the best interests of society. Police are, however, accountable to a range of interested parties, including the government, the courts, the media, individuals and special interest groups representing particular sections of society, and individuals within society who have been adversely affected by police: each of these interested parties has specific areas of policing wherein they can be most effective in holding police accountable.

---

1   The Garda Siochana in Ireland were also briefly politicised in the 1930s when a religious zealot was appointed Chief Constable – he organised pilgrimages to Rome for the force, and later expressed positive support for Nazism.

Independence or control of police

Implicit in the laws which establish police powers is the autonomy of individual police officers in their exercise of those powers. The law, in defining the powers to arrest or search, for example, sets out the circumstances in which a police officer *may* exercise those powers, but does not go so far as to stipulate the circumstances in which a police officer *must* exercise those powers. Furthermore, when these powers are exercised it is only the individual officers who carry out an arrest or a search who are called upon to justify their actions, not their senior officers. The law itself stipulates clearly the conditions which, if met, are sufficient authority for any given police power to be exercised, but there are no conditions set out which require that that power must necessarily be exercised. Once the sufficient conditions are met, the question of whether or not the exercise of those powers is necessary is to be answered by the individual officers who actually exercise them: there is no authority for the vicarious exercise of police powers.

It follows that if the law grants individual officers discretion when to exercise their powers, then an officer can request, but cannot order, another officer to assist in the exercise of police powers. While a number of officers may work together in the search of premises, and one by virtue of rank may be in charge, the individual officers themselves are responsible for their actions, and cannot be ordered to exercise any power for which they, as individuals, are not satisfied that the sufficient conditions have been met. An officer can only effect an arrest, for example, if that officer has sufficient grounds to do so personally: to arrest because some other officer ordered it would be unacceptable to a court.[2] The law renders the officer on the street autonomous with regard to police powers. This is emphasised in Australia, particularly, by the case of *Enever v R*,[3] where the officer arresting the victim rather than the offender in an incident was held to be totally responsible for his actions, and the police force which employed him was found not to be liable for unlawful arrest or imprisonment. Police officers on the streets can neither be ordered to exercise their powers, nor can they be ordered not to exercise their powers: Australian, British and American police officers are all autonomous in this respect.

A strong case can be made out for the autonomy of the police as an organisation to determine policy, strategy and methods of policing. This was established, at least for British policing, by the courts in a pungently expressed ruling by Lord Denning:

---

2   There are some qualifications here: a warrant is an order of the court to arrest a named individual, so if an officer is satisfied a warrant is in existence he or she may, indeed must, arrest that person. Also, if one officer is given sufficient information by another to justify the exercise of police powers, then those powers can be exercised by both. A senior officer in possession of a search warrant can instruct junior officers to carry out the search: if it transpires that there was no warrant and the senior officer lied, the junior officers cannot be held responsible.

3   *Enever v R* (1906) 3 CLR 969.

I hold it to be the duty of the Commissioner of Police of the Metropolis, as it is of every chief constable, to enforce the law of the land. He must take steps so to post his men that crimes may be detected; and that honest citizens may go about their affairs in peace. He must decide whether or not suspected persons are to be prosecuted; and, if need be, bring the prosecution or see that it is brought. But in all these things he is not the servant of anyone, save of the law itself. No Minister of the Crown can tell him that he must, or must not, keep observation on this place or that; or that he must, or must not, prosecute this man or that one. Nor can any police authority tell him so. He is answerable to the law and the law alone ...[4]

This set the judicial seal, so to speak, on the insistence by British chief officers of police from the time of Rowan and Mayne onward that they be free of overt political interference in the way policing was carried out. This is particularly important in 21st century Britain and Australia, where police organisations are large and have some significant answerability to State or national government, but rather less crucial for policing in the United States where police departments are generally smaller and under local government control. The specific terms of accountability and control in each of these nations will be discussed in the following chapters.

There is, however, a great deal of precedent showing the dangers of a large national or State police organisation falling under the control of national or State government. In Spain during the Franco era, while much of policing was local and comparatively benign, the Guarda Civil were established as a para-military policing body answerable only to national government, in effect, to Franco himself. While the local police (and especially the tourist police in resort areas) were easygoing and tolerant of much, even very high levels of, misbehaviour from foreigners in tourist resorts, the Guarda were a very different story. Although they were not particularly obvious to visitors, the Guarda exercised very serious political and social repression over the Spanish people. Merely being a national police force does not, of itself, make the police a means of repression: the Irish national police force, the Garda Siochana, is a very open and accountable police organisation under the control of the Ministry of Justice. The degree of independence the police organisation has from control by the executive government and police answerability to an independent judiciary are critical factors in preventing such repression.

In the modern world, policing cannot be totally independent of government in all matters. For example, policing requires funding, and that funding comes from public money raised in tax or local government revenue and administered by some level of government. Whether the money for policing is raised from local taxes, State or national government budgets or a mixture of these, the ability to increase or withhold funds enables the funding agency to exercise serious constraints upon policing. These funding constraints are, perhaps, no bad thing as a government which supplies

---

4   Lord Denning MR in *R v Commissioner of Police; Ex parte Blackburn* [1968] 2 QB 118, cited in Denning (1977).

unlimited funding to police encourages, so to speak, a cuckoo in the nest which could eventually have power enough to take over the state. Arguably the day-to-day repressive power of the Nazi state in Germany lay with the policing organisations under Himmler and Heydrich, as was the case with Russia's KGB,[5] and their power was such that government acceded to all their demands, and they operated above the law. For the Nazi party to seize and retain power in Germany required the might of the SA and later the SS which received unqualified support from the party in the early stages, but later the power of the policing organisations was so strong that they, rather than the party, effectively controlled the state.

In a modern democracy operating under the separation of powers system described by Montesquieu, all three branches of government can exercise a form of constraint over the police. The executive, as described above, exercises financial control, appoints (and can dismiss) the chief officer and often other senior ranks. The legislature can define police powers[6] and restrictions on those powers, and include in Police Acts or other statutes discipline codes and any other regulations that might be felt necessary by parliament. The judiciary, too, can exercise some control over police, certainly in common law systems, by setting precedent which establishes acceptable police practice. Thus police are constrained rather than controlled by the legislature, judiciary and executive, and within these parameters police retain the right to carry out their tasks as they choose. The line is a fine one, and government starts to control police when finance is provided or withheld for particular policing schemes, or when senior officers are appointed to fulfil the particular whims of the executive. At the extremes, the independence of police from any control and absolute government control of police are both undesirable.

The clearest form of control, especially in the current political climate of economic rationalism, is through stipulative funding, or funding for specific projects. For a government to decide, for example, that drugs are a major problem and to provide additional money in the middle of a financial year to fund a police drug strategy can be seen as a welcome addition to police funding. However, if in setting a police budget the government stipulates that a proportion of the total is only available if used to fund a drug strategy, and states that if the chief officer of police does not produce an acceptable (to the government) drug strategy then that money will be withheld, this comes close to financial control of police operations. The difference between this form of budgetary control, control by asking the chief officer to submit a detailed proposed budget with the costs of strategies allowing the government to approve or disapprove funding for individual projects, and control by telling the chief officer how policing is to

---

5   It is worth noting that two (Andropov and Putin) of Russia's 10 post-Revolutionary leaders had been KGB men, and a surprising number of KGB colonels and generals currently hold regional governorships and other posts in government.

6   In the United States police powers are not solely a matter for legislatures, as legislation must conform to constitutional imperatives. The 4th Amendment, for example, prevents any American state adopting the equivalent of *PACE*.

be done and supplying the money for it is a matter of degree. To supply the chief officer of police with a budget, and to require that the money be used to police effectively and accountably is qualitatively different.

An alternative form of government control is by the executive appointing a particular chief officer whose views on policing accord with those of the appointing body, which almost implies a contractual obligation to carry out policing in the manner required. Once again, this has its dangers, in that once appointed the chief officer may well become the government puppet, placing police firmly under government control. However, particularly in the United States, the body appointing the chief officer of police may be elected on a law and order platform which promises a particular style of policing, and the appointment of a chief officer here may be seen as but one step removed from the direct election of a chief officer. Whatever views one might have of New York's Mayor Giuliani and the policing style of the commissioners he appointed, Bratton and Safir, it cannot be denied that it had enormous popular approval. In situations like these, local policing is more clearly controlled by the population through the ballot box than in the situations more normally found in Australia and Britain where chief officers are appointed on contracts which give security of tenure for the contract period, usually five years. Shorter contracts for chief officers, especially if an extension is stipulated as "performance-related" may place the chief officer under too much pressure to carry out the government's bidding.

Parties with an interest in policing styles and standards

The whole of society has an interest in the way it is policed, but certain groups within it have either more interest than others, or more power to affect the way policing is carried out. Consideration of the interests and influence of particular groups or sections of society will help to establish the role each can play in police accountability. The interest shown in different aspects of policing by various groups can conveniently be divided into two categories – professional and personal interest. The interest shown by politicians, courts, media, etc, is professional in that these groups have duties that affect and are affected by police. Members or representatives of the community, who may be actively involved in police matters like Neighbourhood Watch volunteers, or be members of groups who have, or fear, bad relations with the police, or even be private individuals who have had bad experiences of police, have a personal interest in policing matters.

Professionally interested groups

Perhaps the most important of the professionally interested groups within society are elected politicians, who have already been discussed in terms of control of police by government. Nevertheless, even a back-bench member of parliament has a guaranteed forum, parliament itself, for raising issues about police, and members of the government have even more authority.

At the level of local politics, questions can be raised about police in council meetings, and American mayors are frequently effective commanders-in-chief of their police. In some cities, indeed, the chief of police attends weekly council meetings to answer personally any matters which arise concerning policing,[7] and such meetings, are, of course, open to the public and attended and reported by the local media.

The media themselves have considerable power to hold both individuals and groups accountable, and police are no exception. At worst, the media are self-appointed pursuers of perceived wrongdoers, but at best painstaking investigative journalism can shine a light into dark, corrupt corners and keep it there until something is done about it. The classic example of this is, perhaps, the work of Phil Dickie of the Brisbane *Courier-Mail* and Chris Masters of the ABC *Four Corners* program into corruption in Queensland policing: persistent local publicity and a national television documentary resulted in the Fitzgerald Royal Commission into policing, the downfall of the State premier and two members of his cabinet and the imprisonment of the police commissioner.[8] Other matters brought to public attention by the media are the world-wide television showing of the videotape of the Rodney King beating in 1991 which forced a full inquiry and include police racism and violence in Los Angeles, and the publication in a Sunday tabloid newspaper of photographs of a senior detective apparently enjoying a Cyprus holiday with a notorious London gangland figure, which prompted the Humphries corruption inquiry in London during the 1970s.

On a rather more mundane level, the media frequently report crime stories very heavily, and on slow news days often use local crime items as fillers. The public are fascinated by crime and policing, as the plethora of fictional police series on television indicates, and also the success of "real-life" police series.[9] Although there is a danger of bias, as with any media reporting, unless the media of any society develops a witch-hunt against its police, or decides its police can do no wrong, the media have an important role in maintaining the style of policing acceptable to the public. Even though the police are not formally answerable to the media, if the media choose to make a story out of a particular incident in which police behaved well or badly, then some response from police is called for. If an incident gets media coverage, public opinion is largely formed by the immediate

---

7   This is the case in San Antonio, Texas, for example, where the chief attends but is, of course, not obliged to stay for the whole meeting unless there is actual police business on the agenda.

8   Journalistic investigations over a long period resulted in a television documentary "The Moonlight State" being aired on 11 May 1987. By 26 May the Fitzgerald Royal Commission started hearing evidence, and continued until 9 December 1988. This inquiry will be discussed in more detail in Chapter 10, and the full story is documented in Dickie (1988).

9   "Cops" is a very popular American series on patrolling police officers in various cities, which has large audiences world-wide. A fly-on-the-wall documentary series on Britain's Thames Valley Police during the 1980s received high ratings, and one interview with a rape victim, an object lesson in how not to treat a victim, became so notorious through the appalling conduct of the interviewing officer that it prompted a national review of police procedures.

news story and the subsequent full investigation rarely rates the same level of publicity.

The importance of the media cannot be overestimated, in that it is the prime source of information for the public on all matters of which individuals do not have personal or specific professional knowledge. The public's relationship with its police is largely dependent on how the public perceives its police, and those perceptions are largely determined by the media. For this reason, many large and not so large police services have a fully equipped media department to ensure the police service's responses are available to the media. Despite the verdict of not guilty by the jury in the Rodney King case, the video shown on world-wide television had convinced many millions of people that the police officers involved had carried out an unwarranted and brutal assault, and that the Los Angeles Police Department was under a serious cloud.

For this reason, police organisations have been forced to shed their traditional reluctance to speak to the press, and are more likely to respond to media questions. This is, in some respects, a potentially hazardous course, especially where a criminal investigation is continuing. In Britain, particularly, *sub judice* rules preclude publication of comments which may prejudice or anticipate a court ruling. Unfortunately, the police response to a media inquiry about a particular complaint against police that "[a] full enquiry will be carried out, and to avoid prejudicing that no further comment is possible" is often seen by the public as the response of an organisation with something to hide. While police as an investigating agency are prevented by *sub judice* rules from giving details of suspects, opinions, suspicions or apportionment of blame, few such restrictions apply to members of the public, who often choose to be interviewed giving their own highly coloured eye-witness account of an incident: this account may well be the only one that is heard by the public.

The courts, and by extension other parts of the justice system such as public prosecution departments and defence lawyers, are also interested parties in policing, with significant power to affect police behaviour. In cases of flagrant breaches of acceptable standards of police behaviour, where individuals are subjected to physical or human rights abuses, police officers may appear as defendants in criminal or civil cases to be dealt with by the courts. On a less serious level, the courts may monitor police behaviour towards defendants (and even witnesses) and use the power to exclude evidence in order to impose sanctions on police behaviour. This power varies between jurisdictions, but in general if courts will not accept particular practices as a fair means of obtaining evidence, then police will be forced to obtain evidence by using other means which are acceptable to the courts.

Where prosecutions are undertaken by legally qualified public prosecutors, as in Britain, the United States, and the higher courts in Australia, then the prosecutors also can enforce acceptable police procedures by refusing to prosecute in matters where they feel that the case prepared by police is not unacceptable. This may be because they predict that the courts will not accept certain evidence, and there is insufficient other evidence to support the case, or by being generally dissatisfied with the professional standards shown in preparing cases.[10] Even without a public prosecution system, if defendants are represented in court by lawyers then there is less chance of police malpractice going unnoticed.

Personally interested groups

People who take a personal rather than professional interest in policing fall into two main categories: those who are positively interested in policing, and assist in some way, for example by being a volunteer member of a community policing council or Neighbourhood Watch, and those who are members of groups who feel unfairly treated by police and therefore feel the need to monitor police activities closely. Clearly outright confrontation between the latter groups and police is unproductive to anyone, but any sort of communication between the public and police, however deep the suspicions on either side might run,[11] is better than no dialogue whatsoever.

Involvement of members of the public in policing issues is essential to maintaining the roots of policing in society itself: as a former Police Commissioner for London remarked:

> [T]he effectiveness of the [police] force largely depends on public goodwill and this in turn rests on public understanding. The police in this country have nothing to lose and everything to gain by offering the fullest possible account of their activities. Trust begets trust. (Mark, 1977, Preface)

Public goodwill and support have a very different part to play in determining the manner in which society is policed from the part played by the professional groups discussed earlier. If public support can be maintained, then this provides the grassroots feedback that Bayley has claimed is vital to modern community policing: without it, indeed, there can be no mutual understanding, cooperation and respect between police and community. The reported comment of one 1960s chief constable "sheep never like their sheepdog" (cited in Whitaker, 1964, p 159) indicates a police view of the relationship between police and society which, even if it were true then, is woefully outdated now. It might be convenient for police to carry out their duties to their own standards in their own way with an acquiescent public, but the modern public is no longer acquiescent. The public are not sheep, and the police are not sheepdogs, but (to continue the analogy), whilst

---

10 One of the first consequences of the inception of the Crown Prosecution Service in Britain was its refusal to accept case files which had not been properly prepared, thereby enforcing the correct, if time-consuming, procedure of collecting evidence fully. Police had to drop their previous habit of doing very little in many cases until after the first court appearance in the hope of a plea of guilty.

11 One of the areas of most suspicion concerns the manner in which police treat persons in custody. This has largely been allayed since the mid-1980s in Britain by the lay visitors scheme, whereby community volunteers visit police cells, usually during the evenings, and check on the conditions of persons in custody.

some sections of the community perceive police as rottweilers and other sections see them as poodles, community policing will be ineffective.

Modern policing, then, increasingly encourages public involvement. Even one individual having a small involvement with police in Neighbourhood Watch, for example, can act as a conduit for information from society to its police and vice versa. Community policing would struggle to survive without public involvement on relevant committees. While the effect of legislation and the courts particularly is to set limits to police action, individuals within the community taking a personal interest in policing can effect more positive results in encouraging strategies rather than setting limits. This is not to claim that personal interest groups do not have a role in establishing minimum behavioural standards for policing, but that they, more than any other group, have a chance to influence positive change by promoting more effective and relevant strategies and approaches in policing.

Many, perhaps all, societies contain groups who claim a history of poor treatment by their police. While the most obvious examples are those of particular ethnic groups, others such as homosexuals, hippies, left-wing and environmental activists have all claimed unfair or discriminatory policing practices have been used against them. Police officers have, however, always been recruited from society, and while the police may not mirror society in terms of its ethnic and gender demographics, the vast majority have traditionally come from the majoritarian working class who tend to be monocultural, homophobic, xenophobic and suspicious of intellectualism. It is only within the past few generations that society as a whole has found it unacceptable that members of certain ethnic or cultural groups or those of particular sexual orientation be discriminated against, but members of such groups who have suffered discrimination based on hatred or fear cannot be blamed for feeling that many of these demons of intolerance are dormant, rather than dead.[12]

For good reason, then, many groups are suspicious of police, and this suspicion can only be allayed by police being genuinely responsive to the concerns of these groups. Certain groups in every society are over-represented in the lowest categories of social indices,[13] and since these are the factors which are most commonly associated with criminal activity, such groups tend to come to the notice of police more frequently. While Anatole France was right in his claim that "[t]he law in its majestic equality forbids the rich as well as the poor to sleep under bridges, to beg in the

---

12   The One Nation Party in Australia, with its platform based largely on fear of Asian immigration and Aboriginal funding, is most popular in working-class and country areas. Modern Neo-Nazism in Britain, as in France and Germany, is a blue-collar rather than intellectual phenomenon (unlike in the 1930s when Nazism received support from many members of the establishment), and strikes a chord of recognition if not support from many of the working class.

13   Aboriginal Australians, for example, have lower life expectancy, lower average income, lower percentage of tertiary education, higher unemployment rate, higher incarceration rate and higher incidence of alcoholism and drug abuse problems than any other group in Australian society.

streets and to steal bread", nevertheless those whose duty it is to enforce the law cannot but arrest the poor who are seen to steal bread, even though it might be the rich who are surreptitiously stealing the bakery.

Members of minority groups have a significant role to play, both in drawing to notice systematic police abuses, and in encouraging positive approaches towards policing for their particular groups. This role can only be fulfilled when a mechanism exists for abuses to be reported and dealt with, or for input to be made and genuinely taken into account in planning policing: such mechanisms will be discussed shortly. If such mechanisms do not exist, these interested parties in policing will not go away, but will remain interested if frustrated in their inability to express their concerns effectively.

Individuals belonging to marginalised and easily identifiable groups may also have a personal interest in policing which is engendered by the behaviour of police towards them. If police officers within a society feel able to treat those individuals discourteously, use violence, demand bribes or fabricate charges with impunity, then every member of that society will feel unsafe when dealing with police. In a free society where police are under democratic control in the literal sense of the word, then every individual has a right to feel that police are under an obligation to behave with civility, honesty, and lack of physical abuse. Potentially, every member of society may come into contact with police, perhaps most frequently through a motoring offence or accident, so the expectations individuals have of their treatment by police is crucial to effective policing. Public confidence in police, and a community feeling of ownership of and involvement with police, relies upon the existence of a mechanism for the individual to have allegations that police have behaved less than acceptably dealt with effectively: furthermore, that mechanism must be perceived as efficient and effective, which requires that it be independent.

Accountability

The argument thus far has shown that control of police should lie with society as a whole, and yet this is, in practical terms, not possible. In many respects, the independence of the police as a body is to be valued, yet this independence will itself create social or policing problems.[14] Furthermore, in a modern multicultural democracy everyone has a vested interest in policing strategy, methods and standards, but many have more personal or professional concerns than others. While it is neither right nor possible for groups or individuals to control police, it is right and should be made possible for members of the public to have the opportunity to have their views or concerns heard and taken into account by senior officers deciding

---

14   Aside from the totalitarian problems mentioned here, Skolnick and Fyfe (1994) argue that police abuses can also arise in democratic societies when chief officers of police are beyond the control of government. They cite the American cities of Los Angeles and Milwaukee where police commissioner was a job for life, and police abuses were endemic. This will be discussed in Chapter 12.

operational policing matters. It is for this reason that policing needs to substitute the possibility of control with a system of accountability for each and every aspect of police duty and decision-making at all levels.

Areas of accountability

There are three main areas of accountability to be considered within most policing organisations which are:

- financial;
- operational;
- personal.

All of them are to some extent the responsibility of the chief officer of police. If there is some degree of police independence, then, given the hierarchic nature of police organisations, this translates into a great deal of autonomy for the chief officer, and therefore personal responsibility for any perceived failings in the organisation. Crucial issues in police organisational accountability involve consideration of matters like the appointment of the chief officer, means whereby a chief officer can be dismissed, and to whom (and about what matters) a chief officer is obliged to report.

Financial accountability in policing requires that the enormous cost of policing be recognised within the organisation, and a reckoning made to justify how the money was spent. Although the money ultimately belongs to society, and each individual pays through some form of taxation or another for policing, public money is disbursed by various levels of government, and few people have the desire to examine police budgets in any detail. There are, however some problems inherent in the possibility that financial accountability can become financial control, on the application of the cynic's golden rule "whoever has the gold, makes the rules".

The drift from financial accountability to financial control is, perhaps, multiplied with the trend for sponsorship of some policing activities by local businesses or organisations. If one company, for example, offers funding to sponsor a community policing office and vehicles for a particular suburb, then community policing is totally dependent on that organisation. Without the funding community policing would die in that area, and if the funding remains in the gift of a single donor, then that donor controls it, a wholly unacceptable situation. With multiple smaller sponsors, or large sponsorship from an umbrella organisation like the local Chamber of Commerce, both the independence and financial accountability of police can be maintained.

Operational accountability covers a multitude of decisions concerning policy and strategic planning at organisational level, and operations carried out at local or station level. Policy matters concern the whole community policed by that particular police service, while local or station level operational decisions may have little importance to the wider community. The style of policing, for example whether a police organisation operates a community policing policy, concentrates on a zero tolerance approach, or tries to overlay parts of one or both onto a reactive policing strategy, is of enormous importance to the community being policed, and police organisations need to be accountable to the community for such decisions.

On a local level, particular initiatives or strategies also have an impact on communities for which local senior officers rather than the police executive should be accountable. This is not, however, always the case, as a locally imposed initiative may show problems within a police organisation as a whole. The Rodney King incident in Los Angeles raised questions about the whole ethos of the Los Angeles Police Department, and the subsequent criminal trial of the officers involved raised further doubts about the justice system as a whole. The Scarman Inquiry launched after the Brixton riots concerned not just the police operation that triggered the disorder (wherein police acted lawfully, unlike those involved in the Rodney King incident), but led to legislative changes in police accountability to the public throughout England and Wales.

Personal accountability concerns the way individual police officers behave while carrying out their duties. In many respects, this accountability requirement is answered by having in place an acceptable system of recording and investigating complaints made against individual police officers and an effective discipline system when malpractice can be proven. However, to claim that the behaviour of individual officers is solely a matter of personal accountability is in many respects too simplistic, as a pattern of particular behaviour may signal some endemic problems within the police service itself. If a large number of allegations of particular types of misbehaviour are received against a number of officers, then this suggests a problem for the organisation itself, rather than the presence of a minority of miscreant individuals.

Consider, for example, the case of police shootings in the Australian State of Victoria. Between 1984 and 1995, police in Victoria shot and killed 32 people in separate incidents, thereby accounting for almost half of the total fatal police shootings in the whole of Australia during the same period.[15] There is no evidence that Victoria has significantly more violent crime than its neighbouring State, New South Wales, or other parts of Australia, and there are no significant differences in gun laws or ownership. Each of these shooting incidents was fully investigated and a coroner's inquest was held, but in none of the cases was there any adverse findings against individual police officers. Clearly, it is a matter of individual judgment on the part of a police officer whether or not to draw and use a firearm, but equally clearly there is some disparity between Victoria and the rest of Australia in the exercise of the judgment to use firearms. The number of these incidents during the relevant period and the fact that the individual officers who pulled their triggers were not negligent suggests that the police organisation's policy and training with regard to firearm use

---

15   There were 17 fatal shootings in New South Wales, 6 in Queensland, and the combined total for Western Australia, South Australia, Northern Territory, Tasmania and ACT was 11, a total of 34. Victoria has a larger population than any State except New South Wales. Melbourne has a history of, and a continuing problem with, gang-related crime.

should be held to account for the discrepancy between Victoria and the rest of Australia in the use of lethal force by police during the period in question.

Examples like police shootings in Victoria, or a reputation in particular police organisations (or even stations) for aggressive behaviour, rudeness or racism, go beyond the actions of individual officers, although they, clearly, are accountable also, but become matters of organisational accountability. In addition to matters of policy and strategic planning, senior officers in policing are also to be held accountable for ensuring standards of behaviour by careful recruiting of high quality officers or by training members of the service to the highest standards. Police officers are not saints, and some, for example, will always feel the need to react more physically than others, but senior officers are accountable for general standards of integrity, interpersonal skills and non-violence within the organisation as a whole. For police officers to be accorded professional status, then chief officers must ensure that all officers of all ranks receive not just practical training but continuing education and external professional qualifications relevant to modern policing.[16]

The number of matters for which police are accountable as an organisation and as individuals, and the variety of groups and bodies to which police must be accountable can only lead to a complex series of accountability mechanisms. One issue which is both part of an accountability mechanism and a matter which requires independent accountability is the position of chief officer of police. As a structural hierarchy, individual police officers are accountable to officers senior to themselves in the hierarchy for many of their activities (but not, as Denning points out, all of them): ultimately, all officers answer to the chief officer of police for their conduct. With a chief officer's independence of command of the police comes responsibility for the police organisation as a whole, and ultimately answerability for it to the public:[17] an important aspect, therefore, of police accountability is the appointment and dismissal processes pertaining to the chief officer.

Chief officers of police who are appointed and given tenure certainly have complete independence of command, but have little personal accountability without some form of sanction over their behaviour, which, ultimately, must be the possibility of dismissal.[18] However, a chief officer who is appointed but who can easily be dismissed and replaced must dance to the tune of those in whose power dismissal or continued appointment rests. The appointment and security of tenure of chief officers of police is an

---

16   Increasingly, this seems to involve university studies. This is common in the United States, recruit training in Britain can give advanced standing towards a degree in policing, and two Australian police services, Western Australia and New South Wales have integrated their Police Academies with university campuses.

17   In American policing, particularly, chiefs of police are answerable for their policies. After the Rodney King debacle in 1991, Chief Darryl Gates was replaced by Willie Williams of Philadelphia.

18   This was a problem faced by Grampian Police in Scotland during 1998, where the Police Authority sought to dismiss their Chief Constable, and indeed did so before having the actions ruled *ultra vires*, as such power rested with the Secretary of State for Scotland. The Chief Constable was reinstated, but later resigned.

increasingly problematic matter for police accountability, as, with policing under increasing scrutiny, there is more and more pressure upon chief officers to achieve particular goals. If these goals are set by politicians with an eye to crime statistics then they are likely to be unrealistic and therefore impossible to meet, and no chief officer of police can ever hope to succeed. It may well be an achievable goal to change the manner or style of policing, or to restructure a police service, although police organisations themselves may well resist such change forcefully.

The recent trend in Australia and Britain has been to appoint chief officers of police on a fixed contract, normally for five years, and sometimes extendable for a further five years. In Britain it is common to appoint a chief officer from a different police service rather than internally, something which is rendered easier by there being 43 police services within a relatively small geographical area. Appointing a chief officer from a different police service is, perhaps, more likely to achieve substantial change in the organisation (if that is the goal) as the new chief officer brings no ties, allegiances or a background in the informal behaviour patterns of that particular service. Appointing from another police service is no guarantee of success, however, as recent Australian experience shows. Ray Whitrod received insufficient support from serving members of the Queensland police to root out the corruption endemic in that force during the 1970s, and Peter Ryan was similarly embattled with the New South Wales Police in the late 1990s.

Accountability mechanisms

Not only are there many interested parties and many areas of accountability, but in the three nations primarily considered in this book, Australia, Britain and the United States, the very structures of policing and government vary so that the patterns of accountability vary. Australia has a federal system of government with six States and two Territories, each with its own legal system and each with a single police organisation.[19] The State governments are responsible for policing, each State has a single police organisation, its own system of criminal law (some States having a fully codified criminal law, while other still recognise common law offences also), its own Police Act, and provides its own police budget. Police Commissioners are appointed by the State governor (a titular rather than executive office) although the choice is made by the government, usually after consultation with opposition or on the advice of a committee. Neither federal government nor local government has a significant role in police accountability in the individual States.[20]

---

19 The Australian Capital Territory comprises the national capital, Canberra, and its hinterland, and is totally surrounded by New South Wales. The population of roughly 250,000 is policed by the Australian Federal Police. The ACT is anomalous, for similar reasons to the District of Columbia in the United States.

20 The federal government is, of course, responsible for the Australian Federal Police (AFP), but shows little interest in the uniformed police in Canberra, and directs the AFP as a federal detective body only as another arm of federal law enforcement with customs and other bodies.

The United States is also a federal system, and although there are both federal and State policing bodies, the bulk of the policing is carried out by organisations answerable to local government. Chief officers may be directly elected by citizens of the town, city or county they are required to police, or appointed by the mayor of that locality who in turn is answerable to the electorate. The police budget is taken from local government funds. There is a limited role for State government and a lesser role for federal government in holding American police accountable. Britain[21] has a national system, with a single parliament and 43 local police organisations, but officers from all of the constabularies can exercise their police powers throughout the nation. Each police service has its own Police Authority, an independent body having some local government representatives. Funding is largely from central government, and national standards and requirements are imposed by Westminster. Recent legislative changes in the way British police operate are analysed more fully in Chapter 14.

Legal accountability is similarly diverse. Britain has a single criminal law and court system for England and Wales so judicial decisions which affect police affect all police equally, and statutory formal accountability procedures have common application. Australian police have different, but similar, law and accountability systems in each State, and are bound by judicial decisions of the Full Court or Court of Appeal of each State's Supreme Court. The High Court of Australia's decisions are binding nationally, but few of these decisions have had a major impact on police accountability. Neither Australia nor Britain has a constitutional Bill of Rights, but common law rights of the individual are strongly upheld in all courts, as, of course, are statutory rights, whose essence is equivalent to American constitutional rights.

American police are bound and empowered by State law, local ordinance and judicial decisions in their respective States. However, individual rights, which are the reverse side of the police powers coin, are determined by the United States Constitution, and therefore come within the purview of the federal courts, and, ultimately, the United States Supreme Court. The American federal legal system has a more significant impact on police accountability and in limiting police powers nationally than does the Australian federal law. The Australian desire for State autonomy is such that there is significant resistance to any imposition of formal national standards in policing or the establishment of national criminal law, although informal agreements on these may be reached at meetings of police ministers or commissioners.

---

21 More properly England and Wales. Northern Ireland has its own police service, and different legislation, while Scotland has a number of police organisations and a significantly different legal system. Nevertheless, all are represented in the Westminster parliament, and there are more similarities than differences in policing structures and accountability.

Accountability to government

Police must be accountable to government, but only for particular aspects of policing. There is a tendency for governments to claim that police must ultimately be accountable to them for many, if not all, aspects of their duty. It will be argued here that this tendency may have some dangers for a free society, as, while there are areas of accountability within which it is right that police should be accountable to government and government alone, there are other areas of accountability which should not fall under the government's aegis.

The argument for government involvement in all aspects of police accountability runs thus: police should be answerable to society as a whole; society as a whole elects individuals to govern it; those elected individuals represent society; if police are accountable to the elected government they are thus accountable to the society that the government answers to at the ballot box. While this is certainly plausible, there is a very real danger that a police service that is accountable in all aspects to government may, by virtue of the power of government, rate accountability to government of greater importance than any other form of accountability, and inevitably become accountable only to government. There is only a terminological difference between a police service which is accountable only to government and a police service which is controlled by government, and the dangers of government control of police have been discussed previously in some detail.

There are, nevertheless, important areas where the government, and the government alone, has a role in police accountability. These are:

- financial accountability;
- legislative basis of formal accountability procedures;
- appointment of the chief officer of police.

Financial accountability of police to government is not particularly controversial: since the government controls public money, it is the obvious body to ensure that any money disbursed is used correctly. Dangers do arise when governments use financial control to exercise operational control, but these are averted if police are not operationally accountable to the funding body but to a different body or through different procedures. A government controlling funding can ensure its chosen policing schemes are enforced if police are not operationally accountable to any body other than that government. If, however, police are accountable to society for their operations rather than to government, directly or indirectly, then the government itself may be held to account for not providing sufficient funds for policing schemes approved by society, but not highly favoured by government or for funding government-favoured, but generally unpopular, schemes.

Any system of police accountability may ultimately require legislative force. Police powers and police discipline both require legislative authority, and power to dismiss unsuitable officers must take into account the

201

requirements of State or national industrial relations legislation.[22] With regard to complaints made against police officers, public confidence is gained by having some form of external investigation or review body to avoid the perception of a cover-up which arises when police are seen to be investigating themselves. Whatever system of external supervision of police complaints in used, all systems need legislation to establish both police and public powers and duties, rights and obligations with regard to complaints investigations. If police are to be accountable to the public by a system of consultative committees, these seem to work best if they are established according to parameters laid down by legislation. All these legislative authorities require government instigation and parliamentary debate.[23]

There is a role for government, too, in the appointment of chief officers of police. Unless a chief officer is appointed with tenure, which has been argued to be a dangerous practice (see Skolnick and Fyfe, 1994), whomso-ever has power to appoint a chief officer usually has power in appropriate circumstances to dismiss that chief officer, so that officer is accountable to the appointing person or body for the efficiency and propriety of the police organisation as a whole. If governments do have power to appoint chief officers then this gives those governments a broad, general level of accountability over police operations. It is common, but by no means universal, that government exercises this power: all chief officers in Australia are appointed by governments, and those not directly elected in the United States are local government appointments. In Britain, separate police authorities appoint chief officers, but only in accordance with national government criteria.

Accountability to society as a whole

Society as a whole is concerned with very broad issues in policing. Among these concerns are standards of behaviour such as police integrity, the manner in which incidents are generally handled, including the amount of force each society finds acceptable and unacceptable in carrying out police duties, and the interpersonal skills used by police in their dealings with the public. Also of interest to society as a whole are the general policies in policing such as how heavily armed police should be, whether police should have and use guns, pepper or CS gas sprays, water cannon or tear gas, and whether and in what circumstances a paramilitary police approach is acceptable. In all of these, society as a whole has a right to have its voice heard, and the requirements of society with regard to policing methods and standards must be satisfied. Policing by consent has two aspects: the one most frequently considered is that the public consents to the power of

22   The power under s 8 of the *Police Act* 1892 (WA) is a case in point. The Commissioner's power of administrative dismissal under this section was seen as draconian when it was exercised in some very much publicised cases in 1998, and a compromise was reached whereby the power was amended allowing the Industrial Relations Commission to be appointed an independent arbiter for the use of this power.

23   For American police agencies which are controlled by local government then local ordinance is required, made under enabling legislation of the relevant State assembly.

police in maintaining a peaceful society, but the other aspect is that the police consent to use their powers in a manner acceptable to the society being policed.

Different societies have different policing requirements, and different ideas of what constitutes an acceptable standard in various aspects of policing. The British public, for example, would find the idea of armed police almost universally unacceptable, as would many British police officers, yet the American public would feel even less safe, given the lack of gun controls and prevalence of armed criminals, if their police did not carry sidearms: I suspect only a vanishingly small number of American police officers would be prepared to venture out of their stations without a gun.[24] While violent behaviour by police is not acceptable to citizens in western societies, in some societies it is expected and, indeed, welcomed: victims of crime in Papua New Guinea often complain that police have neglected their duty if physical maltreatment of suspects has formed no part of the interrogation.[25]

The mechanism of last resort for a police organisation to be held accountable to the general public is by means of some form of judicial inquiry or commission into policing. Although at the first whiff of a scandal in policing there will be calls for such an inquiry, in many cases the chief officer of police can be both expected and trusted to deal with the matter. There is no clear defining point at which the malpractice or problems that have come to notice can no longer be considered to be isolated instances, or in the phrase which has become a traditional response to allegations of police corruption "a few rotten apples in the barrel", but has escalated to be indicative of a general malaise within the police organisation. Australian, British and American police organisations have all been subject to external investigation by public commissions which normally publish a report at the conclusion of the taking of evidence or submissions, and, although they might go by different names in the different nations, the reasons for the inquiries and the way in which they are conducted have remarkable similarities.

The main drawback to such inquiries is that they exist only to discover the exact nature and extent of the problem, and have no powers to impose solutions. Thus the Fitzgerald inquiry in Queensland, the Knapp Commission in New York and the Countryman Inquiry in London investigated the extent of police corruption in those particular police organisations, and

---

24 The cultural difference in attitudes to weapons in policing is extremely deep here. Until the issue of long batons which hang visibly from the belt, many officers in Britain chose not to carry the truncheon which was concealed inside the trouser-leg. Indeed, before the mid-1980s women officers in London were not issued with truncheons, so that until the past few years many officers patrolled confidently without any weapon at all. By contrast, many American police officers consider it necessary to carry a firearm at all times whether on or off duty, and one Texan detective, in conversation with the author, equated violent crime with firearms, and could not conceive of serious violence without the involvement of guns.

25 I am grateful to Supt Steve Roast of the WAPS for allowing me access to his unpublished research on this topic some years ago.

made recommendations for prosecutions and suggestions for the future. Power to change a police organisation rests within the organisation itself, starting with its chief officer, who may or may not have been required to resign by the inquiry. While a problem cannot be solved until its nature is precisely known, it is the task of an inquiry to delineate the problem, not to solve it. To expect an inquiry by itself to change policing radically is to expect too much of it, but it may, like the Scarman Inquiry in Britain, be a catalyst for change.

Accountability to sections of society

While all members of society may potentially be harmed by a culture of rudeness or aggression in its police, a culture of racism, for example, directly affects only certain racial minorities. Police, therefore, need to be accountable to particular sections of the community for specific general or local behaviour. Particular policing strategies implemented by a specific police station or region affect the residents of, or visitors to, that region far more than those in other parts of the police service's area. Likewise, particular groups may be affected much more seriously than the rest of the population by a low police regard for them: examples include discriminatory treatment at various times by various police forces towards homosexuals, Green activists, Vietnam War protesters or the women of the Greenham Common peace camp.[26]

The most important requirement of this rather more limited need for accountability is that those groups particularly affected must be provided with some forum to have their views heard and taken into account by police. In some instances, for example racism, the matter may be a problem for the whole police organisation, and must be addressed by a change in policy, or new training approaches. In some instances, the group adversely affected may be so small, or the instances so few, that the matter can be most properly dealt with as a complaint against an individual officer or a small groups of officers under the sort of system detailed below. In matters which fall between the two, then a separate system of accountability is required.

There are two main approaches that police can take towards ensuring the specific rights or lawful requirements of minority groups or local groups are met, although these approaches may well overlap. With regard to minority groups, dedicated community liaison is required, which may take the form of a service-wide community liaison branch or community liaison officers at each station or region. The essential requirement is to establish a means of communication between police and particular sections of the community, which is trusted and seen as effective by both the community and the police. The intention should be to establish forms of

---

26 Greenham Common was, during the cold war, the location of an American air force base for long-range bombers carrying nuclear weapons. For a number of years in the 1980s varying numbers of women peace activists set up camp there, carrying out sporadic non-violent public order offences, until the nuclear weapons were withdrawn.

policing which satisfy the needs of the police service to maintain law and order, and provide a safe environment for the whole community. Community liaison should not be seen as a means for particular sections of the community to stop particular policing strategies to meet their whims, nor for police to insist that unwelcome policing strategies must continue.

The second approach is for the police service to ensure local commanders establish formal lines of communication with representatives of all sections of the community to ensure that policing strategies are developed to meet community needs. If all sections of the community are properly represented and heard, this should ensure that policing strategies and operations do not unduly affect any individuals within the community except those who break the law. This high-level community/police forum requires some formal structure to ensure that it does not fail when senior police officers are transferred, or community members move on. Both these approaches are built into problem solving or community policing styles of policework. While community policing positively encourages the establishment of best policing practice tailor-made for each locality, it also serves to identify and genuinely attempts to eliminate bad practices.

Accountability to individuals

An essential safeguard within policing a democratic society, which gives the public confidence in its police, is the existence of a fair and effective procedure for complaining about individual instances of alleged police misconduct, and having those complaints properly investigated and resolved. As with much of crime and policing, the public perception that the system is fair and efficient is as important as the objective fairness of the system. Investigation of complaints must not only be carried out fully and fairly, but must be perceived as being carried out fully and fairly: justice, in police complaints as in the courts, must both be done and be seen to be done.

The sort of police misconduct that affects the public as individuals is different in many respects from that which causes the most unease within society, which is the fear of a climate of institutionalised violence and corruption in its police. There is a qualitative rather than quantitative difference between an individual being treated badly on the street or after arrest and the routine serious violence used by police in, for example, South Africa of the apartheid era.[27] Equally appalling to society as a whole is the culture of corruption uncovered by the Fitzgerald inquiry in Queensland, or the Knapp Commission in New York. Individuals have a right to expect that they be fairly treated by police, and that if police behaviour towards them is sufficiently bad, avenues exist whereby complaints can be made, and possibly disciplinary proceedings follow against the offending officer.

---

27 The death of Steve Biko is perhaps the best known example, although the hearings of Bishop Desmond Tutu's Truth and Reconciliation Committee have shown irrefutably that this was not an isolated incident, but a single horrifying example of a culture of extreme police racism and violence.

Public confidence in a complaints investigation system comes from the knowledge that any complaint will be rigorously investigated. The comparatively minor nature of most complaints against police suggests that the most obvious first step is an in-house investigation. This is true of any organisation – if a customer in a shop complains about rude behaviour by one of the assistants, the complaint is normally made to and investigated by the manager; only in a serious case is the complaints department at head office likely to become involved. There is no real expectation, nor is there a real or perceived need, for all police complaints to be dealt with through an external body. The way the complaints investigation process is perceived by the public is, perhaps, an even more important issue than its efficiency as determined objectively, since there is a very real public fear that complaints against police will not be taken seriously, and that serious matters will be covered up by an internal investigation. Public confidence increases when the police complaints system provides for an external body to supervise an investigation, or to review the evidence and conclusions drawn by police investigators, especially when this body has both the power and the will to carry out an impartial review, and order a re-investigation if necessary.

In Australia and Britain statutory bodies have been established to oversee internal investigations of complaints against police, while in the United States the system is more fluid because of the great disparity of size in police departments. However, virtually all large police departments have both an internal system for investigating complaints and a review board with non-police community representatives to make decisions on the disposition of complaints. Ultimately, the public needs to feel that a police officer who is violent, corrupt, overtly racist, or otherwise allows personal bias to result in grossly unfair treatment to different sections of society, will no longer be permitted to remain in its police service. Neither the public nor the police service are best served by pro-active techniques which entrap police officers into disciplinary offences, especially where such methods are not tolerated by the courts to entrap criminals. It is clearly wrong for society to be policed by fear and fraud, so it is equally wrong for police themselves to be policed in this way.

Conclusion

This chapter has examined the issue of police accountability in general terms, setting out the parameters of the ways in which a police service can be held accountable to the whole of society by imposing different accountability mechanisms for different aspects of policing, and enabling the police to be accountable to different sections of society and structures within it. This complex but comprehensive system of accountability allows society as a whole to remain in control of its police, while not vesting this control in one or two specific powerful bodies within society.

A caveat must, however, be made regarding the separation of these various accountability mechanisms within small societies with small police organisations. A police department with 50 officers, for example, cannot be expected to maintain a rank structure with six or seven levels, or to have a separate internal investigations section. Likewise, the community it polices is likely to be numbered in thousands rather than tens of thousands, and therefore of a size that interest groups and even individuals can have almost direct accountability over the police officers. Most issues and concerns about police accountability arise in large towns and cities where sheer weight of numbers renders individuals, both police and public, largely anonymous.

CHAPTER 10

POLICE ACCOUNTABILITY IN AUSTRALIA

Introduction

Although each of the eight policing organisations[1] in Australia is respon-sible to a different legal system and Police Act, they are remarkably similar because all but one were established as colonial police forces operating under the British Crown. Remarks made about one police service can, therefore, be expected to be broadly true of the others, certainly with regard to questions of accountability, structure and general ethos. The only police service which did not have a colonial history is the Australian Federal Police (AFP). This has a traditional street policing function only in the area around the national capital, Canberra, the main bulk of its work being the investigation of federal offences, which are mainly white-collar crimes, drug importation, international and Internet crime, etc. The closest inter-national parallel to the AFP is, perhaps, to consider it as a combination of the American FBI and the Metropolitan Police Department of Washington DC, which is nominally a federal government agency doing local police work. The majority of AFP officers are detectives based in State capitals and other cities, are known as agents rather than officers and, except for those officers in uniform in the Australian Capital Territory, have no police rank.

Five of the State police organisations are each responsible for a city of over one million people, a number of smaller towns and cities, and vast rural areas. Tasmania and the Northern Territory differ in that their capitals Hobart and Darwin are much smaller cities, and their populations are lower than any other State. The island of Tasmania covers a comparatively much smaller area. The demographics of the States lead to an imbalance in the police : population ratio, as a two-officer rural police station may have a much higher ratio than is possible in a city, because isolated communities several hundred kilometres apart cannot be policed from a single station in the area, but each must have its own small police presence. In some respects, rural Australia is over-policed, while urban and suburban Aust-ralia is under-policed, despite the crime figures suggesting that this is the wrong way round.

There are no formal nationally set and administered standards for Australian policing, but the small number of police commissioners enables

---

1   The State police of New South Wales, Queensland, South Australia, Tasmania, Victoria, Western Australia, the Northern Territory Police and the Australian Federal Police.

there to be considerable informal contact and discussion of best practice. This tends to establish a reasonably similar approach to policing across the nation. The main mechanism that exists for police accountability, financial and strategic, in Australia is through the relevant State minister for police to cabinet and parliament. All police services in Australia have internal affairs departments to investigate complaints and monitor and improve professional standards, and all governments have the office of the ombudsman to provide an independent review of police complaints procedures. Finally, Australian governments have the authority to institute royal commissions when there is sufficient and continuous public disquiet over policing.

Policing within the Australian political structure

Australia in the early 19th century consisted of the growing colony of New South Wales, with settlements growing up along the coast in each direction from Sydney. Victoria and Queensland had no separate identity until 1850 and 1859 respectively, and the year of the establishment of the Metropolitan Police in London, 1829, was also the year of the foundation of the Swan River Colony, later to become Western Australia. The power in the colony was vested in the governor, who was a nominee of the Colonial Secretary at Westminster appointed by the Crown, and it was entirely natural that the governor should claim the right to control police. The need for the governor to exercise civil power was perhaps given more impetus as the police provided a means of avoiding the problems encountered by Governor Bligh of exercising civil power over a corrupt military body in the Rum Rebellion of 1808. The original colonial Acts creating police forces all specified that they be under the command of a single officer, answerable to the governor. This is a stark contrast to the settled political structure, well-defined city and borough boundaries, and a system of local government and peace-keeping within which policing was introduced in both Britain and the United States.

By the end of the 19th century, each colony had its own single police force, hierarchically organised under the command of one man answerable to the colonial governor, who in turn answered only to the parliament at Westminster. Each colony had its legislative body, whose powers had grown steadily as each colony became firmly established. After Federation, each colony became a self-governing State with its own parliament, and a governor who was still a representative of the Crown, but had a similar relationship to State parliament as the monarch in London had to the Westminster parliament. State governors and the national Governor-General have titular rather than executive power,[2] the political power in Australian States resting with the State premier and cabinet.

---

2   This is, perhaps, illustrated by the actions of Governor-General Sir John Kerr who in 1975 dismissed the Whitlam government, dissolved federal parliament and ordered an election. Debate on whether this was, in fact, constitutional continues: what is certain is that no previous governor had contemplated such action, nor is it likely that such action will be countenanced again.

The Australian Constitution does not permit the federal government any authority over State police,[3] nor does an officer duly sworn in one State have police powers in any of the other States.[4] This does not, of course, mean that the federal government has no influence over policing in any of the States. Canberra can and does establish committees, groups and organisations to develop and promote national strategies on all sorts of matters, including crime, although these cannot be enforced by legislation. However, these national groups are often funding bodies, which can promote the government's crime strategies by offering extra money for policing projects which meet the government's criteria.[5]

This additional funding is by no means a way of exerting control over police through finance. If, for example, a police service wishes to introduce a new or experimental approach to domestic violence or addressing the needs of a multicultural community, then this might qualify for extra federal funding for that initiative. The national government cannot insist that any police service adopts such an approach, nor even addresses national strategies, but it can offer financial inducements for State police to do so. There is no obligation on any police service to apply for federal funding in any particular area, or indeed to apply for any federal funding at all, although it is generally seen as a useful way of supplementing the police budget, and experimenting with ideas without having to sacrifice some established strategy in order to obtain the resources. Federal funding tends to be given for implementation and evaluation of innovative strategies which, if successful, have to be continued out of the normal police budget in subsequent years.

State government and policing

Police in Australia are directly, and almost solely, answerable to their State government. Whereas in Britain police are answerable to their Police Authority, the Home Office and the Inspectorate of Constabulary, and American police answer exclusively to local government or directly to the electorate of the county, until the past few years police accountability in Australia was virtually synonymous with the answerability of the police commissioner to the State police minister. The colonial stipulation that each State appoint one person with responsibility for policing answerable to the governor has evolved into a State police service under the command of a

---

3   The Australian Constitution s 107 states that the federal government has the right to legislate on only those matters designated in s 51. All other matters, including the criminal law and policing, are subject to legislation under the residual powers of individual States.

4   Officers working close to State borders may be sworn in as special constables of the neighbouring State for practical convenience: the communities of Albury, New South Wales and Wodonga, Victoria for example, are separated only by the River Murray, the State border.

5   An example of this is the National Campaign Against Violence and Crime, a federal government body which enables the federal government to be seen to be taking action on the crime problem, and exerts federal pressure on the States by funding particular projects.

commissioner answerable to a government minister with specific responsibility for policing. This minister is, of course, a member of cabinet and thus part of the State's executive arm of government.

The possibility arises, of course, for political control of police by this sort of structure, and, on occasion, this has indeed been the case. In practice, there are some safeguards in the system which have largely served to prevent this. Since the 1960s, as has been discussed already, society has become more aware of police powers and crime has become a political issue, and most States have instituted independent bodies with a supervisory role over police which may well, in the long term, significantly dilute the authority of State government over police. These anti-corruption bodies have been created in the wake of corruption scandals in individual States, for example the Criminal Justice Commission[6] in Queensland was established in the wake of the Fitzgerald inquiry, which will be discussed at length later in the chapter.

Appointments at the most senior levels of policing are nominally made by the governor. Indeed, Australian police officers of the rank of inspector and above are formally given a military style commission from the governor to carry out their duties, and the appointment of commissioners and assistant commissioners requires the formal approval of the governor. However, overtly political appointments are avoided as far as possible by the choice of commissioner being ratified by cabinet with the approval of opposition parties. Practice in Australian police forces until almost the end of the 20th century was for officers to be appointed to very senior ranks after promotion from within that force, although this is now changing. Commissioners of Australia's State police services have been appointed from interstate or overseas on at least half a dozen occasions since 1990, and some assistant commissioner appointments are also being made by lateral entry. This, however, is a far cry from the movement of senior officers between police services which is the rule rather than the exception in British policing.

Although appointments are formally made by the governor, in practice the appointee is nominated by the government of the day. Traditionally, most senior officers who have been considered for or appointed to command of a police force have been granted their commissions and promoted through various senior ranks by governments of varying political complexion, and are therefore broadly acceptable to whatever party is in power. Police officers have traditionally been tenured, even in the most senior positions. In practice the selection of police commissioners has been similar to the selection of judges: the government nominates an individual, who, once appointed, cannot thereafter be easily dismissed so a relatively safe, apolitical appointment has usually been made.

Since the mid-1990s Australian policing has been moving towards a contract system for appointing senior officers. As in British policing, the trend is towards a fixed term of around five years, with an option of

---

6   Now the Crime and Misconduct Commission.

extension for a further similar period by mutual agreement. This gives a commissioner some degree of independence from government, as the maximum time between State elections is usually less than the contract time, giving the electorate a chance to make their views known if a major disagreement arises between a commissioner and the government on policing. Some police services are going further with this trend: the Western Australia Police Service now appoints officers to commissioned rank on contract, although they retain tenure as police officers in their former rank, and the Australian Federal Police now appoint on contract at all levels. It is not entirely clear whether, certainly in the AFP, this creates more instability than continuity.

The traditional picture of the Australian police commissioner has been an individual who is appointed to run a police force after long service in it and complete enculturation in its ways.[7] This is changing, and the modern commissioner has a high profile, a contract for a finite period, a mandate to address particular issues and is under considerable pressure to achieve those goals. Although answerable to the police minister, the contract ensures that the commissioner can resist a considerable amount of political interference.

Financial accountability

Australian police services are directly financially accountable to their respective governments. Most of each State's income consists of that raised by federal government taxation, most notably income tax and GST, and shared amongst the States. There is, therefore, no separate federal allocation of money for funding State police, although it is open to the federal government to make one-off payments to the States for particular purposes. It is, therefore, wholly at the discretion of State governments how much money should be allocated to policing, and it is to the police minister and State treasurer that the commissioner of police must present a case for funding and account for spending. This provides the State government with a direct means of control over police through control of the service's finances more akin to the control of American police by local politicians than to the more general control which can be exercised by the British government.

Financial control has not usually been exercised as a means of curtailing any aspect of police activity, but is more frequently used to supply extra money for schemes the government wishes to see implemented. Policing, like health and education, has traditionally been seen to be a necessary public service and governments have paid more or less what was asked with the occasional boost in funding as a political gesture. Since the 1980s and the introduction of the cuts in public spending of the Thatcher and

---

7   Perhaps the last example of this is the former Commissioner of Police in New South Wales, Tony Lauer. After over 40 years of service and commitment to the New South Wales police, and growing evidence presented to the Wood Royal Commission of misconduct by many officers of almost all ranks, he refused to accept that there was an endemic problem in the service, despite being a man of undoubted personal integrity.

Reagan years in Britain and the United States and its introduction in Australia as economic rationalism, governments have become committed to reducing public spending. Although police budgets have not actually been cut, more is now expected of police without the commensurate financial resources being allocated for the tasks set. The government, for example, may gain significant political mileage from a well-publicised grant of an extra $1.5 million to recruit an extra 50 police officers. However, these new officers will spend the first six months in the Academy and the next six months at least requiring close supervision on the streets before they are effective police officers. The extra money may pay for little more than their training and their first year's wages while they are of little use to the service, and the budget in future years will not necessarily be increased to meet these new officers' salaries.

Long term, government restriction of the general police budget coupled with the release of "top-up" funds for specific purposes or projects reduces the operational independence of the police service, and brings it far more tightly under the control of State governments. If the specific funding is not wholly sufficient for the purpose to be achieved, then part of the general police budget has to be diverted to this purpose, which means something else must be sacrificed. The police commissioner cannot, of course, refuse these additional funds and may have to reduce necessary spending in another area to complete the funding for the new, partly funded project. Although the extra government funds may be perceived by the public as a gift to policing (and is perhaps intended by the government to be seen as such), it nevertheless amounts to an exercise of government financial control over policing strategy.

Policing in Australia is increasingly turning to non-government funding, which has the advantage of financing the initiatives that police wish to establish rather than those that government wishes to establish for them. Community policing is increasingly dependent on sponsorship from businesses or from local councils. This is no bad thing in that it does give this form of policing, which works as a long-term strategy by making police responsive and answerable to the public at a local level, a degree of immunity from governments which tend to be more interested in immediate results. Given, too, that people value something they pay for more than something they do not, if the community has a voluntary financial stake in policing above their tax contribution, they are more likely to take an interest in it. The third major source of funding, as has been mentioned, is federal funding, which, invariably, is for specific projects and is applied for rather than just given, which allows police the option whether or not to apply.[8] A last source of income is the Lotteries Commission, the State Lottery being required to return much of its income to benefit the public. Many community policing projects are funded in this way.

---

8   This, of course, does not apply to the Australian Federal Police, which, as the name implies, is a federally funded organisation, unless the funds are made available by a federal government agency which has no part in funding the AFP.

Operational accountability

Members of Australian police services answer, ultimately, to their commissioners, who, in turn, answer to their police ministers. In general, most police officers have been persons of goodwill, as have their commissioners and police ministers, so the system has worked tolerably well for most of its existence. When there have been indications of problems within policing (or any other public service), the generally accepted response has been an independent inquiry into the problem. In Australia, this has usually taken the form of a royal commission. This does, of course, require the appointment of a commissioner, who is normally a barrister or judge of acknowledged impartiality, by the relevant government. As a judicial officer a royal commissioner has absolute power to investigate within the terms of reference given by the commission. However reluctant the government might be, it is usually well advised to establish a royal commission sooner rather than later, lest the electorate conclude that the government has something to conceal.

Nevertheless, a system that works acceptably because most of the persons operating it are persons of goodwill is one that sooner or later will break down, if only because eventually persons of ill-will will use it to their own ends. Even when systems are manipulated by individuals, the motives may vary from the outright criminal desire for money and power to the "greater good" corruption of an individual who genuinely believes that, in the particular circumstances that pertain, the system itself works against the good of the community, and therefore perverting it is acceptable. It is the former that is to be seen in totalitarian states, but probably the latter which produced the burglary and cover-up of Watergate, the "greater good" being the continuation of the presidency of Richard Nixon.

Australian governments have usually opted for instituting a royal commission when public and political pressure is strong enough. A government which calls a royal commission also sets the terms of reference and the ambit of the inquiry. If the government holds off, there is a risk that, at the next election, the new government, (which, as the recent opposition, was almost certainly the loudest voice in favour of a royal commission) will set its own wider terms of reference for the royal commission. Although royal commissions are by no means rare, they frequently result in a number of issues being raised which were not, perhaps, expected at the outset. The Fitzgerald inquiry in Queensland was instituted to examine endemic corruption in the police of that State, but was very quickly granted an extension to its terms of reference to include political issues also.

The Fitzgerald inquiry had a major effect on the accountability of police throughout Australia, not just in Queensland. It brought to light flaws within the system of accountability of police through their commissioners to government police ministers. Although Fitzgerald inquired into actual events in Queensland, the system of accountability there varied little from the systems in place in the other States, so that the corruption in Queensland could easily have happened elsewhere. For this reason, many of the recommendations of the Fitzgerald report applied throughout Australia. The Fitzgerald inquiry therefore merits detailed discussion: the accountability system permitted police and political corruption to occur, and the recommendations to prevent its recurrence in Queensland should help, if implemented elsewhere, to prevent its occurrence elsewhere in Australia.

The Fitzgerald inquiry and its consequences

GE (Tony) Fitzgerald, QC, a former judge of the Federal Court, was appointed to head a "Commission of Inquiry into Alleged Illegal Activities and Associated Police Misconduct" on 26 May 1987. The terms of reference were extended at the end of June, public hearings ran from 27 July 1987 to 9 December 1988, and the final report was handed down on 3 July 1989. Evidence to the inquiry indicated that there had been significant corrupt dealings in the police force of Queensland for over 30 years, involving a number of officers, some of whom had reached the highest ranks of the police force, and also political malpractice. The eventual report recommended radical changes in policing accountability, together with political changes.

The inquiry covered the period of office of three protagonists as commissioners of police, Bischof from 1958 to 1969, Whitrod from 1970 to 1976, and Lewis from 1976 to 1987. The State premier from 1968 to 1987 was Joh Bjelke-Petersen. The first whispers of corruption were mentions of a group within the police force known as "the rat-pack" in 1959, to be followed by the Gibbs Royal Commission of 1963. The Fitzgerald inquiry brought to light police misconduct that took the form of non-prosecution of illegal bookmaking operations, casinos and brothels in return for large financial considerations.

The evidence disclosed that Commissioner Bischof had been involved in gambling, and had received money which was collected by others of the rat-pack, one of whom, Lewis, was later to become commissioner of police and receive a knighthood. The Gibbs Royal Commission in 1963 had not reported any wrong-doing, in part because its terms of reference had been restricted to matters which were peripheral to the most significantly corrupt activities within the police force. The corrupt practices had had a great deal of time to become established and were endemic before the appointment of Whitrod as commissioner.

Unlike his predecessor and successor, Ray Whitrod had had no connection with the Queensland Police before his appointment as Assistant Commissioner in 1969, followed, a year later, by his promotion. While it would be manifestly untrue to claim that the majority of the Queensland police force were corrupt, there was such a proportion of corrupt officers in positions of influence as to make corruption very difficult to eradicate. The most commonly heard response to allegations of corruption in policing is that there are always one or two rotten apples in the barrel – this invites the reply that, given the choice, most people would reject a barrel with more than a handful of bad apples and insist on one with only sound fruit.

One of the major problems that corruption brings within any police organisation is a lack of trust. Most police officers, like most other workers, have their own views on the worth of their colleagues, and will work best with those with whom they feel most comfortable, usually those who tend to think and act in a similar way. An officer who joins a group and is offered a corrupt inducement may well refuse, but may also find it difficult to report the matter. If the offer is overt, then this implies that it is acknowledged by some senior officers at least, who are also participants. Any attempt to report the matter runs a risk of making a report to an equally corrupt supervisor, which is likely to be positively harmful for the honest officer. An officer at a junior level encountering corruption may well not be certain to whom to report the matter, while Whitrod, an honest officer at the top, had no idea who amongst his subordinates to entrust with the task of investigating corruption.

The more entrenched corruption becomes, the more difficult it is to remove, as it tends to bury itself more deeply to evade discovery, and its proponents gain more and more legitimate power and influence. For corruption to thrive in an organisation, it is not necessary for all to be corrupt, or even the majority: all that is needed is for there to be a sufficient number of corrupt individuals in key positions so that they can keep the rest in line, order the uncompromisingly honest away, and divert those in higher authority from the truth. This last is made easier if the truth is something that those in authority have no wish to hear.

As Fitzgerald pointed out in his report, the Queensland cabinet, and particularly the premier, took a great deal of interest and had direct involvement in all sorts of matters which should have been no part of its political function. In particular, all police appointments of inspector and above were made by cabinet. Although Whitrod had posted Lewis on promotion to a country area well out of Brisbane, Lewis had the support of politicians, and, against the recommendations of the commissioner, was promoted to assistant commissioner by the cabinet, even though over 100 officers were more senior to him. On the resignation of Whitrod as commissioner, Lewis was appointed in his stead. The Fitzgerald inquiry received no evidence to suggest that any politician received money for protection from prosecution from those running vice and gambling in Brisbane, but certainly money was being received by police officers (including the commissioner, Lewis, who later served a sentence of imprisonment), and police received the unqualified support of the government. When the government and police are closely aligned, any substantiated allegations of police corruption affect the public perception of the probity of the government. Therefore, any government not involved in police corruption but strongly supportive of its police has a vested interest in minimising any allegations of police malpractice.[9]

---

9   Dickie (1988, p 52) claims, for example, that one government investigation into crime and corruption instigated by Police Commissioner Whitrod in 1975 and conducted by two senior detectives from London was started late, took considerable time, and the eventual report in 1977 was never released by the government.

Further allegations of police malpractice in Queensland were dealt with by the institution, in 1982, of a Police Complaints Tribunal. While, super-ficially, an independent tribunal might give the appearance of fairness and promise to remove corruption, the structure established by the Queensland police minister was incapable of so doing. The Queensland Police Com-plaints Tribunal was not perceived as impartial because of the offices its members held, the tribunal regularly referred complaints for investigation to the highly suspect police Internal Investigations Unit, and was found by Fitzgerald to be considered impotent by corrupt police. Commentators on police accountability have rightly claimed that:

> Although it was set up to deal with [allegations about police corruption in relation to gambling and prostitution], in practice it took the spotlight off the police and the government in the short term, and worked to protect the police department and the government from future allega-tions of police misconduct. (Landa and Lewis, 1996)

No royal commission can implement change, but can only make recom-mendations which require legislative implementation by government, usually the government calling the commission. The final report of the Fitzgerald inquiry contained a number of recommendations, some of which were no more than the importation into Queensland of sound current prac-tice in other States of Australia. Some of the recommendations were matters which had been under consideration or informally implemented elsewhere, giving other States impetus to maintain and improve these initiatives. The recommendations for Queensland with regard to police accountability do serve very clearly to indicate where the system was at fault, and what steps other States needed to take to change their systems to prevent the endemic corruption Fitzgerald found in Queensland. It must be borne in mind that the faults in the system applied equally to other States, which avoided falling into Queensland's problems either by introducing safeguards before Fitzgerald, or after Fitzgerald but before the problems surfaced. No State or police service in Australia could afford to ignore the Fitzgerald recom-mendations merely by claiming that "it could not happen here": the only basis for that claim was that the recommendations suggested were already in place.

The most obvious reform resulting from Fitzgerald's recommendations was the establishment of the Criminal Justice Commission (CJC), now the Crime and Misconduct Commission (CMC). This is a body completely independent of both government and police (although, like the judiciary, appointed and funded by government), and is specifically designed to deal with all aspects of public sector malpractice, including police misconduct and corruption. Its powers with regard to other areas of the public sector parallel those for dealing with police, but need not concern us here. One unique feature of the CJC recommended by Fitzgerald is that it should be responsible, not merely for supervising or reviewing investigations of com-plaints carried out by police, but for carrying out all such investigations itself. So reprehensible was the Queensland Police internal investigation branch and the government-established Police Complaints Tribunal to oversee it that both were abolished, and the CJC was to both investigate misconduct and report its findings to the Commissioner. The CJC became a rare example of a completely independent system of investigating complaints against police: it is unique in Australia, and no such independent body exists in Britain or the United States, although there are similar bodies in Canada.

The investigative function of the CJC/CMC is undertaken by police officers on secondment, who are carefully vetted and must have considerable experience in investigations. They are not answerable to the commissioner, but to the Chief Executive Officer of the CJC/CMC. This has a number of consequences which do not pertain to police officers who find themselves in internal affairs or their equivalent in other police services. Being on secondment outside the police service removes the stigma of the street police perception that complaints investigators are required to prevent effective police officers doing their job, and avoids the difficult position internal affairs officers can find themselves in once they return to other duties. Except insofar as to have passed the strict requirements of honesty demanded of the CJC/CMC guarantees an ex-CJC/CMC investigator to be free of any possible involvement with corruption, such service is, in theory at least, neutral in its effect on an officer's career.

The CJC/CMC is an anti-corruption body with five separate divisions. According to Landa and Lewis, this, in contrast to other anti-corruption bodies throughout Australia and elsewhere, "allows for an integrated, holistic approach to police misconduct and corruption" (Landa and Lewis, 1996). While other States have anti-corruption bodies and systems for investigating complaints against police, these are split between a number of organisations. The strength of the post-Fitzgerald Queensland system is that it is unitary and completely independent of both police and government. Its one drawback, as Landa and Lewis point out, is that it has no power to institute disciplinary proceedings or review the punishment imposed by the commissioner of police: with regard to discipline, the CJC/CMC can only make recommendations, not insist that the commissioner takes a particular course of action. In the event of evidence being found of criminal wrongdoing, the CJC/CMC can, of course, institute a prosecution through the courts.

The Fitzgerald report recommended other changes in the Queensland Police,[10] some of which, like recruiting policies, regionalisation and the introduction of community policing were concerned more with general policing standards and methods than with introducing or maintaining methods of holding police accountable. Some of the recommendations which do have a direct impact on accountability and a reduction of the power of the State premier or cabinet to influence policing are:

---

10   These are to be found in the report itself (Fitzgerald, 1989), but are also helpfully summarised in Dickie (1988).

- merit-based promotion and annual performance appraisal;
- advertising senior positions outside the State;
- the commissioner to report to the police minister, but a full written annual performance and financial report to be tabled in parliament;
- police informants to be registered centrally, and meetings with them subject to supervision by senior officers.

The issue of promotions is a crucial factor. Almost all police services are in a state of change, if only to keep up with changes in society, and need senior officers to be promoted to command positions because of their ability to lead rather than because of their longevity. While the traditional Australian system of promoting by seniority served to prevent a Commissioner surrounding himself with a clique, and the Queensland system of having all commissioned officer appointments made by cabinet allowed too much government interference and control of policing, an open, merit-based system with due consideration given to a broad range of candidates is most likely to make the best appointments. Senior officers from outside the police service have no personal obligations to other officers, or spectres from their past service to rise up and haunt them. They can, therefore, implement change and ensure best practice without fear or favour. The simple practice of having the commissioner accountable to parliament rather than just the police minister serves to remove the absolute control of the police from the executive government. The move to community policing, although not specifically intended to improve police accountability, has the serendipitous effect of doing so, since the more the police work with the public locally the more answerable they are, formally or informally, to the local population.

Although the registration of informants may seem to be a procedural, and even bureaucratic, step, it does have important implications for preventing corrupt dealings between police officers and criminals. If detectives are allowed to keep the identity of their informants completely secret, then this allows occasions for possible misconduct on various levels. On the most trivial level, an officer can be absent from duty during the working day on the pretext of meeting a fictitious informant, and claim unwarranted expenses for meals, etc purchased for this mythical individual. This is as venial as a business executive lunching with a friend, and claiming the cost on his or her expense account as entertaining a potential client. On the more serious aspect of corruption, an officer found to be in company with a criminal in suspicious circumstances can claim the justification that the matter was a meeting with an informant. Registration of informants provides a level of accountability over an officer's dealing with the criminal fraternity. It need not be a bar to efficiency, as the requirement on the officer to report each and every meeting with an informant, and the results of any information obtained, does not affect the relationship between officer and informant. Meetings with informants which are genuine, when food or drink is bought, information is sought and investigations are assisted, can easily withstand reporting and supervision, and no harm can be done by registering such an informant. Meetings which do not have a positive result for policing because the "informant" is a personal friend of the officer, or are a cover for corrupt dealings with criminals, can more easily be seen as such when requirements to register are in force. The Fitzgerald inquiry was presented with much evidence of corrupt dealings between police and criminals which, as meetings with informants, were unchallenged and unremarked.

The evidence to the Fitzgerald inquiry painted a truly frightening picture of the morass of corruption that can arise within a police force in a democratic nation with reasonably open government. It is, however, important to distinguish between the corruption that arises when the system itself is by its very nature corrupt, as in totalitarian states, and the corruption that arises, as in Queensland, where the system is merely flawed and therefore corruptible. Probably there is no way of establishing a system which is not corruptible in some way, or preventing corruption completely: the best that can be hoped is that corruption can be minimised. Even when corruption in policing or any other organisation is found, it is wrong to assume that all, or even most, are involved in it. One police sergeant who gave evidence at the Fitzgerald inquiry had refused a $400 per month bribe offer, and had retained an unwanted and corruptly given bottle of whisky from Christmas 1982 until the opportunity arose to produce it at the hearing in 1987, when he made this eloquent plea:

> I ask, I implore, all members of the public, the decent members of the public, do not write us off. We are there. The greater percentage of us are honest. We strive, we fight courageously to serve you, to care for you, to keep the streets clean, that you and your family can walk the streets – not frightened, not to be harassed, and if you support us, if you give us the support we need, you will be rewarded by a great body of men and women who will not hold back but will be out there straining to the limits to give you the best police service that I feel you so richly deserve.[11]

Other accountability models

While police officers are, and should continue to be, held personally responsible for their actions, considerable responsibility rests with individual police services and with State governments to ensure that sound, effective systems exist for misconduct by individual officers to be reported, investigated and dealt with fairly. The responsibility is joint, in that the establishment of any internal investigation branch is a matter for the police commissioner, while any legislation regarding external supervision of such a system is a matter for parliament, where such a Bill would be presented by the police minister.

The position of police in Australia's political structure has led to considerable discord at times between government and police commissioners

---

11   Sergeant Col Dillon, evidence to the Fitzgerald inquiry, 17 September 1987, cited in Dickie (1988).

quite unlike that encountered in Britain between police authorities and chief constables, or in the United States between mayors and chiefs of police. Finnane (1994, esp p 38 et seq) describes a number of instances wherein a very public disagreement has arisen between the operational decisions made by a police commissioner and the wishes of the government. These have not been resolved in a fashion which gives a clear demarcation between the principle of police independence from government control and the principle that police are accountable to government. Few of such disagreements have resulted in a clear win by government over police or vice versa, and even when matters have reached such a head that either the minister or the commissioner must go and one has gone, the other has usually followed within a short period of time.

This has left matters more than a little confused as to where the accountability of police lies. Harold Salisbury (Commissioner of Police in South Australia) made the claim that police commissioners were accountable to the Crown – directly to the Queen or her representative in Australia and thereby genuinely independent of government. He had been dismissed in 1977 by the then State premier, Don Dunstan, and a royal commission into the dismissal rejected his claim, and upheld the rights of the government. The Bright Report on policing in 1971, again in South Australia, had rather ambiguously stated that the government should not interfere in the detailed administration of the law, but it had power to intervene. The report failed to define these terms objectively, so that what to the premier appears to be reasonable intervention may well appear to the commissioner as unwarranted interference. Nevertheless, the government has not always managed to exercise its authority over police: in highly public disagreements between police ministers and commissioners in New South Wales and Queensland in 1992 it was the ministers, rather than the commissioners, who resigned.

These rather undignified squabbles between politicians and police are sufficient to highlight the fact that the power of government over police in Australia is not such as to constitute a significant threat to democratic freedom, but the police as an organisation are not so independent as to be, as the Lusher Report[12] suggested, a law unto themselves. Until the 1990s, Australia seems to have muddled through with commissioners and ministers at best leaving each other alone and at worst resolving problems by calling a royal commission to act as a referee, then implementing the commission's recommendations.

In the wake of Queensland's establishment of its CJC, New South Wales and Western Australia both established non-government bodies to investigate corruption in the public sector with particular regard to police corruption. In New South Wales this is the Independent Commission Against Corruption (ICAC), and in Western Australia the Anti-Corruption Commission (ACC), replaced in mid-2004 by the Crime and Corruption Commission. Unlike the Queensland body, neither of these bodies has sole

---

12   Into the New South Wales Police, 1981.

responsibility for dealing with police malpractice, as in both these States police retain an internal investigations branch, and the State Ombudsman also reviews complaints against police. In New South Wales, the Wood Royal Commission showed endemic problems within the New South Wales police service which were totally beyond the powers or capability of ICAC to deal with, and in Western Australia the ACC's secrecy and independence from accountability to judiciary, parliament or executive has led to its perception as a latter-day Star Chamber.[13]

Despite the inadequacies of ICAC and the ACC, the fact that they were established at all is indicative of a desire for an independent body to hold police accountable. In a sense, the government is more threatened by this than police, as a shift of police accountability to another body reduces police accountability to government, yet for police to be accountable to such a body merely spreads accountability more thinly rather than increases it. Problems only arise if more than one body tries in several different ways to hold police accountable for a single aspect of police duty. If any given police activity is to be scrutinised separately by internal affairs, the ombudsman's office, the DPP, an independent anti-corruption body and the commissioner, then this may well increase the paranoia felt by some officers and their representatives in the police union.

The other reforms mentioned in the Fitzgerald Report have become commonplace in policing throughout Australia. The community policing model is commonly found in one of its many forms in all police services, allowing far more informal public input into policing strategies than ever before, which in itself is a form of police accountability. A merit-based promotion system is now normal procedure, and an increasing number of senior appointments are being made of candidates from other police services in Australia and, indeed, overseas. The structure of police operational accountability in Australia has changed significantly since the 1980s, and continues to change. Royal commissions, in particular the Wood Commission in New South Wales, have added impetus to this, the underlying message being that such intermittent investigations are no substitute for the continuous monitoring of policing standards which was not a feature of the traditional Australian policing structure.[14]

Personal accountability

Australian police officers are, in some respects, more highly accountable than their British or American counterparts. Like all police officers, Australian police are ultimately answerable to their commissioner, usually

---

13 One particularly worrying case was that of six drug squad detectives investigated by the ACC in 1997. On information received in secret hearings, which did not necessarily comply with the rules of evidence, a report was submitted to the Commissioner of Police, who suspended the officers, and later ordered them to show cause why they should not be dismissed. The information was, however, insufficient to persuade the DPP to undertake a criminal prosecution.

14 Following the Wood Royal Commission, the government of New South Wales has established an Integrity Commission for its police.

through the internal affairs branch or through the rank hierarchy. The judiciary, too, has a role in police accountability, although its powers are less regularly exercised in Australia than in other countries, particularly the United States. All Australian States except Queensland have an ombudsman with a supervisory function in complaints against police, and most have an anti-corruption body which also investigates individual officers. This multiplicity of accountability systems, coupled with the precedent set in the case of *Enever*,[15] can make the individual police officer feel oversupervised almost to the point of paranoia. Each of these aspects of accountability needs further discussion.

The case of *Enever* was decided in the early years of Australia as a nation, and concerns an officer who, in dealing with a dispute and a minor assault between two parties, arrested the original complainant rather than his assailant. The complainant sued the officer and the police force for wrongful arrest, and the court held that the decision to exercise any of a police officer's powers is that of the officer alone. The office of constable is independent, and an officer is wholly responsible for any decision to exercise the power of arrest. If the arrest is wrong in law, then the officer is liable. It follows that if an officer is wholly responsible, then that officer is solely responsible, and any judgment is against the officer, not the police service. In Britain, police services have long accepted vicarious liability for the actions of police officers, and in the United States a Supreme Court decision has made public bodies responsible for the decisions of their employees:[16] only in Australia can a wrong decision made by a police officer, even if made in good faith, result in the possibility of litigation followed by personal bankruptcy.

Internal investigations

With the exception of Queensland, investigation of complaints against police in Australia is largely carried out by a specialist branch within the police service reporting to the police executive. While these officers are carefully picked within the police service, and usually have commissioned rank and therefore a significant length of service, the investigation remains internal. Complaints investigations are subject to external supervision and review by the ombudsman, and police services place a great deal of emphasis on a full, professional investigation of any complaints made by the public. There are three issues which arise from this system: whether the power granted to the ombudsman is adequate; whether the police services' investigation procedures are adequate; and whether the public now perceive the complaints investigation system to be adequate.

Perhaps the most important principle of modern policing is that police and community should work together, which requires that the public have a great deal of faith in their police. This faith relies, at least in part, on there

---

15 *Enever v R* (1906) 3 CLR 969.
16 *Monell v Dept Social Services*, City of New York 436 US 658 (1978). This is discussed fully in Chapter 12.

being a system for investigating complaints against police which is trusted by the public. There is little doubt that police services throughout Australia fully understand the effect that such an investigation procedure has on their relations with the community, and have accepted the responsibility of improving their investigation procedures giving them due precedence and status within the organisation. While this has, by and large, been accomplished, the task of empowering the office of ombudsman to deal effectively, and to the satisfaction of the public, with complaints against police is a matter for the legislators.

Police officers on the street may well, in the short term at least, take a very jaundiced view of a more thorough and professional approach to investigating complaints against them. In all organisations there are both standards officially required and obligations laid down in the rules which are always more stringent than the normal working practices which are generally acceptable to management. Policing is no exception, so that a thorough investigation by internal affairs will always uncover minor administrative discrepancies or less than perfect practice whether or not there is evidence of the substantive malpractice originally alleged.

From the viewpoint of the officer on the street, then, the increase in professionalism of internal affairs manifests itself as increased supervision, and a tendency for the investigators to dig about until they find evidence of some misdemeanour, however trivial.

In the long term, police officers will become accustomed to the professional standards of a modern police service, and will meet these requirements as a matter of course. In the short term, higher standards need to be inculcated by training or other positive methods to ensure that there is a general agreement in the standard of quality required, and a widespread, genuine attempt to reach it. Without this, a quality control system will not succeed. All too often, the only way that the standards required by the organisation become known is through stringent internal investigations which result in a report which criticises common working practices. This is a reactive approach which just indicates failure and frequently leads to a lowering of morale within a police service, unless accompanied by positive means of achieving higher standards.

The disposition of complaints investigations rest with the commissioner in all States, because the commissioner is solely responsible for discipline. This is even the case in Queensland, as, although the CJC/CMC has wide powers to investigate and collect evidence against an officer, it cannot require the commissioner to take disciplinary action, nor can it override or appeal against any punishment imposed by the commissioner. It is a common feature of Police Acts throughout Australia that the commissioner of police alone is responsible for discipline within the police service, and there are very limited appeal procedures. The CJC/CMC, like anti-corruption bodies in other States, can undertake or recommend criminal proceedings which becomes a matter for the director of public prosecutions rather than the police commissioner. However, when no criminal proceedings are possible through insufficient evidence, or the facts do not justify a charge, then the commissioner of police has full authority to decide whether or not to take disciplinary action.

An important aspect of the commissioner's powers in Australian policing is that which enables the dismissal of any officer in whom "the commissioner has lost confidence".[17] Although this section would appear to be a useful means of removing a corrupt officer from the police service, it is indeed a draconian power for the commissioner to have, especially if there is no appeal procedure following such a decision. Its use can best be justified in cases where corruption is clear but a criminal conviction is doubtful on the evidence available. Corruption usually involves payments made by criminals to police, and to prove this in court often relies on the evidence of the criminal, or on evidence that the police officer and the criminal have been seen together in compromising circumstances. Juries are frequently loath to believe the evidence of criminals, and are usually willing to give officers who claim the meeting was to gain information about crime the benefit of the doubt.

The danger with a commissioner's powers to dismiss an officer for such a nebulous cause as absence of confidence, without the commissioner having to produce evidence of wrong-doing to a criminal court or discipline tribunal, is that it evades all the requirements of procedural justice required in almost every other forum. In the circumstances outlined above, such power may well be necessary, but it is a poor substitute for a carefully prepared case alleging wrongdoing which the officer complained of, as defendant, has to answer. For officers to be required to show cause why they should not be dismissed may be seen as a requirement to demonstrate innocence, which is contrary to one of the fundamental principles of common law. Written notification of the facts on which a commissioner has based the decision to dismiss an officer is a poor substitute for the right to cross-examine witnesses before a tribunal. Such powers may be necessary, but a review procedure must be present to prevent unfair dismissals, and also to comply with the industrial relations procedures which apply to every other worker.

A commissioner's power to dismiss an officer is an important weapon against corruption, and should not be used or repealed lightly. A corrupt police officer is, by definition, not an honourable person, and can therefore be expected to utilise every procedural device available to avoid criminal and discipline proceedings and subsequent conviction or punishment. The power to dismiss such officers prevents their availing themselves of such devices. The other side of the coin is that, if enough hearsay and innuendo exists concerning an officer, that individual may be dismissed unfairly without the opportunity to challenge such evidence as exists. It is by no means clear how procedures can be built into the power to dismiss to ensure it is never misused, but the possibility for misuse through malicious complaints reinforces the need for some form of independent, and possibly judicial, appeal procedure.

17　The wording varies slightly, but this is the general formula which appears somewhere in the legislation governing police in each State.

The office of the ombudsman

The office of ombudsman was established in Australia in the 1970s as an independent investigator dealing with complaints about the public service. The title and role stems from a centuries-old Scandinavian adjudicative post which was seen as a useful means of ensuring probity in the public sector. The ombudsman in each State is independent, government-funded, and reports to parliament.[18] The investigative powers of the ombudsman are set out in legislation, and are fairly wide since the ombudsman's office deals with matters across the whole public service, not just police. The main restriction on the ombudsman is that imposed by the limits of the financial and other resources allocated by the government. Legislative powers vary somewhat between States, but in general the ombudsman has authority to accept and investigate complaints about police misconduct, and to oversee an internal police complaint investigation.

The often confrontational nature of policing means that the vast majority of complaints dealt with by the ombudsman are complaints against police officers, and consequently these are the greatest potential drain on investigators' resources. The office of ombudsman has always been run on a relatively tight budget, which means that no ombudsman's office has the resources to investigate all complaints against police fully and independently, and most content themselves with an independent review of internal police investigations. The ombudsman for Western Australia, for example, generally refers any complaints against police that the office receives directly from the public to the Commissioner of Police, with a direction that an internal investigation is to be carried out and a report sent to the ombudsman within 42 days. Given the professional standards now required of internal investigations and the persistent underfunding of the ombudsman's office,[19] this is the best available compromise, though hardly satisfactory.

A further problem with the system of having the ombudsman oversee police complaints investigation is that the ombudsman has very little power to act. Resources tend to prevent the ombudsman making a full independent investigation, although the commissioner of police can be required to re-investigate or carry out a supplementary investigation on various issues. The commissioner's powers under respective Police Acts predate the ombudsman's powers, so in all cases decision-making rests with the commissioner, and the ombudsman can only advise, not order, a particular course of action. While the ombudsman may not be a completely toothless

---

18   It is, perhaps, noteworthy that Britain also has adopted the idea of an ombudsman, but in a slightly different fashion. Officially known as the Parliamentary Commissioner, the ombudsman is a complaints investigator and adjudicator for the government public service. However, some industry groups have also taken up the idea, and Britain now has a banking ombudsman, insurance ombudsman and various others, all independent but paid for by the national body of the profession in question.

19   Landa and Lewis (1996) remark that, of systems for holding police accountable, "Queensland's Criminal Justice Commission is the exception in Australia in that it has been properly funded since its inception" – clearly they find that the ombudsman's office in every other State is inadequately funded for the purpose of police accountability.

tiger, the lack of real power under the legislation and lack of resources combine to reduce the effectiveness of the office.

Public perceptions

The Australian public probably has less faith in the complaints investigation systems than these systems and police organisations actually deserve. The scandalous behaviour uncovered by the Fitzgerald and Wood Royal Commissions raised serious doubts about the police in Queensland and New South Wales respectively, and the inhabitants of each of the other States could not be criticised for assuming that things were little different there, and police malpractice was merely awaiting discovery. This is fuelled by highly publicised incidents of police misconduct which occur in any police service from time to time. A poor reputation takes a long time to live down, and all Australian police forces have incidents from the past which live on in the public's collective conscience, although most of these should be consigned to history. Australian police still have to live with the public perception of widespread corruption the like of which Fitzgerald identified in Queensland in 1989, even though more than 15 years have passed since the inquiry.

Although procedures for investigating complaints and dealing with corruption have changed significantly, the public is, perhaps, dubious about their efficacy, especially given the apparent powerlessness of the ombudsman. Like all police organisations, Australia's police are not without problems in behaviour, as has been recently highlighted by Chan (1997), in her analysis of racism in New South Wales after the reforms of Avery. Suspicion of police runs deep, especially amongst those who have most to do with them – young people, Aboriginals, the poor and those on the streets. While it should never be suggested that policing in Australia is perfect, nor that current accountability systems are foolproof, public perception of the professional standards of its police is rather below that which Australian police deserve.

What the public see in most States is an internal system of complaints investigation, where the police investigate the police, which generates the fear that this allows the possibility of a cover-up. The external body responsible for monitoring complaints against police is seen as being ineffective, largely because of lack of resources to investigate fully and the practice of reviewing a completed internal investigation rather than instigating its own investigation. The delays, which are inevitable before there is even an investigation report for the ombudsman to review, are perceived as allowing police time to produce a sanitised version of the events complained of, and thus allow police misconduct to go unpunished. This perception is not wholly justified by the systems currently in place in police services: this is not to say that malpractice is impossible, but that it is rendered far less likely to go unnoticed. The current rigorous systems of police complaints investigation are misperceived as being little different from the weak and rightly suspect systems of the past.

Accountability through the courts

Australian police are accountable through the courts in that police evidence describing their actions and exercise of powers is open to be tested in cross-examination by the defence. Police can also be held accountable as defendants in civil courts when they are sued for compensation when their actions are alleged to be negligent or tortious. Both these options exist throughout common law systems, but for a number of reasons are far more effective in Britain and the United States than they are in Australia as a means of holding police accountable. Unlike Britain and the United States, Australian courts recognise no absolute right to legal representation for defendants,[20] and in Magistrates Courts criminal prosecutions are generally undertaken by police themselves.[21] The vast majority of cases are heard at magistrates' court level, which means that most defendants are prosecuted by police, are unrepresented, and the whole case, especially if held before justices rather than stipendiary magistrates, proceeds without a practising lawyer being present. This has the very important effect of reducing the court's ability to exercise accountability over police officers.

The most likely forum for police activities to be questioned is in the higher courts, before a judge and jury, where defendants are far more likely to be represented by counsel. Precedent is set in the court of appeal, so formal rulings on police action are rarely set without the defendant being represented, but this is only part of the story. The court rulings which affect police actions will certainly be disseminated through the police service and will be known to police as well as to practising criminal lawyers, but there is no certainty that lay magistrates or defendants will be aware of them. It is through a lack of legal knowledge that the courts sometimes fail to hold police to account for their actions in dealing with suspects and defendants.

The presence of practising lawyers on either side of a criminal prosecution (but particularly appearing for the defendant) would do much to hold police accountable and maintain the rights of a defendant. As it is, police have the dual role as evidence-collecting prosecution witnesses and as the prosecuting authority, choosing the appropriate charge and presenting the case. Without a separate public prosecuting body there is no review of whether the prosecution is viable, and without defence lawyers little chance of the prosecution evidence being tested fully. The adjudicative rather than inquisitorial role of judges and magistrates in common law courts precludes them from challenging or criticising police on matters not

---

20   There is a limited right to representation, laid down in the eponymous "Dietrich Ruling" of the High Court of Australia, where no prosecution against an indigent defendant in a serious matter can proceed unless the defendant is represented. This ruling is unsatisfactory in that it does not define when a matter is "serious" and does not guarantee legal aid. If a State legal aid body refuses legal aid, the result may be that proceedings are suspended until the defendant can obtain representation.

21   In 1998, the State government of Western Australia considered extending the role of the DPP to all prosecutions, removing police from this role. The proposal was rejected on grounds of cost, although prosecuting lawyers now take an active role in more prosecutions, and are likely to be involved at an earlier stage of such prosecutions.

raised by the defence, and it is only the astute and knowledgeable defendant who can do this.

Although the rule in *Enever* renders police officers individually liable in civil matters, in practice few suits are pursued against police officers. The first and most obvious reason is that police officers are extremely unlikely to have the financial resources to meet any judgments made against them. There is little point in suing an individual who is unable to pay, and most lawyers would be likely to advise potential plaintiffs of this. Furthermore, such legal aid funds as are available in Australia are rarely authorised for plaintiffs in civil suits, rendering this course of action beyond the means of most persons who feel wronged by police action. The no win–no fee system operated by American lawyers has not yet been adopted in Australia.

Conclusion

The system of police accountability in Australia is, as has been shown, reasonably sound, probably better than the public gives it credit for, but not without room for improvement. The best model is undoubtedly the post-Fitzgerald CJC/CMC in Queensland, a well-funded, independent and powerful body which can act for the public in holding police accountable both as a body and as individuals. However, it required both the proven fact of serious police corruption and of questionable government to break the chain of police accountability directly and solely to government. That police in Queensland are answerable to parliament as well as to a police minister, and to an independent body also, is far healthier for the body politic of that State than for police to be answerable solely to government.

Although the current system which gives respective governments far more power to hold police answerable, and thereby leaves far less opportunity for independent bodies to hold police answerable, is effective, it relies on the absolute probity of State governments. There is no suggestion that any current State government is less than acceptable in this sense, but absolutely no reason to suppose that this will always be the case. Only a strong, independent body like Queensland's CJC/CMC holding both police and government accountable can prevent police corruption going unremarked by government. However, the combination of corrupt police and compliant government is bound to recur sooner or later in one of the other States of Australia, and the ombudsmen and anti-corruption bodies there may well be less than effective in dealing with the problem.

As will be seen in discussions of accountability in Britain and the United States in the following chapters, no system is perfect: Australia's means of holding police accountable are grounded in the nation's history and political system, and continues to serve it reasonably well. Since the late 1980s, the accountability of police to government has been reduced, and accountability has been spread more widely to other bodies, and, through community policing, to the public itself, in a more effective manner.

CHAPTER 11

POLICE ACCOUNTABILITY IN BRITAIN

Introduction

Several threads run through all the issues of accountability in British policing,[1] as the same pieces of legislation affect all forces, and some Acts have a major impact in this area. The first important Act was the *County and Borough Police Act* 1856, which established a level of national government supervision over all police forces. A more recent Act of major importance was the *Police Act* 1964, which instituted a number of procedural changes and amalgamated a number of forces. Issues of police accountability at all levels were changed radically by the *Police and Criminal Evidence Act* 1984 (*PACE Act* 1984). Finally, the relationship between police and various levels of government was changed in the 1990s by the *Police and Magistrates Courts Act* 1994 and the *Crime and Disorder Act* 1998. These later Acts are considered again in Chapter 14 with recent and continuing shifts in emphasis in police management.

The first matter to be considered is the position of police in the political structure of Britain. This involves an analysis of the respective roles of the chief officer of police, the police authority, and the Home Office, and the function of Her Majesty's Inspectorate of Constabularies (HMIC). There was a long-established balance between the first three of these which has been significantly altered by the *Police and Magistrates Courts Act* 1994, as will be shown, and the argument here follows various commentators in demonstrating that this adversely affects the independence of police from central government.

The issue of financial accountability is in part answered by looking at whence the money for policing comes. Clearly, those who are responsible for apportioning money for policing have an interest in it, and a right to know how it has been spent. This is by no means the whole story, however, as central government has always supplied some of the funds for policing

---

1   An important caveat, made earlier in this work, needs to be stressed again here. Although "Britain" is used as a shorthand term, much British legislation, in policing as in other areas, applies only in England and Wales: Scotland and Northern Ireland operate under different legislation. Any legal requirements discussed here apply only in England and Wales, although the principles carry over to the other parts of Britain and the effect on the public policed are similar. A comparison can be drawn here with Australian policing, where each State has its own legislation and *Police Act*, yet there is little overt difference to the public between police in the various States and Territories.

yet has delegated the responsibility for ensuring that these funds are used correctly to police authorities. Direct accountability to government changes the pattern of financial accountability. The issue of the possibility of financial accountability being used to expedite operational control is considered also.

Operational accountability in British policing has several facets. The chief officer is answerable to the police authority directly for the operational implementation of policing priorities, answerable also to the Home Office[2] for implementation of national directives regarding policing priorities, and to the Inspectorate for overall efficiency of policing. Superimposed on this is the legal requirement of the *PACE Act* 1984 for BCU[3] commanders to establish community consultative committees and to be held accountable to them for local policing needs, and of the *Crime and Disorder Act* 1998 for the local police commander to work with the chief executive officer of the local authority to develop and implement a crime and disorder strategy. There is clearly a potential problem for the development of policing plans, if the priorities identified by the Home Office, police authority and local community consultative committees are different, or are in actual conflict, or if there are insufficient funds available to address them all satisfactorily, which is quite probable.

The issue of personal accountability of police officers is addressed in Britain by a clear complaints investigation procedure grounded in the *Police Act* 1964 and *PACE Act* 1984, and given credibility by the Police Complaints Authority established in 1985.[4] The courts also have some responsibility for ensuring police behave correctly, by testing the probity of police action in searching, arrest, detention and questioning of suspects when criminal matters are brought before them.

Police in the British political structure

The early history of British policing[5] shows how the national parliament at Westminster both authorised the establishment of police then largely devolved decisions about policing to local committees. The Metropolitan Police was the only British police force ever to be under the direct control of central government, the Home Secretary being the police authority from 1929 until the *Greater London Authority Act* 1999 established a police authority with local government representation. In the formative years of the 1830s, the policing body for London was a comparatively small aspect

---

2   The Metropolitan Police was a special case until 1999 with the Home Secretary as its police authority. This is no longer the case, as a separate police authority for London has been created.
3   Basic Command Unit, formerly known as a division or sub-division, commanded by a superintendent or chief superintendent.
4   The Police Complaints Authority was established on 29 April 1985 under the *PACE Act* 1984 s 83. The Authority replaced the Police Complaints Board which had been established some years earlier to oversee complaints investigations – the Authority was granted significant power under the legislation.
5   See Chapter 2.

of the responsibilities of the Home Secretary, so that Rowan and Mayne could and did establish their autonomy in making policing decisions. Indeed, the Home Office attempt which Mayne rebutted to intervene in police matters was made by an Under-Secretary, Samuel Phillips, a civil servant rather than an elected officer, and thus was in no real sense an attempt to exercise political control over police.

The *Lighting and Watching Act* 1833 permitted ratepayers in towns to establish police forces if they chose, and the *Rural Constabulary Act* 1839 allowed county magistrates the option to establish policing in country areas. The *Municipal Corporations Act* 1835 made it obligatory for boroughs to establish police forces, ensuring that towns and cities were all policed. The introduction of professional policing was thus established by statute, but control of it, once introduced, remained strictly local. The *County and Borough Police Act* 1856 added a level of compulsion to the earlier policing Acts, by rendering the establishment of a constabulary mandatory on rural areas, so that the whole of Britain would be policed by professional officers. The Act also addressed the problems over who was to pay for these new police forces, and how standards of policing could be maintained.

Pay and standards frequently go together. Many counties were reluctant to institute new police, and many of the boroughs merely renamed the members of the old watch policemen, paying them the same low wages: this penny-pinching attitude did not attract the calibre of recruit that was necessary. In all police forces, including the Metropolitan Police, there was a high turnover of officers, with a large number of dismissals for drunkenness and minor infringements of discipline, and a large number of resignations, possibly due to the higher expectations the public held of "new police" that were not held of the old watch.

The *County and Borough Police Act* 1856 addressed all these issues, and established procedures which still hold today in British policing. An Inspectorate of Constabulary was established under the aegis of the Home Office, whose responsibility it was to examine all aspects of all police forces, make recommendations, and issue a certificate of efficiency as to their conduct. To ensure that the system worked, the Act also allowed that 25 per cent of the cost of each police force would be met from the Treasury. The implied stick and carrot was that money would be paid to efficient constabularies – unless the inspectorate was satisfied with standards, no certificate of efficiency would be issued, and government could withhold their contribution to the costs.

Police authorities

Westminster's interest in policing was satisfied by periodic inspection of each force by the inspectorate[6] and by having a measure of control over the

---

6   There remains, of course, the power of the government to establish an inquiry into policing in a particular force, and government was also involved in 1997-98 in the notorious public dissatisfaction in Scotland with the Chief Constable of the Grampian Police.

finance, in effect having the power to cut funding to local governments which did not run efficient police forces. Although 25 per cent of the cost of policing was met by government from 1856, the remaining 75 per cent was raised from the rates (local property taxes), raised by councils. In fact, this precept went up to 50 per cent in 1874, and in 1985 the government contribution was raised above half the cost of policing to 51 per cent. Each police force had its own chief constable, who answered to the police authority. The police authority evolved from the Watch Committee, who had been responsible for the old watchmen. The constitution of this committee might vary, but in general it contained representatives of the magistracy, elected local government members and others who might be elected or co-opted onto it. In keeping with the view that the institution of the new police was of most value to the prosperous urban middle class, the majority of members of police committees until, perhaps, the 1960s were drawn from members of this very group.

There is much in the structure of police authorities and central government involvement to support the view that the police were an instrument of the middle classes. The 1856 Act effectively established the power of the chief constable to determine how policing was carried out, answerable to the triumvirate of the police authority, the Home Office and the Inspectorate. For at least the first century after this Act, almost without exception every person involved in police policy-making was a white, middle-aged, middle class male. The police authorities certainly were of this group, chief constables were often retired senior military men,[7] the Inspectorate consisted of middle ranking civil servants and police officers usually of superintendent rank or above on secondment, and the Home Office's own involvement was through career civil servants.

The separation of the powers controlling police gave certain advantages. Chief constables soon established a clear degree of independence from their authorities, at least in operational matters (see Brogden, 1982) and were able, if they chose, to put their imprint on a force very strongly. Nevertheless, they were appointed by their police authorities, and could be dismissed by them, but only with Home Office approval.[8] Following recommendations made in the Sheehy Report, chief constables are usually now appointed on a fixed-term contract, normally for five years. While the Home Office itself could not dismiss a chief constable, chief constables were answerable to the Inspectorate for the efficiency of their forces, and the Inspectorate reported to the Home Office. A chief constable therefore had to satisfy the police authority, the Home Office and the Inspectorate. Having

---

7 Worcester City Constabulary is a case in point. Its officers during the 1950s were, in general, rather taller than average – this was a direct result of the Chief Constable having been colonel of a Guards regiment, and had a penchant for employing his old soldiers as police officers. Many other police authorities chose retired officers to head their forces.

8 Illustrative of this is the case of Captain Popkess, Chief Constable of Nottingham in 1959. He refused to divulge details of an investigation to his Watch Committee, who suspended him, but Popkess was reinstated by them on the instructions of the Home Secretary. This illustrates both a lack of clarity in the system, and the fact that power over police is divided.

the complete support of all three was, perhaps, a forlorn hope, but a chief constable could afford to challenge one of them if the issue warranted it, provided some support was available from the others. The balance was delicate at times, and relied upon a degree of difference of opinion or priorities, and the possibility of dissent to examine all issues connected with policing.

Two pieces of legislation have done much to upset this delicate balance. The first, the *PACE Act* 1984 opened up control of the police to the public who were most affected by police. This Act required every chief superintendent to establish a consultative committee for the area, and every interest group was entitled to seek representation on the committee. This changed the operational accountability of police, bringing it to a local level, and spreading it across all ethnic and income groups, reducing the power of the traditional oligarchy. The effect of this Act will be examined in detail shortly. The first 10 years of this Act's operation may well come to be seen as the Indian summer of local accountability of police; during the 1990s a number of reports and reviews into policing indicated an insidious shift of control, largely through demands for financial justification of policing strategies. The effect of the *Police and Magistrates Courts Act* 1994 and later legislation in shifting decision-making towards the Home Office is discussed at length in Chapter 14.

Financial control

The injection of money into policing by central government in the 1856 Act was first and foremost a means of getting policing established throughout the nation, and a means of government buying its way into setting national standards. There was certainly no serious attempt to wrest control of policing from local committees to national government, even though national government was paying heavily for policing everywhere. The Metropolitan Police in London was responsible to the Home Office, but the control had traditionally always been slack, despite the fact that most of its budget was met from national funds. Given the size and high cost of the Metropolitan Police, since 1874 central government had probably met over 60 per cent of the national cost of policing rather than the nominal half, yet control had remained with local police authorities. Whatever the cost of policing a town or county might be, if its inhabitants could be persuaded to meet half through their rates, then government would unquestioningly meet the other half.

The Conservative governments in Britain of the Thatcher and Major years from 1979 to 1997 exhibited two important attitudes which have had a profound effect on the control of police: first, a loathing and contempt of local government and, secondly, the desire to reduce the evaluation of everything to fiscal terms. Although almost the first action that the government took upon assuming office in 1979 was to implement the considerable rise in salary and long-overdue pegging of police pay under the Edmund

Davies formula, over the next five years financial and other controls imposed by Westminster on local government effectively cut police budgets, despite the fact that about 85 per cent of this was spent on salaries.

For many years, central government funds had been used to top-up the cash requirements of local authorities when an increase in rates was not feasible. In the 1980s the government instituted rate-capping, which restricted the amount that could be raised locally, and cut, or put restrictions on the use of, central government money available to councils. The effect was that boroughs could not always make available to police authorities their half of the amount of money deemed necessary for policing, since the needs of policing had to be balanced against other needs, for example housing and public works, when dividing up a total income determined by the government. Since many members of police authorities were elected members of local government, they were forced into making decisions about policing that were fiscally driven.

Two questions were constantly being asked about policing from the 1980s on. The first was what the tasks of police actually were, or what they should be. If some of the variety of jobs traditionally undertaken by police could be shown rightfully to belong to some other agencies, then police could be relieved of these and concentrate on their core functions, in the hope that efficiency would improve and costs would be cut. The second question concerned how police efficiency and effectiveness could be measured, and what policing services the public received for its tax payments. These questions were addressed in reviews and reports of the early 1990s such as the Audit Commission Report (1994), the Police Foundation/CSI. Report (Cassels Report) (1994) and the Home Office Review of Police Core and Ancillary Tasks (1995).

The Audit Commission is a government agency concerned with monitoring the financial rectitude of government spending. Although previously the Audit Commission had no brief to examine policing, from 1995 the *Police and Magistrates Courts Act* 1994 requires that police authorities account to the Audit Commission. Police authorities themselves have been distanced from local government:

> Certainly until 1995 Local Authorities had a legal responsibility through their police committees comprising locally elected politicians and magistrates to maintain an adequate, efficient police force for their area. From that date arrangements changed, and Police Authorities became independent bodies in their own right albeit that their legal obligations were not affected. (Walker and Richards, 1996)

Financial accountability *per se* is no bad thing, and with the escalating cost of policing then it is right for police authorities to show how the money is spent. Police services have large capital assets to manage, buildings and vehicle fleets, for example, and the principles of effective management of these are, perhaps, not wildly different from the principles any business would rely on for getting the best value for money from its shops, factories, warehouses and vehicles. What does cause problems is trying to fit policing outcomes into the sort of profit and loss balance sheet to which accountants are accustomed.

Commentators, among them Morgan and Newburn (1997), see dangers in the fiscal approach to measuring police efficiency. Simply looking at how the money is spent, in terms of breakdown into wages, overtime, particular sections of policing, and so on, can easily become an analysis of what individual strategies cost to implement and lead on to a financial examination of operational decisions. The wise chief officer and police authority set aside money for non-specific but likely contingencies such as a major inquiry into a series of rapes, murder, kidnapping or other uncommon, but not unknown, drains on resources. There is already evidence that government can find extra money to meet police needs when it chooses: the miners' dispute of 1984 required national coordination at chief officer level to provide thousands of officers from all over the nation to police the dispute over a protracted period. Policing for the strike was separately funded by national government, and individual police budgets were unaffected.

The model that raises doubts about financial control of police in Britain is that of the health service, where hospitals have become controlled by Health Trusts, which apply tests of financial viability to programs for treatment of patients. Cases have occurred where two hospitals have previously carried out a particular routine surgical procedure, for example hip replacement surgery, but the costs of this at hospital A are significantly higher than at hospital B. Hospital A has ceased to carry out this procedure, since hospital B does it cheaper, and all patients needing this treatment have to go to hospital B, even those living near hospital A for whom travel causes difficulties. If this principle is extended to policing, then it is possible that financial considerations alone will result in particular types of police activity no longer being carried out. Many tests in forensic science are expensive, and fiscal considerations rather than the interests of justice may prevail in the presentation of such evidence to the courts: many police services have developed sophisticated systems of costing to ensure that money is always available to fund the necessary tests for cases deemed sufficiently serious.

One type of police duty which may be diminished on financial grounds is the investigation of vice offences such as brothel-keeping and living off the earnings of prostitution. A successful prosecution for this type of offence requires at least two skilled and experienced officers carrying out observations over a long period, usually several weeks, careful record-keeping and often up to a week for trial, even though the eventual penalty is rarely more than a year or two of imprisonment. The crime is considered victimless and in itself is not viewed particularly seriously by the general public. Such operations would seem to be prime candidates to be written off as not financially worthy of investigation. However, vice observations usually bring to light other more unpleasant matters, such as the involvement of drugs, under-age girls or women from the third world or eastern Europe where violence, threats or addiction are all used to keep prostitutes in a state akin to slavery, rendering vice prosecutions socially desirable even if they are not financially viable.

Police services in Britain are now subject to much more stringent financial accountability than they have been in the past. The object of this accountability has also changed: although the police service is still accountable to its police authority, the police authority is no longer a part of local government but a separate entity. Although the chief officer prepares the budget and requires the police authority's agreement to it, it is the Home Office which determines the aggregate grant.[9] In a subtle but important shift of emphasis, police are now more financially accountable to the Home Office than before, and less financially accountable to local government. If, as has been suggested above, financial accountability is used as a means of affecting operational decision-making, then serious changes will have been made surreptitiously to the accountability and autonomy of police in Britain. This will be closely analysed.

Operational accountability

Operational decisions in policing are considered here to be those taken by officers of the rank of superintendent or chief superintendent which involve short- or medium-term operations in a geographical area rather less than that of the whole police service. Decisions involving the whole force are, clearly, made by the chief officer or executive and are strategic or policy decisions. Officers making operational decisions have traditionally been held accountable for them to the chief officer and thus to the police authority, but also to the police Inspectorate. Police were not directly accountable to the public, and, indeed, the only public involvement before the *PACE Act* 1984 was at several removes insofar as the police authority contained members who were elected to local government.

Before 1984, operational decisions were made to further the plans of the police force, which often were not explicitly stated, and probably no more than a reiteration of Mayne's dictum of 1829. If any given police action gave offence to any section of the public, this was shrugged off as a necessary part of police duty, and the end result, in the form of arrests or seizures of property or drugs, was used as a justification. Events in the early 1980s and the *PACE Act* in 1984 resulted in changes requiring the expressed desires and needs of the relevant sections of the public to be taken into account by local senior officers, and this added a wholly new dimension to operational accountability. It removed none of the pre-existing possibilities for police accountability: the Inspectorate remained, with its power to examine all aspects of policing, and when policing was obviously seriously defective in its approach a royal commission or public inquiry could be held.[10]

---

9   An important cost in the police budget is the matter of pensions. Police pensions in Britain are paid out of current budgets, rather than a pension fund, and the pension bill is rapidly approaching the size of the wages bill.

10   One such inquiry was held by Lord Scarman into the Brixton riots of 1981, and its recommendations led to the establishment of community committees – another such inquiry was held into policing of the Hillsborough football stadium after crowd problems resulted in the accidental deaths of a large number of spectators.

During the 1990s, the Home Office started to set national objectives for policing, and to require that police services address them in addition to the local objectives set by police authorities and chief constables. The *Police and Magistrates Courts Act* imposed a rather different type of operational accountability which can lead to requirements contrary to those raised by consultative committees set up under *PACE*. The effect of *PACE* will be examined in detail, followed by an analysis of the effect of the 1994 Act to establish how operational accountability has undergone major changes in emphasis and direction since 1980.

The impact of the PACE Act 1984

The first direction making police accountable to the public for operational decisions came with the *PACE Act* 1984. Although many senior officers had become used to dealing with community representatives before then, this Act obliged local commanders to set up consultative committees for an interchange of information between police and public. Although not wholly prompted by public disorder, this Act came in the wake of riots in Britain's inner cities, some of which were triggered by a reaction to policing tactics. Most notorious, perhaps, was the stop-and-search drug operation, Swamp 81, carried out in Brixton, South London, which alienated much of the area's West Indian community, and led to violence and destruction on an unprecedented scale. Such an operation would never have been carried out in the circumstances which existed had police management been sufficiently in touch with the community to realise the feelings that it would arouse.

The whole process of establishing procedures for police to consult local communities can be traced back to the Brixton riots. Lord Scarman's report proposed that such committees should be set up, and the Home Office responded in 1982 by giving administrative guidance to police authorities about such arrangements.[11] Among these guidelines were requirements that there should be a flow of information both ways, that local views should be taken into account when planning police strategy and operations, and that membership of the committees should be as wide as possible without being too large to be effective. The requirements of the legislation, *PACE* s 106, made these arrangements mandatory, but did little to direct or constrain the constitution of the committee.[12]

The constitution of police consultative committees (PCCs) and their aims and powers are best seen from the 1982 Home Office guidelines and the Home Secretary's comments during debate on the Bill in parliament.[13] It

---

11 As part of the rebuilding of police community relations in Brixton, the new District Police Commander, Mr Alex Marnoch, had devoted much time to establishing a consultative committee. This became a model for Home Office guidance, as did the lay visitors scheme whereby members of the community visit persons in custody to allay fears of maltreatment of detainees.

12 Section 106(1) reads: "Arrangements shall be made in each police area for obtaining the views of people in that area about matters concerning the policing of the area and for obtaining their cooperation with the police in preventing crime in the area".

13 *Hansard*, Standing Committee J, 22 March 1983.

is clear that the Home Office as the then Police Authority for the Metropolis[14] made directions which that police service must follow, but had, at the time, no authority to make these other than advisory directions to other police services. The Home Office directions to the Metropolitan Police were that police, obviously, should be represented on consultative committees, as should MPs, local councillors, local services such as probation, social services, education, and members of the community. To prevent such committees being overladen with semi-professional committee people, it was expected that the number of community representatives should outnumber police, MPs, councillors and agency representatives. The Home Office made clear that the whole intent of PCCs was to ensure that local needs are to be taken into account when making decisions concerning local policing.

The Act, following the earlier Home Office directions, clearly intended that all relevant sections of the community both give and are given information relating to police operations. There is, of course, nothing in this which requires police to give prior information about operations which might prejudice their outcome, or to suggest that the PCC has any authority to direct policing in its area. Some of the early committees achieved little because of mutual suspicion and unreal expectations. Some representatives of community groups and agencies saw it as an opportunity to instruct police in their job, and specify how chief superintendents should approach particular issues: some chief superintendents saw it as a means of telling community representatives what police had done or intended to do, and showed no interest in their response. The PCCs that worked best seemed to be those where the chief superintendent actively sought out representatives of those sections of the community that were most affected by crime or policing, and involved them as equal partners in planning broad approaches to local policing issues.

Good community consultative committees provide a sound base for community policing to be established. They enable police to determine what the community sees as problems, and enable police either to address these with community support, or explain why they are not policing matters. At least one PCC caused serious frustration amongst its senior police officers because of its habit of raising the problem of canine faeces on footpaths as the most important issue to be addressed, but once it was established what matters were not dealt with by police, productive work became possible.[15]

---

14   The Metropolis, that is the jurisdiction of the Metropolitan Police, is comprised of Greater London, which includes parts of Essex, Hertfordshire, Kent and Surrey but excludes the square mile of the City of London, which has its own police force. The Home Secretary's anomalous position as police authority was replaced by a police authority for London similar to that of other constabularies in 1999.

15   There is a serious point here. In many communities, the public are more concerned about what they see and are distressed by every day, rather than what police deal with every day. The number of people who are confronted by graffiti, litter (or dog faeces) every day far outnumber those who are burgled, assaulted or are victims of other crimes. It follows that what many individuals see as problems for police to deal with are not what police see as part of their duty, and this divergence of views needs to be addressed.

By their very nature, the issues raised by PCCs are local issues. The expectations raised by *PACE* s 106 are that PCCs not only raise local issues, but that these issues are to be addressed in some way by police. There is, after all, no point in establishing a system for interchanging information between police and community about policing matters if no action is taken upon that information. Furthermore, the nature of the PCC meant that the whole community could be involved, with representatives from minority ethnic groups, youth workers, the gay community and others who had previously been totally unheard in any formal committee structure. For the first time, there was a legislatively supported body which provided a forum for the community as it is, rather than just the traditional power groups within it, to have input into policing.

Measuring operational efficiency

British police services had been forced by the government, in Home Office Circular 114 of 1983, entitled "Manpower, Effectiveness and Efficiency in the Police Service", to consider the value they were giving to the public for the money policing cost. This was the turning point from which chief officers of police had to set their minds to justifying their expenditure, and devising indicators of their performance. In order to do this, chief constables needed to provide a far more coherent annual statement of their plans and goals for the coming year, and an indication of how their performance in reaching those goals could be measured. Each police service started producing plans, strategies, and indices of measurement. This also required police services to think carefully about what they were doing, and whether police time was being spent on non-police duties.

A considerable amount of research in policing has shown that police spend an inordinate amount of their time in assisting the public in a variety of ways. Although many, if not most, police officers see making crime arrests as the epitome of policing, dealing with crime is a very small part of what police officers actually do. Very little police time is spent policing pro-actively on patrol, most is spent dealing with calls from the public regarding nuisances, disputes, lost dogs, or one of innumerable other matters which do not involve crime. The cost-cutting argument is that if these tasks are shed from police responsibilities then police could concentrate on crime and other specific police tasks, and increase their efficiency. Furthermore, the need to find indicators of police performance to quantify efficiency is made much easier if performance specifically excludes such matters as finding dogs or arbitrating disputes between neighbours.

Two reports were produced which went some way to defining the police role. The first was the report of a committee chaired by Lord Cassels in 1994, entitled "The Role and Responsibilities of Police", sometimes referred to as the Police Foundation/PSI Report from its joint sponsors. The second report is the Home Office's 1995 Review of Police Core and Ancillary Tasks. The Cassels Report endorses the police service statement of common purpose:

The purpose of the police service is to uphold the law fairly and firmly, to prevent crime, to pursue and bring to justice those who break the law, to keep the Queen's peace, and to protect, help and reassure the community and to be seen to do this with integrity, commonsense and sound judgment.

Perhaps the most notable change here is the relegation of Mayne's "great end" of policing, crime prevention, to second place behind upholding the law. The report also quotes and approves Lord Scarman's comment in his report on the Brixton riots that, in the last resort, public order must be maintained claiming that "public tranquillity ... should be the primary responsibility of the police". While Cassels is keen that police performance should be monitored as far as possible, the report does accept that some important aspects of policing are beyond measurement. This is particularly so in the important areas of public confidence and crime prevention. The report warns particularly against the use of arrest figures as a measure of efficiency: if crime is reduced, arrest rates should, it suggests, go down rather than up, and may be counterproductive:

> [E]ncouraging a high level of arrests per officer [may put] other responsibilities of the police at risk, notably those for reassuring the community, and for operating with integrity, common sense and sound judgement.

Finally, some aspects of policing are, in Cassels view, beyond quantification:

> At a deeper level, how would keeping the Queen's peace be made the subject of mandatory objectives and quantified indicators, or indeed preventing crime? The simple and straight-forward answer is that they cannot. (Cassels, 1994, p 44)

In general, the report accepts that the causes of crime are often well beyond the ambit of police action, hence, perhaps, the approval of the shift of crime prevention to second place below upholding the law. Nevertheless, although crime prevention is a matter for the community, Cassels acknowledges that it works best when the local police take the lead role. There are, perhaps, two reasons for this. The police are the sole agency which records crime, and the agency whose main focus is on dealing with crime. Crime prevention is at the heart of community policing, and is a major issue for police consultative committees. There is an analogy with health here: the medical profession has expertise in dealing with heart disease, knows its causes, has better information than any part of the general public, yet it is the responsibility of the individual to do the right things about diet, smoking and exercise to keep heart disease at bay. If the number of individuals suffering heart disease is not considered as a performance indicator for the medical profession, then there is no reason why the burglary rate should be used as a performance indicator for police.

The Home Office Review of Police Core and Ancillary Tasks also set out to determine what police should be doing, and found there was "little scope for the police service ... to withdraw completely from large areas of current police work". Some tasks, the "inner core" were to be carried out by police constables: typically these tasks involved the use of legitimate force, presumably arrests and searches. "Outer core" tasks were those which could be carried out by police or by others, but under the aegis of police so that the ultimate accountability for error rested with police. "Ancillary" tasks could safely be passed on to other agencies. Unfortunately, the vast majority of police tasks fell into one or other of the core categories, thus leaving very little that could be shed.

The effect of service and national objectives

Clearly, any attempt to make police more efficient by divesting them of some of the tasks they normally undertake is not possible. The next step is to accept all the tasks, but to give some of them priority over others, and to set objectives for dealing with particular policing problems. Since policing problems may well vary from city to city, between city and town and town and rural area, the ranking of policing priorities is a matter which calls for substantial local involvement. Policing has moved well past the era when chief officers held themselves to be solely responsible for operational and policy decisions, and declared their independence from the public or even the police authority in making such decisions. The *PACE Act* 1984 s 106 makes it very clear that members of the local community are entitled, through the PCC, to have their views considered, and police authorities may also be concerned. The Cassels report moves some way to admitting central government involvement here, but only insofar as the Home Office enters into a tripartite partnership or covenant with police authorities and their chief officers, rather than there being any control or direction from one to the others.

If the policing priorities for any given police area are set as a result of consultation and agreement between the chief officer, PCCs, police authority and Home Office, then there is a remarkably high chance of the policing strategies meeting the needs of the community. This creates multiple channels for holding police accountable for operational decisions. However, the *Police and Magistrates' Courts Act* 1994 does not allow for this balanced view. There are several critical issues which enable the Home Office to tip the balance towards directly controlling, or at least possessing a controlling influence on, policing.

First, the Audit Commission Report 1994 finds that the Act allows the Home Office to set national objectives and can direct any police authority to establish levels of performance for those objectives. Chief officers must take these national objectives into account in carrying out policing, and, of course, the Inspectorate has a duty to examine each police service to ensure that this is being done. Secondly, the Act allows the Home Office considerable influence within each police authority by providing that five of the 17 seats will go to Home Office nominees. All but a few police authorities have 17 members, who comprise nine locally elected councillors, three magistrates and five independent lay persons selected by the police authority from a short list of 10 names provided by the Home Office.

This constitutional arrangement of police authorities has obvious dangers. It is reasonable to assume that the nine seats for elected councillors will be filled according to the party political breakdown of the members of relevant local authorities – even where the police service covers an area with more than one local authority. Notwithstanding that voters may swing against the party of national government in local government elections, it is a reasonable assumption that the party of national government will have between three and six of their party's members as councillor members of a police authority. If the Home Office nominates people who are, if not overt party supporters, generally in agreement with government policies, then the majority of the members of police authorities would support the government, and, in all probability, would follow the government line on policing. Only a government punctilious in the extreme would ensure the independence of police authorities by nominating truly independent individuals, or those antipathetic to its views.

Finally, the government's financial contribution to policing and the emphasis on fiscal rather than intrinsic value also allows a measure of control. Reiner (1995) finds that "[t]he new accountability systems replace democracy with accountancy ... the levers of control will be concentrated at the centre", a view not challenged by Morgan and Newburn. Walker and Richards are even more condemnatory in the conclusion to their paper:

> Despite comments to the contrary, it is apparent that the Home Secretary, through the Home Office, will in the future exert greater control over police forces through the imposition of financial constraints, and the setting of national policing objectives and performance measures than has been the case in the past. (Walker and Richards, 1996)

This piece of legislation certainly does not heed the constitutional warning of Jefferson cited earlier to bind the power of government, but is a blatant invitation to central government to exercise much greater control over the police service, one of whose greatest assets is its disseminated local control. The American approach discussed in the next chapter is to reduce the power of police by keeping the size of police organisations fairly small: British policing has traditionally been held accountable to the public by its police authorities being closer to the public than national government is. The *Police and Magistrates Courts Act* 1994 reverses this traditional accountability.

The level of policing most directly affected by this is the superintendent, the head of the basic command unit.[16] The superintendent is answerable through the chain of command to the chief officer and police authority, but also locally to the PCC. Each police service sets its own objectives, which must take into account the national objectives. However, police consultative committees are comprised of local individuals concerned only

---

16   For the argument that follows, I am indebted to a number of superintendents who spent several hours in a lively informal discussion of this issue with me at Bramshill Police College in 1997. Later legislation and its implications seem to polarise this problem even further, as will be discussed in Chapter 14.

with policing local problems, and are likely to take a very dim view of a superintendent who neglects their concerns to address policing priorities set at police authority or national level. Equally, chief officers are going to take a dim view of superintendents who ignore priorities set by them, in order to satisfy the needs of a PCC.

The unofficial consensus among superintendents is that if there is any conflict between the needs of a PCC and the requirements of the Home Office, then all but the most strong-minded will sacrifice the needs of the PCC. If this happens regularly enough over a period of years, then PCCs will cease to be relevant, and the local community will cease to have any involvement in policing decisions. This will have an impact on community policing, and also, perhaps, return policing to the conditions which led to the public disorder of 1981. Certainly, the legislative trend of the 1990s was to reduce the operational accountability of the police to the public and transfer this accountability to national government. Worse still, by making operational accountability part of financial accountability, the way is clear for central government to exercise a far greater control over police than was considered acceptable by Peel, Rowan, Mayne or their successors. The public, quite naturally, will blame the police directly for being monolithic and unresponsive to community needs, and not recognise the constraints imposed upon their supposedly locally accountable police by their national government's policy and fiscal decision-making which has statutory precedence.

Accountability of individual officers

Individual police officers in Britain are held accountable for their actions and the way they carry out their duties in a variety of ways. First, and most obviously, they are accountable to their supervising officers through the rank structure. Secondly, they are answerable to the courts for the way they exercise their powers in those cases which result in a prosecution, and they may also be subject to civil or criminal court proceedings. Finally, they are answerable to the public through a system for recording and investigating complaints made against police by members of the public. The most important piece of legislation holding individual police officers to account is the *PACE Act* 1984 which has something to say about each of the four points mentioned above. The Act establishes a procedure by which a member of the public who is aggrieved by any aspect of an interaction with a police officer can have that interaction examined and impartially assessed, and guarantees the fairness and impartiality of the procedure by external monitoring of it by the Police Complaints Authority.

Complaints and the Police and Criminal Evidence Act

There are two aspects of *PACE* which are to be considered with regard to the personal accountability of police officers. The first is that the Act sets out in great detail the specific powers of police to search, arrest, detain and question individuals, and the Act and its Codes of Practice also set out the rights of individuals who are subject to search, arrest or questioning. The second aspect is that the Act establishes clear rules for the investigation and resolution of complaints, and establishes an independent monitoring body, the Police Complaints Authority. It is worth noting how rapidly the investigation of complaints has grown in importance. Before 1970, the investigation of complaints against police was seen by most senior officers as a tiresome additional duty – during the next few years, police forces established specialist complaints investigation branches, followed by the Home Office setting in place the Police Complaints Board to examine reports of investigations of complaints. Within 15 years, *PACE* legislation had given full authority to an independent body which, as we shall see, is responsible for supervising police in complaints investigations.

The value of the clear description of police powers and individual rights in *PACE* is that this provides an incontrovertible measure for police behaviour. Police actions can be tested against the legislation and seen to comply or fail to comply with its requirements: the Act itself sets rules for police conduct. More importantly, the rules set out by *PACE* cover the sort of issues where police action is most likely to result in conflict with the public, and where most of the serious complaints against police arise. The individuals traditionally most likely to have grievances about police action are those who are stopped and searched in the street, or arrested, or have not been able to contact relatives while they are in custody, or have been released without charge, and the legislative framework of *PACE* provides a yardstick against which both the complainant's and the officer's accounts can be compared to determine the validity of the officer's action objectively.

Many police powers in Britain before *PACE* had been assumed by common law. Powers of arrest and powers of search had been appended to many Acts of Parliament defining criminal offences, but power to question a suspect after arrest, or to detain for the purpose of questioning had never before been specified. Before *PACE*, suspects had had no formal statutory right to consult a solicitor, although those that insisted would, eventually, get legal advice: the Act specified that, on arrival at the station, the right to consult a solicitor would be offered to all prisoners unless certain specified criteria were met, in which case this right could be withheld. The Act was complex, but its principles were clear and sound, and provided a codification of police behaviour regarding suspects and evidence gathering for criminal cases.

The Act also took advantage of the hierarchic structure of police organisations to make individual officers accountable to their supervisors, and to make those supervising officers accountable also. For example, an officer arresting an individual on the street must take the person arrested before a custody officer holding the substantive rank of sergeant at least for detention to be authorised. The sergeant is then held accountable for ensuring that the arrest is justified in law. If the individual is not charged within six hours, a police inspector independent of the case must authorise continued detention: all authorisations must be recorded, and officers making authorisations are held accountable for their decisions. It follows that if an individual is wrongly treated then not only the officers responsible for the ill treatment, but any supervising officers who have made dispensations regarding the prisoner and should have taken preventative action, are held responsible for permitting wrongful treatment of that individual.

Complaints investigation and the Police Complaints Authority[17]

Part IX of the *PACE Act* 1984 is concerned solely with the investigation of complaints against police and the role of the Police Complaints Authority. It provides for informal resolution of minor complaints, full investigation and external supervision of serious complaints, and for disposition by either criminal proceedings in the courts or discipline proceedings within police organisations.

Many complaints made against police officers are fairly petty, for example those involving rudeness or high-handed behaviour which do not amount to aggression, and the person making the complaint will be satisfied with an apology or explanation. In such cases, the Act allows an inspector to make an informal investigation and resolve the matter in a way which satisfies the complainant, is acceptable to the officer concerned, and maintains the reputation of the police service. If such an informal resolution is not possible, for example if the officer's account of the incident flatly contradicts that of the complainant, then the matter is referred for a full, formal investigation. In practice, most minor complaints can be dealt with by informal resolution, especially as any admissions made by an officer at this stage cannot be used in a full investigation.

Full complaint investigations are carried out by senior officers holding the rank of at least chief inspector. Officers have the right to know that an allegation has been made against them and that an investigation is proceeding, and if that allegation is that the officer has committed a criminal offence, then all the rights accorded to a suspect under *PACE* apply to the police officer under investigation, including the right to legal representation while being questioned. In many cases it is by no means clear at the outset whether the investigation is one of a criminal offence or not. A fairly common complaint is that an officer in carrying out an arrest has been aggressive or used excessive force. Since an arrest is by definition an exercise of force, any given amount of force used may, according to circumstances, be justified, excessive, or constitute an assault. Once the investigation reveals that an assault may have been committed, then the police officer under investigation becomes the suspect in a criminal investigation and is entitled to all the rights of a suspect under *PACE*, including the right to legal representation and the right to remain silent.

The Police Complaints Authority has two main functions: consideration of disciplinary charges, and supervision of investigations. In both respects,

---

17   The Police Complaints Authority was replaced by an Independent Police Complaints Commission by the *Police Reform Act* 2002. The older terminology is kept in this discussion of *PACE*, it being the terminology used in that legislation.

the investigator of a complaint will be well aware that the matter will be subject to scrutiny at some stage by the PCA. Once an investigation is complete, the file, with the relevant police service's recommendation as to disciplinary proceedings, is sent to the PCA for its consideration. The Authority has the right to endorse the recommendation, change it, or refer the matter back for further investigation or information. If the matter is one wherein evidence to support a criminal prosecution is revealed, then this may be referred to the Director of Public Prosecutions (DPP) directly, although normally the PCA would consider whether or not criminal proceedings are appropriate.

In serious cases, the Police Complaints Authority will exercise direct supervision over the investigation of a complaint. If it is alleged that death or serious injury has been caused by an officer, then s 87 of *PACE* states that this must be referred to the PCA, and the investigation must be supervised by it. Other serious cases, as specified by the Home Office, must also be referred to the PCA, but the PCA has discretion whether or not to supervise these matters. The chief officer of police may refer any matter to the PCA for it to choose whether or not to supervise the investigation, and the PCA has the power to require police to submit any complaint for its supervision. For example, if a prominent person alleges an assault by a police officer this merits early referral to the PCA, or if a television news item shows what appears to be an assault by a police officer, then the PCA may choose to supervise the investigation, even, perhaps, before a formal complaint is received from the person assaulted.

The Police Complaints Authority therefore makes final decisions on all matters relating to complaints against police. It can choose to supervise any investigation directly, but ultimately reviews every investigation carried out. The Authority may refer any matter which it considers should be resolved by criminal prosecution to the DPP. The DPP may decline to prosecute on legal grounds, for example if the evidence is considered to be insufficient, although the DPP cannot decline a prosecution on grounds of policy. The PCA's impartiality is guaranteed as far as possible by the office of chair being a Crown appointment, the other members being appointed by the Home Secretary.

From the brief description above, the complaints system in Britain should be able to meet the needs of public confidence and personal accountability of police officers. The main problem with the system is its cost, and the time taken to resolve matters. The number of complaints generated results in a considerable amount of time spent by senior officers in investigation: many figures have been bandied about, but, nationwide, it may well be a conservative estimate that the equivalent of one officer in four above the rank of chief inspector is involved full time in complaints investigation. The salary costs alone are considerable, but when the costs of administrative and support staff, offices, and the Police Complaints Authority itself are also considered millions of pounds are spent each year in investigating complaints against police. The sheer numbers of complaints means that a thorough review of each by the PCA will be time-consuming, yet a less than thorough review will lead to lack of public and police confidence in the system.

The role of the courts

The courts, both civil and criminal, have a significant role as independent arbiters of the conduct of individual police officers in particular cases. It is open to any person to sue a police officer who has acted in a manner which may amount to a civil wrong, and also to sue the chief officer who may be held liable for the actions of any member of the police service. Such suits have the effect of pre-empting the complaints investigation process and thus removing the matter from consideration by the Police Complaints Authority. If police are defendants in a civil case, then the complainant is the plaintiff, and any officer investigating the matter cannot interview the plaintiff or the plaintiff's witnesses while the matter remains *sub judice*, since this amounts to representatives of the defendants questioning witnesses for the plaintiff.

The PCA is also excluded from proceeding with cases where a civil suit is pending. Clearly, if the matter is one in which the PCA are not supervising, but reviewing the completed investigation, there is nothing for it to review. If it is a matter which the Authority chooses to investigate, then insofar as the PCA has a judicial function it is inquisitorial. Any findings of the PCA may well have a bearing on the adversarial proceedings in the courts, in that any discrepancy between the two findings could indicate grounds for appeal so it is almost certainly in the complainant's interest not to involve the PCA before the court has heard the matter. Civil suits against police are not particularly common, and are more usually brought after criminal proceedings or following complaints investigation, when liability is frequently not denied and an out-of-court settlement can be reached.

The criminal courts can act as a much more serious check on police behaviour, even aside from those cases where police officers are charged with criminal offences. In any criminal prosecution where a plea of not guilty is entered, then the prosecution evidence is bound to include the action taken by the police officers involved. It is almost inevitable that police action would have been in some, if not all, respects subject to the *PACE Act* 1984, so the criminal courts are in a sound position to monitor police behaviour and ensure compliance with this Act.

The courts have a great deal of discretion in the action they may take when police have acted wrongly, or not in accordance with *PACE*. At one extreme, if evidence has been obtained in a manner which breaches the requirements of the Act, then that evidence may be ruled inadmissible. For example, if a prisoner is interviewed after having been wrongly denied access to legal representation or advice, then any admission made may be excluded. The court has discretion whether or not to exclude prosecution evidence from the jury, although courts are obliged by the doctrine of precedent to follow decisions made in like cases in higher courts. Aside from this, there is no obligation on the court to exclude evidence solely on the grounds of a breach of the Act, allowing the court to decide that the wider interests of justice may be better served by tolerating minor infractions by police rather than enforcing strict rules of procedural justice. This is worthy of contrast to the situation in the United States, where, once the defence has shown that a police search, interrogation or arrest has even minimally breached constitutional rights, the courts are obliged to rule the resulting evidence inadmissible as being the fruit of the poisoned tree.

The courts may, of course, find that the action taken by an officer under *PACE* is perfectly proper, despite a strong challenge against it being made by defence counsel. This is the opposite end of the spectrum from police evidence being excluded because of malpractice, and a court ruling that an officer's actions were lawful serves to weaken any complaint made against police action. However, while an officer's actions might be lawful in a particular case, they may well not meet the standards required by the police service. Furthermore, an officer might breach the requirements of *PACE*, but in such a way that the court chooses not to criticise because of the wider interests of justice. Failure of a court to criticise a police officer's action cannot be taken as tacit exoneration, although a court's criticism may go some way towards substantiating an complaint. In general, adverse comment by the courts in itself is seen as a complaint against police and, if reported, is deemed worthy of investigation.

The courts have an important role in determining police accountability with regard to the *PACE Act* 1984 because many of the Act's provisions contain terms such as "reasonable grounds" (s 1), "not practicable" (s 3), "seriously prejudiced" (s 8(3)(d)), and many other such phrases which can only be understood subjectively. Such terms may well be impossible to define objectively, but judges can and do provide clear examples in actual cases of how these terms are to be understood by the courts. The courts are therefore impartial arbitrators, establishing the correct usage of otherwise extremely subjective phrases, and in establishing the usage of such terms the courts set the parameters for police conduct on behalf of society as a whole. Indeed, the elucidation of terms which have an agreed use rather than a defined meaning is a matter which the courts in common law countries have done through precedent for many hundreds of years, so the test of reasonableness is hardly something new which has arisen with *PACE*.

Discipline

The whole purpose of holding individual officers accountable is that if their actions are unacceptable, then some form of sanction must be possible. Police Acts have always provided for some form of disciplinary action to be taken, up to and including the dismissal of an officer from the police service. Ultimately, if a police officer generally behaves unsuitably, or is guilty of wholly unacceptable behaviour on a single occasion, then the police service needs to dispense with that officer. The current British disciplinary procedure allows for minor punishments, such as fines or reduction in rates of pay, to be imposed by a single senior officer, and more serious punishments like reduction in rank or dismissal to be imposed by a board of three senior officers, before which an officer may have legal representation. Disciplinary judgments can be appealed to the police authority.

There are some important principles arising from discipline proceedings following criminal proceedings arising from the same event. The legal principle of double jeopardy clearly prevents an individual who has been acquitted by the courts to be subjected to a disciplinary hearing on essentially the same evidence, although this, too has been addressed by legislation.[18] Equally clearly, if a court has found a police officer guilty of a criminal assault, then that person almost certainly should not remain in the police service. For British police, criminal behaviour, as shown by a conviction in court, is itself a disciplinary offence, punishable by dismissal. Disciplinary proceedings are not mandatory following a conviction, so an officer who is convicted of careless driving after an accident may face no further action, but one who is convicting of a drink-driving offence, dishonesty or violence will almost certainly be subject to disciplinary action resulting in dismissal from the service.

Conclusion

This chapter has examined three levels of police accountability, and has argued that very sophisticated national systems have been developed which mean that every police service and every police officer is subject to essentially the same constraints on behaviour. Since 1980, all these systems have been subject to major legislative changes which have had significant consequences, some of which are not yet clearly seen, as more time is required for the full ramifications to become apparent. With regard to the individual accountability of the officers on the streets for their behaviour, at least with regard to suspects, standards have been very clearly codified and parameters set. In this regard, the changes have been for the better, and were perhaps even overdue.

With regard to financial and operational accountability, the *Police and Magistrates Courts Act* 1994 has changed previous practice significantly. Police have long been financially accountable to central government, and perhaps rightly so since most of the finance for police comes from central government, but this has been at one remove through independent police authorities. Operational accountability has always been through these authorities, although since 1984 police have been accountable to local committees also. However, the *Police and Magistrates Courts Act* has allowed central government more power in appointing police authorities and more power to insist that the government's national priorities for policing are met, even if this is at the expense of local community concerns. More worryingly, operational accountability is being tied to financial accountability in that police authorities and chief officers may have few funds available to address any tasks other than national priorities.

---

18   *Police Reform Act* 2002.

CHAPTER 12

POLICE ACCOUNTABILITY IN THE UNITED STATES

Introduction

The United States achieves the aim of a publicly controlled, fully accountable police service in a way radically different from that of Australia or Britain, or, indeed, any other nation. This chapter explores why this is so, and what follows from this for policing in the United States. The most immediately startling difference between American policing and policing in the rest of the world is the vast number of policing agencies in the United States. Most nations have national police agencies or, in a federal system, a handful of State police agencies, and perhaps local policing agencies with restricted powers. By contrast, each American municipality or county has its own police agency with full police powers. This plethora of local police departments, coupled with a political system which quite deliberately minimises State or national government control, has some very important consequences for police accountability in the United States.

The reasons for the United States' unique policing structure can be found in the desire for self-determination of the original signatories of the Declaration of Independence, and the constitutional restrictions on the authority of government. Because the establishment of this political framework predated the introduction of police by well over half a century, policing became a matter for local government with minimal State or federal government involvement. The history of American policing shows the key figures in police agencies to be the chief of police and the mayor of the municipality. Local politics can be an excellent means of accountability: Henry claims "American police agencies are (and should be) politically accountable for their activities" (Henry, 2002, p 80), but at its worst local politics in a democracy can facilitate and disguise much more significant corruption than is possible in the larger State or national systems.

The local nature of policing in the United States means that there is little separation of financial accountability from operational accountability. A small police department in a town of 20,000 people is personally accountable to the community, as its 40 or 50 officers are likely to be reasonably well known. In a large city, both police and citizens are more likely to be anonymous in the crowd, and more sophisticated accountability mechanisms need to be developed. As with all matters of policing in the United States, the disparity of policing organisations and the lack of nationally imposed and monitored standards makes generalisation very difficult. Nevertheless, many of the problems arising in policing a large, multicultural city are the same wherever that city might be, and the three cities of Melbourne, Greater Manchester and Los Angeles all have roughly the same population, geographical area, and number of police.[1]

The American political structure

At the heart of the American political and legal system is the American Constitution, which, although claimed by the Supreme Court as a legal document,[2] is the defining document of the nation's political structure. Certain of the sections and amendments to the Constitution together comprise the Bill of Rights, which proclaims the inviolability of the individual over the needs of government. The nation's founders defined the political structure in such a way that it expressly limits the power of government, and implicitly forbids legislation which might contravene any of the provisions of the Constitution. The Constitution can be changed, but it acts as a brake on change within the nation as constitutional change is by no means an easy task or quickly accomplished.

The power of the United States Constitution over legislative change is exemplified by the issue of gun control. Following a shooting in a school in Dunblane, Scotland, in March 1996, wherein a large number of primary school children and their teacher were killed by a single, deranged gunman, the British government (with overwhelming support from across the political spectrum) amended the already highly restrictive *Firearms Act* 1968 to render the possession of almost all guns over .22 calibre and multi-cartridge shotguns illegal. A massacre by another lone gunman in Tasmania the following month prompted the Australian Prime Minister to establish national gun control standards after consultation with each State premier and police minister: each State legislature passed Acts severely restricting gun ownership. Despite many instances of multiple shootings in schools and workplaces in the United States, any meaningful gun control legislation there would infringe the constitutional right to bear arms, a right which much of the rest of the world sees as downright dangerous and completely anachronistic.[3]

---

1   Roughly 3.5 million people and 7000 or so police.
2   In the case of *Marbury v Madison* 5 US (1 Cranch) 137 (1803).
3   The Second Amendment reads "A well-regulated Militia, being necessary to the security of a free State, the right of the people to keep and bear Arms, shall not be infringed". The first part of this seems to imply that arms were necessary for organised defence, presumably at the time against either Native Americans or the British, which is now otiose. It is probably true to say that even if this right were to be abolished, it would be many years before a less gun-ridden America emerged. The number of lawfully acquired guns in the United States is immense, and those who wish to retain them for unlawful purposes are unlikely to surrender them tamely, so gun crime would continue for the foreseeable future.

The very earliest American political writings[4] stress the need to limit the power of government: having achieved independence from a king across the Atlantic, 18th century Americans had no wish to impose on themselves strong national government: the French experience of over-throwing a monarchy to institute a republic, only to substitute this with the Emperor Napoleon a few years later, was to be avoided at all costs. The Tenth Amendment to the Constitution held that all powers not explicitly reserved to the national government were delegated to the States and citizens, permitting the separate development of individual States.[5] It follows that when the establishment of police was considered in the middle of the 19th century, any surrender of control of police to State or national government was to relinquish power from the citizenry to that level of government, and therefore to be resisted strongly.

Although the United States does have a number of federal police agencies (Geller and Morris (1992) list 50 of these), the bulk of police work is done by local police of which Geller and Morris claim more than 14,000 agencies. The actual numbers claimed vary wildly, possibly because it is difficult to determine what constitutes a police agency, and what constitutes a security service. In Britain and Australia the divide between a police and a security organisation can be determined by their authority to carry weapons: security staff are totally unarmed, with a few Australian exceptions for those carrying cash or bullion, and only police are armed. Persons providing security on the railway systems in Australian cities, for example, have neither guns nor batons. In the United States, many universities have campus police who carry firearms, whereas in Britain and Australia their function is performed by unarmed campus security. Counts of American policing agencies may well include organisations which would be called private security agencies in other countries.

Each State also has its own State policing organisation or organisations such as State troopers, highway patrols or the famous Texas Rangers. Even the 50 or so of these State police agencies pales into insignificance against the average of almost 300 local police agencies per State. States may legislate to establish minimum qualifications or standards to be reached before individuals can become police officers, in much the same way as they can establish registration boards for various professions or trades from psychologists to plumbers. However, there are no national requirements, still less is there a national inspection system for police in the United States. For good or ill, control of police within the United States rests almost totally with local government: 90 per cent of the police agencies are local police or sheriff's departments, with 60 per cent of the $50 billion that policing is

---

4   See, for example, the writings of the early political theorists and practitioners, in the "Federalist", originally a regularly published political newssheet, now collated as Hamilton et al (1992).

5   I am grateful to Bob Owens, former Chief of Police in Oxnard, California, and lecturer in policing at the University of Texas, San Antonio, for pointing this out. A similar residuary powers provision is made in the Australian Constitution. The first 10 constitutional amendments, the original Bill of Rights, date from 1791.

estimated to cost being mostly raised and spent by local government (Sheehan and Cordner, 1995, p 12).

The police chief

Chief officers of police agencies at the local level are appointed in one of two ways. Straightforwardly, a town or city mayor may appoint a police chief, or the task of policing may be devolved to the county sheriff. The post of sheriff has its roots in mediaeval England, where the shire reeve, which Anglo-Saxon title became the English word sheriff, was responsible to the king for setting up courts, summoning juries, serving summonses to court, executing court orders and holding malefactors in custody. The post became largely ceremonial in Britain, but remained an important law enforcement position in the American colonies. After independence, the post of sheriff became a directly elected law enforcement position. Sheriffs still retain responsibility for courts, custody of prisoners in county jails and service of legal process, and in rural areas have responsibility for general policing. In some places, municipalities have grown but the elected council has chosen to leave the responsibility for policing with the county sheriff rather than to establish a separate police department.

In discussing the role of chief officer of police, then, chief officer should be understood to mean the person responsible for the local policing agency and thus can be either a police chief appointed by the city[6] or a directly elected sheriff. Local control of police, especially where sheriff's departments are responsible for general policing, renders the role of police chief in the United States one with considerably greater power than chief officers of police in Australia or Britain. In a town of 20,000 people, the police strength would be between 30 and 50 officers of various ranks: in Australia, the senior officer would be a senior sergeant, and in Britain an inspector or chief inspector, who would report through a chain of command consisting of at least three or four ranks to a chief officer; an American town would have a chief of police fully and locally answerable. Although the senior local police officer in Australia and Britain may well be recognised by the residents, even off duty, these officers are not permanent,[7] unlike American police chiefs, who are often long-term residents, known to the townspeople, and often addressed as "Chief".

The very smallness of scale in policing in the majority of police departments in the United States minimises the dangers of the existence of a powerful controlling government agency, but also affords greater local power for the police chief. The resistance to government power implied in the Declaration of Independence has prevented national or State govern-

---

6 In some cities the elected mayor, in others the city manager, who is answerable to the city council, is responsible for appointing a chief of police. In either case, local politicians are answerable for policing at the ballot box. Once again, I am grateful for Bob Owens' elucidation.

7 In Western Australia, for example, a country posting is for two or three years to a particular town, with a possible extension of another year. In Britain, an officer in charge of policing a small town can expect to be moved on or promoted after three years or so.

ment having significant control over the major agency for the expression of civil power, the police. However, an American chief of police is answerable only to the mayor, an elected official, or directly to the local public if an elected sheriff. There are no intermediaries, no such triumvirate of powers concerned with policing as exists in Britain, or designated police minister answerable to cabinet and premier as in Australia, and, in smaller agencies at least, the chief of police is directly accessible by the public.

Chief of police is, indeed, often a more overtly political post in the United States than it is elsewhere, whether they are themselves local politicians who set policy as elected sheriffs and delegate day-to-day policing to a deputy, or are appointed by a mayor in order to police the city in a particular fashion in accordance with that mayor's avowed intentions in policing. For example, Lee Brown was head-hunted by Mayor Dinkins from Houston, where he had successfully introduced community policing, to do the same for the NYPD. Brown had previously been Public Safety Director in Atlanta, taught criminology at university and been a sheriff in Oregon. After his resignation in 1992, Brown worked on drug policy for President Clinton, and, in 2002, was back in Houston as mayor (Henry 2002).

The history of politics in policing

There are two major issues to be explored here with regard to police accountability in the United States: the first concerns the role of police in keeping order in small communities, largely in the south and west, while the other, rather different, issue concerns the effect on policing of institutional corruption in the government of larger cities most common in the north and east.[8] These concerns have arisen through accidents of history. The constitutional authority for self-determination of American communities, as has been shown, enabled policing to be a local responsibility: the further a community was from the seat of power, be it the State capital or Washington, the less interference was possible with locally approved policing methods, whether or not they complied with State or constitutional law. The anomalies that have tainted American policing in the past must be taken into account when considering the reality of policing in the United States today.

As Skolnick and Fyfe observe, "[i]n the broad sweep of American history, the frontier produced the conditions that led to the rationale for the extralegal enforcement of the law" (1994, p 25). Where settlement preceded the formal trappings of social organisation, *ad hoc* enforcement of social norms was necessary, and crude vigilante justice was the only form of policing. However, the establishment of frontier towns, and the need for some form of local government, did not result in the imposition of the

---

8   The east coast was the earliest part of the United States to be colonised by Europeans, so cities like New York and Boston have had longer to grow: the major industrial development was in the North, giving rise to cities like Detroit and Chicago, while the southern and mid-western States have always been largely agricultural, which tends to lower population densities.

necessary legal machinery by the State government, but the entitlement of these communities to elect their own council, mayor, sheriff and, frequently, judges.

Much has been written about the role of police as maintainers of order rather than as enforcers of the law.[9] With the absence of formal courts, the emphasis of vigilante justice was on the preservation of order, which, in effect, meant maintenance of the status quo approved by the majority. Deeper issues such as that of procedural fairness or obtaining an impartial jury or a fair trial took second place to the need for a rugged frontier community to establish cohesion by punishing those perceived to be threatening the majority by their behaviour. Such rough justice is by no means unusual as a means of maintaining social integrity: the harsh punishments for adultery in traditional Islam may well have been necessary to prevent breaking a viable nomadic group of 20 or 30 persons into smaller non-viable units through feuding over illicit sexual relationships. Even earlier, the city states of ancient Greece operated a process known as ostracism, whereby any individual considered to be a troublemaker could be banished for a fixed number of years, usually seven or 10, by popular vote.

The establishment by communities of their own town council, policing and courts without reference to higher levels of government enabled the principles of vigilantism to be legitimised. Rather than concerned citizens getting together to run someone out of town, they could elect a sheriff to do it for them. If that sheriff chose to be pedantic about there being no lawful authority for this, then another, more amenable, sheriff could be elected. There is, indeed, an intuitive appeal in doing the right thing even if it means sidestepping the rules, rather than following the right procedures and risking the wrong result. Such, perhaps, is the appeal of almost every sheriff, if not every character, played by John Wayne. At certain stages in frontier history, the will of the people virtually legitimised vigilante justice, for example in the election of law officers like Judge Roy Bean of Texas, whose court was his saloon, and who claimed to administer "the only law West of the Pecos".

The sinister aspect of this form of policing can be very sinister indeed. As Skolnick and Fyfe remark: "In the South, the line between vigilante justice and official justice was scarcely discernible at all – at least not until the beginnings of the Civil Rights movement of the 1960s and the subsequent demise of the segregation laws" (1994, p 29). Vigilante justice here included lynchings, usually of African-Americans, and if lynchings did not have the active participation of police, at the very least they were condoned by police. Police in a small community are part of that community, and it would be strange if they did not share the hopes, fears and prejudices of that community. Before the Civil Rights movement, however, the voting population was white, and the white, male police force was directly answerable only to the white community. Order maintenance, therefore, included steps to allay community fears, which required, as Myrdal (1941)

---

9   See, for example, Bittner (1990, pp 38–59) on policing skid row. This topic has been discussed throughout Part 2.

reports, that "Negroes [be kept] in their place". While this form of policing is unjustifiable in any century, and is wholly unacceptable in the 21st, the way in which such practices came into being is clear.

Unacceptable but locally approved police practices can continue unchecked when there is a lack of effective supervision of local police by State or national government agencies. The harsh light of publicity which transcends local boundaries has much to do with holding local police accountable for failing to behave in a generally approved manner, but this applies only for serious cases. Perhaps more importantly, since the Civil Rights movement,[10] the voting population of all communities more or less mirrors its ethnic demographics, as do the ethnic (if not gender) demographics of many police departments, tending to eliminate xenophobia from amongst the fears of the general community.

In the larger cities of the United States, the problem of police accountability has presented itself rather differently. Within the bounds of a city, an organised force of several thousand armed men answerable only to the mayor is very much a force to be reckoned with. Indeed, the earliest tasks of city police in the United States was public order in the sense of dealing with riots: for example, in Boston, a police force was established after riots in 1837, and the New York Police had to deal with civil war draft riots in July 1863. Police in cities were monocultural with a vengeance: the perception of the predominance of Irish police officers is borne out by research. Rousey (1983) reports that in 1850 one third of New Orleans police had been born in Ireland, a proportion repeated in other cities like New York, Chicago, Milwaukee, Boston and St Louis.

Between the Civil War and the beginning of the 20th century local politics in many American cities was dominated by corrupt political machines, and order maintenance rather than crime control was the priority of policing. In Los Angeles, for example, utilities like water, power and rail companies were major forces in city politics, as were those who owned and ran the highly profitable, but victimless, vice trilogy of gambling, drinking and sex, all criminal activities but popular among the electorate. The progressives who wished to reform both local government corruption and the police had an uphill struggle to change the law and to have it enforced. Hiding vice operations from the police also hides them from their potential customers, a problem resolved by suborning police with bribes, so that police loyalties lay with local ward leaders and vice operators.

The history of city policing in the United States is of *de jure* local control, but of *de facto* answerability to whomsoever is capable of exercising that local control. With no tradition of police independence or accountability to multiple groups in city policing, street-level police were answerable to a chief, who was himself controlled by those who wielded most power in the city, and to those who were supplementing police pay by bribes. The regularity of these pay-offs remained in the hands of street police: as long as they turned a blind eye, gratitude would be expressed, while police

---

10   This, in practical terms, was effected by federal law enforcement from Washington, ordered into the South by the then Attorney-General, Robert Kennedy.

chiefs could, and did, come and go. Despite numerous attempts at reform, this type of corrupt payment is notoriously difficult to eradicate, persisting in New York, at least, until the heroic revelations of Frank Serpico and the resulting Knapp Commission of 1971.

It follows, then, that a police department of absolute probity cannot exist in a corrupt administration, in that an honest police department will sooner or later turn its attentions to the criminal behaviour of the administration itself. Mercifully, the reverse is true, that a sound and open administration can ensure that the issue of police misconduct does not go away, and can establish systems and policies of openness and public accountability. No police service is without corruption, but corruption can be reduced by a government willing to act against it: the most dangerous case is that of official and police corruption serving to reinforce and protect each other. It is this situation that the Fitzgerald inquiry exposed in Queensland in 1989, and that Vollmer found when he was appointed Chief of Police in Los Angeles in 1923 where:

> [T]he city's graft and corruption were too entrenched for him to make a lasting difference. He saw how effectively gamblers and bootleggers ran the mayor, who ran the city government, and how powerless he himself was to change things. Good government seemed impossible, and the barriers to civic reform Los Angeles itself had erected made a lasting impression on Vollmer. (Skolnick and Fyfe, 1994, p 175)

Operational accountability

The means of establishing operational accountability vary considerably across the United States, and, once again, a clear distinction can be drawn between a small police department and a large one. Justice Department statistics for policing in 1988 showed that the 25 largest police departments employ, between them, nearly 20 per cent of the nation's police officers (95,911 of 555,364), meaning the remainder of the 15,000 or so police agencies average about 30 officers each (figures cited in Bayley, 1992). The whole panoply of internal affairs branches, complaints procedures and independent investigations are not possible in a police agency so small that it does not even boast a detective branch, so methods of operational accountability will be considered for two different sizes of police agency. The criterion of size will be whether or not the police agency is large enough for a separate internal affairs or complaints investigation branch to be considered necessary, the alternative being the investigation of police misconduct by the chief officer.[11] For these purposes, a small police department

---

11 Size may not be the sole criterion for establishing a complaints investigation branch. The Metropolitan Police, London, although over 20,000 strong, had no independent complaints branch until one was instituted by Sir Robert Mark in the early 1970s: there may well be quite large policing agencies which have sufficient public confidence for the behaviour of individual officers not to be perceived as a sufficient problem for a separate internal affairs division to be formed, but this is less and less likely as police departments strive to be seen to be doing their jobs properly.

will be taken to be one of fewer than 50 sworn officers policing a population of under 25,000 people.

Small police departments

A small police department has no room for specialists, either as detectives or as traffic officers or as dedicated community police officers. There is also little room for a complex hierarchic structure as a police department becomes top-heavy with more than 10 per cent of the department supervising others: for a 50-strong organisation, this amounts to no more than a chief, one lieutenant and three or four sergeants. Operational or strategic decision-making is, therefore, likely to be the sole responsibility of the chief officer. Operational decisions, as has been discussed in Chapter 9, should be accountable to the public in general, or to particular sections which are more directly affected than others by those decisions. In small police departments the chief of police is likely to be a known, public figure, unable to exist in isolation from the community being policed. Merely by walking down the main street, the chief of police will be made aware of the concerns of the populace. In many small towns and rural areas the incidence of crime is low, and, providing police are reasonably polite, prompt in attending disturbances of the peace and not too zealous in enforcing traffic regulations, there will be a general feeling of benevolent apathy towards police.

Operational accountability is easily handled, therefore, as the chief of police is easily accessible to the community, and that chief is either elected or answerable to the mayor, who is always elected. Serious public unease about policing operations can be expressed in the local paper, raised at council meetings, used as ammunition by the opposition in council to highlight the mayor's failings which may lead to either the dismissal of the chief of police by the mayor, or the mayor's dismissal by the electorate at the next poll: an elected sheriff is even more readily and directly accountable to the populace. The chief of police is only immune from this if that office is one which falls within some form of public service tenured position: this may well be the case for other officers, but is not usual for the chief. This issue of tenure is important for the authority of the chief of police or sheriff, and relates to the actual power the chief has over officers of lower rank. If, for example, an officer who fails to comply with procedures or directions can be dismissed by the chief, then the chief has both responsibility for the quality of policing and the power to ensure that this is achieved. However, if police officers' jobs are protected by tenure unless some form of gross misconduct can be proved, then it is possible for the members of a police department to choose not to implement an inconvenient plan the chief may have, and, when something has to give, it may well be the chief who moves on.

Although a police department may, for whatever reason, reject a new chief, in general operational accountability is well served by the direct methods outlined above and made possible by a small scale policing system. Usually, if a new chief faces serious problems with a small department it is indicative that either the new chief is out of touch with the needs of the community and its police, or there is something endemically wrong with policing as it is, and drastic measures need to be taken. In many small departments, whoever is deputy to the chief officer holds a great deal of power as a stabilising influence, as this individual is likely to have the same tenure as other public service employees, and to have served under a number of chief officers. This is even more likely to be the case in sheriff's departments, when the sheriff may well be a policy-making local politician rather than a police officer, operational decisions being made by the deputy as senior serving police officer.

Large city police departments

The situation differs greatly in large cities, where police departments may have several thousand officers, and the cities themselves consist of a diversity of areas and population groups. The chief of police is, ultimately, answerable for the police department as a whole to the mayor, but officers in charge of specific sections of the city are not accountable directly to their local population, but to the chief officer. However, the people in each section of the city vote, and if one group feels dissatisfied with the policing it is getting, then this voter alienation may well be felt by local politicians who communicate this to the chief of police, whose own position is in jeopardy unless the recalcitrant captain or lieutenant satisfies the citizens. Police accountability might not, however, be so easily achieved, as politicians respond most to the majority, or to a significantly powerful minority (in voting terms), and it was the fact that the electorate was all white that allowed discriminatory policing in the deep south for so many years.

In very crude terms, then, large city police are, in principle, answerable to the community for operational decisions. The chief of police in American cities has significantly more power than chief officers in Australia or Britain, but is in far more danger of replacement should that power not be used to the satisfaction of the mayor, who is wholly reliant on the voters. The mechanism for accountability is crude in the sense that the accountability is to the city population as a whole rather than to specific sections of it, even if some sections might be more seriously affected than others.

Consider a hypothetical large city of a million people which is divided into 10 police precincts, each with roughly 100,000 population, and each under the command of a captain. These 10 precincts vary in nature, but one, Precinct J, has the highest rate of crime, lowest socio-economic indicators, more drug dealers, graffiti, etc, rendering it a very unpleasant area. The chief of police is working hard to establish a problem-oriented approach to policing, and the communities of nine of the 10 precincts all feel their problems originate in Precinct J. While community policing is starting to make progress in Precinct J, as in the other precincts, and the precinct captain is building a rapport with local leaders, an election is looming, and the opposition candidate for mayor is mounting a "get tough on crime" platform.

The captain in Precinct J is convinced that current long-term programs are having an effect, albeit a gradual one, as is the chief of police. However, the mayor, responding to public opinion from outside Precinct J, wants policing to suit the majority, and asks the chief to do something quickly and effectively (preferably with high publicity) about crime in Precinct J. The captain in Precinct J is likely to have job security as a public employee, but can, of course, be moved from J to one of the other precincts or to a captain's post at headquarters, while the chief's position relies on the mayor: a new mayor will appoint a different chief of police, and the current mayor is unlikely to be re-elected on current policing policy with regard to Precinct J. It is likely, therefore, that answerability to the public *outside* Precinct J will determine the style of policing within that precinct, whether or not it is the choice of its residents, or the best long-term option for them.

Although this hypothetical model is over-simplified, it serves to demonstrate how accountability to the public through the mayor is a blunt instrument. The city as a whole may get its stated requirements met, but this does not guarantee that the individual policing needs of each part of the city are actually met. In many cities, there are pockets of high-crime areas dotted about the place, and in very few places is crime the first matter in an election campaign. It follows that a chief of police doing a competent job is likely to remain in post after a change of mayor, especially if that chief is willing to accede to any changes in policing that the new mayor wishes to make. It is not even necessary that the population of a city approve positively the policing they receive: what matters is that the majority do not actively disapprove of the way in which policing is carried out, mere apathy towards policing is sufficient.

Police reform

Aside from corrupt practices, the other allegation which is regularly levelled against police is violent or racist conduct. Quite frequently the two are combined, as, for example, in the infamous Rodney King incident. There the two crucial features were the savagery of the beating inflicted on Rodney King, and the suspicion that African-American claims that violence is a regular feature of police conduct towards their people (but much less frequent towards white Americans) are justified. Neither corruption nor brutality is acceptable in modern policing, and a number of persons who have been chief police officers in various cities are cited in the history of American policing as having made their mark in the reform of police practices.

The issue of violence in policing is a problem of degree: as has been argued, coercion is a defining characteristic of policing, while the legitimate use of force, even deadly force, is at times a necessary form of coercion, yet excessive force or brutality is unacceptable. There is a problem which arises when one tries to categorise precisely what force is excessive, or what constitutes police brutality. As one analysis so aptly puts it: "Like hard-core pornography, we may not be able to define it, but we know it when we see it" (Skolnick and Fyfe, 1994, p xvi) They further argue that, for the cities as well as the frontier, vigilantism is interwoven with legitimate policing, and at times the two have been difficult to distinguish. An important part of policing is order maintenance (Scarman, 1981), and, as Bittner has argued about policing skid row, at times order maintenance has been the major policing task. This order maintenance may be carried out through the benign manipulation of the criminal law, as in Bittner's example of the skid row police officer arresting a drunken and temporarily affluent inhabitant to prevent him being mugged. At its worst, however, order maintenance may also involve physical violence towards members of the public being meted out by police as a form of "summary justice".

Skolnick and Fyfe indeed argue that institutionalised violent behaviour, in particular towards members of ethnic minorities, has been a feature of both American police history and recent, arguably current, police practice. There is a perception among the American public and some, at least, of their mayors and their police chiefs, that protecting the public and preserving the peace is a hard task involving violent people, and on many occasions a violent response is called for. As will be demonstrated shortly, some mayors and police chiefs have been outspoken on this issue. Police officers on the street can be expected to show a violent or racist attitude if they have the overt support of their chief or their mayor even more than if they assumed that such support was covert within the police department itself.[12]

Effective reform of policing (where it is needed) in American cities relies on three factors all being present together: a reforming chief of police; a reform-minded mayor or local council; and support from senior officers within the police department for reform. Reform cannot be achieved overnight, so sufficient time must be given to the chief of police to implement a reform agenda. Frequently, only one or two of these factors has been present, and some notable figures in police reform have been more famous for their ideas implemented elsewhere than for their personal success in achieving change. If a prophet is without honour in his own country, a reforming police chief is often without recognition in his own city. August Vollmer, for example, instituted professional methods into the small police department in Berkeley, California, but was unable to succeed in Los Angeles because local government corruption was too entrenched. His ideas, however, were influential on policing elsewhere through his participation in President Hoover's 1929 Wickersham Commission on law and policing.

Problems arise, too, when positions within the police department just below that of chief are tenured by civil service regulations, although the

---

12   Uelman (1973, pp 1-65) in an analysis of a number of California police departments found that the number of fatal shootings by police depended more heavily on the policies of the department chief than on other factors.

chief of police is an untenured political appointment. In such circumstances, a police executive team which does not support the reform strategy can very effectively destroy or at least seriously weaken it, whatever the chief of police tries to do. Such officers have a great deal of power in the police department, cannot be removed by the reforming chief, and often are at a high enough level that they cannot be moved into backwater tasks. One observer (Miller, 1991) has claimed that this was the situation faced by Philadelphia's Commissioner Willie Williams during his reform process; the problem remained unresolved when he moved to Los Angeles to take over from Chief Darryl Gates. This problem is not confined to the United States, as was discovered by Ray Whitrod, who was unsuccessful in reforming the Queensland police in the early 1970s against what was later shown to be endemic corruption involving both government and police.

Instances of police reform in the United States usually involve the importation of a reforming chief officer, rather than promotion of a refor- mer from inside the department concerned. This is logical, as an aspiring chief who has spent a whole career in one police department is likely to be imbued with that departmental ethos and no other: if the department is in need of reform, then it is unlikely to come from someone who knows no other policing, but if the department has a culture of change then it is unlikely to need serious reform. Change must, however, be kept in per- spective: police agencies (and this is probably the majority) which have been providing a sound but unexceptional service and implementing new ideas a little after they have been implemented elsewhere and shown to be valuable, and working in accordance with the needs of their communities usually have little need of wholesale reform. Gradual improvement is better and less traumatic for the police and the city than radical change.

Case studies in police accountability

In general, the system of operational accountability of police in the United States works reasonably well in that chief officers of police can be, and are, replaced, as are the mayors to whom they are answerable. Both the need for the system, and the fact that it is not perfect, can best be illustrated by the cautionary tales of occasions where police have not been fully accountable for operational decisions to the communities that they are responsible for policing. Skolnick and Fyfe (1994) discuss a number of police departments in great detail with regard to violent acts committed by police so flagrantly that they are, and know themselves to be, above the law.

One such breakdown of accountability was in the city of Philadelphia, during the mayoral term of Frank Rizzo. The mayor's stated intention was to deal harshly with criminals, and, as a former police commissioner of the city, even the US Justice Department report (Thrasher et al, 1979) claimed it was unclear how much the mayor was directly responsible for police department decision-making. There was certainly an unholy alliance between the mayor, the police commissioner and the police department, whereby police who shot or injured criminals were actively protected by both the police department and the mayor. Fatal shootings by police increased annually, but dropped by two-thirds after Rizzo completed his maximum permissible terms of office (figures from Skolnick and Fyfe, 1994).

Problems also occurred in Los Angeles, where police chiefs were traditionally appointed from inside the force, and, unusually, had tenure. The televised beating of Rodney King[13] led to a world-wide furore over what was seen as a culture of police violence within the LAPD, after which Willie Williams was appointed in July 1992 as a non-tenured chief. Ironically, tenure resulted from a suggestion by Vollmer when he found that his work as chief was hampered by his being answerable to a corrupt local administration, and, after his departure, the independence of police was secured by the tenure of the chief. Although the first chief to take advantage of this, William Parker, stamped out corruption over his long term as Commissioner, he did so by creating a semi-militaristic police agency, and subsequent appointments from inside the force reinforced this model. Skolnick and Fyfe report that another city, Milwaukee, which also had a tenurable position as chief of police and a policy of promoting from within, faced considerable similar problems with police violence. Both Los Angeles and Milwaukee have since replaced tenure with contracts for their chief officers.

The highest profile recent example of a police department operating on the directions of a popularly elected mayor was New York City in the 1990s. Mayor Giuliani was elected in 1993 and re-elected in 1997 with an increased majority, the reduction of crime in the city being a major plank in his election platform. Although the majority of New Yorkers are, apparently, in favour of the style of policing his appointed chiefs of police introduced, it is by no means certain that the whole community felt that way, particularly African-American and Hispanic New Yorkers, whose younger community members figure prominently in arrest statistics. While no criminal who is arrested as a result of any policing strategy is likely to approve of that strategy, law-abiding members of minority groups may well feel that those policing strategies which result in increasing numbers of arrests of minorities are discriminatory policing.

Personal accountability

The question of a police officer's personal accountability is, in many respects, dealt with differently in the small police organisations from the way in which officers are held to account in the large city departments. Much as the matter of financial accountability of the police organisation is difficult to distinguish from organisational accountability in small towns, so, too, does the personal accountability of police officers in a small

---

13   The violence against Rodney King took place on 2 March 1991 and the trial of the officers responsible was held in May 1992, when rioting followed their acquittal by a jury in Simi Valley.

department become a significant part of the accountability of the organisation as a whole.

In all hierarchic organisations, those persons with supervisory or executive authority bear responsibility for ensuring that those under their command act correctly and efficiently. In a small police department, the chief should know each member of the department personally, set standards and ensure that they are maintained. Where the department is too small to have an internal affairs or complaints department, this task should be part of the duties of the chief of police, or whomsoever is second in command. For a police department in a small town, the rank structure provides one of the most effective means of holding individual officers accountable for their actions.

It also must not be forgotten that the community being policed, if it is small, may be able to exert considerable pressure on individual police officers to conform to the norms of that community. While policing by consent is usually taken to imply that those policed will always outnumber the police, in a small community a police officer who consistently behaves in a manner objectionable to that community can be subject to criticism and informal sanctions. An officer who is rude or aggressive still has to live in the community, which can react in a thousand small ways: the local shop-keepers may have sold out of the best produce when the officer calls, or the garage does not quite finish repairs on the officer's car in time for the weekend, and so on.

In a small community, human interaction is unavoidable, and serves to ensure that police behave in a fashion acceptable to the community. The community may not actually be right, however, and an officer who attempts to enforce an unpopular law may be subject to the same social pressures as one who behaves rudely. In reality, the forces at work here which ensure that individual police officers do not exceed their authority and act in an acceptable fashion are the very same peer group pressures which caused police in the past to condone or participate in vigilantism when members of the community found the due process of law inadequate, inconvenient or contrary to their desires. The principles of democracy require that the wishes of the majority be carried out, but civil rights require that needs of individuals and minorities be respected. Democratic policing means that the law be upheld equally for all, not that order be maintained for the benefit of the majority. Any statistician knows that a small sample may not extrapolate to the whole population: the most dangerous aspect of local control of policing is that the small size of a local community may result in a local majority demanding a form of policing which cannot be provided within the requirements of State and federal law and the Constitution.

Officers policing small communities can, therefore, be made accountable directly to the community, or, indeed, members of the community can hold the chief of police accountable so strongly that the chief's own job is in jeopardy if the recalcitrant officer is not disciplined or dismissed. Even if the community distrusts an officer rather than has hard evidence of misconduct, that officer is unlikely to receive any help or support from the community in investigating offences, so that that officer's efficiency is diminished. A small police department cannot afford to carry an officer whose performance is noticeably below standard, and this becomes an operational issue for the chief of police.

Accountability through the courts

American police officers are held accountable through the courts in three particular ways: the obligation on judges to exclude as evidence any piece of information which follows from a legally untenable police action; the emphasis on the constitutional rights of every individual, and the possibility of police being found culpable for violations of these rights in a federal court; and the chance of a police officer being a defendant in a civil suit for civil rights violations or other damages claims. Each of these three has significant differences from the accountability of Australian or British police officers to the courts.

Consider a search carried out by a police officer where the reasons for that search (the "probable cause") are found by the court to be insufficient. American courts have no discretion here: not only must evidence of the search and items found be excluded, but everything which follows, such as questions and admissions relating to the item found, must be inadmissible. This is far more stringent than the rule applied in Australian or British courts, where, if officers exceed their powers, the courts have discretion to exclude the evidence but may admit it in the interests of natural, rather than procedural, justice. Although this rule is intended to prevent searches of dubious legality being justified *post hoc ergo propter hoc* by the discovery of prohibited material, it is uncertain whether this really achieves its object. Experienced police officers will be fully aware of what the Supreme Court means by prior cause, and also aware of what their local courts will accept as evidence justifying a search, and can be expected to have all the right answers for the district attorney or the judge. If a police officer knows what a court expects to hear, that can be written into the evidence somehow: a London detective attending a class in 1985 on the new procedures for dealing with suspects under the *Police and Criminal Evidence Act* 1984 explained his unusual level of interest thus – "if I know the rules, I know how to write the script". A rigid exclusionary rule may, therefore, do no more than encourage police officers to doctor their evidence to meet the requirements of the court, knowing that if, for example, the probable cause for a search is challenged, there is unlikely to be independent evidence of the dialogue between police and the suspects.

The whole issue of constitutional rights is almost exclusive to the United States within common law systems.[14] While rights are taken seriously, and the preservation of individual liberty is no less important as

---

14 Canada now has a Bill of Rights, but Australia, Britain, New Zealand and other common law countries rely on statutory rights or on common law rights harking back through centuries of precedent to Magna Carta.

a fundamental principle of law in Australia or Britain than in the United States, constitutional rights outweigh every other legal matter in importance. In the phrase of the legal theorist Ronald Dworkin, "rights are trumps". No infringement of a person's constitutional rights, however petty, can be overlooked by the courts in the interests of wider issues of justice or fairness within the trial procedures, and even a very minor infringement of rights can "trump" any piece of evidence, however important to the case.

There are two practical aspects of American law which serve to make civil suits against police officers a more common means of holding police officers accountable than in Australia or Britain. In 1976, federal statute permitted judges to include in the costs of successful plaintiffs reasonable attorney's fees. This was a more certain method for lawyers to be paid for acting for a plaintiff, as the contingency fee where attorneys settled for a percentage of the sum awarded by the court could mean that even a win in a police malpractice suit meant the lawyer did not break even, as courts are markedly reluctant to award a large amount of damages to a plaintiff who is perceived as a criminal. The second important factor is a Supreme Court case, *Monell*,[15] which decided that if an employee of any agency violates an individual's constitutional rights, then the agency itself has vicarious liability for that infringement. It follows that if a police officer is sued for constitutional rights violations, then the city or county can be joined to the suit, ensuring that at least one defendant has the financial resources to meet the judgment, and there is every likelihood that a public body will negotiate an out-of-court settlement of the suit. These two factors together are a suitable encouragement for lawyers to take likely cases on a "no win, no fee" agreement knowing that a win or a settlement will be profitable. There is now a large and growing civil rights bar in the United States. Neither of these factors is present in the Australian or the British legal systems: the *Enever* ruling means Australian police services have no vicarious liability for their officers' malpractice, and Australian and British lawyers have consistently rejected "no win, no fee" agreements on principle, legal aid often not covering civil cases for the plaintiff.

In many cases, the American system of a civil suit against police malpractice is a sound method of holding individual officers accountable. The victim of police malpractice receives compensation, the city which has paid out can be expected to charge the damages to the police budget, and the officer responsible should suffer the wrath of the police department and probably also disciplinary proceedings. On this logic, a complainant's lawsuit will result in punishment of the officer concerned and just as salutary a lesson for other officers as a formal complaint and discipline proceedings, with the additional benefit for the complainant of a significant sum of money. It is, perhaps, hardly surprising that many more complainants of police behaviour in the United States follow this procedure than do so in Australia or Britain.

---

15   *Monell v Department of Social Services of the City of New York* 436 US 658 (1978).

At its best, a successful civil suit against a police officer shows the officer, the department and the city what behaviour is unacceptable, and even stipulates the degree of unacceptability by putting a dollar value on the harm done. Since both the police officer and the department as employer are jointly liable, the judgment ties personal and operational accountability together. An officer who behaves badly is criticised formally by the court, the police department pays the bill and can deal with the officer further by internal discipline, training or dismissal. If a number of officers are criticised by the courts for similar behaviour, and the police department faces a number of expensive suits, then this shows clearly that there is something at fault with the ethos of the organisation, and policy changes or further training are necessary.

There is a danger, however, that unless the police department does take action against an officer whose behaviour has resulted in a judgment against it, individual officers will see their behaviour as being indemnified by the department, and do nothing to change it. A line of argument often heard from hard-bitten street cops of all nations is that real policing involving dealing with the public and making stops, searches and arrests, which is bound to upset people from time to time, and therefore leads to complaints (and lawsuits). It follows that only those dealing with the public get complaints, the corollary of which is that those officers getting complaints must be doing real policing, and the really tough street cops sometimes even claim that the number of complaints is an index of both workrate and effectiveness.

If a police department pays out in court judgments and settlements without taking action against the officers whose behaviour gave rise to those matters, then this gives official recognition and approval to the argument of the street cops outlined above. Comparisons of settlements from various police departments show that the per capita cost of lawsuits in 1990, calculated by dividing the total paid in judgments by the number of officers in the department, is three times as high in Los Angeles as in New York or Chicago, and nine times as high in Detroit (Mitchell, 1991).[16] Skolnick and Fyfe (1994) examine a number of cases in Los Angeles, as a result of which they argue that, at least until the retirement of Chief Gates, the attitude towards lawsuits had the effect of condoning, rather than condemning, such behaviour. They cite the case of the McDonalds Bandits, where LAPD action resulted in three out of four suspects being shot and killed, and a lawsuit filed with a judgment for punitive damages of $44,000 against Chief Gates and the officers involved in the shooting. This sum was paid directly from city, rather than police, funds.

If the police department, and in the Los Angeles case above, the city, behave in this fashion, then significant doubts are raised about the real accountability of police. The major fear members of the public have about

---

16   The figures for 1990 cited are that Los Angeles and New York paid about the same amount of money, $11.3 million, although the NYPD has three times as many officers as the LAPD, Detroit paid $20 million with two-thirds the number of officers as the LAPD, while Chicago paid half as much as LAPD with 50 per cent more officers.

making a complaint against police officers is that an internal investigation will produce a whitewash or a cover-up, where the public's concerns are minimised. While a successful civil suit shows the police department that the community's most powerful impartial arbiter, the justice system, has stated that certain behaviour is unacceptable, the refusal of a police department to take remedial action is extremely disturbing. For a police department to pay the damages then maintain business as usual is not a covert cover-up, but an overt statement to the public that, although the behaviour of its officer might be unacceptable,[17] nevertheless it will not be changed. Such an attitude on the part of the police department effectively negates any accountability of individual police officers to the public for their actions, and renders the police organisation a law unto itself, which is compounded if the city council also colludes in shielding police officers. It can easily be envisaged that a mayor elected with a mandate to get tough on crime may appoint a chief of police with an attitude that results count more than the means of obtaining them, and officers on the street almost have a licence to behave as they choose, provided they do not breach the criminal law or departmental regulations.

Few large police departments in the United States take this attitude, and most consider a judgment against them in the courts to be a criticism of police actions, and take steps to modify their officers' behaviour. In general, the principles of policing by consent apply: in return for the citizenry accepting the necessity for being policed and consenting to it, the police in turn show sensitivity to the needs of the community, and consent to police accordingly. Most police departments of any size recognise the need for a system to record and investigate complaints made by citizens, and the need to have this system itself transparent to prevent any claims that complaints are covered up.

Complaints investigations systems

The usual caveat for discussing American policing – that each police organisation operates its own system in its own way – applies with regard to complaints, internal affairs and professional standards. There are no national standards for police behaviour, or even national police powers other than those that result from decisions in the Supreme Court. Foremost among these in police usage is *Terry v Ohio*,[18] which is usually taken by police to authorise a personal "pat-down" search on arrest of suspicious persons who might be armed and dangerous. Supreme Court judgments not only clarify suspects' rights, but also police powers.

---

17 There is an important question about whether the whole of the population considers this behaviour unacceptable. There is a considerable popular opinion, often to be found on talk-back radio programs, which holds that offenders deserve everything they get, and finds nothing reprehensible in police violence towards those who are violent or disorderly.

18 392 US 1868 (1968).

The vast majority of complaints against police are relatively trivial, and not the sort of matter that even a litigious society like the United States would waste the time of the courts with in a civil suit. As elsewhere in the world, American police are more likely to be accused of being rude, aggressive in manner, or rough in their handling of suspects, than vicious or corrupt. To some extent, American police tend to handle suspects in a manner which, although acceptable to the American public, is generally rougher than Australian or British police. The reasons are twofold: there is a far greater likelihood of a suspect having a weapon, particularly a firearm, in the United States than elsewhere, so police officers take their personal safety even more seriously than police in other countries; and it is standard American police practice to handcuff every person arrested, whereas this is normally only done with violent offenders or those who are likely to try and escape in Australia and Britain.

City police departments have, for many years, had internal affairs departments to investigate complaints against police officers from the public or deal with internal discipline cases. As elsewhere, the public desire for the process to be transparent has resulted in most cities establishing a Police Board to adjudicate such matters. Police officers in most departments have some sort of trade union which negotiates on behalf of its members, and can represent their interests in defending complaints from the public. The membership of the police boards vary considerably from city to city, but, in general, there are representatives from the police executive, police union, city council and independent representatives of the public. The number of members, and whether the preponderance of numbers is with the police or the citizenry, are the main variables. The object of such boards is to allow some independent supervision of the resolution of public complaints against police, although the general public are rarely allowed into the hearings.

There are some pro-active schemes in policing to forestall complaints, and also to allow more stringent action should matters reach the police board. San Antonio, for example, has a counselling system for officers whose behaviour comes to notice, either from a complaint or from observation by senior officers. Officers who have domestic or financial problems, or are drinking heavily, or have some other personal difficulties which are adversely affecting their duties may be diverted into some sort of assistance program, or a short-term transfer to less stressful duties before serious consequences befall the officer or the public. If these programs are successful, then the officer's problems never reach the stage of a police board: if unsuccessful, the police board can more justifiably decide that there is no alternative but to dispense with the officer's services. Some police officers, of course, may ultimately be unsuitable for police service, and the chief of police needs to be able to sack them. This power is not available in all departments, but the alternative, which is to suspend an officer indefinitely without pay, does exist. It is particularly important if the police service is heavily armed that the only officers allowed on the streets are those that can be trusted not to use their weapons unnecessarily, or even to use them as a threat to the public.

Conclusion

For a number of reasons, the subject of police accountability in the United States is far more difficult to generalise about than police accountability in Australia or Britain. At its best, it works as well as any system in place in those countries, but, like any system that relies on a comparatively small number of people in a small area, it can be open to abuse. This applies equally in small police departments as in larger ones, as has been shown. One of the most interesting aspects of police accountability in the United States is that in small police departments financial accountability and the personal accountability of individual police officers becomes subsumed into the operational accountability of the police department, and for this the chief officer of that department becomes personally responsible. To be a chief of police in the United States carries a much higher career risk than to be a chief officer elsewhere, as with this responsibility goes the implied threat of dismissal for lack of achievement. The reality of running a police department in the United States is that the chief must meet expectations to retain that appointment, but that sometimes too little emphasis is placed on precisely how those expectations are met.

The role of chief of police often has a high profile in the large cities, and the more local politicians run election campaigns on law and order grounds, the higher the profile of the police chief is likely to be. Police officers who reach chief constable or commissioner rank in Britain and Australia are likely to have devoted their whole careers to policing, even though they may well have gained high academic qualifications in so doing, while their American counterparts are likely to have a much more varied and political curriculum vitae. Much further down the rank structure, while the character of the British police officer is based in the popular myth of the stolid, friendly, trustworthy and essentially non-confrontational figure epitomised on television by Dixon of Dock Green, so, perhaps, the American law officer paradigm is the Western sheriff as the lone hero. Although this John Wayne figure was willing to bend the rules and cut red tape in order to achieve the ends of justice, he was just as benign to the public as George Dixon, gave the villain a fair chance and used the minimum of physical force. Imperceptibly, the police hero moved from this image to that of Clint Eastwood's Dirty Harry, a detective who dealt with crime and criminals in an uncompromisingly violent fashion, but was still seen as a hero for solving the case, usually by killing the perpetrator, thereby avoiding any awkward questions about the legality of his actions at any subsequent trial.

The perception, and probably the reality, is that American cities are more violent than cities in Australia or Britain, and that American police of necessity must use more force to uphold the law than their Australian or

British counterparts. Nevertheless, police accountability must be maintained to prevent the maintenance of law and order descending into guerrilla warfare between police and criminals: a police service which does not conform to the policing standards expected by its community and established by the law is criminally dangerous.

PART IV

POLICING IN THE 21ST CENTURY

CHAPTER 13

ISSUES IN CRIME IN THE 21ST CENTURY

Introduction

The impact of new technology at the end of the 20th century and the beginning of the 21st has produced some changes in the type of crime committed: some of these crimes are wholly new, created by the technology itself being put to criminal use, while some are old crimes in new guises, crime, like other aspects of life, being made easier by new technology. These technological crimes will be closely examined in this chapter. The main vehicles for these changes in crime are computers and the Internet, the aspects of information technology which provide the ability to conduct financial and other transactions without using cash or personal contact between individuals. Information technology also facilitates international or transnational crime, which, because police and courts have always been restricted in their authority by geographical and jurisdictional limitations, has always been difficult to address.[1] Despite increased airport security since 2001, it has never been easier to move quickly around the world, so these two factors have changed transjurisdictional crime from being a comparatively rare occurrence to a serious law enforcement problem.

There are four particular types of crime considered in this chapter as examples of new problems for policing. The first is Internet crime, which includes crimes which were inconceivable before the advent of the world-wide web, and old crimes which, when committed using new technology, are now much easier to commit or are less easy to detect. The second is the criminal aspect of globalisation, international or transnational financial crime. Thirdly, people-smuggling is examined. Although this is a transnational crime, it is worthy of separate consideration as it is a crime against persons, in its worst aspects a 21st century version of the centuries-old tradition of slavery. Finally terrorism is considered. Although all these crimes are serious and important matters, it will be argued that they are, nevertheless, crimes which will have a direct effect on only a miniscule proportion of the population. While the images of the destruction of the World Trade Center had an impact around the world, the crimes that directly affect people in their own lives are still the quality of life offences, graffiti

---

1   There has always been such crime. In a 15th century case, a dispute arose between a British sea captain and a British wine merchant over a consignment of claret, where the act alleged had been committed at the port of embarkation. A British court in Islington (now an inner London borough) gave itself jurisdiction by declaring the offence to have been committed "in the town of Bordeaux in the County of Middlesex". Such inventive solutions are no longer acceptable.

and drug addicts in the street, petty theft and vandalism. Police efforts against "quality of life" crimes are largely driven by political requirements and the need to convince the public, through the media, that action is being taken, even though for a variety of reasons these efforts are less than effective.

Internet crime

Little hangs on the distinction whether a crime is wholly new, or an old crime in a new guise. To steal or falsify another's credit cards and to use their PIN or passwords for financial gain is a modern version of the crime of fraud: the crime is essentially the same as that committed when a mediaeval clerk authenticated a false document with his master's personal seal to his own advantage. The difference lies in the level of anonymity provided by the Internet for the perpetrator and, often, jurisdictional problems for any subsequent prosecution. The mediaeval victim would know which people had access to the personal seal and the false document had to be produced personally to another interested party to gain money or goods, making it reasonably easy to identify the offender. In the 21st century a credit card may be used fraudulently over the web or telephone by an offender who never meets any other person in the course of the criminal transaction. Such offences may go unnoticed, and even if reported the location of the offence may be difficult to pinpoint, while the criminal, the victim, and the goods obtained may all be in different jurisdictions. It is still the same, centuries-old crime of fraud, but rendered almost impossible to detect or prosecute by information technology and its inherent anonymity.

Pornography and paedophilia

These two crimes are considered together not because of any inherent similarity between the pornographer and the paedophile, but because both these offences have been made much easier to commit, less easy to detect and more profitable by the advent of the Internet. Pornography is by no means a new crime. Without wishing to debate the distinction between erotica and pornography here, one can easily imagine an oral tradition of erotic verse: Eskimo Nell may have an equivalent in an Icelandic saga or Homeric ode, and erotic art has been found on the walls of Pompeii. After Caxton, the next major advance for the pedlars of erotic or pornographic material was the invention of photography and cinematography. This still, however, required specialised equipment (and skill in its use) for the production of films and printed material and a network for the transport, storage and sale of contraband books, magazines, films and videocassettes. Obscene publications take as many resources to distribute and sell as any other publication, and when found by police, whether in storage or in transit, can be seized as physical evidence. As with any other contraband material, there are certain locations at which they are at high risk of discovery, for example at the place where they are made, at cross-border customs posts, at distribution centres where they are stored in bulk and at the point of sale to the public. Modern technology minimises such risks of discovery by enabling the distribution of material in electronic rather than physical form.

The digital camera and the Internet when used together enable family photographs to be transmitted instantly around the world, downloaded and reproduced endlessly with easily used equipment available at any number of high street or mall retailers. This very same technology also allows pornographic images to be produced and sold across jurisdictional borders without ever having tangible form: the technology makes no distinction between a family photograph and a pornographic image, and electronic transmission provides no opportunity for inspection by, for example, a police or customs officer. Communications technology did not generate a new type of pornography, but allows pornography to be produced with minimal production facilities or technical assistance, and to be distributed and sold online, the material being downloaded directly onto the purchaser's computer in private. Nothing is physically made or transported, so there is nothing to be found by police or customs: production, distribution and purchase of pornography are so nearly undetectable that the risks are now minimal, while profits are still vast.

Pornography prosecutions have always been difficult for police, not least because there is no objective definition of the term. Investigations into pornography for a number of years have concentrated on material which is provably harmful to its participants, which increasingly has come to mean sado-masochistic images where some individual has suffered real, not simulated, serious injury, and images of children. This is the point at which pornography and paedophilia intersect: it is impossible to create pornographic images of children without the children involved being sexually abused in the process. Adult participants in pornographic material may be willing or may be coerced, but every child participant is a victim of serious abuse, and can never be considered to be a consenting party.

Paedophilia has, since the 1990s, become the newest horror crime foremost in the public mind. The public mind is rather muddled, however, perceiving the greatest danger to be that of the sexual predator, often assumed to be lurking in Internet chatrooms, and expressing outrage over allegations involving the Catholic priesthood, while being apparently unaware (or unwilling to accept) that the most likely source of abuse is still a member of the child's family circle. These different matters require different action. Allegations which have been made against clergy are most typically allegations of serious and systematic abuse carried out some years ago when the victims were children, made now when the victims are adults. Australian allegations concerning the Christian Brothers involve orphaned children[2] sent from Britain in the care of the Catholic Church during, or in the years following, the Second World War who were

---

2   Not all were without living parent or family, but were given into the care of the church by relatives who were unable or unwilling to care for them.

physically and/or sexually abused. Child abuse is not, therefore, a new phenomenon. It has, however, come to prominence because society's attitudes have changed to encourage discussion, no subject being taboo. While the sexual abuse of children has never been condoned by society, it has long been denied, and systematic physical abuse of children was not only accepted but approved until the last quarter of the 20th century: the practice of caning in orphanages, reformatories and schools, which was abolished finally in the 1970s was no less than institutionalised state-sanctioned violence against children. The vociferous minority who wish the practice to be re-introduced, and court and legislators who are still ambivalent about physical punishment of children indicate that old ideas die hard. Slapping a spouse to enforce one's will is now, rightly, considered to be an assault and is no longer acceptable: if such violence between spouses is now viewed as a serious issue, then the same type of violence as punishment of a child must, logically and ethically, be equally (if not more) unacceptable. In its panic over the dangers of the Internet the public seem to ignore the fact that most instances of child abuse, physical and sexual, occur within the family, and intuitively, it would be surprising if most of those who use violence against a spouse would see any reason to refrain from violence against a child.

To the public mind, every time a child uses the Internet, he or she is in danger of being corrupted by accidentally visiting a pornographic website, or falling prey to a paedophile lurking in a chat room to groom victims and lure them away to appear on the web in pornographic images. This is, of course, a possibility, but, arguably, not such a common occurrence as to justify the panic and fear that it generates. The most obvious point to be made about pornographic websites is that they are there to generate profit – the images that are to be found by searching the net are lurid and titillating, indubitably unsavoury and unsuitable for children, but the explicit material is only to be obtained upon payment, ie on entry of credit card details. While an adolescent might borrow and use a credit card for such a purpose, this will only remain undetected for a few weeks until the credit card statement arrives. There may well be some danger in chat rooms, but in the main they are used by members of like-minded groups, and discussions are trivial if not utterly boring to the casual visitor. The 1950s equivalent of chat room users may well have been the radio hams: in his famous television sketch, Tony Hancock raised a Japanese radio ham, compared the weather in Tokyo and East Cheam and signed off.

For every advantage that the Internet (or any other technological advance) brings, there is a darker application. Websites can be devoted to any topic, and enable individuals with something in common to find each other to their mutual advantage. A website devoted to military history enables old soldiers to swap tales of (British) National Service spent in Egypt after the Suez crisis of 1956, and to renew contact with people not seen for over 40 years. The very same system enables groups that are far from innocuous to establish contact and mutually reinforce their antisocial beliefs or criminal tendencies. The clear message of support groups of all sorts, on the web or in live meetings, is to tell the individual "You are not alone – other people feel the way you do – you are not wrong to feel this way". This is a helpful message for those in despair having been diagnosed with a particular medical condition, a harmless message when found in a website for, let us say, the Flat Earth Society, but potentially harmful if the website is, for example, racist, terrorist or paedophile in content.

One of the most difficult and unpleasant facts regarding the children whose images are to be found on paedophile websites is that the adult perpetrators are most commonly either the child's parents, or known to the child's parents. To identify the child is usually to identify the offender, which leads to a relatively straightforward investigation for detectives in a child abuse unit. However, identifying the children involved in a piece of child pornography can be almost impossible, as investigators are often unable to determine even the country in which any given pornographic image is made. The other problem for an investigation is that such websites create a network with a multitude of abusers, child victims, and purchasers of material. The sheer numbers of users of such websites creates a herculean task for policing. The task is, however, worth undertaking as each victim is a child in misery, pain and despair, not, as in most crimes, an individual or an institution which has merely suffered financial loss.

The scale of the problem is shown by an American investigation into the Landslide website, which provided access to child pornography. The website provided data on 390,000 subscribers in 60 countries. There were 35,000 subscribers in the United States and over 7000 in Britain (Jewkes, 2003). Each individual merits investigation, but each investigation requires not just ordinary policework in tracing the suspect and obtaining a warrant but specialist skills and considerable time in examining each computer's hard drive fully, especially if information is encrypted. The task is not impossible, but does require a very large commitment of specialist investigators and the allocation of huge budgets to do little more than scratch the surface of a world-wide problem. This issue will be taken up again a little later.

Transnational crime

Transnational crime is as old as national and jurisdictional borders, from the first time a person stole another's possessions in one tribal area and bartered them in another. The essence of transnational property crime is that a commodity can be obtained in one jurisdiction and sold in another at a profit when the obtaining, the selling or the transport of the commodity is illegal. In some offences, such as smuggling goods whose possession is lawful in each jurisdiction, the profit is generated by taking goods across the border and avoiding taxes or duty. In other cases, goods may be freely and legally available in one jurisdiction but not in another, and the profit is generated by legal purchase, transport across the border and illegal sale, for example the trade in alcohol between Canada and the United States during the prohibition era. In the case of the illicit drugs trade, possession and sale is illegal in almost every country, but if the raw materials such as opium and cocaine are only available in a few parts of the world and the demand for the commodity is worldwide, the crime, of necessity, becomes international.

Whatever schemes can be devised to facilitate international trade and legitimate travel will, inevitably, be available to facilitate international criminal enterprises. The Maastricht Treaty removed internal barriers within the European Union so that there are now no border checks between member countries. While this improves social and business travel and speeds the transport of goods by road, rail and sea it also makes life easier for the criminal. A car stolen in France disguised with false Belgian registration plates can be driven into Germany with no routine checks. The car may contain property stolen in Holland, which can be transported to another jurisdiction where it may even not be defined in law as stolen property (and, even if it is, is unlikely to be so listed by police), and sold with a much lower risk of detection.

The prevalence of air travel also increases the possibility of virtually undetectable minor crime, for example straightforward theft. Once a piece of baggage is checked in at the start of a journey, its owner may not expect to see it again until the final destination, during which time it may have been transferred several times. Travelling from, for example, Kalgoorlie, Western Australia to Zurich involves changes of aeroplane in Perth, Singapore and Heathrow, and if the bag fails to arrive in Zurich it may have been genuinely lost in transit or stolen at any one of the transfer points. Had it been stolen, no later investigation could possibly identify the thief, as detection could only occur in the unlikely event of a more or less random search catching the offender in possession of identifiable property. Even then, the possibility of a successful prosecution is reduced if the owner cannot conveniently attend the relevant police station or court – if significant travel expenses are involved, then neither the victim nor prosecuting authorities are likely to be willing to pay the costs of the case.

Identity theft

In many nations, all citizens have long been obliged to carry national identity cards, and non-citizens required to carry identification and proof that they are legally entitled to be in the country. Even before the Maastricht treaty, national identity cards of member states were acceptable as travel documents within the EU. Since roughly the mid-1980s, the need to have proof of identity, even in countries such as Australia and Britain which do not issue national identity cards, has both become more important and has changed subtly in character. Every individual now has two forms of identity, one which might be termed financial or computer identity, which is usually assured by PIN and password codes, and the physical identity proven by workplace evidence like passports, driving licences and photographic identity cards issued by employers. Both sorts of identity can be stolen, with rather different effects for the individual. Such crimes are not rare: it is estimated that 750,000 US citizens had their identities stolen for financial gain in 2002 (Jewkes, 2003).

The greatest risk of financial loss occurs, not surprisingly, with the theft of financial identity. Once a victim's financial identity can be obtained, this can be used to obtain money not only from the victim's own bank and credit card accounts, but also by obtaining credit in the victim's name from other institutions. While 50 years ago one's ability to borrow money rested upon one's standing with the bank manager, now almost every adult has a bank account and at least one credit card, and the ability to use these without defaulting on payment creates a good credit history. Credit ratings are determined and maintained by independent credit reference organisations, their information being sold to any institution which offers credit. It is worth noting the difference between being creditworthy 50 years ago, and being creditworthy today. Fifty years ago, a bank manager would inquire not only into the individual's history of borrowing and repayment, but into current debt and income, ie the ability to repay. Today, an individual's credit rating will be good provided that money owed has been repaid without default or court order, with no consideration being given to the ability to repay further loans. An individual can easily obtain further credit using fresh loans to repay existing debt, which can create a social problem when financial systems allow individuals to sink further into debt. The provision of inquiry-free credit also allows criminals an easy way to obtain money in another person's name.

A criminal takes some risk in using a stolen credit card as there is no way of knowing whether it is near the owner's credit limit, which will cause the transaction to be rejected. However, by assuming an individual's financial identity fresh loans and credit cards can be obtained, and those credit cards used in the country of origin, overseas and over the Internet up to the agreed limit. These cards are perfectly legitimate even though they are fraudulently obtained, so there is nothing to indicate that there is anything amiss with the transaction when they are presented at a retailer. In fact, if an individual needs a way of paying secretly for goods or services,[3] then if a card is obtained in this fashion and the bill paid regularly, the user may never be identified.

The problem with identity theft is that it is cumulative. Once one document has been obtained, obtaining others becomes much easier, the first document being used as proof of identity for others. With a little devious thinking, it is possible to obtain a complete identity in a false name. It has for many years been something of a joke in France that if one loses one's French identity card it is both easier and cheaper to obtain a forged replacement to use until the original expires than to face the bureaucracy

---

3   Examples of such uses may be to obtain goods over the Internet without being traced: pornography is an obvious example, but it also allows travel and accommodation to be booked in a false name. Cash is anonymous, and is unquestioned for most purchases unless large sums are involved: however, cash transactions are rarely accepted for car hire and hotels, and are impossible on the Internet.

and penalties involved in getting a legitimate replacement. However, once a false identification is obtained, it can be used to obtain other, legitimate, documents, such as a driving licence, to open a bank account, obtain a passport and so on. The original false document can then be discarded. It is quite possible for victims to be unaware that other persons are sharing their identities: in 2003 a British tourist was arrested and held in South Africa, his details having been circulated by the FBI as a wanted man. It was found that a criminal, as yet unidentified, had taken his identity 14 years earlier, and had committed numerous frauds in his name. The victim, a man in his 70s, spent several weeks in custody before his innocence could be demonstrated to the satisfaction of the FBI.

The United States and Australian governments are in the process of introducing passports with biometric information included in an attempt to ensure that a passport cannot be altered or used by anyone other than the holder. The British government is intending to take the process a stage further and introduce identity cards. There are possible shortcomings, however: if a document does have unforgeable biometric information in it, this information requires some sort of computerised reader for the document and a device for scanning the individual to check this fully. While such equipment may be installed at fixed points, such as immigration controls at airports, it will almost certainly not be readily available to police officers on the street or to staff in shops, banks, etc. In many instances, identification will rest on the traditional recourse of comparing a face to a photograph, and the problems that have long existed with photographic identification will continue.

A rather different policing problem arises with the theft of financial identity. Provided an individual has taken reasonable steps to protect against theft, such as not releasing a PIN, and reporting any physical theft of credit cards as soon as possible, the financial cost of such crime is borne by the bank rather than the individual. Rigorous checking of applications for credit would reduce very significantly the number of fraudulently obtained credit cards, but few financial institutions seem prepared to do this. The opposite seems to be the case, judging by the number of offers of credit, many of them "pre-approved" that appear regularly in almost everyone's mail, and the fact that a new credit card can be issued within a couple of weeks of the application being sent. It would seem that, to the major banks and financial institutions, losses to fraud are more than offset by the increased profits generated by readily accessible credit. Banks do, however, have increasingly sophisticated internal security and investigation processes, which are often triggered by computer reports of apparently anomalous transactions in accounts. These serve to reduce losses, and are considered cost effective, but on a cost/benefit analysis the sort of rigorous checks on creditworthiness which would reduce criminal activity are not considered viable by financial institutions.

People smuggling

People smuggling is becoming a *bête noire* of many governments throughout the world, but has a number of aspects which need to be considered separately. The common factor is illegal migration, whether the migrants in question consider themselves refugees fleeing an oppressive regime, whether they are seeking work and financial security, whether they have been cheated by those transporting them, or, worst of all, are unwittingly destined to a life of virtual slavery in a foreign land. The persons arranging the movement of such people do so for financial reward although, as with the drugs trade, those making the biggest profits are rarely those taking the risks. Contrary to popular fears, people entering a foreign country as terrorists rarely need or use people smugglers to assist them.

For Australia, the issue of people smuggling, in the mind of the general public, is inextricably linked to the contentious "children overboard" affair just before the 2001 election, the rescue of a number of people of Middle Eastern origin from an unseaworthy vessel by the Norwegian ship the *Tampa* and the subsequent argument over where they should be landed, and the sinking of the SIEV X in international waters, all in the same year.[4] The claims of the migrants involved were that they sought refuge in Australia from repressive regimes in Afghanistan, Iraq, Iran and other countries in that region, and that all had paid, often considerable sums, for their passage. The policing issue of border protection became a priority issue for the government, and involved the Australian Federal Police, Customs and Navy. Much less heavily publicised are operations by New South Wales and other police organisations which have found numbers of young women, usually of Asian origin, who are working as virtual prisoners in brothels. These women, often naïve country girls, believed they were coming to Australia to do domestic work, on the understanding that part of their pay would be used to fund their (illegal) passage, but on arrival have found themselves forced into the sex industry with all their earnings kept to pay for their passage, food and shelter. They are, in effect, slaves.

This latter form of people smuggling, taking girls or young women for the sex industry in another country, has always happened, particularly in poor Asian countries like Burma, but has burgeoned into a world-wide problem since the 1980s. The collapse of the Communist Bloc and war and genocide in the former Yugoslavia have led to massive poverty and instability in parts of Eastern Europe. One way out of poverty for Eastern Europeans is to find some way of escape to the rich nations of Western Europe. Women can be tricked into believing they will find work as nannies or waitresses in Germany or France, and are smuggled into those countries on the understanding that they will pay their traffickers out of their wages. On arrival, they find themselves trapped into working in brothels without papers, contacts, or more than a rudimentary knowledge

---

4   For an account of this, see Marr and Wilkinson (2003).

of the language. This is exactly the same phenomenon as occurs with Asian girls in Australia, although Eastern European girls may be better educated.

Many legal and illegal migrants from the third world do genuinely find more lucrative work in developed nations than is available at home, and send money home to their families. One of the largest sources of foreign currency in the Philippines, for example, is money sent home by women working in hospitals and hotels in America, Europe and the Middle East, usually as nurses or domestic staff. There is a darker level at which migrant workers are exploited to the extent of virtual slavery, as was seen in early 2004 in Morecambe Bay, in north-west England. Here nearly 40 people were trapped by an incoming tide and drowned while collecting shellfish. They were found to be migrant workers from rural China, brought to Britain illegally, and working for gangmasters who apparently paid derisory wages and kept the workers in appalling conditions. Tragedies like this, and the occasional container lorry whose human cargo has suffocated en route, are the visible tip of an extremely large and profitable iceberg of crime which involves its victims in personal suffering rather than mere financial loss.

The problems posed for police by people smuggling have many parallels to the problems of the illegal drug trade. The problem is huge, solvable only by international co-operation, and involves victims and some participants living in deep poverty. Persons who are starving, or earning only a few dollars a day, may well risk their lives for $US3000, and an inconsequential sum to the organiser of a smuggling operation may well be a bribe too large to be refused by a border guard in a poor country.[5] To be dealt with effectively requires an investment of expertise and resources by the richer countries to which the people (or drugs) are heading, and co-operation by the country of origin and possible transit countries. Like paedophilia and drug trafficking, people smuggling is a crime involving human misery rather than financial loss, and therefore unquestionably merits consideration as an international policing priority: however, supplying funding for effective action, as opposed to window-dressing for the popular vote, seems to be low on every Western government's priority list.

Terrorism

Terrorism has been high on the policing agenda since the destruction of the World Trade Center in September 2001, the Bali night club bombings the following year and the Madrid train bombings in March 2004. These three attacks by extremist Muslim suicide bombers are particularly horrific because of the scale of the attacks, the numbers of deaths caused and the almost banal normality of the targets: people working in ordinary white-collar jobs, tourists on holiday and commuters travelling to work. However,

---

5   On 1 May 2004 enlargement of the EU allowed some of the poorest countries in Europe to join. Once across the EU border, there are no further checks: French border protection may, therefore, rely ultimately on the vigilance of an Estonian border guard.

terrorism is by no means a new crime, and terrorist organisations have been active in various parts of the world since at least the 1970s. It is worth comparing the terrorists of the 21st century with their counterparts of a generation earlier to assess the most effective police response.

From 1969 until the Good Friday agreement of 1999 police in Britain, especially in Ulster and London, worked with a constant awareness of the threat of the Provisional IRA. During the 1970s, European police also had to contend with the Baader-Meinhof Gang, the Red and Angry Brigades, the Red Army Fraction, ETA (Basque separatists), and Palestinian groups such as Black September. Although there were some very high-profile attacks, including spectacular airline hijacks, the attack on Israeli athletes at the Munich Olympics in 1972, the kidnapping and murder of the Italian politician Aldo Moro by the Red Brigade in 1978 and the Harrods bombing just before Christmas 1983, the death toll for each individual attack rarely reached double figures. Furthermore, each terrorist group developed a more or less settled pattern of behaviour in selecting targets and making bombs.

Consider, as an example, the Provisional IRA, the terrorist organisation which, with ETA (the Basque separatists), has had the longest continuous history of attacks. In Northern Ireland itself the situation was one of pro-tracted guerrilla warfare, much like the Palestinian Intifada, and terrorist attacks on mainland Britain involved fairly obvious targets. The vast majority of PIRA bombings were in London, and almost all involved government, or at least establishment, targets. The Guildford and Birming-ham bombings targeted pubs commonly frequented by army personnel, and the Brighton bomb was aimed at the ruling Tory party's annual con-ference. In London, the most common targets were army or government establishments[6] or individuals, the Harrods bombing being something of an exception.

Twenty-first century terrorism has a rather different aspect. The victims of the attacks in New York, Bali and Madrid were ordinary people doing ordinary things. The World Trade Center, although a significant feature of the New York skyline and, as its name suggests, a symbol of American entrepreneurialism, was a block of offices not essentially different from the office towers found in every major city in the world. The tourist bars in Bali could have been in the Greek islands or any other holiday destination, and many cities have, like Madrid, extensive commuter rail networks. The numbers of people killed are also far higher than in 20th century terrorist attacks, provoking a sense of revulsion and fear far more significant than earlier terrorist groups have achieved. As a result, since 2001 terrorism has provoked world-wide fear, and has required a major response from

---

6   A good example is the bombing of an unoccupied Territorial Army building in Ham-mersmith, West London, in December 1979. On the evening this occurred, the Territorial Army building a few miles away in Shepherds Bush was the venue for a local police Christmas party, and the Hammersmith building was to host a similar event the following week. Officers attending both parties (which included the author) felt lucky to escape a bomb which had been placed at the wrong location, or on the wrong day.

governments. This is so even for countries which might rightly consider themselves at low risk. New Zealand, for example, has, because of its non-nuclear stance, for many years refused access to the American Navy and is neutral except in UN peacekeeping activities, yet the Bali attack showed that the risk for countries which might consider themselves unlikely targets is not negligible. Even though the vast majority of airline flights are at low risk, airline security throughout the world has been increased enormously, and at great cost. Auckland and Zurich are highly improbable targets, yet any travel between these two cities will involve stops at cities which are at much greater risk, so security at both end and intermediate points must be equally good. Twenty-first century terrorism has also created the fear of chemical or biological attacks on cities, against which precautions much be taken.[7]

Every police service in Australia, Britain and the United States has been required by national government to make provision for terrorist attacks including the possible use of chemical and biological agents, requiring the purchase of specialised equipment and training in its use. Policing responses to the threat of terrorism have two aspects: preparation for a possible terrorist attack, including preventative security measures and emergency planning for the event of an actual attack, and investigative measures to discover and arrest terrorists before an attack can be carried out. Investigative measures are primarily a national responsibility rather than the responsibility of local police agencies: in Australia the AFP and security agencies and in the United States the FBI and CIA have leading roles. In Britain the security agencies and the Anti-Terrorist and Special Branch of the Metropolitan Police with their residual experience of IRA-related terrorism have national responsibility, but work closely with local constabularies.

Large city police services can fairly easily make risk assessments and train some officers in emergency management. Whether they be called SWAT teams, Territorial Response Groups, Special Operations Groups or have other designations, large city police agencies have groups of officers who operate in groups of 10 or 20 as a team, and can add special training for terrorist attacks to their training for other emergency duties. Local officers can be expected to take special note of potential targets in their area to improve security, and local disaster plans have existed for years for incidents at sports stadia and tourist attractions, for example. Problems arise in deciding how much equipment smaller agencies in particular should be required to purchase, and the extent to which local or rural police officers should be given training to deal with terrorism. Unnecessary training can be a significant waste of police officers' time, reducing the number of officers available for normal duties and stretching already inade-quate budgets. Throughout the course of the cold war, the Metropolitan

---

7   Throughout the Second World War there was a great fear of gas attacks, and every British citizen was issued with a gas mask. The technology certainly remained from 1918, but no such attack ever took place. Poison gas attacks have, however, been made more recently by Saddam Hussein against the Kurds, and by Japanese terrorists on the Tokyo subway.

Police in London, in common with many other police agencies, had on-going training in police responses to a nuclear attack. This consisted of a one-day course every three years or so: no officer could discern any change in the syllabus in the time between one of the co-called "Nuclear Ned" days and the next, nor was the course likely to be of any real use in nuclear war. Even this minimal training commitment took the equivalent across the force of 8000 officer days per year: any putative anti-terrorist training commitment will likewise result in a small but significant reduction in the number of officers available for normal duties.

For different reasons, countries like Australia, the United States and New Zealand face a much more difficult problem in deciding how to involve police in anti-terrorist precautions than densely populated European countries. Britain, which may well consider itself to be a likely target for terrorists, has few places which are far from a large city with the resources to deal with a terrorist attack. The Avon Constabulary in the West of England includes Bristol, a big city which can muster the resources mentioned above, but which could also supply assistance to neighbouring constabularies well within the hour were an attack to take place in Gloucestershire, Somerset, Wiltshire or South Wales. New Zealand may reasonably consider itself to be at relatively low risk, but some preparations must be made, and with its low population spread over two islands, it is not feasible to base all the anti-terrorist resources in Auckland. It is, however, problematic to decide whether to split resources between Wellington, Dunedin and other smaller cities or to duplicate them.

The United States, as has been made clear elsewhere, has a plethora of small, independent police agencies: although it is likely that somewhere in the nation would be targeted by terrorists, the chances of such an attack in, for example, the back country of Arizona is extremely small.[8] While many low-risk towns and counties may safely leave terrorist precautions to the State policing agencies and the FBI, there is still a danger and a need to make some provision for an attack. The situation is different again in Australia: most of the nation's policing resources are concentrated in the five large capital cities, but the distances involved to other centres is huge. One can easily name high-risk targets in Sydney, Melbourne and Canberra, and possible targets in Adelaide, Brisbane and Perth. However, Bali has shown that centres for tourism can be a target, which raises the potential threat levels of, for example, Cairns and Broome. These are small towns whose emergency services would be completely overwhelmed by a terrorist attack, yet their capital cities, which are the only centres large enough to have adequate resources to assist, are two or three hours distant by commercial jet.

There is another point, perhaps more political than strictly policing, which must be considered regarding terrorists. There is a great deal of

---

8   It is worth noting that the worst bombing attack before 2001 in the United States was perpetrated by Timothy McVeigh, an American-born ex-soldier in the unlikely venue of Oklahoma City.

pressure internationally for nations to co-operate in tackling terrorism, leading to the danger that a government might declare a particular organisation terrorist for its own purposes, and seek international help in dealing with what might be no more than internal opposition. Proverbially, one man's freedom fighter is another man's terrorist: there may be little doubt into which category the Baader Meinhof gang, the IRA and al Quaeda belong, but it is by no means clear whether the Zimbabwean opposition or Kashmiri separatists are terrorists, or resistance fighters against oppressive regimes. In this context, it should be remembered that in the mid-1980s Margaret Thatcher explicitly stated that the ANC was a terrorist organisation, and therefore the imprisoned Nelson Mandela was, presumably, a terrorist. While history, which is written by the victors, will distinguish for posterity between terrorists and freedom fighters, the label "terrorist" is at present applied by governments and the media.

When taking precautions against terrorism nothing is more certain than that more successful attacks are inevitable. While precautions are necessary, and will divert or minimise some incidents, a great deal of time and energy will be wasted by police and others in anti-terrorist precautions in places which will never be targets. Conversely, however many precautions are taken in suspected target areas, some attacks will be successful. The vast majority of precautions taken against terrorists will, in hindsight, be either be too little or too late, and most will be completely unnecessary.

Choosing the crime issues

The crimes discussed in this chapter are matters which will never impinge directly on the vast majority of the population, yet they are serious matters unquestionably worth significant police attention. They are also matters which, if they are to be addressed effectively, could drain the financial resources of any police agency. It is, therefore, worth examining the driving forces that put these issues so strongly on the policing agenda, and looking at one of the perennial problems of crime prevention, distinguishing the fear of crime and the reality of crime. The crime problems for which Peel introduced modern policing emphatically did not include terrorism or paedophilia, but theft, burglary, street robbery and disorder which are not greatly different from modern "quality of life" offences. Among the major fears the public have are the fear of terrorists and the fear of child sexual predators.[9] The statistical probability of oneself or one's child being a victim of such crime is extremely low, but the crimes are of such enormity that fear of their occurrence is, nevertheless, real and serious. The biggest fears we face are always fears of things which cannot be prevented. Consider a parallel. All parents fear the death of their child: the biggest fear for the parents of new-born babies is that of SIDS. This will strike perhaps 200 of the 250,000 or so babies born in Australia each year, and far more children

---

9   I acknowledge here that most sexual offences against children are carried out within the family circle, so the fear of this crime is the much less common occurrence that a child will be molested by a stranger.

die before maturity of other diseases or accident, yet the horror of SIDS, the unexplained and unpreventable tragedy, is the greatest fear.

Crime as a political issue

While the public fear of terrorism may be unreasonable, nevertheless it is a very serious public issue. There is a general feeling that the government should take steps to deal with or prevent terrorism: the public have no clear idea of what might be effective against terrorism, but require that something be done. Whether the action genuinely improves public safety or not, if the fear of terrorism is allayed then government can claim a degree of success. There is little doubt that the terrorist attack on commuter trains in Madrid was instrumental in the electoral defeat for the Spanish government a few days later, the government being blamed for making Spain a target by participating in the Iraq war. Government action may even take the form of apportioning blame, with hindsight, for the failure to prevent terrorist attacks. At the time of writing (May 2004) the United States Congress is holding an inquiry into the intelligence available and government action taken before the destruction of the World Trade Center to determine, particularly for survivors and relatives of victims, whether the attack could have been prevented. To apportion blame to particular agencies may persuade the public that a problem identified is a problem solved, and might just help to reinstate public confidence.

As in all criminal activities, a balance has to be struck between effective police action, and individual liberties which are taken for granted. Police could clear up a great deal of crime if, on the Saturday before Christmas, they sealed off any shopping mall and systematically searched every person therein. There would be considerable amounts of stolen property recovered, together with fraudulently used credit cards, possibly drugs and weapons, and if names are checked not a few wanted persons would be arrested.[10] However, such operations have a grave impact on civil liberties, and would be severely disruptive to people going about their daily lives in a lawful manner, and so are generally unacceptable. The public will, however, tolerate much more stringent legislation directed at the threat of terrorism, for example increased security procedures at airports, and even accept the detention of suspects without trial.

Immediately after the attack on the World Trade Center on 9 September 2001, the governments of Australia, Britain and the United States all rushed to create new anti-terrorist legislation. The UK, for example, despite having created new non-IRA terrorist legislation in the *Intelligence Services Act* 1994 and the *Terrorism Act* and the *Regulation of Investigatory Powers Act* 2000, published the Anti-terrorism, Crime and Security Bill on 12 November, which became an Act of Parliament on 13 December, less than 100 days after the Al Quaeda attack (Matassa and Newburn, 2003). This Act creates

---

10 During an investigation into the murder of a number of prostitutes in Shepherds Bush, West London, in the 1960s, the area was swamped with police in a "stop-and-search" operation. This yielded an extraordinary number of arrests for unconnected matters, and a general reduction of crime in the area.

the possibility of internment of suspects without trial, and a number of such prisoners have been held at Belmarsh Prison just outside London. Far more widely known is, of course, the American camp at Guantanamo Bay, Cuba, which has, since 2001, been used to detain suspected al Quaeda personnel and others without trial. The legal validity of such detentions is at best dubious, and the effect on civil liberties of such hasty anti-terrorist legislation is not seriously challenged by the general public, who view the incarceration of government-designated dangerous people as a pragmatic necessity to preserve their safety.

The aims of anti-terrorism legislation are, it is claimed, sixfold (Wilkinson, 2001):

1. Prophylaxis – dealing with underlying problems
2. Deterrence – creating severe penalties for particular offences
3. Increasing powers – for international co-operation, search, seizure, etc
4. Symbolic action to express public revulsion
5. Enhancing public security
6. Suppressing terrorist organisations.

Numbers 2, 4 and 5 all have some similarities to the justifications for punishment for criminal offences listed in criminology texts: deterrence of offenders, expression of society's disapproval of criminal acts, and imprisonment to protect the public from dangerous offenders. Since terrorist attacks are currently being carried out by suicide bombers, it is fairly clear that any anti-terrorist legislation will have not the slightest impact in these three areas. Similarly, no legislation directed at the internal affairs of any Western nation can possibly hope to address the underlying grievances and problems in the Middle East that lead to Islamic terrorism.

Potentially, the most effective aspect of the type of legislation under discussion here is its ability to increase police and intelligence powers to investigate, arrest and bring terrorists to trial, and in the suppression of terrorist organisations. These are, however, not without a very real cost to individual liberties. There is a danger, too, that legislation rushed through parliament to deal with a perceived threat from Islamic terrorists may be used at a later stage against groups whose danger to the polity is far less generally accepted. There have been a number of instances where former terrorists have become accepted and internationally respected governments: the ANC in South Africa became the democratically elected government no more than 10 years after it was denounced by British Prime Minister Margaret Thatcher as a terrorist organisation, and some of the founders of the state of Israel, including later, well-respected prime ministers, were deemed terrorists by the British government which, in the aftermath of the Second World War, controlled what was then known as Palestine. A number of states around the world are in turmoil – Haiti, Zimbabwe and Liberia spring to mind as examples – and, while their governments might describe any violent opposition as terrorists, it may not be helpful to anyone for foreign governments to automatically acquiesce and invoke their own anti-terrorism legislation against these groups. The independence of East Timor from Indonesia was obtained only by the Australian government rejecting the Indonesian claim that the independence fighters were terrorists.

It may well be that the rush to pass anti-terrorist legislation has, as its most politically important aim, the fourth item in Wilkinson's list, the symbolical expression of public revulsion at terrorist attacks. This symbolism is not addressed at terrorists, however, who would no doubt completely ignore it, but at the populace of the state who fear becoming victims of terror and are mollified by the feeling that something is being done. If this is the case, it follows that the more draconian the powers and punishments, the safer the public will feel, leaving questions of procedural fairness and legality aside.

The effect on police

Police have ample reason to be wary of legislation introduced at short notice to address a problem which is causing alarm to the public. In the mid-1980s the British press carried almost daily accounts of the horrors of adolescents sniffing glue, and the fact that police had no power to deal with the problem. A piece of legislation, the *Intoxicating Substances Act* 1985, was hastily drafted to the relief of the public. Police officers intending to make use of it discovered that the offences contained in it applied only to shop-keepers selling glue, etc and were extraordinarily complex to prove. Only a few prosecutions were ever undertaken, one of which involved five days of observation on a shop: on conviction, the penalty imposed was a moderate fine. The most common problem with such legislation is that hasty drafting can allow serious flaws to be overlooked, rendering it difficult or impos-sible to implement. The *Intoxicating Substances Act* has been little used since its provisions are difficult to understand, and the problem to which it was addressed has now, if not disappeared, at least changed its nature such that the legislation is of little value.

It is by no means obvious what powers police could be granted that would significantly improve their ability to fight terrorism. The law in all countries contains provisions for search of persons and premises, and it is difficult to imagine what acts potential suicide bombers or terrorists could commit that are not offences under pre-existing legislation. There are ample powers to search for firearms and explosives, for example, with or without a warrant. Legislation to detain terrorist suspects for an extended time for questioning may sound impressive, but a trained, fanatical terrorist is unlikely to confess or offer useful information if kept in custody for even a couple of weeks, unless the detention is accompanied by lack of food, water, sleep, or some other form of coercion which, even if it falls short of actually being torture, is illegal in liberal democracies.[11]

---

11 Allegations have been made of mistreatment of prisoners in American custody in Bagh-dad, Afghanistan and Guantanamo Bay where undue coercion seems to be preliminary to, or part of, interrogations. The situation is still unclear at the time of writing, May 2004.

The introduction of legislation to expedite international co-operation in dealing with terrorism and, presumably, the other international crime issues discussed earlier, may well be of real value in providing for formal sharing of information and assistance. One of the more intractable problems in policing is the unwillingness of individual officers to share information, and rivalries between different policing organisations and practitioners. There has long been a gulf between the FBI and local police agencies in the United States, and a similar, though not so large, gap between Australia's State and federal police agencies, so it is only to be expected that there would be suspicion and mistrust of international agencies, and little co-operation until personal relationships are established between individual officers. Mistrust is likely to be exacerbated if information flows one way, rather than being freely traded, as happens when one agency claims a lead role in the investigation, and treats others as subordinate. This is, of course, just another version of the ill-will that can exist in any police agency between local and headquarters departments. Street detectives may be required to share information with, for example, the drugs squad and vice versa, but in practice far more useful information is supplied to head-quarters squads than is returned to local officers.

Every police officer's dream is to work on a squad which is supplied unhesitatingly with sufficient staff and equipment. This can only occur when the inquiry has such a high profile and such urgency that no hierarchy can cavil at the cost lest it be thought to be jeopardising the inquiry. The fear of terrorism is such that governments are very keen to announce the establishment of new anti-terrorist squads, especially if they involve international co-operation, without considering the cost. In truth, the cost of re-deploying several hundred detectives, even with the necessary supporting equipment, office space and ancillary staff, is relatively modest compared with the cost of deploying a battalion of troops. However, anti-terrorism squads are under tremendous pressure to succeed, pressure which may be counter-productive in the long term. During the 1970s, Britain's anti-terrorist squad had a remarkably high clear-up rate for IRA bombings, and IRA trials at the Old Bailey captured the headlines for weeks. The public had been badly frightened and arrests and convictions were demanded. Juries at the time were looking for reasons to convict, and convict they did without questioning the evidence, but as time went by more and more of these convictions were adjudged unsafe, and reversed on appeal, albeit 10 or more years after conviction.

The 1984 *Police and Criminal Evidence Act* (*PACE*), had it been in force at the time, would have done much to prevent the evidence which was later disputed and rejected being put before the original juries in those IRA trials. *PACE* provides eminently sensible safeguards for the rights of persons in custody, rights which apply to all suspects, regardless of the nature of the crime for which they were arrested. Legislation which is introduced to strengthen police powers to deal with terrorism must not permit practices which, in some more peaceful later time when there is less public hysteria, a higher court finds so unacceptable that terrorist convictions are overturned.

To provide a mechanism for expeditious arrest, detention and conviction of suspects when an atmosphere of concern, if not outright fear, exists can only bring both the police and the justice system into disrepute if that mechanism is shown, at a later stage, to be flawed, unjust or inimical to human rights.

Another problem for police concerns the cost of anti-terrorism measures at a local level. A major national anti-terrorist squad will be funded by central government, although detectives seconded to it may still be paid by their own police service. However, if State or local police agencies are required to purchase equipment or train officers, this is by no means a negligible expense. Police budgets are already tight, and may be severely stretched if anti-terrorism provisions are required. Suppose that extra training on terrorism is proposed for every member of a police agency. It is a matter of simple arithmetic to calculate the cost of abstracting officers from duty for even a one-day seminar. If there are 20 students and two instructors for each group undertaking training, 100 officers can attend every week, at a cost of 110 officer days away from operational duty. An officer working a normal 8-hour day, 40-hour week with four weeks' leave works a basic 240 days per year. Two hundred officers undergoing one day's training costs 220 officer days, almost the equivalent of one officer less on the street for a year. To train 4000 is to lose the equivalent of 18 officers for a year. To keep police numbers on the street up requires paying other officers overtime to cover the gap, which, even at modest penalty rates, is the equivalent of an extra 20 officers' salaries for a year. It is doubtful if a single day's training can have an real effect on improving police responses to terrorism, but can be used as extremely expensive window-dressing to persuade the public that police are doing something to counter the fear of terrorist attacks.

Terrorism creates a problem in that it places extra demands on police without any increase in resources to meet them. Just as it is impossible to measure how effective police are in preventing crime, so it is impossible to measure how effective police are in preventing terrorism. There is absolutely no doubt that police throughout the world, especially in nations like the United States, Britain, Australia, Spain and other European countries, are doing their utmost to prevent terrorist attacks. Despite these police efforts more major terrorist attacks resulting somewhere in great loss of life are inevitable and will be remembered, but attacks successfully prevented by police will be forgotten by the public, even if they ever knew. The Harrods bombing on 17 December 1983, in which a 15kg device killed five people and injured 91 is part of history: that a 5kg bomb had been found and safely detonated a few hundred metres away three days earlier is forgotten (Williams, 2002 pp 83-85).

Crime issues for the public

The general public is aware of the crime issues discussed above through the media, but the media are ambivalent in their treatment, sometimes viewing these matters as law and order, ie policing issues, and sometimes as straightforward political problems. It is only to be expected that the public have similarly mixed attitudes. The problem this raises for police is that the public have not changed their view of the most important crimes requiring police attention: these are still the same quality of life issues, graffiti, burglary, drug abuse and drunkenness in public places. These, in the public mind, are the matters which should be at the heart of police activity, and police will be criticised if these matters are neglected. While the government might see fit to add anti-terrorism to the tasks of police, the public might well resent police resources being taken from the issues they see as the real crime problems.

The public certainly require action on the crime issues raised in this chapter. What they are not prepared to accept is that this action be taken at the expense of other crime issues closer to home. While Jewkes describes paedophilia as "the moral panic of the age" (Jewkes, 2003, p 517), it would appear that governments are unwilling to commit the necessary resources to dealing with it. The scale of the problem is shown by the example of the paedophile website given earlier: 390,000 subscribers world-wide actually means 390,000 suspects to be interviewed, and presumably, 390,000 offenders to be prosecuted. The police services in Britain instigated Operation Ore in May 2002 to deal with 7272 cases reported, ie 7272 active paedophiles known to be living in the country. Although police estimated the costs of preliminary routine work to be over £2 million, the Home Office view was that the inquiry must be managed from within existing police budgets.

The sheer cost of the multitudinous investigations necessitated by the American information meant that in nine months, only 1200 arrests were made, and only a few cases taken to court (Jewkes, 2003). Although this amounted to no more than a token effort, the publicity attendant on these few successful prosecutions may well be sufficient to mollify the public that the issue has been addressed. If it is brought home to the public at a later stage how ineffective the response was in investigating the huge number of suspects on the database, it is doubtful that the blame will be laid at the door of government for failing to provide sufficient resources: more probable is that police will be blamed for insufficient investigation. For the moment, the public are either unaware of the scale of the problem,[12] or content with the prosecution rate that is being attempted. Certainly, the public in general would not tolerate a diminution of police activity on the street (there is a general feeling that there is too little of this anyway) in order to provide resources for investigation of Internet paedophiles. Extra funding, in the public's view, must be provided by government.

People smuggling is seen by the public, certainly in Australia and Britain, as an immigration problem for government rather than an inter-

---

12 While operation Auxein in Spring 2004 appeared successful, with a number of arrests and the suicide of a number of suspects, it may well be that, once again, these represented just the tip of the iceberg of offences, and many other named suspects remained uninvestigated.

national criminal operation with major social implications and links to other criminal activities. In Australia, the discourse uses terms like "illegals" and "queue jumpers" with the implied fear of terrorists infiltrating Australia in small boats, rather than being a discussion of refugees and humanitarian issues (Marr and Wilkinson, 2003). Similarly, the British tabloid press highlights the problems of Romanian gypsies begging and stealing, and, since the expansion of the EU in May 2004, threatens a flood of Eastern Europeans quite legally entering the country and claiming welfare. On this view there is nothing to persuade the public that people smuggling is a police matter, and therefore not an acceptable use of police resources. Other forms of international crime are viewed in the same way, a matter for someone else to sort out, not a matter to be dealt with at the cost of local police services.

However, any matter which a government nominates for police action can only be dealt with at the cost of some other aspect of policing. Police budgets have been tightened considerably over the past 20 years, such that for a number of years there has been no fat left to trim, nor room to manoeuvre to find extra staff or resources. If government directs police to address a particular issue without providing sufficient extra funding, this can only be achieved by a reduction of police activity elsewhere. Even when extra funding has been provided for a new initiative, or an increase in staff, a contribution has always been required from existing police budgets. I doubt whether there is any recent scheme in policing (or in health, or any other social service) which has been completely funded by new money from the government. While governments might fund multi-agency investigative teams to prevent terrorism, and provide some equipment to local police to use in the event of a terrorist attack, there are always a number of ancillary costs (training, storage, transport, etc) which must be met out of existing inadequate budgets.

It is in these situations of police responding to new issues that a conflict of priorities may arise. The public's priorities remain the same: the crime which they feel requires the maximum police attention is the crime that they see, and which impinges upon them directly. The public are afraid of terrorists, but have no real belief that they themselves will ever be a terrorist target. They loathe paedophiles, but have no expectation that their children will ever become victims. Something must be done about both these categories of criminal, but not at the expense of more police on the streets to prevent graffiti. This might not be a logical approach, but it represents general public feeling. Police, meanwhile, must meet (and be seen to meet) this public agenda, but also meet the very much more structured targets set by government for their activities. Despite police forces becoming services, and genuinely attempting to provide the policing the public requires, it is the government agenda that drives policing, not the problems identified by the public or by police themselves, and government budgets which restrict the scope of police activities.

CHAPTER 14

CONTROL OF POLICING

Introduction

Since the 1980s, economic considerations have been given increasing importance by governments of every political hue to the extent that economics is now of far more importance than any social considerations,[1] and has led throughout the world to a reduction in the scope of the welfare state. In recent years, the police budget has become the most important factor in determining the scale of police activity, while crime and policing have become increasingly political issues. Government control of, for example, health provisions, seems to have cost reduction rather than quality of health care as the most important aim. There has been a simultaneous drive by governments to control the spiralling cost of policing, by encouraging, amongst other things, a vast increase in various forms of private policing, from traditional uniformed security guards to mobile patrols, and sometimes very sophisticated investigative work within specific industries or agencies. This chapter will examine the pressure which constraints imposed by government as a funding body and politically determined performance criteria put on senior police management to provide a professional policing service which meets the requirements of the public it serves and protects.

Governments now publicly state that the panacea for the ills of policing (and other public service agencies) is a radical change of management policy. A great deal of the restructuring of police agencies, indeed almost all restructuring to improve the efficiency of public institutions from hospitals to universities, seems to involve new management plans in the image of the management procedures of large profit-making businesses and an emphasis on the financial accountability of senior officers, with the somewhat naïve belief that, if the management procedures are right, everything else will fall into place. The theory that once management is redesigned all the problems of policing will be solved is questioned here. The main aim of this book has been to examine what police are doing, should be doing and how they should be doing it, not how policing should be managed or financed. Determining the functions of police is logically prior to examining the management structure of police agencies: a factory may perfect its

---

1   Consider, for example, President Clinton's aphorism "It's the economy, stupid".

management process, but if it continues to produce transistors in the microchip age, it will be doomed to bankruptcy. A further important issue is the threat to the principle of police independence and autonomy posed by the ever-increasing answerability of police management to government strictures, targets and constraints. It is unclear whether or not this disturbing trend is a temporary phenomenon or the thin end of a rather more sinister wedge of complete government control of policing.

Police as a service

We have now become accustomed to the term "police service" rather than "police force" being used of police agencies, and there is little doubt that it expresses the desired relationship between police and public much more clearly. Police officers have always provided a service to society, and, indeed, have prided themselves on so doing. For police to acknowledge themselves to be supplying a social service is, I will argue, to acknowledge that they are part of the welfare state. It is somewhat ironic that police finally accept that they are part of a state structure at the very time that that structure is under threat in Australia, Britain and elsewhere.

The most basic requirements of life are food, shelter and personal safety and security, followed very closely by health and education. In mediaeval Britain, these requirements were met by the church which provided care for the indigent and sick, the Elizabethan Poor Laws placed obligations on the parish to do likewise for those with no family to support them, and various charitable foundations gave food and shelter to those too old or sick to work, even if all these provisions were rudimentary. Personal security and safety were assured by a judicial system which could provide everyone with redress for wrongs, the cornerstone for which had been laid in 1215 by Magna Carta and developed over the centuries. The state had responsibility for the court system, but otherwise the rudimentary mediaeval roots of the welfare and justice systems were no part of government responsibilities. In the middle part of the 19th century the state started to take responsibility for welfare, when British, European and other governments began to concern themselves directly in education, Poor Law reform, regulations for workplace safety, and, in Prussia, the first worker's compensation insurance. The first recognisable modern police bodies date from about the same time, an indication that the modern state was also prepared to take responsibility for ensuring the safety and security of its citizens.

In the modern industrialised world, food, water, and security are taken for granted, and when a country descends into chaos, as happened in the former Yugoslavia in the 1990s, these are the very things the loss of which is felt most urgently by its people. In this context, it is no surprise that the coalition forces in Iraq in 2003 stated that the re-establishment of police was as great a priority as the restoration of electricity and water supplies. In the modern, democratic world, police are required to do far more than simply maintain order. Order can be maintained by sheer brute force, as any number of totalitarian regimes have shown: in some, like Stalin's Russia, terror became a government monopoly. Modern, democratic police agencies need to maintain order peacefully, remaining answerable to the public for the manner and scope of their actions. From the 19th century onwards making a complaint to police provided a means of free access to the criminal courts for every member of the public, and as Bittner, amongst others, has shown clearly, police also provide a free impartial arbitration service for petty disputes (Bittner, 1990). The actual tasks undertaken by police have been discussed in Chapter 6 and elsewhere, but every piece of research on the subject has shown that pure law enforcement occupies a relatively small proportion of police working hours.

State health systems originally provided only basic medical care to the sick, but soon progressed to encompass vaccinations and regular health checks for children and pregnant women. A 21st century health system places considerable emphasis on preventative medicine,[2] and links with other social services and support agencies. There is a parallel with modern policing here, where the emphasis on crime prevention (in Britain, the wider term "community safety" is used (Crawford 2003)), obliges (in Britain the obligation is statutory) police to work with local and community groups. Policing is a state (or at least local government) run task, and is now overtly concerned with the welfare of society. Any police agency that considers itself to be a service (and many that retain the old designation of a force) can, with good reason, be called part of the welfare state.

Many of the traditional ways in which police have operated, particularly their patrolling functions, have almost disappeared, or have been gradually taken over by other groups. There are probably currently very few serving police officers who have patrolled an appointed city beat on foot at their own discretion during a tour of duty. Since the introduction of radios and cars in the 1960s the patrolling officer has been less and less able to determine the route the patrol should take, or choose the tasks to complete. The widespread use of radio cars means that a police patrol now consists of answering calls from the public interspersed with short periods of fairly aimless driving while awaiting the next call. Not only did the police patrol at the officer's discretion disappear, but social changes brought about the disappearance of a variety of other persons who provided semi-formal authority and a conduit for information to police officers they knew only in passing. Buses have long ceased to have conductors, few trains have guards, no parks have park keepers, yet all these posts provided a level of surveillance and control which prevented anti-social behaviour or, at the very least, provided a number of conscientious individuals willing and able to call police (Jones and Newburn, 2002).

There are some signs that this particular wheel is to be re-invented, at least in Britain, with the establishment of community support officers under the *Police Reform Act* 2002. These persons have limited enforcement powers

---

2   Albeit that this is often intended as a cost-saving measure. In the health context, dentistry as a preventative expedient is rarely available as a state benefit in either Australia or the UK.

but are expected to patrol, to issue penalty notices for minor disorder and minor traffic matters and to deal with anti-social behaviour. Local authorities in Britain and Australia have instituted patrols in conjunction with, or to supplement, police, and public transport systems, particularly commuter trains, in many cities have security staff with limited powers to enforce regulations. This in itself is not completely new: limited enforcement powers existed for some of the categories of person who formerly provided a level of social control; park keepers in Britain, for example, were authorised to seize cigarettes and matches from children under the age of 16 under legislation for the protection of children. It is worth noting that none of the former semi-formal authority figures like park keepers and bus conductors were paid from police funds, yet British community support officers, although cheaper than police, are paid from police budgets.

It follows that police officers on patrol may eventually have less responsibility for the lower levels of social control. Although non-police patrol schemes are in their infancy, whether they have responsibility for dealing with all instances of minor disorder will depend on whether, for example, they are equipped with radios, or, indeed, whether the public are willing to accept them to settle disputes. If community support officers are in radio contact with a police base, they may be assigned to deal with minor disturbances reported to police by the public, although, of course, it is open to individual police services to implement a policy that any call to police must be dealt with by police. However, any calls for assistance which may or may not fall within the ambit of any designated non-police patrol will continue to be dealt with by police officers. This leaves at one end of the scale the most serious incidents, involving a crime or where there is the possibility of an arrest being necessary, and at the other the least serious, the matters which require no law enforcement action but where some other service or welfare need requires police attendance. The police will always remain a 24-hour emergency service, available when all other services are out of hours. It may well be that as financial constraints cut the availability of specialist social services, the welfare role of police will grow rather than diminish just because they are always available.

Government control of police

It has already been shown in Chapter 9 that governments have an important role to play in police accountability, and those arguments will not be repeated here. There is, as was shown in Chapter 1, a dynamic tension between police, the law and society where a balance of control must be reached for the maintenance of a civil society. There have been a number of changes in the attitude of government to police, most notably in Britain since the election of Tony Blair's New Labour government in 1997 where a number of Acts of Parliament intended to address the perceived problem of rising crime have, as will be shown, made quite fundamental changes to police strategic planning.

The sheer number of police agencies in the United States, most of which are under fairly close control by local government (or, in the case of elected sheriffs, by a local electorate), has made State or federal government control less feasible, except where drugs or terrorism is involved or constitutional rights are contravened. In the case of drugs, since the establishment of the DEA (Drug Enforcement Agency), the introduction of RICO (Racketeer Influenced Corrupt Organizations) legislation which allows the seizure of the proceeds of (frequently drug-related) organised crime, it is the bait of extra money in the form of extra federal funding for police departments which adopt federal drug initiatives, that persuades American police to follow federal government policies. With regard to terrorism, there is both the carrot of extra federal funding for police activities which are specifically directed against terrorism, and the stick of criticism from the Department of Homeland Security for failing to do enough to combat terrorism and the stigma that failure to act effectively is, by implication, insufficiently patriotic.

In Australia there are signs of an increasing desire of governments to involve themselves in policing, even though they have not yet done so to the extent that the British government has. The federal government certainly has little direct effect on Australian State policing. Its greatest impact is on the Federal Police, which is a comparatively small organisation that it controls directly, and on specific national policing projects which are federally funded, this being additional money to that given to police in State budgets. Examples of these are the National Crime Authority (now the Australian Crime Commission) whose officers are drawn on secondment from other police agencies to deal with organised, interstate crime, and various drug and anti-terrorism national task forces. While the federal government can set up any number of such national bodies, it has no power to coerce, only to seek to persuade (usually with the offer of additional funding), State governments over crime and policing matters. This was seen most clearly in the wake of the Port Arthur massacre, when the Prime Minister promised more restrictive legislation on the possession of firearms, a promise not within his power to keep. A meeting of State justice and police ministers and police commissioners reached a general agreement with the Prime Minister on the principle of tighter gun control, and each individual State drafted new, but distinctly different, firearms legislation.

Australian State governments, however, do show an increasing tendency to involve themselves more and more in aspects of policing which might properly be left to commissioners. Considerable pressure is frequently brought to bear on commissioners by government and the media, which is always quick to shine a spotlight on any high-profile public servant facing criticism. This is particularly the case, it seems, with commissioners who have not been promoted from within their State's police organisation but have been brought in from elsewhere. The most obvious example of this is Ray Whitrod, appointed from Victoria by the Queensland government to clean up corrupt elements in its police force. There was an atmosphere of mutual mistrust between Whitrod and his executive team, and a marked lack of support from the government, some members of which were themselves later implicated in corrupt activities by the Fitzgerald inquiry.

More recently, the two Commissioners of Police in Western Australia appointed during the 1990s, Bob Falconer (a Victorian) and his successor Barry Matthews (from New Zealand), faced challenges on all sides. Commissioner Falconer implemented a major program of change in the teeth of opposition from within the organisation itself, continuous adverse comment from the local press, and at best lukewarm support from government. His successor implemented no major upheavals, but continued the re-evaluation and change process instigated by Falconer, accepting the principle that to meet the needs of a changing society, policing itself must be in a state of constant gradual change. Commissioner Matthews also faced very public disagreements with the police minister, often over comparatively trivial operational decisions such as opening hours for police stations, which have usually been considered purely internal policing matters.

This issue of night closures of police stations exemplifies the problem of political interference in minor matters. An eminently sensible decision was made to restrict the opening hours of some suburban police stations to allow more police officers to be available for patrolling the streets. Very few members of the public set foot in a police station from one year to the next, and then only for routine form-filling or general advice and never for urgent matters, which are done by phone: only the lonely, insomniac or psychologically disturbed find it necessary to visit a police station during the night. This decision was followed by a public outcry for stations to remain open 24 hours per day, there being a perception that fewer manned police stations somehow meant fewer police officers rather than more on patrol, despite the best use of police resources being fewer rather than more officers in police stations.[3] The police minister, for whatever reasons, supported the public view, although neither police nor the public are best served if irrational populist or other political considerations are allowed to overrule professional judgments made on operational or policy matters.

The most glaring Australian instance of political and media interference in policing occurred in New South Wales, during the commissionership of Peter Ryan from 1996 to 2002. The reason for appointing a commissioner from outside the State, in this case from Britain, was the shadow of the Wood Royal Commission's findings of entrenched corruption within the NSW Police. An outsider at the helm was guaranteed to be untainted by corruption findings, and Ryan's appointment was central to the State government's strategies on law and order and police corruption. Ryan personally became an important figure in the 1999 State election campaign, and policing in general came under challenge as a matter of importance to

---

3   Nineteenth century police stations were placed in busy shopping streets, many of which are now backwaters with the introduction of shopping malls, and the most visited modern police office facilities seem to be those placed in shopping centres and sharing their opening hours.

both political parties. While there was a great deal of popular public support for Ryan, almost unheard of in a society where police commissioners have been public servants rarely in the public eye, there was a great deal of opposition from within the police service itself, and sections of the media. Alan Jones, a radio talk-show host who, like Rush Limbaugh in the United States, speaks for a small but vociferous reactionary minority and claims more political influence than he probably possesses, consistently pounced on Ryan's errors, real or perceived. In the months before Ryan's resignation relations between the newly appointed police minister and the commissioner over almost every issue were abysmal, such that it became obvious only one could continue in his post.[4]

It is noteworthy that neither Falconer nor Matthews sought the customary extension of contract, and Ryan resigned two years before his contract was due to expire. All three had approached the task of running a large police service as thoughtful, professional police officers, and, while working within financial and other constraints, sought to make policy decisions based solely on what a lifetime's experience in policing suggested would provide the best police service to the public. For their political masters, other considerations applied.

Government and policing in Britain

The Home Office in Britain has, since the *County and Borough Police Act* 1856, maintained a level of control over policing by the stick of supervising standards through the HM Inspector of Constabularies and the carrot of funding for policing. National government has also long set and maintained training and promotion standards, and for many years some training, especially for officers over the rank of inspector, has been carried out nationally. This trend has continued, and now almost all police training is carried out to nationally set criteria and to measurable performance standards: I do not suggest that ensuring a consistently high training standard is inherently undesirable, and for lower ranks does not in itself devolve authority significantly from individual police services, but rigid Home Office control of training for senior officers has inculcated officers in operational command (ie superintendent and above) with no alternative to Home Office thinking (Reiner, 1995).

In a number of ways, which have grown in number and strength since the mid-1990s, the trend during and since the last quarter of the 20th century has been towards creeping nationalisation in policing. While the *Police and Criminal Evidence Act* 1984 (*PACE*) obliged police to establish community consultative groups to determine as broad a consensus as possible for planning local policing policy and strategy, this could well be the last ditch stand for local decision-making in policing. *PACE* placed an obligation on divisional commanders[5] to discover the policing needs of the

---

4   For Ryan's own detailed account of his time in New South Wales, see Williams, 2002.
5   Divisions and sub-divisions are, in modern terminology, Basic Command Units, but remain under the command of a superintendent or chief superintendent.

community being policed, and gave authority for local policing policy to be set in accordance with them. Later legislation has changed this substantially. Furthermore, the number and importance of Home Office policy circulars to police has increased. While these had been issued for very many years, until the 1980s they were generally few in number, and were usually considered advisory documents. Since then, their numbers have increased dramatically, and have become de facto policy directives (Jones, 2003), documents that senior police officers now treat as if they were flagged "ignore at your peril".

The Home Office moved another step towards increasing control of police with the *Police and Magistrates Courts Act* 1994, which allowed the Home Office to set national policing targets. It is by no means a bad idea to set targets for police (or, perhaps, any other agency) over one, two or more years, although the perils of rigid adherence to over-ambitious plans were amply demonstrated by the five- or ten-year plans of Stalin's Russia and Mao's China. However, the idea that all parts of the country necessarily face the same crime or policing problems is extremely dubious. Any police officer who has served in more than one area of a large city is aware that each has different demographics and require different policing approaches, and inner city areas like Brixton, London and St Pauls, Bristol, with high crime and unemployment have little in common with affluent suburbs like Finchley, and even less with quiet holiday towns like Tenby in South Wales or villages in rural Worcestershire. The government took this "one size fits all" target-setting and planning approach a stage further in the *Police Reform Act* 2002, which allowed the Home Office to publish a national policing plan, with related objectives and measurable targets, and a Police Standards Unit to monitor performance (Jones, 2003).

Although the *Police and Magistrates Courts Act* 1994 did provide a new structure for police authorities, their power to set the agendas for their police is trumped by national objectives and plans. If a Police Authority chooses to ignore national objectives as irrelevant to local needs, the Home Office still retains control of funding which is under threat if national (Home Office) priorities are not met. Funding is watched closely, so while a police service might receive enough funding to address the objectives and targets in the national plan, there is unlikely to be enough spare money to address any additional local needs. While the Home Office may have always been the single most important source of control over police, it now overwhelms any local controlling body both by exerting financial control and by claiming legislative power to overrule police authority decisions.

The main source of police input into policy-making is ACPO, the Association of Chief Police Officers, which, Jones suggests, has "transformed itself into a more effective policy-making and lobbying body" (Jones, 2003, p 615). This certainly has the potential to challenge Home Office directives, but if, as has been suggested, its members have been immersed in Home Office thinking during their higher leadership training and are reliant on Home Office approval for promotion, its effectiveness in opposing government may be limited and its willingness to do so weakened. Apart from *PACE*, since the 1970s every change in the way policing is run in Britain has diminished the input from, or the decision-making capacity of, every representative body except national government, which in itself influences the planning and decision-making of senior police officers.

Cost driven decision-making

Since the 1980s many governments' approach to policing, health, education and other aspects of the welfare state has changed in that everything is assessed primarily in terms of its financial cost rather than its intrinsic value to society. Government departments are now to be run in accordance with the business model, which has inherent problems of applicability to the public sector. The *raison d'être* of any business is to make a profit, while the purpose of policing, public health and education is to provide a service whose value is socially, rather than financially, quantifiable. A manufacturer of bicycles can easily calculate the cost of making each item, add on a percentage for profit and sell bikes, and the public have a choice whether or not to buy, so their willingness to purchase affects the price. Such is the way business economics work. While the cost of investigating a crime and bringing a prosecution can be calculated, or the cost of a hip replacement or heart surgery easily assessed, it is impossible to place a monetary quantification on the value such matters have to individuals or the community. The public are uneasy about the public health system for the same reason they are uneasy about policing: they see these services as less effective than they could be or need to be, and, in the case of the health service at least, inadequate in comparison to its past performance. Adequacy, not cost-effectiveness, is the primary consideration for the public.

Another problem with applying the business model to the provision of police services by the state is that criminal justice is an important state monopoly; emergency health provision is a near state monopoly. Individuals can decide whether or not they want bicycles, and, if so, which bicycle they want at what price. They do not choose whether or not to become victims of crime, or to have a heart attack or stroke, but when this happens they require the police or health service to be available immediately. To be violently attacked in the street will create in the victim an urgent need for hospital treatment and criminal investigation, and there are no immediate alternatives to state health and police services. To imagine a business parallel to this is to conceive of an individual being suddenly placed in a dangerous, involuntary state of bicyclelessness which can only be satisfied by the immediate provision of a free bicycle, a quite bizarre situation.

Police are rightly one of the emergency services, since their services are, to a large extent, those that the recipients need because of untoward circumstances, not through any positive choice in the matter. Most of us would rather go through life not needing the professional services of a police officer, any more than we would choose to require the services of a heart surgeon or a dentist, but are glad that these professionals are available when the need arises. We have no real idea what we would be prepared to pay for such professional services on the open market, although we may well have an awareness of the limits to our ability to pay. The most heart-breaking stories of medical need are those where a child is dying for want of specialised treatment which is only available overseas at a cost which is beyond the family's means: for a child to suffer and die of an incurable disease is a cruel and unavoidable fate, but for a person to die through inability to pay for treatment is the more cruel for being avoidable for those with money. Most medical treatment has always been too expensive for the average member of the public, and sophisticated modern medicine on demand is completely beyond the means of any except the very rich: it is only the intervention of state health provision or private medical insurance which makes it accessible to the vast majority of people.

There is a parallel between the cost of health care and the cost of policing. Modern forensic science and crime scene analysis can do a great deal to establish the facts of a crime, and a great number of crimes can now be cleared up which, in the past, were left unsolved. DNA analysis alone has resulted in identification of suspects, fresh charges and convictions in old cases[6] where blood or body fluid samples are available, as more and more samples are taken from suspects and persons on conviction. These new techniques often require considerable expertise and equipment, and, unlike Sherlock Holmes' examinations of cigars and ash, bootprints and reconstructions, can be extremely costly. Very many people are avid watchers of detective series on television, both fictional and documentary-style reconstructions of cases. There is a general public awareness that traces can be found which can link an individual to a crime scene and thereby prove a case, though there is little corresponding awareness of the cost of such procedures. In some cases, for example in domestic burglaries where electronic equipment, cash, and other (insured) items of no sentimental value are taken, the public are willing to accept that an investigation will be limited to dusting for fingerprints and circulating details of property stolen, but victims of more personal crimes are unwilling to accept that a cash limit might be placed on the investigation. Even fewer people are willing to be told their own crime is so minor that it does not merit the cost of investigation and is merely to be recorded.

The cost factor does, however, loom large to police management. In the past, when senior officers were asked to save money, the immediate response was to limit overtime and cut the mileage of police vehicles, but now budgetary constraints are much more wide-reaching. Every aspect of policing is now fully costed at both organisation and station level, and all spending is watched carefully. Costs can be (and are) accurately quantified, but this is only one half of a costs/benefit analysis. Unfortunately, benefits

---

6   These new techniques are also laying to rest cases which have been disputed for years – in Britain, a muted campaign protested for years that James Hanratty was wrongly convicted and executed for a particularly vicious rape and murder. DNA evidence 40 years later proved his guilt.

cannot so easily be financially quantified: there is no basis on which one can even begin to calculate how much the arrest of a burglar, robber or rapist is worth, and at what point a murder inquiry should be wound up because of its cost. It has never been possible to determine police output in terms of the number of crimes prevented, nor a measurable increase or decrease in public peace and safety, still less to put a monetary value upon these imponderables.

Police management can make an accurate assessment of the costs of an investigation, but has not reached the stage where serious (and comparatively rare) crimes like murder or rape are considered too expensive to investigate fully; however, the less serious offences which have the most important effect on the quality of everyday life are subject to financial constraints on investigation. The parallel with health is again clear: those few who suffer heart attacks receive immediate, costly, life-saving treatment without question in public hospitals, but the majority whose lives are impoverished by hernias, arthritic hips, psychological problems and other diseases which are not life-threatening but merely debilitating, face delays in treatment caused by the financially restricted availability of resources. These costs are not avoided but merely deferred as treatment will, eventually, have to be provided. If crime is not cleared up, or even investigated, then this can encourage further criminal behaviour.

Managerialism

The ethos of determining police services by cost rather than by need has led to a new managerial approach to police command for all ranks from inspector upwards in Australian and British policing and for lieutenants and above in the many police departments in the United States, especially those following the Compstat process. Despite what has been said above about the difficulties of quantifying the value of policing, the model of business management adopted requires that policing outputs be assessed, which has led to an obsession with crime and arrest rates, these being the most obviously quantifiable aspects of policing, although there is considerable feeling among criminologists that these are seriously flawed measures. The Compstat process, as Henry (2002) describes it, makes matters worse by taking what is at best an imprecise measure, crime rates, and uses changes in them over very short periods of time, even weekly changes, to determine policing strategy. We shall return to Compstat shortly.

Policing is generally felt to be an expensive undertaking, and police funding is, rightly, no longer seen by anyone as taken from a bottomless pit but should be spent carefully in a controlled, planned manner. In principle, the requirement that police should improve their efficiency and effectiveness is sound, but problems arise with any attempt to give substance to these nebulous aims by choosing criteria according to which police efficiency and effectiveness can be measured. Objective criteria by which the success or otherwise of many police activities can be measured are difficult if not impossible to find, so alternative measures are needed. The British Home Office and the Compstat process places great emphasis on comparative assessments in the absence of more objective criteria. This involves recourse to some fairly arbitrary standards which are nominated as benchmarks. These standards and measures then become a measure of acceptability for those who have achieved them, or a target for those who have not, and the basis for comparisons between police agencies, divisions within police agencies, and performances of agencies or divisions over time.

Another phenomenon to be seen in public service management, following the example of business management, is the development of a plethora of buzz-words and jingoistic phrases.[7] In Britain, for example, a "Quality of Service" program in policing was launched in 1990, and a "new public management" system introduced under which the "status, power and, more importantly, the autonomy of the professional were increasingly questioned; claims to the right of self-regulation were increasingly difficult to sustain" (Long, 2003). After the election of the New Labour government in 1997, "Best Value" government reforms were introduced and later given legislative force, which required local authorities (in the context of policing, police authorities) to undertake "Best Value" reviews and prepare "Best Value" performance plans for each financial year. Although "Best Value" sounds good (it is a phrase which has been used in advertising almost as long as advertising has existed) it is flexible in meaning. "Best" suggests the highest quality, which is what the public desire from its police, while "Value" is usually synonymous with "cheap", which is certainly what a cost-cutting government requires. Consider for a moment Operation Ore, the paedophile inquiry mentioned in the previous chapter. Best policing, which the public would opt for, given the choice, is a full investigation of all 7272 cases (in effect, 7272 paedophiles) reported to the British police. Value, for the Home Office as funding body, is that the matter be investigated within current budgets. The result is limited but well-publicised police activity which results in some convictions, but is unlikely to deter the majority of uninvestigated offenders, or satisfy the detectives who see hundreds of paedophiles needlessly at large, rather than a handful in prison.

Although the new public management system has as one of its priorities an emphasis on achieving results rather than administering processes, a great deal of police management time is now spent (wasted, some would claim) in developing processes to measure results, reporting on performance and preparing fresh plans rather than dealing constructively with policing issues. Much as a student under pressure will sacrifice the ideal of

---

7   A good industry example of this is banking, which now advertises banking "products". Banks actually produce nothing, but provide a service: this service is dropping, since with the closure of branches, ATMs and Internet banking, the bank customer is, in effect, being forced to do the work that bank employees formerly did. Banks now provide DIY banking only, seeking to persuade customers that this is "an improved product", for which they charge ever higher fees: it is no coincidence that banks as institutions are now unpopular and mistrusted.

gaining knowledge to concentrate on the issues that will appear in the exam, so police management under pressure is likely to set aside anything that will be costly to investigate and will not fit the target parameters for the annual report. Nothing can be fudged so easily as crime statistics: while the Home Office refused extra funding for Operation Ore, it remained a national investigation, not appearing in crime statistics. Had the 7272 cases all been recorded as reported crimes by the respective constabularies, it would have caused a dramatic increase in the number of unsolved cases of serious sexual offences in every constabulary and created a media outcry.

Compstat

The Compstat process[8] and its accompanying phrase "zero tolerance policing", was one of the best known changes in policing in the 1990s. It was introduced in New York by Commissioner Bratton, who had been appointed by Mayor Giuliani upon his election in November 1993. The concept of zero tolerance was that which excited the public imagination, first in New York then, very rapidly, throughout the world, although a detailed exposition (Henry, 2002) of the New York policing revolution shows that the heart of the process was managerial.[9] Henry points out that the Compstat process is primarily one of information-gathering as a basis for planning, a process which, he demonstrates, can be adopted in areas other than policing, and he cites several cities in the United States which have adopted and adapted the Compstat process to improve local government agencies.

In the early 1990s New York had, and was perceived by its inhabitants to have, a major crime problem which was increasing. There were underlying problems in policing, management and strategic planning since the collection of city-wide crime statistics was laborious and outdated, and resulted in statistical information routinely being made available only after lengthy analysis, when it was frequently too late to be of direct use. The acronym Compstat refers to the *comp*uterisation of crime *stat*istics, and the first stage in this process is the recording of crime on computer, and the weekly collation of these records. As computer technology and the process itself became more sophisticated, the information recorded grew to include many relevant non-crime statistics, such as staffing issues like sickness and complaints made against police in each precinct. In essence, the development and use of Compstat as a data source is a prime example of information-led policing, since it uses information technology to analyse crime, collate individual crimes in different precincts, develop crime patterns which can indicate linkages to show the work of single offenders or

---

8   I am grateful to Vince Henry for his full, detailed insider's account of the Compstat process both in conversation in 1997 and in his recent book. The factual accounts in this section are drawn almost exclusively from his work: analysis and criticism are mine.

9   Henry makes only one passing reference to zero tolerance in over 300 pages. The full title of his book, *The Compstat Paradigm – management accountability in policing, business and the public sector* indicates the emphasis which is placed on management.

teams, and allows resources to be targeted effectively to deal with crime. As Henry explains it, "many of the principles and practices of good policing that came to be part of Compstat had long been in the repertoire of effective cops; they were simply not in the agency norm [of the NYPD]" (2002, p 245).

The weekly Compstat reports and meetings show how Compstat is used as a management tool. A Compstat report, issued to each precinct commander and the police executive, is compiled each week from raw data, providing basic unanalysed statistical information with, for example, the actual number of crimes reported, arrests made and the percentage change in each since the last report. There is a separate page for each precinct, and comparisons by week, month and year to date. A different part of the report also ranks "in descending order, all patrol commands by the number of crimes committed and arrests effected" (Henry, 2002, p 251). This ranking is a much more positive, even aggressive approach than formerly, when "Precinct Commanders were not so much challenged to reduce crime as to ensure their crime increases were not as substantial as other commanders' increases" (Henry, 2002, p 261) which institutionalised mediocrity by the acceptance that the crime problem was insoluble and efforts to address it hopeless. A further part of the Compstat report which can be seen beside each precinct's crime report is its Commander Profile report, which covers non-crime issues for each precinct, including such items as sickness, overtime, injuries, complaints, response times, etc which give an indication of the commander's management abilities. This, too, is in a format which allows direct comparison between precincts, even though their demographics may be so totally different as to render comparison meaningless.

The weekly Compstat meeting is attended by the senior executive of the NYPD, precinct commanders and other operational middle managers, and requires precinct commanders to present a detailed report on the state of crime and other issues in their command, and provides them with a positive opportunity to "impress executives and other personnel ... with [their] knowledge, leadership talents, crime-fighting abilities and overall career potential", as well as to "publicly communicate their needs and, in doing so, to place some of the responsibility and some of the accountability on the executives" (Henry, 2002, p 267). It is also an opportunity for the executive to publicly challenge and question each commander on their presentations, and on the manner in which their precinct is run. Henry stresses the importance of these meetings and their positive aspects as a transparent management tool, and a genuine weekly opportunity for middle management to address senior management on policing issues, and a way of creating a leadership dialogue rather than the familiar pattern of management by diktat from the executive.

Although as Henry describes Compstat meetings there are elements of both stick and carrot, the carrot being the opportunities to give public praise to individual commanders for innovative strategies and individual officers of lower ranks whose commanders have recounted their particularly noteworthy exploits, the presence of the executive and the generally confrontational tenor of the meetings suggests that the stick may well predominate. In the absence of genuine objective measures, and to avoid the complacent mediocrity which can arise from designating any level of crime as tolerable, the NYPD has used Compstat to adopt a comparative measure of crime. There is but a small jump from comparative to competitive and, if too much hangs on the results, competition will, inevitably, become unhealthy. In an effort to avoid the disapprobation of the executive and humiliating criticism at Compstat meetings, there is a very real risk that crime and other statistics may be manipulated at precinct level, and, if the executive accept and publish these figures, they become complicit in the deceit.

Crime will always occur despite the best efforts of police, educators, social workers and security personnel, and no true objective measures of police efficiency yet exist. Crime reduction is not the sole indicator of good policing: nations with the lowest crime figures are often police states or other repressive regimes where the populace is unwilling to have any dealings with police, even if they are victims of crime.[10] Repressive policing and draconian penalties for offenders may well reduce recorded crime, but they are hardly techniques which are worthy of emulation in a democracy. There is a danger in policing that too great an emphasis on reducing crime rates and increasing arrest rates will lead to bureaucratically creative means of improving the statistics. Ways can be found to hide unwelcome truths, especially in crime statistics: a broken window, for example, may well have been caused by a burglar attempting to enter premises, but can be written up as accidental damage, on the basis of insufficient evidence to prove that it was deliberate. If there is a drive to increase arrests in a particular station or branch, then there can be internecine squabbles over where the credit for particular arrests lie. At an operational level disputes over the credit for arrest in order to boost the figures of one group over another, detectives over uniformed officers, or one station over the next, invariably result in a lack of co-operation and bad feeling between groups of officers, and a fall in morale which diminishes the effectiveness of policing throughout the organisation.

The Compstat process does indeed seem to have unpleasant consequences for any commander with increases in crime to report. The Compstat comparative rankings can be seen as a weekly league table, and while it may be appropriate for football fans to agonise over the position of their team after the weekend results and call for the coach to be sacked after a poor run, it is by no means obvious that such cut-throat competition is an appropriate way to run a police service. If the level of competition amongst management is such that a premium is put on results, serious problems will arise: pressure put on middle management will be passed down, and

---

10   Rape is virtually unknown in fundamentalist Islamic nations like Saudi Arabia, where to admit to being a victim of this crime is to risk public disgrace for the victim and her entire family, ruining the victim's chance of marriage. Police in some nations require bribes even to accept crime reports.

pressure will in turn be put on lower ranking officers to improve their performance. This in itself may be no bad thing, but if the pressure imposed reaches an unhealthy level on middle management, then unhealthy pressure will be put on lower ranks. Such pressure to satisfy the need for arrests will inevitably lead to procedural short-cuts and abuses at street level, or even manufactured evidence and false confessions. Pressure to reduce reported crime may well lead to police officers on the street persuading victims not to report their crimes, or to take the report and re-classify it as a less serious allegation.

While weekly analyses of crime can be enormously helpful in making informed decisions on tactics and deployment, they may not always be valid measures of crime trends, nor of the ability of middle management. Furthermore, if managers are to be held accountable for their performance week by week, this does not encourage any strategic planning, or inventive special operations to meet specific needs that require some time to be successful: only the implementation of short-term reactive measures are encouraged. The Compstat process is antithetical to any long-term approach to police planning. The converse also holds: if police agencies adopt the approach of working with the community and building partnerships to reduce crime, as police agencies in Britain do, then this can only take place if short-term variations in the crime rate are ignored. A long-term strategy will not yield immediate results and cannot be expected so to do.

Pressure on police management

While Henry is correct in his assertion that a management mindset which tacitly authorises mediocrity is to be avoided, too much pressure on middle management to meet short-term goals can encourage this very mediocrity. At the same time as command has been devolved downwards so that local senior officers have far more responsibility for the manner of policing in their area, their actions are more tightly constrained than ever and inspectors and superintendents (lieutenants and captains in the United States) are subject to far more accountability procedures than ever before. While no direct instructions are issued from headquarters about what planning is to be done and how policing strategies are to be implemented in the area, local commanders are bombarded with circulars, performance targets, budgetary limitations, agency-wide initiatives on specific crimes which must be addressed, short and medium term reporting requirements and possibly a weekly Compstat meeting to address. A local commander may be severely criticised for not complying with all these requirements, yet any truly innovative strategy is likely to challenge at least some of them. The pressure on middle management in policing is higher than it has ever been, and likely to increase rather than decrease, so that the only safe option for police superintendents is to comply strictly with all the circulars issued, and avoid innovation lest it fail and blight their careers.

A police superintendent can be expected to have at least one eye on future career prospects and promotion. A successful innovation will help this considerably, but an innovation which is unsuccessful, even though something useful can be learnt from the manner of that failure, is a considerable handicap in the promotion race: it is less risky to comply and not come to notice than to innovate and fail. In a climate of bureaucratic constraint and government pressure, there is very little true autonomy given to superintendents and the pressure on these officers serves to stifle any genuine innovations in policing, or any potentially valuable but unproven strategies to deal with crime which would require time and manpower to implement. It is also worth noting that most senior police officers joined the service to be police officers, and, had they wished to acquire and use accountancy or business skills they would have joined a different profession. The system itself, while its rhetoric encourages change, makes genuine innovation both extremely risky and very difficult to accomplish. Police middle management may well not contain many mediocre police officers, but any system which constrains their actions and imposes increased accountability thereby discouraging individual initiative encourages a culture of safe but mediocre management and rewards the strategy of avoiding criticism by avoiding mistakes.[11]

Police and privatisation

For at least 20 years, police senior officers have responded to the call for more police on the streets and the need to save costs by moving police officers from non-operational to operational duties and filling their non-operational roles with unsworn staff. The rationale is that police officers are most effectively employed on operational duties which improves service to the public while at the same time making a significant financial saving, since clerical or other unsworn staff are usually paid a lower salary than police officers, especially police officers with significant length of service. Police agencies have repeatedly re-assessed police officers on non-operational duties, such that many years ago most police agencies reached a point at which any police function that could be carried out by unsworn staff was no longer done by a police officer. Police agencies, particularly in Britain, are now moving even further, in hiving off major police-related tasks to private agencies. This practice is not restricted to police, in that many governments are to a greater or lesser extent ideologically committed to privatisation or outsourcing within the public service. However, the discussion here will be restricted to the impact of privatisation on policing, rather than discussion of the ideology or its impact on other public services. In Britain, some aspects of policing which have been removed from the direct control of any police service include the maintenance of criminal records, prisoner transport between police stations, courts and prisons, and some police training.

---

11   I am grateful to Bill Boaks of the Western Australia Police Service for insights on this from his current research on the opinions of police middle management.

In many cases, the effects, aside from the immediate financial implications, of privatising particular police activities may be delayed. In some cases, for example prisoner transport in London, the transition was covered by a core group of police officers who retired to continue in their old jobs under a new, private company, which employed a retired senior police officer to implement the contract: in other cases, serving police officers may be seconded to a government unit under contract. One serious difficulty with privatisation, especially of such a sensitive area as criminal records, is that private companies and public servants have completely different rationales for carrying out their tasks. At risk of tautology, the role of a public servant is to provide a service to the public, and, despite a proportion of time-servers, the ethos of policing is to work for the public interest, with any other factor, such as cost, being subordinate. Private companies, however, exist solely to make a profit, and working practices are planned in accordance with a cost/benefit analysis where the public interest is of secondary importance to profits. As a comparison, when publicly owned utilities such as the telephone system are privatised, there is a heavy emphasis on profitability, and a consequent rise in prices, often with a decline in service.

More troubling issues are those where problems of accountability arise. Police officers are bound by a firm discipline code as well as, in many cases, a code of ethics, and thus are personally accountable for transgressions. Police agencies are likewise responsible for the bad behaviour of police officers if this can be shown to be the result of organisationally tolerated malpractice, lack of training, etc. This has been seen most vividly in Britain in the Metropolitan Police response to allegations of institutional racism in the wake of the bungled investigation into the murder of Stephen Lawrence.[12] If, however, there is malpractice on the part of an employee of a private company, then that person is accountable to the employer, unless there is some direction to the contrary. In the case of privatisation of prisoner transport in Britain, legislation was drafted to authorise security staff to detain prisoners, and included rules on custody of prisoners. Without such steps, an individual working for an organisation carrying out some police function under contract is not accountable to the public as a police officer would be.

There is also a danger that accountability may fall between the individual, the private employer and the police or government organisation to whom the company is contracted. Shared accountability can mean that no one individual or agency can be held responsible, or, even worse, accountability may fall between the cracks, and no-one at all can be held accountable. This may be the case with regard to suspected terrorists and other prisoners held for interrogation in Iraq, Guantanamo Bay and Afghanistan. Although they are in military custody, the matter is not

---

12   Stephen Lawrence was a black teenager murdered in South London in 1993, and an inquiry into the botched police investigation reported in 1999 that it found evidence, *inter alia*, of "institutional racism and a failure of leadership by senior officers" within the Metropolitan Police.

wholly dissimilar to police accountability issues. At the time of writing (May 2004) investigations are under way into the abuse of prisoners by United States military personnel in Iraq and Afghanistan. There are some allegations[13] of interrogations complying with neither the Geneva Convention on prisoners of war nor the standards required by the courts in democratic nations being carried out by members of contracted private security organisations rather than by members of the CIA or US military intelligence. There are clear accountability procedures for members of military intelligence, who are military personnel and thus subject to military discipline, and CIA staff who are answerable to the United States government, yet employees of private companies (who in earlier conflicts such as the 1960s Congolese war of independence were called mercenaries) are not subject to either. Furthermore, the United States criminal law does not hold in Iraq, and American contract workers have immunity from Iraqi civil law, at least for the time being. These circumstances provide an extreme example of accountability issues, where, if the allegations are proven, private contractors apparently have *carte blanche* for any activities, however unacceptable, that they might indulge in. Although an extreme example, this case does indicate that privatisation has potentially troublesome issues regarding accountability, which must be addressed before contracts are agreed. Such problems cannot be ignored for reasons of ideology or expedience.

Policing partnerships

Partnerships between police and other agencies, although not privatisations, involve some devolution of control over policing matters. Such schemes which involve police in crime prevention partnerships with other agencies, particularly local authorities, are particularly common in Britain, where they have both government and legislative approval. The rationale is that crime is not just a matter for police, but is a problem that has its roots in social issues that are well outside the ambit of police action. If the problems and social issues are addressed by a number of agencies acting in concert, then there is a real chance of improvement. However, immediately questions are raised about funding and control of such projects, inter-agency issues start to appear. It can be said, perhaps cynically, that when a working party is mooted, people hear the word "party" and agree to join; when the time comes for action, they hear the word "work" and disappear.

Any organisations which could usefully participate in a crime prevention partnership, including the police, currently operate under considerable financial constraints. Although the individuals involved may have a genuine desire that the project succeed, none of the agencies from which they come has any spare resources to contribute, and individuals are

---

13   I stress that this issue is in its early stages at the time of writing, and information on it comes mainly from the British media, particularly the *Guardian Weekly* and the BBC, relatively trustworthy sources but both consistently expressing criticism of the United States foreign and military policies in Iraq.

expected by the agency they represent to minimise outlay to any multi-agency project, and all hope that their own agency's necessary parsimony will be made up for by the contributions of the others. The issue of contribution of resources is also linked to the issue of control of the project – the agency which takes the lead is expected by the others to make the highest contribution of resources, and the agency which makes the highest contribution of resources is likely to use that contribution as a means of controlling the project. If there is a genuine spirit of co-operation, and the successful outcome of the project is given primacy, a multi-agency part-nership approach has a good chance of success.

Harry Truman's doctrine of accountability was that "the buck stops here", meaning that the individual in charge of any venture, large or small, takes the praise or the blame depending on the outcome, and is responsible for all other individuals engaged in the venture. However, in a multi-agency project or some other joint enterprise, it is far more difficult to apportion the accountability of ultimate responsibility for failure to an agency or individual. If the project succeeds, the praise can be shared, but if it fails each agency involved will seek to shift responsibility to the others. It is tempting to hold the acknowledged lead agency ultimately accountable, but in practice no agency has any formal control over the staff of another agency, so has no way of enforcing compliance with its own directions. For example, in a joint venture between the police and education departments, police cannot answer for or exercise control over education department staff and vice versa. It follows that one organisation cannot be held respon-sible for errors made by another. If and when multi-agency projects go wrong, each organisation can blame the others, thereby spreading the responsibility or avoiding blame completely.[14]

Police partnerships with other agencies may well be effective if established in the spirit of co-operation and with a clear understanding of the responsibilities of each agency. However, the public continue to see crime as the primary responsibility of police. It follows, then, that any unsuccessful crime reduction initiative in which police participate will be seen as a failure for police rather than for any other participating organi-sations. There is a real danger for police credibility here: by participating in partnerships they risk being perceived as being fully accountable for projects over which they have only partial control.

Private security as private police

Much of the reduction in public services other than policing has come by governments persuading or coercing individuals to provide for their own welfare. The original intention of the welfare state was to provide edu-cation, medical care and retirement pensions funded out of taxes, and

---

14   This seems to be the case with the British railway system, where, on privatisation, different companies became responsible for track, signals, services, etc. The system is in complete disarray, with each company shifting the blame for incompetence and negli-gence, which in some instances has led to loss of life, to others.

people were led to believe that their tax payments entitled them to health care, education for their children and a pension when they were too sick or too old to work. This was certainly the case in Britain and Australia in the latter half of the 20th century, less so in the United States which had ideological resistance to the welfare state. However, government in Australia and Britain now follows a "user pays" policy, where individuals are legally obliged to make private provision in a superannuation fund for their retirement (with no protection from government in the case of failure of such funds), and are very strongly persuaded to take out private medical insurance.

The growth of the private security industry is, perhaps, an example of the "user pays" policy applied to policing. An important aspect of "user pays" is that it entitles the payer to choice in the type and level of service provided. The majority of users of private security are private companies, although some are employed by local government, or government agencies. Security officers employed by wholly private companies are those typically seen in shopping malls, on factory estates, and handling cash or valuable property in transit. These security companies vary considerably, some being highly reputable and responsible companies operating nationally or internationally[15] employing many thousands of security officers, while others are much smaller local companies. If a security company is supplying security under contract to, for example, a shopping mall, then its security officers have a duty to fulfil the security needs of the mall owner, which is linked to the profitability of the mall itself. The interests of the security company and the mall management are wholly financial; while this might not always be at odds with the public interest, public and business interests are never identical, and sometimes not even similar.

Increasingly, local authorities are turning towards security patrols for housing estates and parks under their control.[16] Many public transport authorities have also established patrols to keep order and create a feeling of security on trains and buses. All levels of government in Britain and Australia are committed to the contracting out of services, and a large number of security activities are undertaken by the major security companies on behalf of some local authority or public body. There is a difference in accountability between security officers employed in this capacity, and those employed on behalf of a profit-making organisation. Although the security officers themselves are still primarily answerable to the company which employs them, they serve that company best by meeting the security needs of the local authority or other public body. These security needs are concerned with crime prevention in the public

---

15 In Britain, for example, Securicor and Group 4 are well known and respected, as are MSS in Australia: Chubb Security is international.

16 The London Borough of Wandsworth introduced its own security patrols in parks and council estates in the late 1980s. Many other boroughs in Britain and Australia have followed suit over the past 10 years. In the United States, policing is locally based anyway, but a number of public bodies such as universities and hospitals, as well as some hugely expensive enclosed housing estates, have their own security or police bodies.

interest, rather than with ensuring that some enterprise is profitable, so private security officers employed in public undertakings should, ultimately, find themselves answerable to a public body rather than strictly private interests.

Consider the objectives of security guards who are deployed at a shopping mall. In general, their functions are to prevent rowdy behaviour, eject people who are abusive or drunk, perhaps deal with shoplifters, and to liase with the public emergency services when necessary. They are answerable ultimately to their employer, who may well be a major security company, but on a direct daily basis they answer to the management of the shopping mall. Since the mall exists to make a profit for its owners and this profit is dependent on the profitability of the shops within it, then the *raison d'être* of the security staff is to create a safe atmosphere in which the public will spend money, and the success of security officers is judged by whether or not they achieve this. Very little concern is given to the way in which this atmosphere is created, provided that paying customers are not discouraged from spending freely.

The very success of private security companies means that this has become an important growth industry. Not only do large shopping malls employ security guards, but so too do an increasing number of residential estates, and some late-opening shops, chemists for example, that perceive themselves as at high risk of criminal behaviour. Like the nightwatchmen that security guards have replaced, security staff are usually unskilled and low paid. The low rates of pay need to be maintained if private security is to remain significantly cheaper than an expanded police service. As a result of a high fear of crime, and perhaps at the behest of insurance companies, local authorities, groups of small businesses and even groups of citizens are employing private security.

Increasingly, private security companies are not just taking over isolated tasks, but are moving into activities which previously were the province of police, for example patrolling and checking burglar alarms. There have been instances where private security guards take no action in the event of an alarm or a crime being committed other than calling police. Police must of necessity work more frequently and closely with security officers. To achieve this successfully, security companies' standards must be commensurate with policing standards, both in achieving the desired outcome, and in maintaining operational criteria, notwithstanding that their staff may have less education and significantly lower wages than police officers.

Accountability of private security

There is very little control, regulation or licensing of security staff, despite the growth of the industry and the amount of power they might have. In Australia police clearance is required for individual security personnel, but this amounts to little more than a check that the individual has no criminal record under the name given in the State in which registration is required.

In Britain the *Private Security Industries Act* 2001 regulates and licenses companies that provide private security under contract, but does not include large businesses' directly employed internal security staff. Licensing procedures are limited, in that they can ensure that private security personnel have no criminal record and have undergone specified training, but the Act has no jurisdiction over working practices or employers' directions to staff.

The only real controls over private security personnel are the criminal law and sanctions by their employers. If a security guard assaults an individual in the line of duty then a prosecution can ensue, and a security guard faces, ultimately, dismissal for behaviour that is not acceptable to the company employing that guard. Like the police, security personnel have a direct involvement with the public but, unlike police, they are not answerable to the public. Police officers are answerable to the public in ways which have been discussed in detail both for what they do and the way in which they do it. Security personnel are answerable for what they do to their employers, and the only public accountability is that which applies to any citizen, in that if a security officer breaches the criminal or civil law, then that individual may be held accountable before the courts.

If a security guard, in dealing with a disorderly individual in a shopping mall physically assaults that person then a criminal charge may be possible, but if the guard is verbally abusive or ejects the individual in an unnecessarily forceful manner, then there may be no procedure for registering complaints or holding the security officer answerable. It is even possible that the mall management approve and encourage forceful ejections. The security staff of any shopping mall are expected to give priority to the interests of the management, which are to maximise profit, and not necessarily to safeguard the public interest. Profit is increased by increasing the number of paying customers in the centre, which may be achieved by excluding those who are genuinely unruly or disruptive, or those who are unacceptable to shopkeepers or management. This category will include any individuals or groups such as the homeless, the young or bizarrely dressed or members of ethnic minorities, who may offend or upset those patrons who are more likely to spend money. The crucial question for the management may well be the amount of money which is spent, rather than the standard of behaviour exhibited – some of the best hotels are known to tolerate extremely bad behaviour from rock stars and others who spend vast sums of money in their establishments and pay for damage caused despite the effect on other customers. The point here is that private security personnel have a duty to management rather than to the public, and will enforce company policy rather than the public interest whenever there is a conflict between the two.

Private crime investigations

A number of government agencies and private companies now have highly sophisticated investigative branches, which deal with both internal security investigations and, increasingly, investigations of the public insofar as their activities affect the company or agency. In the government sector, the Customs, Post Office and Tax Office have long carried out investigations in their own areas, and other agencies have also commenced or increased their investigative activities, for example into welfare cheats or fraud involving prescription drugs. Prosecutions may or may not follow from these investigations, the Tax Office in particular placing revenue above punishment, but such decisions are made by a public agency answerable to parliament, and the public interest is generally given priority.

The immediate reaction to the term "private investigator" is that of a seedy individual working for divorce lawyers. The private investigations discussed here are those carried out by large companies on the public, for example bank and credit investigations. Despite there being government regulations concerning reporting of certain bank transactions in an attempt to identify tax fraud and money-laundering operations, most of the bank investigations concern attempts by staff and customers to defraud the banks themselves. The decision by shops to move to self-service, having goods on display for customers to pick up and carry to a cash desk both increased sales and decreased the number of staff needed (thereby lowering costs) but encouraged shoplifting and created the need for store detectives to prevent it. Similarly, the move by banks to make credit and loans easier to obtain have increased profits but have also encouraged fraud. Banks now have sophisticated systems to monitor transactions (all of which are, of course, recorded on computer) and detect fraud.

The response of bank investigators to fraud is not always to identify and prosecute offenders. The aim is to discover the manner in which the fraud was perpetrated in order to take steps to prevent a recurrence, and, in the longer term, to assess the cost of prevention and its effect on profits. Much as shoplifting in major stores can be prevented by the reintroduction of sales counters and restricted access of customers to goods, which will in turn increase costs and reduce sales and profits, so credit inquiries may reduce fraud but also reduce profits. Prosecutions may even be counter-productive, in that the exact method used by the perpetrator is publicised in court, showing the flaws in the bank system to other potential offenders.

It may well be the case that bank investigators reach some sort of compromise with the more enterprising perpetrators of frauds again the banks. In the field of computer crime, the most important information a hacker has to offer is the way in which computer security can be breached. While not every hacker becomes a computer security consultant, the old adage about poachers and gamekeepers has its 21st century equivalent. The decision whether or not to pass the results of investigations and the identity of suspects to police for prosecution is taken solely on the basis of the interests of the institution which can reasonably consider itself the victim, not of the public interest. In most cases of any type in which police have evidence of an offence the public interest and the victim's interests are indistinguishable, and the decision whether or not to prosecute depends heavily on the victim's willingness to proceed. If police have investigated, they then know the circumstances and can inform the prosecuting authority when the public interest differs from the victim's wishes. In the case of private investigations where the victim chooses a solution other than prosecution, then neither police nor any other public agency have knowledge of the case in order to overrule the decision. Such cases might be extremely rare, but it is possible to envisage money being obtained by bank fraud to be used as capital for other crimes, for example terrorist attacks. The bad publicity generated by a prosecution may well reduce the bank's revenue even more than the original crime against it.

Conclusion

The argument in this chapter has been that in a variety of ways decisions about policing matters are being taken away from police. Government interference has resulted in an erosion of police autonomy at a time when police accountability is at its highest. Unless genuine decision-making power is devolved, the devolution of authority to middle management does no more than create potential scapegoats within the intermediate ranks. What recent trends have shown is that police in Britain are no longer allowed to set pragmatic goals but are expected to meet politically motivated government targets. The cult of statistically driven management and financial control bodes ill for policing, as it serves to stifle innovation. Policing in the past was criticised for its rigidity and unwillingness to change traditional practices, but the last two decades or so of the 20th century saw police agencies shake off organisational inertia and undertake major changes in their approach. The start of the 21st century has seen policing aware of the need to change, but unable to do so through external constraints.

CHAPTER 15

POLICING THE 21ST CENTURY

Introduction

This chapter looks at the effects the changes discussed in the previous two chapters have had on the majority of police officers in the lower ranks performing operational duties, and on the public with whom they come into contact every day. Street crime has, in essence, changed little over the history of policing (indeed, over the history of the human race) as people have always fought each other, stolen each other's property, abused alcohol (and now also drugs) and generally indulged in the various forms of anti-social behaviour which are at the root of much of a police patrol officer's work. In looking at policing from the perspective of a 21st century police officer it is pertinent to examine the aetiology of crime first.

The factors that make policing the 21st century different from policing the 19th or 20th centuries include the impact of new technology, particularly information technology. As in most other aspects of life, technology has had a cataclysmic impact in policing, but the question arises in all endeavours, including policing, whether the technology is properly used to address needs more efficiently, or whether the way the tasks are carried out is modified to accommodate the new technology rather than the needs addressed. Certainly in some spheres of activity the use of new technology itself changes the way the activity is performed. An example of this effect is the use of Powerpoint and similar software. Its use is now expected in conferences and other presentations and is effective in making points through key words and phrases, so academics in particular who use Power-point are persuaded by the limitations of the technology to sacrifice lucid argument, discussion and explanation, which should be essential to their work, in order to comply with the format of the software.

The pressures felt by police middle management that have been ana-lysed in depth in the previous chapter also have a serious impact on police officers patrolling the streets which will be considered here. Officers on patrol are, and always have been, constrained by the law and answerable through the police hierarchy, but are also answerable directly to the public through the obligation to respond to their requests. The only explanation which has traditionally been automatically accepted when a police officer fails to carry out the duties assigned by a senior officer is that an urgent request from a member of the public required immediate action. The dichotomy between street and management police officers has been remarked on by a number of commentators (for example, Reuss-Ianni and Ianni, 1983), but if government pressure on police management is felt as pressure on street officers requiring them to operate in a manner which is consistently at odds with the direct policing demands made of them by the members of the public they meet and serve, then this divide may become both deeper and wider.

Social problems and crime

The discussion in Chapter 3 on the causes of crime argued that crime was not just a police problem but was a problem for society as a whole, and that action on such matters as unemployment, health and education, which would have a significant effect in reducing crime, could only be undertaken by national or State governments. The two social factors which have the most direct impact on street crime are unemployment and the use of drugs. Although these two are by no means the only important factors which are causally responsible for crime, they are, perhaps, the most intractable, so much so that it is difficult to imagine what life would be like without drug use and unemployment being at the problematic levels they have reached over the past 20 or more years. Insofar as these two factors are an intrinsic part of modern life, the current level and type of crime may be as much a 20th century bequest to the 21st as communications technology, laser surgery, and high levels of personal affluence for some. This argument is not intended to suggest that the world is settling into an anarchic abyss, in Hobbes' words a "war of all against all", and that policing is doomed to failure, but to show that there may well be social factors which prevent even the most promising approaches to policing being as effective as they deserve to be, and that any economic benefits of less than full employment have a social cost of some magnitude.

Although the 19th century had its share of drunkards, opium smokers and laudanum addicts, perhaps the biggest single criminogenic factor then was purely and simply poverty. Even a cursory glance through the records of crime in the magistrates' courts in British towns and cities, or the offences for which individuals were transported to Australia, shows a depressing list of petty thefts of clothing, food, and small items worth only a few pence when sold or pawned, truly crimes of desperation. This pattern of crime was no less true in American cities of the same era. Poor people worked, stole or starved, poverty also forced women into prostitution, and, although working was preferable, many of the poor were forced by circumstance into crime to stay alive at some stages of their lives. The provision of state welfare in modern societies tries to ensure that none shall be so destitute as to die for want of food or shelter, but this is not universally available. The 19th century Irish who fled the potato famines and sought work in the United States or Australia, and the Welsh who left the mining towns of the Rhonnda for Patagonia, have their modern counterparts in the migrants and refugees from countries where there is war, repression or rampant poverty who travel across the world seeking work and any means, legal or otherwise, to ensure the survival and safety of themselves and their families.

Drugs and society

Society's attitude towards drugs has changed radically over the past half century. The traditional distinction, that drugs are either medicinal and lawful, or harmful and unlawful, is no longer viable, and the view that alcohol and tobacco, being socially acceptable and a suitable source of revenue, are therefore not really harmful drugs is no longer widely believed. The clear distinction which society once held between drugs which are harmful and illegal and alcohol and tobacco which are a feature of everyday life no longer exists.[1] This has not led to a desire to proscribe alcohol (or tobacco), since the problems this caused in the United States during the prohibition era remain as a salutary lesson, and because government income would fall dramatically without alcohol and tobacco taxes, but has led to questions about the value and consistency of laws which attach serious penalties to the use of recreational drugs whose dangers are thought to be no greater than those attached to tobacco and alcohol.

While the younger generation of the 1960s was experimenting with unlawful drugs, particularly cannabis and synthetic drugs like LSD and amphetamines, medical science was establishing causal links between tobacco use and a number of diseases, particularly of the heart and lungs. While there remains little controversy over the addictive and life-threatening dangers of such drugs as cocaine and the opium derivatives, the perception of cannabis as a dangerous drug has diminished and the perception of the dangers of tobacco and alcohol has grown. Health education campaigns have focused on the risks attendant on the use of tobacco, and while in the 1970s any non-smoker who expressed a complaint about smokers in the workplace or restaurants would be considered unsocial, now the act of smoking itself is considered antisocial. Most workplaces, restaurants and shopping centres prohibit smoking,[2] forcing smokers today to gather in forlorn groups outside. Similarly, the safe drinking limits which are being promoted to prevent alcohol abuse in the 21st century are well below those which would have caused a person to be termed a heavy drinker in the 1970s. The dangers of alcohol are made ever more explicit in links being drawn between alcohol use and personal injury (through crimes of violence and accidents of all types) and the high percentage of work in hospital accident and emergency departments that is alcohol-related. While deaths through overdose of illegal drugs or drug-related murders are

---

1   This history of drug laws in the United States is described in Hagan (1985). The pattern in other nations is similar, except for the prohibition of alcohol, although the chronology varies somewhat.

2   Legislation to ban smoking completely in enclosed public places is now quite common, and smoking in pubs and bars is now banned in a number of places, from New York to the Republic of Ireland.

newsworthy, there are no less alcohol-related road fatalities in Australia each year,[3] and deaths among the 1960s generation of cannabis users are far more likely to be related to tobacco use or alcohol abuse than to the consumption of cannabis. The very clear view that society had in the first half of the 20th century that some substances were to be classified as illegal drugs because they were extremely dangerous to the individual and society, while other substances which caused health or other problems but were socially acceptable, legal (and could be highly taxed), has changed.

There are two phrases in common use which seem to sum up society's ambivalent feelings towards what constitutes a drug, and what sort of drug use ought to be severely punished. The first phrase is "recreational drug" and the second "drug of choice". The first phrase connotes that an individual may, on certain occasions such as at a party or relaxing at the weekend, indulge in drug use which might well be expensive but, provided it does not cause harm to others or interfere with the individual's capacity to continue a normal working and family life, is socially acceptable and should not be illegal. The second phrase is often used in relation to the consumption of a glass of beer or wine or a cup of coffee or a cigarette as an acknowledgment, perhaps, that many people accept that they require some sort of stimulant or relaxant on various occasions during working hours or in social activity. It seems difficult to justify legislation which renders the possession or use of some substances unlawful while the purchase of other substances, which are acknowledged as equally if not more harmful, is a lawful source of government revenue.

The argument that some currently unlawful drugs such as cannabis have far fewer deleterious effects than lawful substances like alcohol and tobacco has considerable strength, and logic dictates that, to maintain consistency, either alcohol and tobacco use must be penalised in the same way as cannabis use, or cannabis use should be decriminalised. Many of the persons in positions of authority in the 21st century are likely to have used cannabis at some time in their youth,[4] if not continued its use intermittently as a recreational drug ever since, and almost certainly know many contemporaries who have smoked the drug. Any legislative decisions about cannabis will therefore be based, at least in part, on the personal knowledge and observation of the legislators. The problem with this argument for the decriminalisation of cannabis as a drug which has fewer harmful effects than tobacco or alcohol is that cannabis is not the only such candidate for decriminalisation. If the criterion for decriminalisation is to demonstrate

---

3   In Western Australia, for example, there have been in the order of 80 deaths from drug overdose per year over the past 10 years, and a murder rate of about 30 per annum (many of which are alcohol related) for several decades. By contrast, the death rate in road accidents is about 200 per year. More than half the drivers involved in fatal accidents have more than the legal amount of alcohol in their bloodstream. The figures are not precise, but do serve to point out the comparative dangers of the various substances.

4   Several political leaders have made equivocal statements about this, typically admitting having tried cannabis once or twice at university, or, famously, "smoking but not inhaling". These admissions contradict assertions that drug use automatically ruins the individual's life.

that a drug has fewer harmful effects than tobacco, then a case can be made for the decriminalisation of many of the new designer drugs. Although there are deaths from the consumption of ecstasy and other such drugs, they are comparatively few given the estimated level of use of these substances.

There is no longer a clear demarcation line between harmful and addictive drugs and those that are perceived as the relatively benign "recreational" drugs. The increasing practice of testing for drugs in the workplace is a de facto recognition that recreational drug use is fairly common and the range of organisations instituting such tests indicates how prevalent drug use is among employees in all types of occupation. Recreational drug users have often claimed that the effects of their drug use is temporary, and does not result in loss of efficiency at work the following day, and this seems to some extent confirmed by the insistence by employers on drug tests for employees at random, not restricting drug testing only to those employees who have come to notice through underperformance or unusual behaviour. Almost everyone has at some time had to cope with a colleague with a hangover, or an inability to stay awake after an all-night party, but the after-effects of other drugs is not always so obvious.

The ambivalence of society towards drugs creates a number of problems for police in dealing with drug offences. Although many members of society feel that there is nothing seriously wrong with the straightforward possession of certain drugs, there is, nevertheless, a desire that suppliers of drugs be prosecuted, notwithstanding that individuals cannot use drugs which they have not previously obtained from a supplier. The most feasible way for drug suppliers to be traced is if they are named by their customers, which is where drug prosecutions usually start, and drug possession is most easily detected by police among those who are careless and less surreptitious than others in their approach to obtaining drugs. The easiest way to tackle a drug supply chain is to start at the bottom and work up, which means arresting drug users, a strategy which runs contrary to the widespread public feeling that for police to charge individuals with simple possession and process them through the justice system is often carried out as an exercise to improve statistics and a waste of time and money.

The most commonly used illegal drug amongst all age groups and all classes of society is cannabis, and the articulate, middle-aged, left-over hippie is as readily characterised as a cannabis user as someone with a career in the arts, a member of a bikie gang or an African-American from the ghetto. Despite the prevalence of cannabis use, police will have difficulty finding legitimate reasons to justify searching an individual who knows, and plays by, the rules of police procedure, who is articulate or circumspect, so they are unlikely to stop such people. The persons most likely to be stopped in the street by police, searched for drugs and eventually arrested are the unsophisticated, inarticulate and less intelligent, which characteristics often typify the young, particularly those from minority groups or of low social status, and those who have dropped out of school. It follows that police drug prosecutions are often seen as trivial at best and racist at worst, being most often directed against the young and vulnerable or members of minority groups.

The ambivalence of society towards drugs suggests that a large proportion of the users of illicit drugs are maintaining otherwise law-abiding, productive lives. One of society's modern stereotypes is the young financial trader amassing great wealth while using cocaine to stay awake and track the world's markets. The link between drug use and other crimes is that illegal drugs are expensive, and users without significant legitimate incomes will commit crime to obtain the money to buy drugs. Among society's other stereotypes is the picture of the typical burglar as a 15-year-old breaking into houses in order to obtain money or property to sell to obtain money for drugs, thus the whole juvenile crime problem can be blamed on drugs. While a significant proportion of crime, particularly juvenile crime, is committed by people with a drug habit they cannot afford, this crime issue cannot be dealt with effectively unless the question why such a large number of young people feel the need for drugs in the first place is addressed. This, however, is a major social question, not one that police should be expected to deal with.

There are two entirely different aspects to the question of illegal drug use in the 21st century. One aspect is relatively harmless to society, that a fairly high proportion of people who do not consider themselves criminals indulge in the recreational use of unlawful substances, acknowledging that they are putting themselves at some health risk, but arguing that these risks are comparable to (or lower than) the risks from indulgence in tobacco or over-indulgence in alcohol, both of which are legal. Such individuals treat the drug laws as they would, perhaps, speed limits and see their law-breaking as a technical rather than criminal matter, reliant on arbitrary legal definition. The second aspect of the drugs issue is that of a rather different group within society which also indulges in the use of unlawful and expensive substances, both the recreational drugs used by the first group and other, more harmful and addictive drugs. The difference is that this group of people is unable to afford its habits and turns to crime to fund them. The first group come to the notice of police only rarely and then usually by accident, but the second group has become a major and highly visible crime problem.

The debate about drugs and crime has become highly politicised, and police are asked to deal with the problem at its source, the suppliers and importers. While this is undeniably important, supply only answers demand, and there would be no complex supply network if there were not a large and profitable pool of drug users as customers. The illegal drugs trade is so large and profitable that even the most draconian police measures are unlikely to succeed, and such measures might bring with them many of the problems that American society and its police faced during the 1920s and 1930s in maintaining the prohibition of alcohol. The drug problem could be reduced by reducing the demand for drugs, but this is rarely addressed, since it means discovering what is lacking in so many people's lives that drugs are needed to fill the gap, and why so many young people in almost every country of the developed world are so disenchanted and alienated that they feel the need for drugs, then addressing these social issues.

If society continues to deal exclusively by way of punishment or incarceration with those individuals whose level of drug use is such that they resort to crime, rather than addressing the reasons for their addictive behaviour, then the drug problem on the streets is likely to become, if it is not already, beyond the ability of police to control. It is, clearly, intolerable that much of the crime in society results from the need of some of its members to support a drug habit. It is far more likely to be a productive crime prevention strategy to determine and address the reasons why individuals feel the need for drugs and to rectify this need rather than merely to punish their offending behaviour. Addiction to anything is difficult to cure, as the number of celebrities repeatedly undergoing rehab shows, and is better prevented. Inquiring into the social causes of drug addiction and addressing those causes is, perhaps, the only way to address the drug-related crime problem which police and the criminal justice system are currently powerless to deal with effectively.

Unemployment

Although no-one starves in the welfare state, neither do those who live solely on welfare have a high standard of living. In the 21st century employment patterns have changed: individuals can no longer expect to have a job for life even if their work performance with an employer is satisfactory, and everyone is likely to have to change jobs, if not careers, several times before retirement, which itself may well come later than was common in the latter half of the 20th century. In the modern technological world many of the tasks which required less skill, were repetitive, or required manual labour, are now carried out by machines or computers rather than people. As early as the 1940s this was noted by one British philosopher, Bertrand Russell, who saw nothing sacrosanct about the five-day working week, and suggested that technological change could permit a four- or even three-day week (Russell, 1960). Russell's view was that technology would provide an opportunity for those not required to carry out laborious tasks to shorten their working week and enrich their increased leisure time.

Rather than spreading the work about as Russell suggested so that the same number of workers have to work fewer hours, new technology has been used to reduce the workforce significantly. Among the buzzwords of the 1990s was downsizing, and in many industries reducing costs has become synonymous with laying off workers. The political and social arguments concerning whether full employment is good or bad for a nation's economy are of no relevance here: what is of concern is the effect that the significant and apparently irreducible level of unemployment in most societies has on crime. The matter would be less problematic if unemployment was not an almost permanent state for many individuals. If the level of unemployment affected different people at any given time, for example if many people spent short periods out of work between jobs, so that the individuals who are unemployed today are likely to be in work in a month or two when different individuals might be unemployed, it would be easier for individuals to deal with. It would, perhaps, create less social problems if most people were to be unemployed some of the time than some of the people to be unemployed most of the time.

For the 19th century unemployed it was a case of steal or starve. For the long-term unemployed of the 21st century starvation has been replaced by subsistence,[5] although anything more than the bare necessities may be inaccessible other than by crime. Certain members of the long-term unemployed are unemployable, in the sense that any employer seeking to fill a vacancy would choose almost any other applicant before them. From the employer's viewpoint if there are any other candidates for a job there is no point in even considering a person who has been in prison, is an alcoholic, a drug addict, mentally or physically ill, illiterate, without a fixed address or with heavy tattoos or body piercing that the employer finds distasteful. These characteristics have been discussed before: they were described in Chapter 3 as commonly found amongst individuals who fall foul of the justice system. The same characteristics which render an individual unemployable are those very characteristics commonly found in those who commit crime. Even if it is disputed that the link is causal, it is clear that the same indicators of social deprivation which are commonly found in persons who are unemployed for such a long period that they feel themselves to be unemployable, are also found in persons who commit crime. The weakest conclusion that can be drawn is that the larger the pool of unemployed and unemployable individuals becomes, the more likely it is that crime will increase.

The bleakest prognosis of unemployment and crime is that many nations in the 21st century will have a significant and increasing proportion of their population who are unemployed as well as exhibiting other forms of social disadvantage, and many are unlikely ever to be employed in other than casual or temporary work. These individuals are likely to commit crime to supplement welfare payments, then will be arrested, imprisoned, released to further unemployment and continue the cycle. There is a parallel here with the issue of drugs discussed earlier. By failing to address the reasons for individuals becoming drug addicts and implementing preventative measures, the pool of drug users who commit crime is undiminished and, indeed, growing. Failure to address the problems that cause a significant number of members of society to be almost constantly unemployed creates a further, and partially overlapping, pool of individuals who are likely to indulge in criminal enterprises.

There are, then, two important sub-cultures, which overlap to some extent, for whose members crime is part of their normal way of life. These,

---

5   There are, indeed, political moves to remove unemployment benefit from the long-term unemployed, in the United States at least. This presupposes that every person is employable in some capacity, and that jobs exist for everyone, which is patently not currently the case.

the sub-culture of drug users and the sub-culture of the almost permanently unemployed, comprise a significant proportion of the population, and cause a considerable amount of crime. They are beyond policing in the sense that arrest and imprisonment as a consequence of their actions are as much a part of their lives as an increase in income tax is a consequence of a pay rise for those in work.[6] It is unrealistically utopian to suggest that social issues could be addressed so that no-one would wish to take drugs and that no-one would be unemployed, but the tacit acceptance by society of the existence of a drug culture and the existence of long-term unemployment has, as a corollary, the inevitability of the crime problem created by members of these sub-cultures. A point will be reached, if it has not been reached already, where the best efforts of the police and the justice system are powerless to prevent these individuals committing further offences.

Organised, complex crime

A further problem for police in the 21st century remains the issue of organised, complex crime, which can be characterised as being a highly profitable, continuous enterprise with the persons in charge removed from personal involvement in any specific criminal act. The individuals at the very top of a drugs syndicate are as likely to be found with packets of heroin in their pockets as executives of General Motors are to be found doing a shift on the production line. Although many sorts of crime can be organised, the most usual examples are highly profitable continually repeatable offences, the most prevalent being drug distribution followed by gambling and consensual sexual offences like prostitution and pornography.

There is a structural parallel between organised crime and legitimate business whose implications are worrying. Many small and thriving businesses are only viable as long as the persons who set them up remain in charge, and many cease to operate when their principals retire or move on to something new: few restaurants, for example, maintain their character and clientele after a change of ownership. As long as criminal organisations have the character of small businesses, police can succeed in destroying the structure by removing the key individuals at the top. Even a large criminal organisation such as that established by the Kray brothers in the East End of London during the 1960s collapsed on the conviction of the Kray twins, and the complex web of corruption in Queensland was destroyed by the Fitzgerald inquiry and the trials which followed it. The perception that any criminal enterprise will collapse if the individuals running it can be brought to justice is difficult to change, and even as late as the mid-1980s London's then recently retired Assistant Commissioner (Crime) made the claim that even the most serious criminal gangs could be destroyed by arresting the ringleaders (Kelland, 1986).

---

6   Every police officer who has worked the streets of a city has encountered prostitutes, flypitchers, or gamers who see the regular small fines of the courts as a form of income tax, and for prostitutes, at least, being arrested is an opportunity for a night off.

Unlike small businesses, large businesses generate a life of their own and continue over a long period of time with different participants: General Motors would survive even if half its executives were sacked and the rest reshuffled. There is a structural parallel between large, legitimate corporate bodies and organised crime syndicates in the way they are run. The CEO of a large corporation is answerable to the shareholders for the efficiency and profitability of the corporation, and ultimately responsible for decisions made at a lower level of the organisation. However, it is not reasonable to expect the CEO to have knowledge of, for example, the dismissal of a driver, clerk or factory hand, or the delivery of goods. Although morally the person at the top of a criminal enterprise is equally as guilty of a crime committed by that enterprise as the individuals who actually carried it out, like the CEO of a corporation, the head of a crime organisation is almost certainly unaware of the day-to-day minutiae of its operations. Although the ways the enterprises are run have similarities, the legal burden of responsibility is dramatically different.

The status of major corporations as legal entities gives their directors and officers duties and responsibilities in law, making them answerable through legal process in the courts for actions taken by the corporation itself, or less senior members of its staff. A criminal organisation has no such legal status, and a successful criminal prosecution of the individuals at the top will have to prove that they had direct personal knowledge of specific crimes or had direct, rather than moral, responsibility for the activities of the organisation. To produce evidence of this and meet the burden of proof for criminal cases is extremely difficult, and, even if successful, the criminal organisation will remain dangerous if it can survive the removal of key individuals, and does not collapse upon their arrest or conviction. The struggles that Italian and American police and prosecutors have had in order to deal with the Mafia effectively have shown that there is a point at which an organised crime structure may be strong enough to withstand the arrest and prosecution of large numbers of its members, even those who are in charge.

There are two particularly difficult problems in trying to eliminate organised crime by the criminal prosecution of its leaders. The first is that it is very difficult to find sufficient evidence against individuals who are concerned with the direction of criminal activities of their actual involvement in specific crimes. Al Capone, associated in everyone's mind with major crime in Chicago in the 1930s, and undoubtedly responsible for many crimes both personally and by virtue of his control of a criminal organisation, was only ever convicted of tax evasion. Perhaps even more surprising, amongst all the records of the Third Reich there are no documents or other material available to prove that Hitler personally authorised or acknowledged the Holocaust.[7] The second point is that even if such

---

7   This is not a denial of Hitler's undoubted responsibility for the Holocaust, but an observation that the formal documentary evidence which might have been expected, and would be required by a court, is lacking.

evidence is forthcoming against particular individuals, a conviction may not be sufficient to destroy the criminal organisation. One might hypothesise, using the example of the Third Reich rather differently, what the result would have been if one of the plots to murder Hitler had succeeded. From the time in the mid-1930s when the Nazis consolidated their power, there were a number of individuals who could have succeeded Hitler, and after some internecine disputes one of them would inevitably have taken over. The death of Hitler is unlikely to have brought an early end to the war, and the Third Reich would have continued, if rather differently, under Goering, Heydrich, Himmler or Borman.

Not all large-scale criminal enterprises have an organisational structure like General Motors, which sells its products through a chain consisting of manufacturer–wholesaler/importer–distributor–retailer–purchaser. An alternative structure is that of equally legitimate organisations like Amway, which operate a distribution network whereby the products are bought by major distributors, then immediately shared among the next level of distributors in lesser quantities and so on down the distributor chain until the products reach their eventual users. This structure has much in common with the distribution networks of criminal drug dealing enterprises, whereby large quantities of drugs are split and sold, split further and sold on so that at each successive lower distribution level more people have smaller quantities of drugs until they reach the street user. The larger the quantity of drugs that any individual buys and sells, the larger the profit but also the larger the risk if caught. As with legitimate sales organisations with the same structure, if people drop out of the distribution chain, there are always others ready to step in or move up the chain, so that the organisation itself is little affected. The potential for profit in organised crime is so enormous that, whatever the risk, someone will be prepared to take it, and if the organisation is constructed so that it can continue after losing its leaders then it will be almost impossible to destroy.

With regard to street crime, then, the 21st century police officer will continue to fight the same battles in the same way, because neither the crimes nor the people that commit them have changed in any significant way. The underlying factors which cause crime – human need, human greed, love, hate and anger – are a part of the human psyche. Exacerbatory factors like poverty, unemployment and the drug culture are well beyond the control of police, who can only attempt to deal with their results. Organised crime, likewise, remains ineradicable although not totally beyond restraint.

Police behavioural standards

One of the many matters the 20th century has bequeathed to the 21st is the awareness of police malpractice and corruption, and the need for police agencies to be seen to be taking steps to prevent and remove it. Police behaviour has been under intense and continuing scrutiny since the 1960s, and police services are taking an increasingly positive approach to the improvement of behavioural standards. One such initiative is the introduction of an ethical code rather than continued reliance on formal discipline to punish incidents of bad conduct by police. The development of an ethical code sets a positive standard of behaviour which each individual should strive to attain, whereas a discipline code, like the criminal law, enforces the minimum standard of acceptable behaviour. An ethical code is, therefore, a far better basis for improving professional standards as it aims for the best, rather than accepting the barely permissible mediocre.

The best means for police to reduce malpractice and corruption are through the education and personal development of officers to establish the required standards of honesty and integrity, and through the recruitment by the organisation of persons of the right standards and ethnic diversity to meet the community's needs. Despite these efforts, corruption can never be completely eradicated (Johnston, 1992) but will always be present in all organisations, including police. It has even been argued (Klitgaard, 1989) that there is a point at which the costs of the eradication of corruption exceed the benefits which can be expected of continuing efforts to eliminate it. However, the frequently repeated police response that cases of unacceptable behaviour are the work of "a few bad apples" is no longer sufficient to satisfy a sceptical public, and police now, rightly, need to justify the contention that corruption, violence, and racism are indeed rare, and not the norm for police behaviour.

The reputation of policing depends to a large extent on its relations with the public, and to this end, if for no other, complaints investigation must continue to be taken very seriously indeed. One effect of the implementation of procedures for dealing with corruption or other unacceptable behaviour within the police service is that it serves to highlight corruption and create the impression that the problem is growing. As Johnston expresses it: "Just as police work can create an appearance of a crime wave simply by producing more arrests, reforms can produce the appearance of increased corruption simply by turning up more evidence of it" (Johnston, 1992, p 161). There are some indications that a general improvement of ethical behaviour through education results in a shift in police culture which in turn leads police officers on the streets to take action against colleagues who breach the required standards. While at one time, perhaps, violence towards a refractory prisoner on arrest was a fairly common practice by some officers to which the rest turned a blind eye, such behaviour is no longer generally accepted. The general view of violence towards prisoners has moved from acceptance through tacit disapproval to private remonstration with the perpetrators, and in some police services, officers have arrested violent colleagues for assault.

It is, perhaps, ironic that while the requirements for police to behave correctly are more stringent than ever, legislative provisions for the rehabilitation of offenders, which require that criminal convictions be ignored after a lengthy period of law-abiding behaviour, can mean that old convictions for minor matters are no longer an absolute bar to joining the police service. Many police services will accept mature applicants for the police service who have had a minor brush with the law in their youth. This merely reflects the realities of modern society, where people are driving regularly in their teens, drug use is widely accepted and most young people have had the opportunity to collect motoring infringements and experiment with recreational drugs. It would be unrealistic to deny that almost everyone has broken the law in some way by the time they reach their early 20s, either through speeding, experimenting with alcohol or tobacco below the legal age, smoking cannabis or some adolescent act of dishonesty out of bravado or peer pressure. Some individuals are caught and prosecuted but most escape, the difference between them often being as much a matter of luck as character. The important question regarding an individual's suitability for the police service concerns the individual's current ethical standards and behaviour – not whether the individual has ever been caught breaking the law, but whether that person as an adult continues to disregard the law.

Elitism and corruption

Some of the most serious examples of corruption involving groups of officers, rather than malpractice by individuals within a police service, arise within elite squads. There is a tendency for such groups, isolated from mainstream policing partly from choice and partly from force of circumstance, to work to their own systems and standards rather than those imposed by the police service itself. If unchecked, these pragmatic variations can become outright bad practice or lead to what has been termed "noble cause corruption". Such an elite squad can persuade itself that the ordinary rules which apply to others do not apply to it, and that the only way it can operate is by its own procedures, which no-one but members or ex-members of the squad can understand fully.

Among the more dangerous practices of elite squads is their need for frequent involvement with criminals. Although such relationships may be justified to obtain information, collect evidence and arrest criminals, they are clearly fraught with the possibility of corruption. The trend in modern policing is to ensure absolute propriety by requiring that all dealings with informants be carefully recorded and supervised. The argument presented by elite squads is that the nature of their work and the seriousness of the crimes they investigate mean that normal procedures are too transparent to protect their informants, and it is thus impossible for them to work within operational regulations and maintain the necessary level of confidentiality in their inquiries. Arguments for special consideration have been used by elite squads in the past, and have resulted in some very successful operations in which criminal enterprises have been destroyed which would not otherwise have been possible. Unfortunately, members of such squads have, perhaps equally as often, been found to have indulged in widespread malpractice and eventually brought discredit upon their police service.

The very profitability of organised crime when coupled with modern information-driven investigative methods creates a rather different form of corruption in 21st century policing, the selling of information. In modern major inquiries the hub of the inquiry is likely to be the computer wherein the information is held. Investigations into major criminal organisations require a large team of officers and a computer system, and even smaller investigations into criminal gangs are likely to use a computer system. The only police action which can have any but the most peripheral impact on such criminal enterprises is that of investigation by specialist squads, and the only persons who can gain access to information about the inquiry are the members of those squads. It follows that, if a criminal enterprise has foreknowledge of an investigation in progress, especially in its early stages, that organisation can take such action as will prevent a successful prosecution.

Large-scale criminal enterprises are more likely to need warning of major investigations being undertaken than they are to need an official blind eye to be turned to their street activities such as illegal gambling or drinking clubs. Corruption in the past typically involved a whole network of police being paid off individually, and an offer of regular payments in the hundreds of dollars[8] was usual, and was rejected out of hand by honest police. The profit generated by the drugs trade, for example, is such that the amount of money available to pay for information is huge, and large one-off payments for information may be made. An offer of two or three times an officer's annual salary for a single corrupt act, untraceable, and perhaps even paid into an offshore bank account, would be sure to tempt someone to supply information, and only a single accurate source is necessary. In the same way that one or two criminals giving information to police can lead to a successful operation, one or two police officers passing information to criminals or destroying crucial evidence may ruin one.

Technology and the police

We have seen in Chapter 4 how motor vehicles and telephone and radio communication changed the way policing was carried out in the second half of the 20th century. The question for the 21st century is how computer technology will affect the way policing is done. Police in the Western world are, like most organisations, now totally reliant on computers. A great deal of police activity and interaction with the public is automatically recorded on computer through the dispatch systems which allocate calls from the public to police officers on patrol. Police make computer records of crime reports, arrests, and other information on crime and criminals to which some or all officers can gain access, and they also have access to information on other computers, for example some government records and vehicle registration details. Police also record a great deal of information

---

8   Sgt Col Dillon's evidence to the Fitzgerald inquiry was that he had been offered and refused $400 per month in the 1980s not to investigate certain premises, and sums of that order, when adjusted for the purchasing power of the dollar over the years, were usually the going rate in police corruption of this type.

themselves, all of which can be used for crime detection, crime prevention, and as a supervisory tool for management.

The primary business of policing, as seen by the traditional patrolling officer and all detectives, is the arrest of offenders, and many police officers see the main function of information technology as a means of improving the chances of identifying and locating a suspect and producing evidence to prove the case in court. The whole panoply of fingerprint and DNA identification, crime scene forensic techniques and offender profiling have become crucial in this enterprise. The use of computer terminals in police vehicles to make checks on persons and cars has led to an increased rate of arrests of persons wanted on warrant or otherwise (Chan, 2003, p 659) as instant access to vehicle and criminal records allows police officers to identify and gain an insight into the person they are dealing with, sometimes even before they have effected a vehicle stop.

There is a very real danger that such use of computers can foster an over-reliance on computer information. Police powers to stop and search require grounds for action before the stop. These grounds may sometimes be provided by the computer check. When a stop is carried out before seeking information from the computer, there must have been a pre-existing level of suspicion in the police officer's mind. If the officer's suspicion is automatically dispelled when the computer check produces a negative result this suggests that that officer is over-reliant on technology, since a more alert officer will accept this information, but continue questioning the suspect thoroughly, realising the possibility that the vehicle may be so recently stolen that not even the owner knows it has been taken, or the driver may have given a false name, possibly supported by false identification.[9]

Insofar as modern technology assists the process of catching and providing evidence against criminals, it has the wholehearted support of every police officer. There is rather more suspicion about the use of information gathered by police being disseminated to the public or interested parties to minimise the risk of crime. Police officers are notoriously territorial about their information and its sources, and, while they are always willing to draw from the common well of information, they are far more reluctant to contribute to it. While crime patterns generated by a computer might be hard evidence of criminal activities at a particular time and place, these can be used either to target police resources into making arrests or disseminated to the public as crime prevention advice to prevent further offences. In any given case a choice has to be made how information can be used to the best effect, and it is often by no means clear whether crime prevention or arrests will be the more suitable option: arrests certainly create better statistical results.

---

9   US social security cards, driving licences and student ID cards are sold as "novelty" documents on the web for about $150. Although mainly in demand in the United States for under 21s to buy alcohol, the documents produced may well convince a police officer making a cursory check.

Consider some hypothetical examples of crime around a path between a railway station and a residential estate which, although somewhat over-grown, can be used as a short cut by persons on foot. In the first instance, the area around this path becomes a haunt of drug addicts, and there are a high number of reports of muggings of passers-by. The best response is almost certainly crime prevention by clearing up the area and installing lighting, etc. In the second case, the area around the path is quiet, but there a number of reports of indecent assaults at dusk on young women walking home, consistencies in both description and method indicating a single offender. Here, surveillance over a few evenings should result in the arrest of an incipient rapist, although this does leave unwitting potential victims at some risk. These two examples lead to fairly obvious decisions, but it is easy to imagine realistic cases where the best approach is far less clear. Suppose that over a few weeks there are a number of muggings, handbag snatches and thefts of mobile phones on this path, and the suspects are des-cribed in a variety of ways. It is by no means obvious whether surveillance and arrest or preventative publicity and strategies would be the better choice. If police action would lead to the arrest of all or most of the offenders, ie if at most a small gang of offenders is responsible, then such action would be worthwhile, although again there is a risk to potential victims, but the number of offenders beyond which judicious pruning of bushes and improved lighting to prevent future crimes would be the better option is impossible to judge.

Once any information is released into the public forum, there is little point in using it as a basis for police surveillance, as the chance of an arrest will be reduced. For the police officer whose main aim is to make arrests, releasing information to the public would seem both a waste of a good opportunity to catch criminals and a breach of faith by police management. For a police officer committed to community policing and working with the community the release of such information is precisely what police work should be about. One of the key phrases used about modern policing is that it is "information led", but information has always driven police work: the difference now is that the modern police agency has so much more accurate information collated by experts than ever before, and a responsibility to work with the public directly, rather than as an agency working on the public's behalf. This can lead to hard choices about how information is to be used, whether released as a crime prevention strategy, or retained confi-dentially as a crime detection tool. In the examples above, as in many other real cases, information can be used for one purpose or the other, rarely both.

The third use of information gathered and held on police computers is as a management tool. The previous chapter has shown how computer generated reports hold middle management accountable under the Compstat paradigm, but any police agency with a computerised dispatch system and personnel records can use such information to hold lower ranks accountable also. Whatever a computer records it records with complete accuracy, and that record is incontrovertible if it is made automatically by the computer, just as, for example, the time, date and place is printed on an ATM, credit card or EFTPOS transaction. Whenever a call is made to police the time and date is recorded automatically, as is the time it was allocated to a police patrol, the time arrival at the scene was reported, and so on. Any such call will later require the police officer attending to enter a result on the computer by making a report. A fair proportion of calls to police have always been from persons who just need informal advice, are mistaken about the subject of their call, or are mildly delusional, and such matters were in the past recorded informally. Now all calls logged on the computer (in effect, all calls received) need a full report to be made and entered on the computer showing the result. The quantity of reporting, and thus of supervisory checking of reports, has increased since the advent of computer technology (Chan, 2003).

While in the past police officers on patrol could answer calls and were aware of supervision by patrolling sergeants, there is now a feeling that the computer knows where officers are and what they are doing at all times, a feeling compounded where there are GPS systems in patrol cars. While police supervising officers may well not have either the time or the inclination to make thorough checks on officers on patrol, the fact that the technology is available for them to do so can increase the gulf of suspicion between street police and management. The important feature of an inter-action between police officers and members of the public is the quality of that interaction, the manner in which the incident was handled and the accuracy of the officer's report, the sympathy shown, the help offered and the advice given. No computer can record these important qualitative matters, only the cold facts like time of arrival and departure, nature of the call and the result. A computer will record the facts that the caller was mistaken about hearing gunshots, and the officer attending discovered this within seconds yet spent 45 minutes at the scene; nevertheless, the time might have been wholly necessary to convince a frail and frightened elderly person that it is safe to go to bed.

Policing is embracing the new technologies, not solely out of necessity, but because there are easily recognised advantages for police in their use. Technology is not without its problems, though, and brings with it hard choices to be made about the best way it can be used. Computer systems are powerful tools, and policing, along with the rest of 21st century society, still has much to learn about their use and abuse. The collection, retention and use of information is central to good policework but has implications for personal privacy both as a policing tool and as a management tool which are best resolved in advance rather than as a response to specific situations. These are issues for many aspects of 21st century life and not just for policing and government, although the sheer volume of government and police information and the effect such sensitive information has to impinge upon the individual places an increased responsibility on police to ensure their procedures are sound, particularly with regard to the security of criminal records and information about continuing major investigations.

Autonomy and the officer on the street

The police officer on the street has traditionally had considerable auto-nomy, although this has diminished with the increase of technology. Except for a chance encounter with his sergeant, the 19th century policeman answered only to the members of the public he encountered from the time he walked out of the police station until he returned. The introduction of police boxes, motor vehicles, radios and now computerised despatch has gradually whittled away this autonomy ever since. Police officers have always been aware of three factors affecting their activities: the needs of the public who, either personally or by phone have called on them for assistance; the orders and requirements of the police hierarchy and the con-straints of the law on their actions. These have formed at times an uneasy troika, but now there may be major conflicts of interest between the first two.

The previous chapter described in some detail the effect that financial constraints, government-imposed strategic plans and managerial answera-bility have had on police commanders in charge of divisions. Such plans are intended and claimed to give a better service to the community by police, and as such are imposed by senior officers on police officers on the street. Members of the public generally know little and care less about the arcana of policing, their only concerns being the news from the media about crime and their personal experience of police, which in most cases is infrequent. The discussion here concerns interactions which are instigated by the public, usually when they request police assistance, rather than the far more frequent occurrence of police-instigated interactions, the most com-mon of which are traffic stops.

The public have grown to expect that whenever they call police, a patrol car appears within a very short time to deal with their problem. The availability of instant communication by telephone and radio has fostered this belief, together with numerous crime series on television where police always attend instantly. Furthermore, the public expect police to have some solution to offer to their problem, whether it be a police matter or not. Police officers on the street have, by and large, viewed themselves as servants of the community, and have striven to answer even the most trivial of requests. Police are quite used to being at the beck and call of the public in this way, as well as being under the control of their supervising officers, carrying out the tasks they set. Police and other emergency services (including hospital medical staff) have always had these two controlling forces, management instructions and public requests and needs. They respond to each according to urgency, and are perhaps the only agencies in which management has accepted that its directions are not automatically given priority.

With a great deal of pressure on them to achieve results in specified areas, management in policing is now forced to exert its authority more strongly over police officers in the lower ranks, reducing their availability to the public. The public care nothing for this, and continue requesting police assistance as before. Police officers who see it as their primary duty to give their best response to the public will continue so to do, although this may be increasingly at odds with the requirements of management. The pressure on police management to meet targets in particular aspects of policing will result in an insistence by senior officers that police on the streets concentrate their efforts on these specified issues. The public will continue making calls for assistance, which may or may not be about these same issues, and police officers on the street will be required to make some sort of response, whether or not it is considered valuable by police management.

While formerly police inspectors and superintendents were willing to accept that particular directions given to patrolling officers had not been met because of contradictory requests by members of the public, pressure on middle management may now mean an insistence that compliance with management instructions has priority over responding to public requests. This could well lead to a decrease in morale among street duty officers and a deepening gulf between management and street police. Street police may come to feel that management strategies, plans and targets actively impede the provision of service to the public, and it is they, not the management, who will bear the brunt of public dissatisfaction. Police officers have always worked in an atmosphere of hostility and suspicion from some sections of the community, and have no liking for policy decisions which, if implemented will serve to alienate even more members of the public.

We have seen that too much government involvement in policing, as exemplified by legislation and other directives in Britain, has minimised the importance of local involvement in police policy-making and strategy-setting. The same pressure brought down to street level risks separating police officers from the individuals they serve at the point at which police interact with the public. Street police officers are caught in the middle here, under direct, personal pressure from both management and the public when it is increasingly difficult, if not impossible, to satisfy both. The malaise that appears in other parts of the welfare state, particularly health and education, where economic and strategic considerations increasingly seem more important than direct delivery of services seems to be moving into policing, unwanted by both police and society.

Concluding remarks

There are a number of themes running through this book to be drawn together and reiterated here. One important factor which distinguished the policing tradition established by Peel, Rowan and Mayne from the law enforcement that preceded it, and from the state police systems operating in Europe at that time, was that law enforcement was independent of government, and operated for the benefit of the people not their rulers. Despite some wavering at various times in various places, this principle remained, and has been adopted by other democratic nations. Montesquieu's doctrine of the separation of powers described the British political system, in the century before the establishment of modern policing, as a paradigm of government because it shared power between the executive, the legislature and the judiciary. Policing elsewhere rested firmly under the control of the executive, yet this system was rejected by the British parliament. It is all the more disquieting and disturbing that, at the start of the 21st century, the British government seems to be moving away from this fundamental principle by increasing its control over policing unnoticed by society or many of the police officers who serve it.

The most important principle of policing established by the Peelian tradition is that police are not to be placed under the control of any arm of government, but are to be independent of, although answerable to, all arms of government. There may be some executive direction, but the legislature provides police with their powers, and the judiciary provides supervision over the exercise of these powers. Policing by fear, which was a feature of the European police systems that the Westminster parliament specifically rejected, had to be avoided by Peel, and his new system became that of policing by consent. Modern policing has always had as a minimum requirement the tacit consent of the community to be policed, and has operated best when it has the active help of the community.

Although this book has dealt specifically with police within the common law traditions of Australia, Britain, and the United States, the principle of policing by consent has been adopted by the police of every democratic country in the world. The pejorative term "police state" signifies a nation where the police are strictly under state control, and the extent to which police are independent but answerable serves as a useful indication of the extent to which that nation recognises human rights. Whenever any state violates its citizen's human rights, one of the main instruments available for it to do this is its police force. The principle of policing by consent underpins any modern community policing strategy, and these strategies are to be found, not just in the affluent nations of Europe, North America and Asia, but in some of the worlds poorer emerging nations like Bangladesh and Zambia.[10]

One of the most encouraging changes in policing in the past 25 years has been the development of the concept of policing by consent into policing in partnership between police and the community. For the crime problems of any society to be addressed, police need more than the consent of the community to do their job – more, indeed, than just the support of the community. What is needed is that the police and community work together in addressing crime, and more and more police and community partnerships are being forged. The forms these partnerships take are as diverse as the communities being policed, but this is of no matter: the important issue is that the public and the police work together. The citizen patrols of the Volunteers in Policing scheme in San Antonio, Texas may feel

---

10 There are some extremely effective community policing efforts being made in the grinding poverty of the shantytowns on the outskirts of Lusaka, for example. I am grateful to one of the instigators of these schemes in the 1990s, Supt Nancy Kaona, for supplying information on this.

little in common with penniless Zambians building a police station in their own shantytown, or with Aboriginal community patrols dealing with anti-social behaviour by taking disruptive community members off the streets of country towns in Australia, but all are working positively and practically with their police to counter crime and unacceptable behaviour in their communities.

For a community to accept these close working arrangements with their police there must be an atmosphere of mutual trust. Trust in police can only be earned by high standards of police propriety and a system of police accountability in which the community can have faith. It is for this reason that a large part of this book has been devoted to a discussion of accountability mechanisms: without police being fully accountable for all their actions, the community may well withhold some, at least, of its support. The police are a part of the community, and have a great deal of specialist knowledge to offer to a community problem-solving approach to crime and anti-social behaviour. This specialist knowledge can be a more valuable contribution to community-based crime prevention than the specific coercive powers which police also possess, although it is these powers which set police apart from the rest of the community.

The history of policing from 1829 to the present has shown great and continuing changes in society which have brought about significant changes in both the nature of crime and the demographics of the criminal. Crime has always been a part of society, and the aetiology of crime varies with the nature of that society. In some respects, the type of crime prevalent in modern society is the price it has to pay for its progress in other areas. As an example of this, affluent, modern technological society provides many homes with a variety of valuable, portable electronic equipment such as TVs, CD players, DVDs, computers and cellular phones, and changes to family structures and work patterns mean that these homes are often empty during the working day. Domestic burglary is now both easier and more profitable than it has ever been, so an increased burglary rate can be viewed as one of the hidden costs of affluence and microchip technology.

The nature of the average criminal has changed too. The proportion of crime committed by juveniles increased dramatically over the last quarter of the 20th century, and there is no sign of this trend abating. In the 19th century much street crime was a result of abject poverty, and, from the perspective of lives lived in the safety of the welfare state, we may well now feel sympathy with many of the criminals of that era. Faced with the choice of stealing or starving few of us would choose to starve. At the start of the 21st century, starvation, in Western countries at least, is no longer a cause of crime, although relative poverty is still a major social problem, while the amount of crime committed to support a drug habit has risen dramatically. The well-fed citizens of the 19th century showed little concern for the social evil of poverty, and little sympathy for the petty criminal sentenced to flogging, transportation and gaol. In modern society punishments may be less harsh, but nevertheless societies of the 21st century show little sympathy for their drug addicts, and vote-winning political strategies for getting tough on crime show very little concern for, or even recognition of, the underlying social problems which give rise to poverty and the youth drug culture.

Whatever the changes and pressures, policing must remain true to its roots. The police are part of the community, and must remain committed, now more than ever, to achieving their goals through working within the community using community-based problem solving approaches to crime. The precise strategies used are as diverse as the communities being policed and the crime problems they face, and systems of accountability are as diverse as the political structures they operate within, but any system which works must be counted as a success for that community. There is, at bottom, only one criterion by which policing will eventually be judged: whether or not the whole community being policed considers it successful.

BIBLIOGRAPHY

Albrecht J (1998) "A 45% Reduction in Index Crime: Examining the Secrets of NYPD's Success" Academy of Criminal Justice Sciences Annual Meeting Albuquerque (unpublished)

Ascoli D (1979) *The Queen's Peace* Hamish Hamilton

Avery J (1981) *Police – Force or Service* Butterworths

Australian Bureau of Statistics (1998) *Trends and Issues* Nos 11 and 15 (1998) "How the Public See the Police, an Australian Survey" Canberra

Bayley D (1989) "Community Policing in Australia" in Chappell D & Wilson P (eds) (1989) *Australian Policing – Contemporary Issues* Butterworths

Bayley D (1992) "Comparative Organisation of the Police in English-speaking Countries" in Tonry M & Morris N (1992) (eds) *Modern Policing* University of Chicago

Beresford Q & Omaji P (1998) *Our State of Mind* Fremantle Arts Press

Berlin I (1969) *Four Essays on Liberty* Oxford UP

Bittner E (1990) *Aspects of Police Work* Chicago

Brewer J, Guelke A, Hume I, Moxon-Browne E, & Wilford R (1996) *The Police, Public Order and the State* 2nd edn Macmillan

Brogden M (1982) *The Police: Autonomy & Consent* Academic Press

Cassels J (1994) *Report of an Independent Committee of Enquiry into the Role and Responsibilities of Police* Police Foundation/Policy Studies Institute

Chan J (1997) *Changing Police Culture – Policing in a Multi-cultural Society* Cambridge UP

Chan J (2003) "Police and New Technologies" in Newburn T (ed) (2003) *Handbook of Policing* Willan UK

Chappell D & Wilson P (eds) (1989) *Australian Policing – Contemporary Issues* Butterworths

Chappell D & Wilson P (eds) (1996) *Australian Policing – Contemporary Issues* 2nd edn Butterworths

Crawford A (2003) "The pattern of policing in the UK: policing beyond the police" in Newburn T (ed) (2003) *Handbook of Policing* Willan UK

Cumming E, Cumming I & Edell L (1964) "Policeman as Philosopher, Guide and Friend" *Social Problems* Vol 12

Denning T (1977) *The Discipline of Law* Oxford UP

Devlin P (1965) *The Enforcement of Morals* Oxford UP

Dickie J (1988) *The Road to Fitzgerald and Beyond* UQP

Ekblom P (1998) *Safer Cities and Domestic Burglary* Home Office Research Study 154 UK

Edwards CJ (1997) "The Future of Rights and Democracy in a Multi-cultural Society" *Rechtstheorie Beiheft 17 Rule of Law*

Farrell G (1988) "The Development of the Community Patrol Officer Program: Community Oriented Policing in New York Police Department" in Greene G & Mastrowski S (1988) *Community Policing – Rhetoric or Reality* Praeger

Finnane M (1994) *Police and Government* OUP

Fitzgerald G (1989) *Report of the Inquiry into Possible Illegal Activities and Associated Police Misconduct* Government of Queensland

Geller W & Morris N (1992) "Relations Between Federal and Local Police" in Tonry M & Morris N (1992) (eds) *Modern Policing* University of Chicago

Gill A (1977) "Aboriginals, Settlers and Police in the Kimberley" in *Studies in W.A. History* UWA

Goldstein H (1979) "Improving Policing: A Problem-Oriented Approach" in *Crime and Delinquency* 25

Goldstein H (1990) *Problem-Oriented Policing* McGraw Hill

Gottfredson M & Hirschi T (1990) *A General Theory of Crime* Stanford UP

Graef R (1989) *Talking Blues* Collins

Greene J & Mastrowski S (1988) *Community Policing – Rhetoric or Reality* Praeger

Hagan J (1985) *Modern Criminology* McGraw Hill

Hamilton A, Madison J & Jay J (1992) *The Federalist* Everyman

Hayek F (1960) *The Constitution of Liberty* Chicago UP

Hazlehurst K (1987) *Ivory Scales: Black Australia and the Law* UNSW Press

Henry V (1996) "Re-aligning Police Discretion and Accountability Structures to Support Effective Problem Solving and Reduce Crime" Queensland CJC conference paper (unpublished)

Henry V (2002) *The Compstat Paradigm* Looseleaf Law Pub

Hobbes T *Leviathan* Penguin

Home Office (UK) (1995) Review of Police Core and Ancillary Tasks

Home Office (UK) (1998) British Crime Survey 1997

Jewkes Y (2003) "Policing Cybercrime" in Newburn T (ed) (2003) *Handbook of Policing* Willan UK

Johnston M (1992) "Corruption as a Process: Lessons for Analysis and Reform" *Police Studies* Vol 15 No 4

Jones T (2003) "The governance and accountability of policing" in Newburn T (ed) (2003) *Handbook of Policing* Willan UK

Jones T & Newburn T (2002) "The Transformation of Policing" *British Journal of Criminology,* 42: 129-46

Kelland G (1986) *Crime in London* Grafton

King H (1956) "Some Aspects of Police Administration in New South Wales" *Journal of the Royal Australian Historical Society* Vol 42

Klitgaard R (1989) *Controlling Corruption* University of California Press

Landa D & Lewis C (1996) "Making Police Accountable for Their Conduct" in Chappell D & Wilson P (eds) (1996) *Australian Policing – Contemporary Issues* 2nd edn Butterworths

Lane R "Urban Police and Crime in 19th Century America" in Tonry M & Morris N (1992) (eds) *Modern Policing* University of Chicago

Livingstone K (1988) *If Voting Changed Anything, They'd Abolish It* Fontana

Long M (2003) "Leadership and performance management" in Newburn T (ed) (2003) *Handbook of Policing* Willan UK

Mark R (1977) *Policing a Perplexed Society* George Allen & Unwin

Marks J (1990) "A Freer Market for Heroin in Australia: Alternatives to Subsidising Organised Crime" *Journal of Drug Issues* Winter 1990

Marr D & Wilkinson M (2003) *Dark Victory* Allen & Unwin, Sydney

Marshall G (1965) *Police and Government*

Matassa M and Newburn T "Policing and Terrorism" in Newburn T (ed) (2003) *Handbook of Policing* Willan UK

Mawby R & Wright A "The Police Organisation" in Newburn T (ed) (2003) *Handbook of Policing* Willan UK

Miller W (1991) "Will the Force Be with Him?" *Philadelphia Enquirer* 3 November 1991

Mitchell J "$11.3 Million Paid in LAPD Abuse Cases" *Los Angeles Times* 29 March 1991, cited in Skolnick J & Fyfe J (1994) *Above the Law: Police and the Excessive Use of Force* Free Press

Morgan R & Newburn T (1997) "The Future of Policing" *Criminal Justice Matters* Winter 1996-7

Morgan R & Smith D (eds) (1989) *Coming to Terms with Policing: Perspectives on Policy* Routledge

Mukherjee S & Dagger D (1990) *The Size of the Crime Problem in Australia*

Myrdal G (1941) *An American Dilemma: The Negro Problem and Modern Democracy*

Newburn T (ed) (2003) *Handbook of Policing* Willan UK

Nozick R (1974) *Anarchy, State and Utopia* OUP

Oakeshott M (1983) "The Rule of Law" in Oakeshott M *On History and Other Essays* Cambridge

Plato *The Republic* Penguin

Punch & Naylor (1973) "The Police: A Social Service" *New Society*

Reiner R (1991) *Chief Constables* OUP

Reiner R (1992) *The Politics of the Police* 2nd edn Harvester Wheatsheaf

Reiner R (1995) "Counting the coppers" in Stenning P (ed) *Accountability for Criminal Justice: Selected Essays* University of Toronto

Reiner R (1996) "Looking Through the Glass (of a Crystal Ball) Darkly" *Policing Today* Vol 1 No 5

Reiss A (1992) "Police Organisation" in Tonry M & Morris N (1992) (eds) *Modern Policing* University of Chicago

Reuss-Ianni E & Ianni F (1983) "Street cops and management cops: the cultures of policing" in Punch M (ed) *Control in the Police Organisation* Cambridge, MA

Rousey D (1983) "Hibernian Leatherheads: Irish Cops in New Orleans 1830 – 1860" *Journal of Urban History*

Russell B (1960) *In Praise of Idleness* Routledge KP

Sanders A & Young R (2003) "Police Powers" in Newburn T (ed) (2003) *Handbook of Policing* Willan UK

Scarman, Lord L (1981) *The Scarman Report: The Brixton Disorders* HMSO

Sheehan R & Cordner G (1995) *Police Administration* 3rd edn Anderson

Skolnick J & Fyfe J (1994) *Above the Law: Police and the Excessive Use of Force* Free Press

Storch R (1975) "The Plague of Blue Locusts: Police Reform and Popular Resistance in Northern England 1840-1857" *International Review of Social History*

Thrasher, Tiefer, Fleetwood & Lechner *Report of Investigation of Misconduct of Philadelphia Police Force and Recommendation* US Department of Justice memorandum 30 April 1979 cited in Skolnick J & Fyfe J (1993) *Above the Law: Police and the Excessive Use of Force* Free Press

Tonry M & Morris N (1992) (eds) *Modern Policing* University of Chicago

Trahair R (1987) "Organised Crime: A Global Perspective" *Australian and New Zealand Journal of Sociology* November

Uelham G (1973) "Varieties of Public Policy: A Study of Police Policy Regarding the Use of Deadly Force in Los Angeles County" *Loyola of Los Angeles Law Review* 6

Walker N & Richards N (1996) "Service Under Change Current Issues in Policing in England and Wales" *Police Studies* Vol 19 No 1

Whitaker B (1964) *The Police* Penguin

Wilkinson P (2001) *Terrorism versus Democracy: The Liberal State Response* Frank Cass, London

Williams S (2002) *Peter Ryan – The Inside Story* Penguin, Australia

Wilson J & Kelling G (1982) "Broken Windows" *Atlantic Monthly* March 1982

TABLE OF STATUTES

TABLE OF CASES

INDEX